HASTINGS LAW LIBRARY

3 5012 00154 6161

"America's lea[...]elf-help legal
info[...]★

—YAHOO!

W9-BNT-127

LEGAL INFORMATION ONLINE ANYTIME

24 hours a day

www.nolo.com

AT THE NOLO.COM SELF-HELP LAW CENTER, YOU'LL FIND

- Nolo's comprehensive Legal Encyclopedia filled with plain-English information on a variety of legal topics
- Nolo's Law Dictionary—legal terms without the legalese
- Auntie Nolo—if you've got questions, Auntie's got answers
- The Law Store—over 200 self-help legal products including Downloadable Software, Books, Form Kits and eGuides
- Legal and product updates
- Frequently Asked Questions
- NoloBriefs, our free monthly email newsletter
- Legal Research Center, for access to state and federal statutes
- Our ever-popular lawyer jokes

Quality LAW BOOKS & SOFTWARE FOR EVERYONE

Nolo's user-friendly products are consistently first-rate. Here's why:

- A dozen in-house legal editors, working with highly skilled authors, ensure that our products are accurate, up-to-date and easy to use
- We continually update every book and software program to keep up with changes in the law
- Our commitment to a more democratic legal system informs all of our work
- We appreciate & listen to your feedback. Please fill out and return the card at the back of this book.

OUR "NO-HASSLE" GUARANTEE

Return anything you buy directly from Nolo for any reason and we'll cheerfully refund your purchase price. No ifs, ands or buts.

RECEIVED

MAY 0 6 2004

LIBRARY
HASTINGS COLLEGE OF THE LAW

Read This First

The information in this book is as up to date and accurate as we can make it. But it's important to realize that the law changes frequently, as do fees, forms, and other important legal details. If you handle your own legal matters, it's up to you to be sure that all information you use—including the information in this book—is accurate. Here are some suggestions to help you do this:

First, check the edition number on the book's spine to make sure you've got the most recent edition of this book. To learn whether a later edition is available, go to Nolo's online Law Store at www.nolo.com or call Nolo's Customer Service Department at 800-728-3555.

Next, because the law can change overnight, users of even a current edition need to be sure it's fully up to date. At www.nolo.com, we post notices of major legal and practical changes that affect a book's current edition only. To check for updates, go to the Law Store portion of Nolo's website and find the page devoted to the book (use the "A to Z Product List" and click on the book's title). If you see an "Updates" link on the left side of the page, click on it. If you don't see a link, there are no posted changes—but check back regularly.

Finally, while Nolo believes that accurate and current legal information in its books can help you solve many of your legal problems on a cost-effective basis, this book is not intended to be a substitute for personalized advice from a knowledgeable lawyer. If you want the help of a trained professional, consult an attorney licensed to practice in your state.

1st edition

Prenuptial Agreements:

How to Write a Fair and Lasting Contract

by Attorney Katherine E. Stoner
& Shae Irving, J.D.

NOLO

HASTINGS COLLEGE OF LAW LIBRARY

KF
529
Z9
S76
2004

First Edition   APRIL 2004

Editor   LISA GUERIN

Illustrations   MARI STEIN

Cover Design   TONI IHARA

Book Design   TERRI HEARSH

Proofreading   ROBERT WELLS

CD-ROM Preparation   ANDRÉ ZIVKOVICH

Index   THÉRÈSE SHERE

Printing   DELTA PRINTING SOLUTIONS, INC.

Stoner, Katherine E., 1947-
    Prenuptial agreements : how to write a fair and lasting contract / by Katherine E. Stoner
and Shae Irving.--1st ed.
        p. cm.
    Includes index.
    ISBN 0-87337-996-9 (alk. paper)
    1. Antenuptial contracts--United States--Popular works. I. Irving, Shae. II. Title.

KF529.Z9S76 2004
346.7301'662--dc22

                                                                    2003064967

Copyright © 2004 by Nolo.
All rights reserved. Printed in the USA.

No part of this publication may be reproduced, stored in a retrieval system, or transmitted in
any form or by any means, electronic, mechanical, photocopying, recording, or otherwise
without the prior written permission of the publisher and the authors. Reproduction prohibitions
do not apply to the forms contained in this product when reproduced for personal use.

Quantity sales: For information on bulk purchases or corporate premium sales, please
contact the Special Sales department. For academic sales or textbook adoptions, ask for
Academic Sales, 800-955-4775. Nolo, 950 Parker St., Berkeley, CA 94710.

Acknowledgments

This book would never have been written without the foresight, enthusiasm, and patient support of our friends at Nolo, especially Janet Portman and Jake Warner. Nor could we have done justice to the sheer breadth of the legal landscape without the diligent research efforts of Ella Hirst. Thanks also to Tom Hannah for his work on the preliminary research.

We are indebted to Lisa Guerin for her editorial assistance, and to André Zivkovich for his sharp-eyed suggestions and his help with the CD-ROM. Our gratitude also goes to Terri Hearsh, a talented and patient book designer, and to Robert Wells for his careful proofreading.

Special thanks to Anne Lober, Peggy Williams, and everyone at Divorce Helpline for providing a wonderful meeting place halfway between our homes in Pacific Grove and Berkeley—many good ideas were hatched in those rooms.

A personal note of thanks from Kathy goes to her law partners and staff for their interest and support, and to Mickey for hanging in there. Shae wants to thank everyone at Nolo for making it a joy to go to work each day.

Finally, we'd like to thank each other. Rarely does a collaboration proceed with as much grace and good humor as this one did.

About the Authors

Katherine E. Stoner is a certified family law specialist with the firm of Stoner, Welsh & Schmidt in Pacific Grove, California. Her practice focuses primarily on family law and mediation. She is the author of *Using Divorce Mediation* (Nolo, 1999). She is on the training staff of the Center for Mediation in Law in Mill Valley, California, and an adjunct faculty member at Monterey College of Law, where she has taught community property since 1980.

Shae Irving is the author of *Medical Directives & Powers of Attorney for California* (Nolo, 2003) and a co-author of *Quicken WillMaker Plus* (software from Nolo). Irving joined the editorial staff at Nolo in 1994 after receiving her law degree at Boalt Hall School of Law at the University of California at Berkeley, and has edited numerous Nolo books including the best-selling *Plan Your Estate* and *Nolo's Simple Will Book*.

Table of Contents

Appendixes

A How to Use the CD-ROM

B Worksheets

C Clauses for Building Your Prenup

D Summary of State Prenup Laws

Index

Introduction

How to Use This Book

This book is all about prenuptial agreements—called "prenups" for short. We tell you what they are, what you can do with one, and how to make one that's right for your relationship. If you're planning to be married, you and your fiancé can use this book to decide whether or not you want a prenup, what terms to include in it, and how to put those terms into a legally binding document.

A. How This Book Can Help You

If you are thinking of marrying and considering a prenuptial agreement, the information in this book can help you sort through the myriad questions that naturally arise. For example, you might have misgivings about exploring the idea of a prenup with your beloved for fear of appearing coldhearted or mercenary. Maybe you aren't sure if a prenup is what you really need. Or perhaps the two of you have decided you want a prenup but you don't know how to start putting it together.

If you even leaf through the first few chapters of this book, you will see that there are definite benefits to making your own rules about the financial aspects of your marriage instead of leaving everything to the laws of your state. Although prenups aren't for everyone, you can successfully use them for the following purposes and more:

- coordinating and supporting your estate plans, to be sure that family property passes as you wish
- specifying ground rules for buying and owning property together, and
- avoiding potentially divisive issues that could arise if you ever separate.

In addition, while a prenuptial agreement may not seem like a very romantic project, working together to consider and choose the terms of a prenup can actually strengthen your relationship. After all, marriage is a partnership in every sense of the word. Learning how to deal respectfully and constructively with each other about finances is a benefit in itself. So even if you conclude that you don't need a prenup, using this book can help you converse with each other about the important—and sometimes challenging—financial matters that are sure to arise in the course of your marriage.

B. Using This Book to Draft Your Own Prenup

In the chapters that follow, we take you step by step through the process of making a prenuptial agreement, from deciding whether to have one to preparing a final written agreement customized to your situation and designed to stand the test of time. Throughout the book, we provide worksheets to help you assess your finances and goals. We also include sample clauses that you can tailor to meet your needs. When it's time to put your prenup together, you can use the CD-ROM at the back of the book to cut and paste the clauses you've chosen into a final agreement.

To help you see how this works for actual people, we follow three couples through the entire process. You'll meet Ted and Grace, Karen and Russ, and Steven and Freda—though these aren't their real names—in Chapter 1. You'll have a chance to see how they deal with each stage as they come to it, and you'll be able to read selected parts of the agreement each couple signs. In addition, there are a host of other fictional couples who make cameo appearances to illustrate particular points that may arise as you negotiate and draft your agreement.

C. Our Assumptions

We have written this book with a distinct—and firmly held—point of view on the subject of prenuptial agreements. In the interest of full and fair disclosure, we want you to know up front just how we view this subject.

We think that a prenuptial agreement is more than just a legally binding contract. It is the material and financial counterpart to wedding vows.

When you marry, you make what you expect and hope will be a lifetime commitment to be there for each other in every way. Your prenup should support and reflect the spirit of partnership with which you approach your wedding vows.

Prenups aren't always negotiated in this spirit, but we believe they should be. Not only that, we think this is the best way to ensure that a prenup will be binding in court, should a serious dispute ever arise.

This means we're making certain assumptions about how you will approach your prenup. They are:

- you want to be fair
- you are prepared to make full disclosure about your property and finances
- you are willing to communicate about finances, and
- you'll each work with a lawyer.

Let's look at each of these assumptions more closely.

1. You Want to Be Fair

Forgive us for stating the obvious. Of course you want to be fair. However, there is often more to "fairness" than meets the eye.

In our view, a prenuptial agreement is fair if it meets two criteria:

- fair terms—that is, what you agree to benefits both of you (it's not one-sided), and
- fair process—meaning that you negotiate the agreement fairly (you don't subject each other to undue pressure or coercion).

As for the first of these criteria, it will be up to the two of you to decide what's fair and what's not. In fact, you may discover that each of you has a different take on what's best in your situation. It may take some talking and a little compromising to come up with an agreement that seems fair to both of you, but we think you'll find that it's well worth the effort.

Having a fair process means taking the time to make sure that both of you participate in making the agreement and that neither of you feels pressured into signing an agreement you're not comfortable with. Fair process is the basis for our second, third, and fourth assumptions, discussed next.

A prenup that meets both criteria of the fairness test—its terms are equitable and you've mutually negotiated it—is most likely to stand the test of time in your marriage. An agreement that fails the fairness test will at best be an unhappy reminder that you put away and hope to forget about. At worst, it may permanently erode the trust between you and your betrothed, and it could even be the source of bitter and expensive court battles in a later divorce.

On the legal front, courts in most states will not enforce a prenup that it finds to be unfair in one or both aspects. So paying attention to fairness also makes it more likely that a court will enforce your premarital agreement, if it comes to that. As you use this book, you'll learn how to prepare an agreement that's fair.

2. You're Prepared to Make Full Disclosure

Our second assumption is closely related to the first. A premarital agreement is most likely to be viewed as fair—by you and by the courts—if it is based upon complete and accurate financial information. This means that you should both disclose everything you own (including approximate values) and all of your debts (including any obligations from a prior marriage, such as child support or alimony). We are not alone in considering full disclosure basic to fairness. Virtually every state requires that any premarital agreement be accompanied by complete written disclosure of both parties' financial circumstances.

As you work with this book, we'll help you figure out exactly what you own and what you owe. We'll also give you detailed information to help you prepare the written financial disclosures that will accompany your prenup.

3. You're Willing to Communicate About Finances

Let's face it: Although most of us marry for love rather than money, marriage is a financial partnership as well as a spiritual, emotional, and physical union. Sooner or later, the two of you will need a workable understanding about how to handle your finances, even if it's just day-to-day stuff like whether to have a joint bank account or who will pay the bills. This means that you'll want to be able to communicate well about money and finances.

If you intend to sign a premarital agreement, good communication about finances is not just desirable, it's essential—*before* you sign. If your communications aren't clear, it will be next-to-impossible to come up with a written document that truly represents a mutually negotiated agreement between the two of you.

Bringing up the topic of money can be hard. Having a sustained conversation about it is even more difficult. At a time when romance is on your minds, talking about money can feel like a comedown. And just the thought of disagreeing can be enough to make you avoid the subject. Maybe it feels awkward to discuss old debts when you're in the process of clearing them up and you're confident that they'll soon be ancient history. Or maybe it's your fiancé who has the outstanding debts and you hesitate to bring up an embarrassing subject.

Whatever the reasons, money and finances can be a difficult topic for many of us to broach. If this is true for you and your betrothed, don't be alarmed, but don't let it be an excuse to delay the inevitable, either. Straight talk between you is essential—the sooner the better. If you need help, we provide lots of tips on how to have good conversations about money, and guidance for working with financial or couples counselors if you get stuck.

4. You'll Work With a Lawyer

If you want to end up with a clear and binding pre-marital agreement, you should get help from a good lawyer. In fact, you will need two lawyers—one for each of you. That may sound surprising in a self-help legal book, but it's true. Here's why:

As we'll discuss in the next chapter, our Anglo-American legal system views marriage as a matter of contract between two consenting adults. The terms of the "marriage contract" are dictated by the laws of the state where the married people live, unless they have a premarital agreement containing different terms.

The laws governing marriage contracts vary tremendously from state to state. In this book, we provide some general information on each state's laws relating to prenups, and we give you some tips on doing your own legal research. (See Chapter 4 and Appendix D.) However, if you don't want to invest your time learning the ins and outs of your state's matrimonial laws, a lawyer who knows the intricacies of those laws will be an important resource. She or he can help you put together an agreement that meets state requirements and says what you want it to say.

This explains the desirability of having one lawyer, but why two? That's because prenuptial agreements are still scrutinized by the courts, sometimes very closely. If you want your agreement to pass muster, having an independent lawyer advise each of you can be critical. While most courts don't require that each party to a prenup have a lawyer, the absence of separate independent advice for each party is always a red flag to a judge. On a practical note, having separate legal advisors can help you and your fiancé craft a lasting agreement that you both understand and that doesn't leave either of you feeling that you've been taken advantage of.

That said, it's best not to ask your lawyers to start writing up a draft or final agreement until the two of you have agreed on its essential terms. You should also put those terms in writing—either in a written outline or a draft agreement created using the clauses in this book. A prenup prepared by a lawyer who isn't working from terms you've both agreed on is likely to be one-sided and adversarial. If you provide your lawyers with an outline or draft prepared by both of you, the whole process—and the final document—will be more balanced.

All of this assumes that you select and use lawyers who are not only competent and experienced in matrimonial law but who are also capable of supporting the two of you in negotiating and writing up a loving, clear, and fair agreement. You also don't want to spend a fortune on lawyers doing background work you could handle yourselves. Finding the right lawyers can take some time, but it's worth the effort. This book gives you some suggestions on how to find and work with good lawyers in a way that both cuts your costs and supports your relationship. (See Chapter 7.)

D. Icons Used in This Book

Throughout the book, the following symbols will help you along.

 Slow down and consider potential problems.

 Take advantage of an important tip.

 Consider talking with your lawyer or another expert.

 You may be able to skip some material that doesn't apply to your situation.

 Go to these sources for more information about the particular issue or topic discussed in the text. ■

1

A Prenup Primer

"Prenup" is an informal term for "prenuptial agreement," a written contract created by two people before they are married. A prenup typically lists all of the property each person owns (as well as any debts) and specifies what each person's property rights will be after they are married.

In this chapter, we'll show you how prenups work and what you can accomplish by preparing one. We'll also explain the steps involved in making a prenup from deciding whether or not you really need one to finalizing a binding contract.

A Prenup by Any Other Name

In some states, a prenuptial agreement is known as an "antenuptial agreement," or in more modern terms, as a "premarital agreement." Sometimes the word "contract" is substituted for "agreement," as in "prenuptial contract." For the sake of brevity, we'll stick with "prenup" in this book, but occasionally you'll find us using one of the other terms if it is appropriate.

A Note for Same-Sex Partners

Legally sanctioned same-sex relationships similar to marriage are now recognized in several states, and other states may follow suit. Same-sex couples who are planning to enter into a legal partnership face many of the same basic concerns confronted by couples about to marry. Addressing these issues in a written "pre-union" or "pre-partnership" agreement may be as desirable for a same-sex couple as for a couple planning to marry.

If you are in a same-sex partnership and want to write up a property agreement before making the relationship official, you can use this book to create your agreement. When you get to Chapter 4, be sure to familiarize yourself with any ways in which the laws of your state might be different for your relationship by doing your own research or consulting a competent lawyer.

Then, when assembling your draft agreement, adapt the sample clauses by substituting the words that fit your relationship for those that apply to a marriage. For example, you might use "partner" instead of "spouse," "union" or "partnership" instead of "marriage," and "partnership property" or "property of the union" instead of "marital property" or "community property."

A. How Prenups Work

People have been making prenuptial agreements for thousands of years. Scholars tell us that the practice dates back to the ancient Egyptians, and that prenups have existed for many centuries in Anglo-American tradition. In previous times, the parents of the bride and groom negotiated the agreement on the new couple's behalf. These days, engaged couples do their own negotiating, although family members often exert influence behind the scenes (especially if family money is involved).

Contrary to popular opinion, prenups are not just for the rich. While prenups are often used to protect the assets of a wealthy fiancé, couples of more modest means are increasingly turning to them for their own purposes. For example, a marrying couple with children from prior marriages may use a prenup to spell out what will happen to their property when they die, so that they can pass on separate property to their children

and still provide for each other, if necessary. Without a prenup, a surviving spouse might have the right to claim a large chunk of the other spouse's property, leaving much less for the kids.

Couples with or without children, wealthy or not, may simply want to clarify their financial rights and responsibilities during their marriage. Or they may want to avoid potential arguments if they ever divorce by specifying in advance how their property will be divided. Prenups can also be used to protect spouses from each other's debts, and they may address a multitude of other issues as well.

Exactly what you decide to do with your prenuptial agreement depends on your particular circumstances and wishes. But before getting into the specifics of what you want to accomplish with a prenup, it's wise to have a basic understanding of what you're doing when you make this type of contract. To put it briefly, you're deciding how you each want your property to be treated—during your marriage, when you divorce, or when one of you dies—rather than letting your state's law make these decisions for you.

1. Making Your Own Rules

If you don't make a prenuptial agreement, your state's laws will determine who owns the property that you acquire during your marriage, as well as what happens to that property at divorce or death. (This property is known as either marital or community property, depending on the state. We explain these terms in more detail in Chapter 4 and Appendix D.) State law may even have a say in what happens to some of the property you owned before you were married.

Under the law, marriage is considered a contract between bride and groom, and with that contract comes certain automatic property rights for each spouse. For example, in the absence of a prenup stating otherwise, a spouse usually has the right to:

- shared ownership of property acquired during marriage, with the expectation that the property will be divided between the spouses in the event of a divorce or at death
- incur debts during marriage that the other spouse may have to pay for, and
- share in the management and control of any marital or community property, sometimes including the right to sell it or give it away.

So what do you do if some of these laws—called marital property, divorce, and probate laws—aren't to your liking? Enter the prenup, which in most cases lets you decide for yourselves how your property should be handled.

As part of making your prenup, you'll review your state's laws to see how your own preferences for property ownership, division, and distribution compare with the state's rules. If you find that state law already provides the type of property treatment you wish, there may be no need to make a prenup. But if you find that the state's plan won't meet your needs, you'll probably want to go ahead and craft your own agreement. (In Chapter 4 and Appendix D, we discuss state laws in more detail and tell you how to find the laws for your state.)

Head off disputes by making a prenup if your state's law is unclear. When you familiarize yourself with the laws of your state, you might feel that they'll work just fine for you. But keep in mind that the law isn't always clear or predictable. Going without a prenup can increase the likelihood that there will be contentious and expensive court battles at the time of a divorce or even after death. Often, the law says something that seems straightforward enough at first glance, but it turns out that there's room for argument on the finer points. If you agree in advance on a fair approach to things like separate vs. shared ownership of property and inheritance rights of the surviving spouse, you can save yourselves and your inheritors the risk of legal expense, uncertainty, and acrimony by making a prenup.

Making Sure Your Prenup Is Valid

As prenuptial agreements become more common, the law is becoming friendlier toward them. Traditionally, courts scrutinized prenups with a suspicious eye, because they almost always involved a waiver of legal and financial benefits by a less-wealthy spouse. In the days when married women had far fewer legal rights than today, many courts believed that a woman was at too great a disadvantage when negotiating with her prospective husband. Even more unacceptable legally was a prenup that spelled out the couple's rights in the event of a divorce. Prior to 1970, such an agreement was considered unenforceable in all states because it was seen as a way to encourage divorce.

As divorce and remarriage have become more prevalent, and with growing equality between the sexes, courts and legislatures are increasingly willing to uphold premarital agreements. Today, every state permits them, although a prenup that is judged unfair or otherwise fails to meet state requirements will still be set aside. Because courts still look carefully at prenups, it is important that you negotiate and write up your agreement in a way that is clear, understandable, and legally sound. As you progress through the steps in this book, we'll show you how to avoid the pitfalls that could invalidate your agreement.

2. What a Typical Prenup Covers

Every prenup is unique to the couple that signs it. However, to introduce you to what a prenup can include—and what you might accomplish with yours—this section offers a list of typical prenup provisions.

Most prenups begin with a brief description of each party's circumstances—such as age, occupation, any children, and maybe even intentions for future employment or education. And prenups almost always include disclosures of both parties' finances—that is, assets, liabilities, and incomes. (These disclosures are usually attached to the end of the prenup as separate lists.)

Beyond that, what appears in the contract depends on your preferences. Here are some provisions that couples commonly include:

- A provision that each spouse's separately owned property will remain his or her sole and separate property during the marriage. (Sometimes this refers only to assets owned before the marriage, but it can also include property acquired during the marriage, especially gifts and inheritances.)
- A provision confirming that each person is responsible for his or her own premarital debts.
- A waiver of the surviving spouse's legal right to claim a share of the other spouse's separate property at death.

Here are some other typical but less common provisions:

- A provision that all property acquired by a spouse during marriage will be his or her separate property, and that there will be no marital or community property to be divided in a divorce or upon death.
- An exchange of property for the waiver of property rights, sometimes including one or more of the following:
  - payment of a certain amount of money (either right away or according to a specified timetable)
  - life insurance coverage, or
  - establishment of a trust for the spouse who is giving up his or her rights.
- A provision spelling out how property will be divided in the event of a divorce.
- A provision requiring each party to sign documents after the marriage reaffirming any waivers contained in the prenup. (This usually applies to waivers of rights to retirement benefits or an interest in real estate.)
- A provision specifying how household expenses will be paid.
- A provision that the agreement will automatically terminate on a certain date in the future, often called a "sunset clause."

Some prenups also include provisions that are enforceable in some states, but not in others. The most notable examples are provisions waiving alimony if there is a divorce or legal separation, and the so-called "bad-boy" (or bad-girl) clause requiring financial compensation if one party is caught cheating on the other.

In addition to the typical provisions, many prenups contain terms that are tailor-made to the couple's circumstances. For example, there might be an agreement that the couple will own a home in certain percentages, or perhaps the couple will promise to take turns supporting each other while obtaining an education.

Finally, every prenup contains standard clauses that go into all agreements of this kind. Lawyers often call these clauses "boilerplate" (a newspaper term referring to preset or syndicated features). The boilerplate in a prenup would most likely include clauses naming the lawyers who represented each party, a statement about who prepared the agreement, the agreement's binding effect on the couple and their inheritors, which state's law will apply in any legal dispute over the agreement, and other terms relating to the legal interpretation or enforcement of the agreement.

This material is just to get you started thinking about the issues that might be involved when you set out to make a prenup. In Chapter 2, we discuss in much more detail what a prenup can—and can't—do. And in Chapters 5 and 6, we provide plenty of sample clauses that you can include in your contract.

B. How to Make a Prenup

From getting started to getting married, there are eight basic steps to making a prenup. Here, we introduce you to each in turn, and explain how this book helps you along the way.

1. Start Early

Begin planning for your prenup as soon as possible—at least three months before the wedding. If you wait until the last minute, you may not have time to decide what you want and get it done in time. (An agreement signed after the wedding is not a prenup. It is a post-nuptial—or postmarital—agreement, and is covered by more stringent legal rules. See Chapter 9, Section F.)

Plan to sign your prenup about a month before the wedding. The closer you get to that all-important day, the more likely it becomes that your agreement won't stand up in court later.

Before signing, you should allow a couple of months—or longer, if you can—for talking together and figuring out the details of your agreement, getting it reviewed, and putting it into final form for signing.

Although it's possible to plan and finalize a prenup in less than three months, moving too fast will add un-needed stress and could doom your efforts to create a clear and fair agreement.

A premarital agreement is a binding legal document. It's true that some prenups get thrown out of court because they were signed at the last minute, but that doesn't mean yours will be. If you have reservations about a proposed agreement, don't sign it with the hope that you can get out of it later. You never know exactly what a particular court or judge might do.

2. Decide Whether You Need a Prenup

If you're reading this book, you've probably already decided that a prenup is what you want. Even so, it doesn't hurt to take a little time to examine your situation (together, if possible) to figure out if a prenup is what you need. Chapter 2 is devoted to helping you decide whether a prenup is right for your situation.

3. Agree on the Specifics

Once you've decided to go forward, the next step is to figure out exactly what your agreement should say. This involves doing some list making and some soul search-ing, both separately and together. Clear communication is essential to success in this endeavor, and it doesn't hurt to know a little about constructive negotiating, too. Chapter 3 explains how to decide on the specifics of your agreement, and Chapter 8 offers tips on commu-nicating and negotiating.

4. Create a Draft Agreement

As Chapter 3 explains in detail, you'll almost certainly be better off if you have your final prenuptial agreement written up by a lawyer. A good lawyer can ensure that you put together a contract that meets the requirements of your state and says exactly what you want it to say. In fact, as we explain later, you will greatly improve the odds that your prenup will stand up in court if each of you has a separate lawyer review and sign off on the agreement.

Even if you take our advice and work with lawyers, you'll save expense—and wear and tear on your nerves—by taking the time to write down what you've agreed on. That way, you'll both be in sync on the fine points before you ask a lawyer to prepare the final agreement. You'll also minimize the risk of having a lawyer put together a one-sided agreement that doesn't reflect what either of you wants. You can use your draft to check the lawyer's work, making sure nothing's been missed or misunderstood. Of course, if you elect not to use a lawyer to write up the final agreement, then your draft will eventually become the document you sign.

Chapters 5 and 6 provide a format for your prenup, with sample clauses covering the most common situa-tions and suggestions for customizing your agreement.

5. Write Up the Final Agreement

After you've made a draft agreement, each of you should read it carefully to see whether you need to make changes to it. Once that's done, you'll either prepare the final document yourselves or hire a lawyer to help you; the best way to proceed is to hire separate lawyers for each of you. Chapter 7 takes you through the process of finalizing your prenup, including suggestions for finding good lawyers and tips on how to work with them.

6. Show the Agreement to Your Lawyers

Whether you've prepared the final agreement yourselves or with the help of a lawyer (or two), the next step is to have your separate lawyers review the agreement to confirm that it's legally sound. (We discuss the importance of having separate lawyers review your agreement in the Introduction to this book and in Chapter 7, Section B.)

7. Sign the Agreement

Signing the agreement should be something you remember without regret. Plan to sign at a time when you can pay attention to the moment. If the agreement will be notarized, you'll need to arrange to sign when a notary is available. You may also have to contend with your lawyers' schedules, so it's important to plan ahead. You may even want to make a ceremony out of the event, or you might plan a little celebration afterward—just the two of you. Whatever you do, after the hard work you've done getting to this point, do what you can to make signing the agreement a relaxed and positive experience for both of you. (Chapter 7 provides more details about signing your prenup.)

8. Enjoy Your Wedding

Your wedding day promises to be one of the happiest moments of your life. When you get there, put away this book, file away your prenup, and enjoy the day. Our best wishes will be with you. ■

Is a Prenup Right for You?

You may be wondering whether you really need or want a prenup. If so, this chapter can help. Here, we explain what you can and cannot accomplish with a prenup. We also outline a step-by-step approach you can take to decide whether a prenup is right for your particular situation.

We've designed this chapter so that the two of you can read and use it together. We will also show you how to adapt this process for individual use, if that is more comfortable for you.

If you know you want a prenup, skip ahead. To get right to the specifics of what your agreement will say, turn to Chapter 3.

A. What You Can Do With a Prenup

When deciding whether you want a prenup, you might find it helpful to consider the kinds of things that you can—and cannot—do with this type of contract. Prenups are most often used to:

- keep finances separate
- protect one or both spouses from the other person's debts
- support an estate plan by agreeing to provide for children from prior marriages or to keep family property in the family
- define who gets what in the event of separation or divorce, and/or
- clarify each person's responsibilities after marriage

Let's take a closer look at each of these possibilities.

Each state has its own laws about what can and cannot be covered in a prenup. This chapter gives you general rules about what you can and can't do, but you'll need to check the laws of your state to be sure that what we say here applies to you. For an overview of state laws, see Chapter 4. For a summary of the laws in your state, see Appendix D.

1. Keep Your Finances Separate

Every state has laws designating certain kinds of assets accumulated during marriage as marital or community

property, even if these assets are held in the name of just one spouse. If a couple divorces or when one spouse dies, the marital or community property will be divided between them, either by agreement or by a court.

If you want to avoid having some or all of your individual accumulations during marriage divided up, you can do so with a premarital agreement. The prenup can be customized to fit your situation. For example, if you want to keep absolutely everything separate, you can specify that no assets accumulated during your marriage will be considered marital property. Or you can specify that certain types of property or items that you plan to acquire will be separate property and the rest will be marital property, or vice versa.

Steven and Freda

Steven, a sales manager, and Freda, a schoolteacher, are considering a prenup. They are in their mid-30s and this is a first marriage for both of them. Steven watched his brother Tom go through a bitter divorce two years ago. Tom told Steven he had better have a prenup to protect the property he owns before the marriage. When Steven mentioned the idea to Freda, it occurred to her that she might also want to use a prenup to keep her own premarital assets separate.

Rules for retirement plans. Most retirement plans require a separate written waiver of spousal death benefits—that is, one spouse's right to receive money from the plan if the other spouse dies. The waiver cannot be signed before you marry and must be on a form provided by the retirement plan. Your agreement can spell out your intentions to waive spousal death benefits, but you or your spouse must also sign the necessary form after you are married.

2. Protect One or Both of You From the Other Person's Debts

Some of us bring debts, as well as assets, to a marriage. If there's no prenup, creditors can sometimes turn to marital or community property to satisfy the debts of

You can't hide property. Every state has laws making it illegal to give away your own property to protect it from debt collectors. These laws are known as "fraudulent transfer" laws. While you can use a prenup to protect your fiancé's separate property from your debts, you probably cannot save your own assets from your creditors by transferring ownership to your fiancé. If one of your goals is to protect each other's property from your separate debts, good legal advice from a competent lawyer may be especially valuable.

just one spouse. But if you want to make sure that saying "I do" does not mean saying "I owe," you can use a prenup to limit your liability for each other's debts. Your prenup can specify who will be responsible for any debts you bring to the marriage. You may also be able to place certain assets out of the reach of bill collectors by designating those assets as the separate property of the person who does not owe the debt.

Karen and Russ

Karen and Russ are both in their late 40s and about to get married, each for the second time. They live in California, a community property state. Karen is a veterinarian who has two teenage children. Russ is a bookkeeper who has a six-year-old daughter. Each of them owns a home. After they marry, they plan to rent out Russ's house and live at Karen's place.

Both Karen and Russ want to protect their property from the other person's debts. Although Karen's veterinary practice is quite successful, Karen and Russ want to be sure that there will not be any liens placed against Russ's home if a disgruntled patient sues Karen or if her business runs into financial troubles.

They are equally concerned about protecting Karen's assets and income from Russ's business debts and any child support obligations to his ex-wife.

Karen and Russ may be able prevent these problems by using a prenup to designate their assets and earnings as their separate property, and to spell out their intention to be responsible for their own debts.

3. Provide for Children From Prior Marriages

A prenup is helpful (perhaps essential) if either of you has children from another relationship and you want to make sure that your children inherit their share of your property. Consider the following examples.

Ted and Grace

Ted, age 70, is a retired real estate developer. He owns several parcels of commercial real estate as well as his own home, which is furnished with valuable antiques and artwork. Ted has three grown children. Grace is 48 and has worked for the past fifteen years as a county social worker. She owns her own home and has a modest retirement plan from the county. She has no children of her own. Ted wants to make sure that Grace will be comfortably provided for if he dies first, but he also wants to make sure that his property will revert to his children after Grace dies.

Without a prenup, Ted can do some estate planning and make a will or trust that lets Grace use (but not actually own) Ted's property during her lifetime, with the assets going outright to Ted's children when Grace dies. But even with a good estate plan in place, Grace could still be entitled to a share of Ted's estate, as Ted's surviving spouse. If Ted and Grace agree, Grace can waive her rights, in a binding premarital agreement, to take the share of a surviving spouse. This guarantees that Ted's estate plan will work the way that Ted intends.

Karen and Russ

Let's go back to Karen and Russ, introduced above. Karen's divorce settlement with her first husband states that each of her two children is to receive at least $50,000 from her estate if she dies before the youngest child turns 25.

Even if Karen makes sure that her will sets aside $50,000 in a custodianship for each child, Russ's rights as a surviving spouse could affect Karen's estate plan unless they sign a prenup in which Russ agrees to waive those rights.

4. Pass on Family Property

In a prenup, you list all of the property each of you owns at the time of your marriage. If your property includes something you want to keep in your birth family, whether it be an heirloom or a share in a family business, you can specify that item in your prenup and the two of you can agree that it will remain in your family. This can even include property that you expect to receive in a future inheritance.

Ted and Grace

Many of the antiques in Ted's house are family heirlooms. Ted wants to leave some items to his children and let Grace enjoy the use of all the other items until she dies, at which time they will also go to his children. Ted can designate the items going to Grace and to his children in a will or trust. Then Ted and Grace can use a prenup to list Ted's family heirlooms so that there will be no question about which items in the house were Ted's and which ones belong to Grace.

On her side, Grace owns a 10% share of a family farm, together with her mother and sister. Her mother is planning to give Grace and her sister a larger share of the farm over the next few years. Grace and Ted can include in their prenup a statement that Ted waives any spousal claim to Grace's current and future share in the family farm so that Grace's will or trust can leave her share to her sister.

Follow through by making your estate plan. In addition to using your prenup to waive inheritance rights and state your intentions for passing on your property at death, it's vital that you prepare the estate planning documents—your wills, living trusts, and so on—that actually transfer your property as you intend. See Chapter 9, Section D, for more information about estate planning.

Reassuring Family Members

Sometimes the main impetus for a prenup comes from your grown children or other family members. Your children may worry that they will be left out when you die. Other family members may fret over possible dilution of the family wealth. Still others may be concerned about messy disagreements after you are gone. Even if you know that there is no reason for alarm, you may decide to reassure your nervous family members by spelling things out in a prenup.

On the other hand, it is important that you not let others dictate what is best for the two of you. As we have said before, a prenup should reflect your marriage commitment to one another. This may mean balancing your concern for family members with your best interests as a couple. It may take some careful thinking, discussion, and planning. For help, see Chapter 8.

---

5. Define Who Gets What If You Divorce

As mentioned earlier, without a prenup, state law will specify how your property will be divided if you ever divorce. These laws may dictate a result that neither of you wants. (Chapter 4 provides an overview of how state divorce laws work.) You can use a prenup to establish your own rules for property division and avoid potential disagreements in the event of a divorce.

Talking about what would happen if you divorce can be a touchy subject, likely to raise at least some anxiety in most people. However, if you are comfortable talking about the possibility of a future divorce, spelling out your rights in advance can be a wise thing to do. In fact, you may be surprised to find that talking about these things brings the two of you closer together. You might want to try turning the subject on its head: You're not really planning for divorce, but practicing honest communication about important issues such as money, property, and family—skills that are likely to *prevent* divorce in the long run. And if you ever do part ways, the work you've done on your prenup will almost certainly make the passage easier.

> **EXAMPLE:** Daniel and Chanee plan to buy a house together. Chanee's parents have agreed to give them the money for the down payment. In the state where Chanee and Daniel live, the law is not clear whether the gift from Chanee's parents is considered joint property or Chanee's separate property. Furthermore, state law says that in the event of a divorce, even if the down payment were found to be Chanee's separate property, she would be entitled to reimbursement for only the amount of the down payment, without appreciation, unless she and Daniel have a written agreement stating otherwise.
>
> In talking about this, Daniel and Chanee agree that if they ever split up, Chanee would get back the money from her parents, plus appreciation if the value of the house goes up after they buy it. Chanee and Daniel ensure that their agreement about the down payment will be carried out in a divorce by including it in their prenup.

Some people use a prenup to simplify potentially complicated property issues. This can save money and time if there is a divorce. It can also streamline the settlement of your estate by clearly specifying what will belong to the estate and what will belong to the surviving spouse.

Karen and Russ

Naturally, Karen and Russ hope to stay together. They expect Karen's veterinary practice to provide both of them with a comfortable lifestyle and retirement savings as they grow older, supplemented by Russ's more modest earnings as a bookkeeper.

Karen and Russ are also aware that under state law, a portion of any increase in the value of Karen's veterinary practice will be considered community property. This seems fair to them, especially since Russ contributes his time to the veterinary practice by doing the books on the weekends.

Karen's lawyer has advised her to put into the prenup a formula for calculating the community property share in Karen's practice. According to the lawyer, there are numerous methods for computing community property rights in a business at the time of divorce. Settling on the most appropriate method in advance will eliminate the possibility of a long and expensive duel between experts in a contested divorce case. This can also cut down on expenses of probate, since the community property share of Karen's practice might need to be determined then, too.

6. Clarify Each Person's Responsibilities During the Marriage

We have already discussed how you can use a prenup to keep your finances separate, to protect yourselves from each other's debts, to support your estate plans for your children or family property, and even to spell out your rights if there is a divorce. There are countless other uses for a prenup, depending on your circumstances and what the two of you want. Here are some examples of other matters people include in their prenups:

- procedures for deciding whether to file joint or separate income tax returns, or for allocating income and tax deductions on separate tax returns
- who will pay the household bills, and how—for example, each of you might take responsibility for paying certain bills from your separate accounts, or you might agree to pay all bills from a joint account, into which you deposit equal or proportionate contributions
- whether to have joint bank accounts and, if so, how you will handle them—for example, you might agree to create several joint accounts for different purposes (household expenses, savings, vacations, taxes) and decide how you will make contributions to each
- agreements about specific purchases or projects, such as buying a house together or starting up a business

- how you will handle credit card charges—for instance, whether you will use different cards for different types of purchases, what kinds of records you will keep, and how you will make payments
- agreements to set aside money for savings
- agreements for putting each other through college or professional school
- whether you will provide for a surviving spouse—for example, in your estate plan or with life insurance coverage, and
- how to settle any future disagreements—for example, you might agree to hire either a mediator or a private arbitrator.

As you can see, most topics covered in prenups are financial. However, some people are tempted to include nonmonetary matters in their premarital agreements as well—from critical issues such as having children to more mundane matters such as who's responsible for household chores. We recommend against this, for reasons discussed in the next section.

B. What You Can't Do With a Prenup

As we said at the beginning of this chapter, there are some things you cannot accomplish with a prenup. State laws differ as to what matters are considered off-limits. However, as a general rule, any agreement to do something that is illegal or against state-defined public policy will be considered unenforceable—and may even jeopardize other valid aspects of the premarital agreement.

The Protest Prenup

One of the most unusual prenups in history was signed by Lucy Stone and Henry Blackwell on their wedding day in Massachusetts in 1855. At the time of their marriage, both were well known as antislavery abolitionists and as proponents of the growing movement for reform of property laws affecting married women.

In those days, the laws of most states considered a married woman a legal nonentity. If she owned any land when she married, it stayed in her name, but her husband had sole rights to manage and sell it, and any profits belonged to him. She was prohibited from owning or acquiring any new property, and she was barred from entering into any legal contract. She had no right even to use her own name if she chose to, since the law considered her identity to be incorporated into that of her husband.

In this context, Henry Blackwell and Lucy Stone, who objected to those laws, stood before their assembled wedding guests and recited a "protest" they had written together. In it, they declared their mutual affection and commitment to become husband and wife. They then stated their objection to the laws giving custody of the wife to the husband and prohibiting her from having an identity of her own. They stated their belief that marriage should be an equal partnership and they agreed that if any difficulties arose between them, they would submit the matter to a mutually chosen arbitrator rather than to a court of law that refused to recognize a woman's equal human rights.

After the wedding, Lucy Stone cut back on her public speaking and activism in order to devote her time to being a wife and mother. However, she and her husband left their mark in the annals of marital property law. Their written protest, which was sent to local newspapers, helped further the cause of reforming property laws. By the end of the nineteenth century, most states had adopted some form of a "married woman's property act."

Meanwhile, Lucy Stone set an example by retaining her maiden name, although she often had to add the phrase "wife of Henry Blackwell" to sign legal documents or to avoid scandal when registering at hotels with her husband. Women who followed her example by keeping their maiden names were known as "Lucy Stoners," a term that endured well into the twentieth century.

For practical reasons, you should also keep non-financial matters out of your prenup; there are better ways to address issues that are strictly personal.

1. Agreements That Violate Public Policy

Your state may block you from including a number of issues in your prenup. For example, no state will honor agreements limiting or waiving future child support. The same holds true of agreements limiting future custody and visitation rights. This is because state lawmakers consider the welfare of children to be a matter of public policy and do not enforce any private agreements that would impair a child's right to be supported or to have a relationship with a parent in the future.

In some states, a similar public policy limitation applies to agreements waiving alimony—also called spousal support or separate maintenance—if there is a divorce. Other states permit such waivers, so you will need to know what your state laws say if you are considering this kind of agreement. (See the summary for your state in Appendix D.)

A third example of a public policy limitation is any agreement that would "promote" divorce. At one time, many courts viewed any prenup specifying how things would be divided up if the couple were to split as void and unenforceable because it promoted divorce. The modern approach allows such agreements, but judges in some states still take a hard look at them. If the agreement appears to offer a financial incentive for divorce to one party, it may be set aside.

The Case of the Dubious Dowry

In a famous California case called *Marriage of Noghrey*, the court threw out a premarital agreement specifying that the wife would receive a house and half of her husband's premarital separate property if they divorced. The prenup was arranged by the families of the bride and groom, who were members of a traditional culture where a husband could divorce his wife at will and the wife could not. In that culture, a prenup guaranteeing a wife a substantial divorce settlement was designed to discourage a husband from divorcing his wife. But in California, Mrs. Noghrey was able to sue for a no-fault divorce a few months after the wedding. She then tried to claim the property specified in the prenup. The court invalidated the premarital agreement because it violated public policy by giving Mrs. Noghrey an incentive to file for divorce. (See *Marriage of Noghrey*, 215 Cal.Rptr. 153 (1985).)

2. The Practical Limits of a Prenup

Even if your prenup does not contain anything that is illegal or against public policy, there are practical limitations to what you can do with a prenup. While you can take care of the most obvious and most important aspects of your finances, there is no way you can—or should—anticipate every possible contingency that might arise during your marriage. A better solution to the "what ifs" of your future together is to periodically review your prenup to see if it still makes sense or if changes are needed to bring it into line with your new circumstances. For more on this, see Chapter 9.

You also shouldn't try to dictate every aspect of your personal life in a prenup. While we think that communicating about what's important to each of you is a vital part of preparing for marriage, a prenup isn't the best place to address lifestyle agreements—that is, matters such as who's responsible for taking out the garbage and what kind of schedule you will keep around the house, or whether you will have kids and, if so, how many.

Nonmonetary agreements aren't binding in court, and in fact they could cause a judge to take your entire prenup less seriously. Rather than including such matters in your prenup, you may find it helpful to simply make a list of your most important concerns and discuss them together. If you want to take it a step farther, you can underscore your commitment by writing down your personal agreements in a separate document—perhaps in a letter that each of you writes to the other, clarifying your intentions and wishes.

Here is a partial list of nonfinancial matters that sometimes find their way into prenups, but that we believe are better dealt with separately. Of course, the possible issues are endless and you may well think of many that aren't mentioned here:

- responsibility for household chores—from laundry to cleaning to car care
- use of last names after you marry
- agreements about having and raising children, such as birth control, having children, children's names, child care responsibilities, and education
- how you will relate to in-laws or stepchildren, and
- whether you will have any pets and who will be responsible for them.

However you approach your personal agreements, be sure to leave yourselves plenty of room to experiment and discover together. As long as you cover the basics, the rest will probably take care of itself, especially if you stay current and communicate with each other as you go along.

C. Will a Prenup Work for You?

Whether to have a premarital agreement is as personal and unique a decision as whether to marry in the first place. Only the two of you can call this one, and even so, you may think differently about it now than you will in a year—or two, or 20. Here, we'll take you through several steps to help you figure out whether a prenup is what you need. First, we'll briefly list the main advantages and disadvantages of prenups. Then we'll walk you through some basic questions to help you decide whether a prenup is right for you and your fiancé. Finally, we offer some suggestions for talking together about what you've discovered—and about whether you want to continue with the process of making a written agreement.

1. Consider the Pros and Cons

Before getting to the specifics of your situation, it can be helpful to review the general pros and cons of making a prenup. We'll start with the good news, then we'll take up a couple of the downsides.

a. Benefits of a Prenup

We've already mentioned some of the main benefits of having a prenup, but here's a quick list to remind you. Making a prenup can:

- protect your separate property
- support your estate plan
- define what is considered marital or community property
- reduce conflicts and save money if you divorce
- clarify special agreements between you, and
- establish procedures and ground rules for deciding future matters.

In addition, remember that creating a prenup may strengthen your relationship. While people often focus on the fact that negotiating a prenup can be potentially divisive, it is easy to lose sight of the fact that communicating about money matters can actually improve the quality of your marriage. Even if you do not end up signing a written agreement, just sitting down and hashing out the basics about money and property can eliminate misunderstandings that might otherwise derail your marriage.

How can you tell whether negotiating a prenup would help or do damage to your relationship? Obviously, there's no way to know for sure. But you probably have a pretty good sense of how well the two of you can talk now about money matters. You probably also know your own temperament. Are you the type to plan in advance and confront things directly, or are you more inclined to let things take their course and deal with problems if and when they arise? How about your fiancé: Does she or he like to plan or take things as they come?

Balancing such intangibles against your legal and financial objectives will help you decide the right course for you. Remember, sooner or later you and your intended will be talking about money. If you think you can handle it, most psychologists and legal experts would tell you there's no time like the present.

Everybody's Got an Opinion

Many experts who work with couples in conflict—and those familiar with statistics on divorce rates—believe that having a prenup strengthens a relationship. Some even believe prenups should be mandatory. Why? Because making a prenup forces a couple to grapple with the difficult but necessary questions of money and property. By working through money issues in advance, couples start out their economic partnership on a firm foundation.

Other experts say prenups are not all that useful: they cite examples of couples who put away the prenup once it is signed and never look at it or think of it again.

Interestingly, very few scholars believe prenups are harmful. Nevertheless, the idea meets with resistance among many couples. Not only does having a prenup run counter to our romantic ideas about love and marriage, but there is also the potential for dissension and divisiveness. A couple negotiating a prenup may even discover that they have such fundamental differences that they decide to call off the wedding. While some would say that it's better to find out about such differences sooner rather than later, others disagree and argue for a wait-and-see approach. You and your fiancé must consider this question and be the final judges of whether negotiating up front is likely to help or hurt.

b. Disadvantages of a Prenup

While there is a lot to be said for a carefully considered, clearly written prenup, there are some downsides to consider before proceeding.

i. It's Not Romantic

Let's face it, a prenup is not romantic. Being engaged conjures up images of candlelit dinners and walks in the moonlight. Although marriage is a financial partnership as well as romantic one, if you feel that discussing anything as mundane as property and finances will mar an otherwise beautiful time of your lives, you may not be candidates for a prenup.

ii. The Time May Not Be Right

The need for a prenup is partly a question of timing. The issues covered in a prenup will probably arise sooner or later in your marriage: money management, property rights, responsibility for debts, estate planning. And if your marriage does not work out, you will certainly need to deal with divorce decisions. If you decide to have a prenup, you will confront many of these issues now, at a time when your relationship is still new and perhaps untested. The process of discussing what goes into a prenup could be unpleasant and stressful, leaving one or both of you with bad feelings about the relationship. (If now is not the time to make a written agreement, you may be able to make a contract after you marry—called a "postnup." But postnups have their own disadvantages. See Chapter 9 for more information.)

iii. State Law May Protect You Without a Prenup

It may be that the laws of your state do a fine job of accomplishing what you want. For example, you might live in a community property state where assets owned before marriage are separate property and all assets accumulated during the marriage are community property that is owned 50-50. If this is essentially what you would want in your prenup, or maybe even better than what you expected, why go through the hassle, expense, and possible unpleasantness of negotiating a prenup? Still, you will want to be certain that you're not facing any special circumstances where your state law is unclear. Proceed to the next step to take a careful look at your situation.

2. Examine Your Situation

Now that you have an overview of the basic uses and considerations—pro and con—of a prenup, you are ready to focus on the specifics of your situation and figure out if a prenup is what you need.

Step One: Take a Prenup Quiz

If you are not sure whether you would benefit from a prenup, ask yourself these questions. If you and your fiancé are using this book together, each of you should answer the questions that apply to you. If you are doing this on your own, answer as many questions as you can for both of you.

	You	Your Fiancé
1. Do you own any real estate?	_____	_____
2. Do you own more than $50,000 in assets other than real estate?	_____	_____
3. Do you own a business (with or without other partners)?	_____	_____
4. Do you owe more than $10,000?	_____	_____
5. Are you currently earning a salary of more than $100,000 per year?	_____	_____
6. Have you earned more than one year's worth of retirement benefits or do you have other valuable employment benefits, such as profit sharing or stock options?	_____	_____
7. Does one of you plan to pursue an advanced degree while the other works?	_____	_____
8. Will all or part of your estate go to someone other than your spouse?		

If you or your fiancé answer yes to any question, there is a good chance a prenup would be helpful. If you answered no to all the questions, you might still benefit from a prenup, but having one might not be as critical for you.

Step Two: Identify Important Issues

Jot down on a piece of paper a list of the things you might want to include in a prenup, such as separate property identification, decisions about how you will handle money and property while you are married, retirement benefit agreements, and agreements about how you want to leave property at your death.

Common Prenup Topics

Here's a quick reminder of some of the issues that can be included in a prenup:

- separate vs. joint property
- estate planning issues such as providing for children from prior marriages or leaving family property
- how to handle a separate business
- retirement benefits
- nonresponsibility for the other person's debts
- who gets what if you separate or divorce
- procedures for filing tax returns, including allocating income and deductions
- who pays household bills—and how
- whether to have joint bank accounts and if so, how to manage them
- agreements about specific purchases or projects, such as buying a house together or starting up a business
- how you will handle credit card charges
- agreements to set aside money for savings
- agreements for putting each other through college or professional school
- provisions for a surviving spouse in your estate plans or through life insurance coverage
- how to settle any future disagreements, such as with the help of a mediator or by a private arbitrator acting as judge.

Step Three: Assess Your Comfort Level

Next, ask yourself this question. On a scale of one to five, how comfortable am I with the idea of having a prenup? A one is not comfortable at all and a five is very comfortable.

If you gave yourself a one or a two, try to identify the reasons for your discomfort. If it is because you are uncertain how the terms of a prenup might compare to your legal rights without one, you may want to investigate the laws of your state before making your decision. (See Chapter 4 and Appendix D.) If you are pretty sure you want a prenup and your discomfort comes from fear of starting an argument or offending your fiancé, then you might take this as an opportunity to practice talking about difficult matters in a loving way, using some of the techniques we discuss in Chapter 8. You may even find it helpful to work on your communication and negotiation skills with a counselor who specializes in premarital counseling. (This is also discussed in Chapter 8.)

If you scored a three, four, or five on the comfort scale, you are ready to start talking specifics with your fiancé. Even so, bear in mind that every good conversation involves some give and take. Don't assume that you and your fiancé will see eye-to-eye on everything, especially when you first start talking. Allow plenty of time to talk—and be willing to get help if you need it.

3. Share Your Thoughts

If you think you want a prenup and you have been using this book by yourself up until now, then it is probably time to broach the subject with your fiancé. If the two of you have been using this book together, it will be a natural progression to share with each other what you've learned about your attitude toward a prenup.

If one or both of you has some interest in a prenup, then you're ready to work on the specifics and you can move on to Chapter 3. But before you do, you may want to read through Chapter 8 for some specific suggestions on communicating and negotiating.

If you've been working alone so far and you're ready to raise the topic with your fiancé, how to proceed is a matter of individual style and preference. You probably know better than anyone what is best. Some people prefer a direct and forthright approach. Others will want to introduce the idea more slowly and indirectly.

It may be that you have both concluded that a prenup is not for you. In that case, you can close this book and go back to planning your wedding and honeymoon or just enjoying your time together.

Ted and Grace

Remember Ted? He is the direct type. When he approached Grace about a prenup, here is what he said, "I've been thinking about our financial future and how best to provide for you and

protect you from hassles with my kids when I die. I've heard that having a premarital agreement is a good way to do this. What do you think? Can we talk about it? I've got a good book about prenups, and a few suggestions and ideas. Let's arrange a time to take a look at this together."

Karen and Russ

Karen's approach was similarly direct. Here is what she said to Russ: "I went to see my lawyer about the contract with the new vet we're hiring. We talked a little about coverage for the office when you and I are gone for the honeymoon and she told me that we really should have a prenup to spell out what happens to the practice if I die or if we get divorced. I know it's not a very pleasant subject to have to deal with, but we probably should talk about it soon."

Steven and Freda

Steven favored a more indirect approach when talking to Freda. Here's how he got the ball rolling: "You know, I'm starting to realize that there is a lot more to getting married than just planning the wedding. The human resources manager at my office said there are a lot of forms that I'm going to have to sign after we're married, including beneficiary designations for my retirement benefits and insurance forms. You've probably got similar paperwork to deal with at school. Maybe we should sit down sometime soon and go over all this stuff together." Freda and Steven then arranged a time to talk. When they met, Steven brought up his brother's remark about protecting the property he already owns. This led to a conversation about using a written premarital agreement to specify that all the property owned by Steven and Freda before their marriage would remain their separate property.

These are just a few examples of how you might approach the subject of a prenup. Again, there is no one right way to do it. You will know best what will work for you. The most important thing is to clearly and kindly express what you want—and to be open to your fiancé's point of view. ■

Deciding on the Specifics

Once you've decided you want a prenup, you'll need to hammer out the details of your agreement. But where to start? Unless you've been through this before, you're probably not sure how to proceed. This chapter provides a step-by-step approach to figuring out what to include in your prenup.

A. Evaluating Your Situation

Crafting a prenup begins with a conversation about what you want the written agreement to accomplish. To prepare for that important conversation, we suggest that you make a few notes about your financial situation and your goals for the prenup. These notes will help you stay on target when you talk. They will also be useful when you compile the written financial disclosures for the prenup and prepare an outline of terms to include in the prenup itself.

1. Inventory Your Finances

A prenup establishes guidelines for your financial future together. A good way to start thinking about choosing those financial guidelines is to get a clear picture of your current financial circumstances. Then when you sit down to discuss the prenup, you will have a solid base of information from which to work.

To help you develop a clear picture of your finances, we suggest that you and your fiancé each prepare a financial inventory. When you've finished, you will share your inventories as you decide what your prenup should say about property ownership and other financial issues. Your financial inventory will also be the basis of the written financial disclosures attached to your prenup, so it's a good idea to make the inventory as complete and accurate as possible.

To prepare your inventory, you can use Worksheet 1 (available in Appendix B or on the CD-ROM at the back of the book) or you can choose some other format (see "Don't Reinvent the Wheel," just below).

Don't Reinvent the Wheel

If the inventory we're describing sounds familiar, that's probably because you've already made one. Many of us have prepared a personal financial statement (or net worth statement) for some other purpose. Or you may have assembled your financial information when applying for a mortgage or other loan. If you still have a copy of that financial statement or loan application, you can use it as a starting point and simply update it as needed.

Even if you haven't previously prepared a financial inventory, you may have access to one without realizing it. For example, many personal finance software programs—such as *Quicken* and *Microsoft Money*—have the capacity to generate net worth reports and income/expense (cash flow) statements. If you already keep track of your finances with a computer program, you may be able generate a complete report at the push of a button. (You could also take this opportunity to start keeping track of your finances through a software program. Then you can update the information and print out a report whenever you need it.)

If you want to stick to pad and pencil, and if you don't have a favorite format, our financial inventory worksheet may suit you just fine. Choose whatever method works best for you. Just be sure to include the basics that we discuss below: what you own, what you owe, how much you make, and how much you spend.

Have you already done an inventory? If you've already prepared a thorough inventory, you can skip the rest of this section and go on to Section 2, "Examine Your Credit History and Spending Habits."

Whatever format you use, we recommend that you each complete a separate financial inventory, even if you and your fiancé are working through this book together. Set aside a quiet time. Have your financial records and a notepad or keyboard at hand. Go through your records and make an inventory of your current finances. The inventory should include the following information:

- **Assets.** List all of the property you own. Put down an estimate of current market value next to each asset.
- **Debts.** List all your outstanding debts and write the current balance due next to each debt.
- **Income.** List your current annual or monthly income. If your income comes from more than one source, such as wages, interest, and dividends, indicate your income from each source.
- **Expenses.** Estimate your household and personal expenses. Separate the expenses into categories such as housing, auto, food, and other personal expenses. You can use average monthly amounts or annual figures.

If this is your first attempt at preparing a personal financial inventory, here are some guidelines to follow.

a. Listing Your Assets

An asset is any property you own that has value, including cash, real estate, individual items of property, and money that others owe you.

When describing and valuing your assets, you should be as thorough, specific, and accurate as possible. Obviously, we don't expect you to list everything you own down to your paperclips and the leftovers in your fridge, but you'll want to make sure to include everything that's important to you—financially or sentimentally. (See Worksheet 1 to jog your thinking about what you might include in your inventory.)

Categorize assets to save time. You don't need to list every item of property separately—you can use categories for similar types of property. For example, you might list all of your household furnishings, linens, kitchenware, appliances, and the like as "household goods." You can then estimate the total value of all of the items in that category. Do the same with other assets, such as automobiles or bank accounts. When

you prepare the written disclosure that will be attached to your prenup, you may decide to be more detailed with some assets, but that's not necessary at this stage.

Specify your ownership percentage. If you own less than 100% of an asset because you share ownership with another person, indicate your percentage and the value of your share.

Use market values. Include your best estimate of the current market value of each asset or category of assets. If you have a obtained a recent appraisal, that can be a good point of reference. Here are some tips that may help you determine the value of particular items of property.

- **Real Estate.** You can use classified ads in your local newspaper (or an online equivalent) as a starting point in determining the value of real estate. In addition, you can check with a local realtor—as a way of promoting their services, many realtors provide a complementary "property profile" based on a computer search of similar properties in the local multiple listing records.
- **Vehicles.** You can get the wholesale and retail values for vehicles from one of the "blue book" type services available online or at your public library, or you can check with a dealer.
- **Household Goods.** Classified ads are good sources for valuing large household items.
- **Stocks, Bonds, and Mutual Funds.** If you own investments like these through a broker, your monthly or quarterly statement will show their values as of the statement date. You can obtain current values from your broker, from any daily newspaper, or from one of the many stock trading websites on the Internet.
- **Small Businesses.** If you own all or part of a small business—that is, one that is not publicly traded on the stock market—determining the market value of the business may be tricky, unless you just purchased the business or recently had the business appraised for some other reason, such as applying for a loan or buying out a partner.

  Appraisers use many different methods for valuing businesses. Some methods are as simple as multiplying the yearly gross receipts of the business by a certain number (typically a number between 1 and 4, depending on the type of business).

Other methods are much more complicated. Which method to use depends on the circumstances and the type of business. If you don't have recent data on the value of your business, you can ask your accountant to help. The accountant may have an easy way to estimate the market value of your particular business. If not, the accountant can give you a balance sheet showing the "book value" of the business. Book value first considers the original cost of the assets owned by the business, then adjusts that amount for depreciation and outstanding liabilities. Book value may not accurately reflect the market value of the business assets, nor will it take into account the intangible "goodwill" value of the business. Nevertheless, it is a good starting point for your discussions about a prenup, and it can be replaced by a more accurate market value later, if you decide that is necessary. If you do use book value, make a note of this on your inventory.

b. Listing Your Debts

A debt is a legal obligation to pay money now or in the future. A mortgage is a debt, as is a car payment. The amount owed on a line of credit is a debt, along with any other amount borrowed and not yet repaid. Unpaid taxes are considered a debt, along with any penalties and interest that have accrued. Bills that get paid in full when due, such as utilities and insurance premiums, are in a sense debts too, until they're paid. But you don't need to include those recurring monthly bills in the "debts" section of your financial inventory unless they are overdue. The same is true of revolving credit arrangements or credit card charges; don't list them unless the balance due is more than what you will pay off in the current month.

A special category of debt is any obligation owed to a former spouse—or to the other parent of your child. Include child support and alimony (spousal support) obligations on your list of debts, even if you are current in your payments. If you owe a property settlement or reimbursement payment under a divorce decree (judgment), include that in your list. Sometimes a divorce

decree requires you to do something other than pay money. For example, you may be required to maintain dependent medical insurance coverage for your children. Or you may have to keep a life insurance policy for your children or your former spouse. If so, list those obligations, too. Even though they are not technically debts, these obligations should be considered when you decide what goes in your prenup.

c. Listing Your Income

The financial inventory you are preparing should include a reasonably accurate picture of your current income from all sources. If you filed a federal income tax return for last year (Form 1040), and if your income hasn't changed significantly since then, you can put down the same amounts that appear in the income section of your return. The income section of our financial inventory worksheet includes the most common income categories, with a space to insert others.

If your income in any category has changed significantly since the time covered by your last income tax return—or if you haven't filed an income tax return recently—then you'll need to insert the current amounts, using whatever records you have, such as pay stubs or monthly investment statements. This may involve converting monthly or quarterly figures to yearly amounts.

Sometimes income varies substantially from year to year. This is particularly true of business or investment income. If this is your situation, take a look at your annual income for the last three to five years and come up with a reasonable average. Indicate that average on your worksheet.

d. Listing Your Expenses

Unless you and your fiancé are already living together, you don't necessarily know what the other spends on housing, food, clothing, and other personal items. After you marry, you will be partners in spending as in other aspects of your financial life together. Sharing with each other a summary of your current expenditures will help you assess differences and similarities in spending patterns, so that you can decide whether to include an agreement about budgeting in your prenup.

Because your monthly expenses will probably change after you marry, you don't have to go into great detail when listing your expenses. Just summarize your expenses in major categories. Our financial inventory worksheet breaks expenses down in four categories: Housing, Transportation & Auto, Necessities (including food, clothing, and medical expenses), and Other (such as entertainment, travel, gifts, and so forth). Feel free to be flexible in your approach; you may come up with different categories that work better for you. You can insert a total amount for each category or break down a category into smaller ones, as we do on the financial inventory sheet.

Because some expenses are the same each month while others change, you may decide that annual figures, monthly amounts, or perhaps some other time period, such as quarterly or year to date, give the most accurate numbers. Any approach will work, as long as you indicate which one you're using.

2. Examine Your Credit History and Spending Habits

In addition to sharing information about your assets, debts, incomes, and expenses, the two of you should have an honest discussion about your credit ratings and your spending and saving philosophies. Knowing this information will help you decide how to structure key provisions of your prenup. And if you have had credit problems in the past, the sooner you bring this up the better. Putting off this discussion is not a good way to start your financial partnership, even without a prenup.

To prepare for your conversation about spending and credit, continue your separate inventory process by taking a look at your individual credit history and your own approach to spending and saving.

a. Credit History

The best way to start investigating your credit history is to order a copy of your current credit report. You can get one from a local credit bureau or other credit reporting agency, or from one of the many reporting services available on the Internet. Often, you'll pay a small fee for the report, but in some circumstances you can obtain a copy of your credit report for free. Either way, you can use the report to get an accurate picture of your creditworthiness.

Credit Reporting Agencies

You can order your credit report from any of the three major credit bureaus listed below:

Equifax
P.O. Box 740241
Atlanta, GA 30374
800-525-6285
www.equifax.com

Experian
National Consumers Assistance Center
P.O. Box 2002
Allen, TX 75013
888-397-3742
www.experian.com

Trans Union
Consumer Disclosure Center
P.O. Box 1000
Chester, PA 19022
800-888-4213
www.tuc.com

Cleaning up your credit. Nearly 70% of credit reports contain at least minor errors—and many contain mistakes that can seriously damage your creditworthiness. If you haven't checked your credit report recently, this is a good time to review it for errors and make any necessary corrections. For detailed information on checking your credit report and cleaning it up, see *Credit Repair*, by Robin Leonard and Deanne Loonin (Nolo).

In addition to getting a copy of your credit report, we recommend that you jot down the answers to the following questions about your credit history. (We've included a worksheet for you to use to note your answers; see Worksheet 2 in Appendix B or on the CD-ROM.)

1. Have you ever been sued for failing to pay a debt? If so, give details (when, by whom, what court, amount of the claim, and the outcome).

2. Do you currently owe any debt that is more than 60 days overdue? If so, specify the debt and the amount you owe.

3. Have you been turned down for a loan or credit card in the last two years? If so, give details (when, by whom, and the reason given for the denial of credit).

b. Spending and Saving Habits

After you have taken a look at your credit history, spend some time thinking about your financial philosophy. Are you a saver or do you spend money as fast as you earn it? Do you believe in borrowing to take advantage of financial opportunities or are you more comfortable keeping spending within the limits of your income? Knowing the answers to these and similar questions will tell you and your fiancé a lot about how you will approach spending decisions in your marriage.

To get started, answer the following questions. This will give you a snapshot of your own financial philosophy, both in theory and in practice. You can record your answers on Worksheet 2, if you like.

1. On a scale of one to five (one being least important and five being most important), how important is it to you to set aside savings on a regular basis?

2. On a scale of one to five (one being least comfortable and five being most comfortable), how comfortable are you with going into debt to take advantage of an investment opportunity?

3. Do you usually pay bills early, on time, a little late, or very late?

4. Of the following methods, which ones do you use to pay bills and everyday expenses (list all that apply):
   - cash
   - check
   - automatic transfer from a checking or other bank account
   - credit card
   - other (specify).

5. How many credit card accounts do you currently have?

6. Do you pay credit card bills in full each month? (Always, Never, Sometimes, Occasionally)

7. How often do you balance your checkbook? (Always, Never, Sometimes, Occasionally)

8. Do you participate in a voluntary savings program?

9. Have you set aside money in a savings account or other investment (including retirement accounts) in the past 12 months?

10. How many secured loans have you obtained in the past 12 months? How much money did you borrow?

11. How many unsecured loans have you obtained in the past 12 months? How much money did you borrow?

12. Is there any other information you consider significant in analyzing your spending and saving habits?

3. Scan the Financial Horizon

The next step in your financial self-assessment is to look at the road ahead. Are you planning a major investment sometime soon—such as buying a house or starting a business? Will you be changing jobs or going back to school in the foreseeable future? Has a parent or other relative informed you that you will be the recipient of a substantial inheritance?

If possibilities such as these appear on your financial horizon, it's important to think about how they might affect what you say in your prenup. For example, you may not own any separate property now, but if your parents have informed you that you are the beneficiary of a trust, you may want your prenup to identify any property or funds that you receive from the trust as your separate property.

Here are the questions that will help you focus on upcoming financial developments. If you like, you can jot down your answers on Worksheet 3 (in Appendix B or on the CD-ROM).

1. Do you plan to make a major purchase or an investment of more than $5,000 in the next two years?

2. Are you planning a career change in the next two years?

3. Are you planning to retire from your current occupation in the next five years?

4. Are you planning to enter a college, vocational, or professional school in the next two years?

5. Do you expect to receive a significant inheritance or gift in the next few years?

6. Do you know of any other approaching events that are likely to affect your financial status?

4. Identify Your Goals

After you complete your financial inventory, focus on what you hope to accomplish in the prenup. Your goals will likely fall into one or more of these categories:

1. Keeping some or all of your property separate.

2. Protecting yourself from your fiancé's debts.

3. Clarifying each person's financial responsibilities after you're married—from dealing with taxes to allocating responsibility for household expenses or financing professional educations.

4. Supporting your estate plan—especially providing for children from prior marriages or passing on family property.

5. Providing for each other after one of you dies.

6. Defining who gets what if you divorce.

Within these general categories, your goals will be unique to your situation. You may also find that your goals change or that you add new goals after the two of you explore things further. At this point, your list of goals is merely a starting point for your discussion about the prenup.

As you list your goals, consider which ones are most important to you and note these on your list. Doing this will help you settle on the essential terms of your prenup.

You can each use a copy of Worksheet 4 (in Appendix B or on the CD-ROM) to record your goals and note which ones are most important to you.

Ted and Grace
Ted has two primary goals in writing up a prenup with Grace:

1. He wants to be sure that marrying Grace will not interfere with his plan to leave the bulk of his estate to his children and grandchildren.

2. He wants to protect Grace and his children from arguments with each other over his estate after he dies.

Karen and Russ
When Karen considers a prenup, she comes up with these main goals:

1. Protecting her separate assets, including the veterinary practice, from Russ's child support obligations.

2. Settling on an equitable approach to Russ's potential community property claims on the practice and other assets if she and Russ divorce.

3. Ensuring her ability to carry out her previous divorce agreement to provide an inheritance for her children if she dies before the children reach age 25.

B. Talking It Through

After completing the steps outlined above in Section A, make copies of all four worksheets so that you have a set and your fiancé has a set. Now you are ready to sit down together and exchange the information you've compiled about yourselves. Follow the approach outlined in the remaining sections of this chapter. For more detailed help on talking together and negotiating the terms of your prenup, see Chapter 8.

1. Share Your Results

You may be a little apprehensive about the conversation you are about to have. This can be especially true if the two of you haven't talked much about finances up until now. Here are several simple things you can do to help your conversation go smoothly.

a. Choose the Time and Place With Care

Optimize your chances of having a productive and relaxed discussion by setting aside enough time to go over all four worksheets without feeling pressured. A couple of hours should do it. And be sure to select a time when you are not too tired or stressed from other demands.

Pick a place that's comfortable and free of distractions. Some people find a quiet nook in a favorite coffee shop. Others prefer the kitchen table or some other setting at home. Choose whatever location will be conducive to a relaxed and distraction-free discussion.

b. Pace Yourselves

Some people can easily review their worksheets in a single conversation. Others prefer to conduct the conversation in segments. Choose whatever approach seems right for the two of you and be prepared to adapt if you need to go slower or faster. There is no "right" way to go about it. Just be sure you allow enough time to cover everything thoroughly and thoughtfully.

c. Take Turns

You and your fiancé probably do not have identical financial profiles. One of you may be more wealthy than the other, or you may have significant differences in what you owe. It is important to learn about your differences (and similarities) without feeling embarrassed or uncomfortable. To stay on the right track, consider taking turns when sharing the contents of your worksheets.

For example, Ted might start by showing Grace his financial inventory (Worksheet 1). He would answer any questions Grace has about the financial information on the inventory. Grace would then show Ted a copy of her Worksheet 1 and they would discuss his questions about it. Then Grace would start first with Worksheet 2, and they would continue to alternate in this way through all four worksheets.

d. Stick to the Facts

At this point in your conversation, your goal is to understand each other's financial circumstances and perspectives as clearly as possible.

As you talk together, you may begin to uncover some differences between you, not just in the financial specifics but also in how you approach decisions about property and finances. If so, resist the temptation to short-circuit the information exchange by minimizing or quickly negotiating away these differences. First, get a firm grasp on the reality of your separate finances and how you approach them. Stay honest, even when your approaches appear to differ. Then, when you really understand each other, you'll be ready to look for mutually acceptable ways to reconcile any differences in your points of view. It's worth hanging in there even if things get a little bit uncomfortable; the result will be a prenup that works for both of you.

2. Agree on the Basics

After you cover all the information in all four worksheets, you'll be poised for the next step in making a prenup. This step, like the preceding one, will take an hour or two. As you did when exchanging information, pick a time and place that will be conducive to a relaxed but focused discussion. Pace yourselves by breaking the discussion into two or three different sessions if necessary, and take turns expressing your views.

Each of you should have your list of prenup goals (Worksheet 4) in front of you. Together, go through the goals each of you identified for your prenup. Highlight or mark each goal that you both want your prenup to meet. If you disagree about a goal, make a note of that and set it aside to return to later.

Think about what you might include in your prenup to meet each of the goals you have agreed on. Then write down what you want to put in your agreement. For example, Ted and Grace want to ensure that the bulk of Ted's estate will pass to Ted's children when he dies. So they agree that their prenup should include waivers of surviving spouse rights that could interfere with that goal. (Chapters 5 and 6 will supply the clauses you need to cover each goal in the prenup itself.)

Use Worksheet 5 to record your results. (You can find it in Appendix B and on the CD-ROM at the back of the book.) Here's a sample worksheet to show you how Ted and Grace listed the essential points for their agreement.

Once you have gone through all the goals once, ask yourselves whether there is anything else you'd like to include in the prenup. Add any additional items to your list in Worksheet 5.

1/10/2004
Date Prepared

Ted Beckford and Grace Nelson
Your Name

Worksheet 5: The Basics of Our Prenup

1. Premarital assets will be:

   ☑ Separate property

   ☐ Marital property

   ☐ Community property

   ☐ Exceptions or special provisions (specify):

2. Assets we acquire during our marriage will be:

	Separate	Marital Property	Community Property
a. Real estate purchased during our marriage	☑	☐	☐
b. Each person's salary earned during marriage	☑	☐	☐
c. Retirement benefits earned during our marriage	☑	☐	☐
d. Stock options and other employment benefits earned during our marriage	☑	☐	☐
e. Any increase in the value of a premarital business	☑	☐	☐
f. Other investments made during our marriage	☑	☐	☐
g. Joint bank accounts (see below #3)	☑	☐	☐
h. Other: _____			

3. Special provisions concerning assets acquired during marriage. Details:

   Joint bank accounts: Funds will be shared in proportion to contributions. Reconcile each January.

   Gifts to each other will be separate property of the person receiving the gift.

4. Our prenup will provide the following regarding each person's premarital debts. Details:

   Each person's debts are his or her sole responsibility.

5. Our prenup will provide the following regarding business debts or other debts incurred during marriage. Details:

   Consult with accountant each year—compare filing jointly and separately then pick the most

   advantageous. If separate returns allocate all past income and deductions to each, each pays own taxes.

   Ted pays all accountant's fee's and all taxes on joint returns. Any refund to person who paid tax.

6. Our prenup will spell out a process for deciding whether to file joint tax returns and how to allocate income, deductions, taxes, and refunds. Details:

   Both waive all surviving spouse rights.

7. Our prenup will define each person's responsibility for household expenses. Details:

Ted will pay all. Deposit necessary amount in joint checking account.

8. This is how our prenup will support our intended estate plans (this may require waivers of surviving spouse rights).
Details:

Both waive all surviving spouse rights.

9. Our prenup will provide for our estate plans to include the following terms. Details:

Ted's trust will leave $250,000 to Grace plus the right to stay in the house and $3,000 per month for

one year.

10. Our prenup will provide for support of the surviving spouse. Details:

See above.

11. Our prenup will specify what should happen to our property if we separate and divorce. Details:

_N/A_

12. Our prenup will limit, avoid, or provide for alimony if we separate and divorce. Details:

Ted waives alimony. Grace gets $3,000 per month to age 62, unless she remarries.

13. Our prenup will include other agreements that apply if we divorce. Details:

    N/A
    _____
    _____
    _____
    _____

14. Other provisions of our prenup. Details:

    N/A
    _____
    _____
    _____
    _____
    _____
    _____
    _____
    _____
    _____
    _____
    _____
    _____
    _____

Next, go back to the goals you disagreed about. Do you still disagree? (Sometimes what initially looked like a conflict can be easily resolved after you've talked about other matters and taken a second look.) If you still differ on a particular goal, decide how you will resolve those differences. (See Chapter 8.)

After you have completed these steps, Worksheet 5 should constitute a pretty good list of the basic elements of your prenup. Congratulate yourselves on a job well done and take a break before you continue.

C. Will Your Prenup Pass the Fairness Test?

Now that you've outlined what you want your prenup to say, you're almost ready to start preparing a draft of the document itself. But before you proceed, you should take the time to check two important things:

- Are you on your way to making an agreement that's fair?
- Will the laws of your state (or federal law, if it applies) serve you just as well as a prenup?

In this section, we'll explain in detail what you must do to make an agreement that's fair. Chapter 4 is devoted to helping you understand the laws that affect prenups.

You'll remember from our discussion in the introduction to this book that we consider a prenup to be fair if two things are true:

- the terms of the agreement are fair, and
- you've negotiated the agreement fairly, without subjecting each other to undue pressure or coercion.

Here are some tips to help you create a prenup that meets both parts of the fairness test.

1. Fair Terms

Take some time to make sure that the plan you've outlined for your prenup is well balanced, so that you won't make an agreement that obviously disfavors one of you. And commit to reevaluating the terms of your agreement periodically, even after you've signed it. If your circumstances change significantly, what's fair now could seem otherwise later on. (See Chapter 9 for

more information on giving your prenup occasional check-ups.)

What's Fair?

Courts take different approaches when deciding whether or not a prenup is fair. Some look only at how the agreement was negotiated (see "Section 2," below), but most give at least some consideration to the terms of the agreement itself. Courts commonly consider the following factors when analyzing the fairness of a prenup; these factors may help you decide whether your planned agreement feels truly fair to both of you. Think about:

- your goals in entering the agreement
- the amount of income and property that each of you owns
- your family relationships and obligations
- your education, occupation, and earning capacity
- the expected contribution one of you will make to the education, training, or increased earning power of the other
- your future needs
- your age and health (physically and emotionally)
- your expected contribution to the marriage (pay careful attention to the value of contributions such as caring for the house or children), and
- your ability to support yourself after divorce or the death of your spouse.

The last of these factors is particularly important. Consider your plan in light of what might happen if the two of you divorce or if one of you dies. If your prenup would leave one of you struggling to make ends meet while the other—or the other's heirs—are well off, you've clearly got some balancing to do.

⚠ Making an agreement that appears imbalanced. We don't recommend it, but you may find yourself wanting to make an agreement that seems to disproportionately benefit one of you. Be aware that some courts will assume that such a prenup is fraudulent, putting the pressure on you to prove otherwise. For example, a court might be inclined to overturn a prenup in which a much less wealthy fiancé gives up all of his or her rights to spousal support in the event of a divorce or waives all inheritance rights. You'd have to show that such an arrangement was actually fair. If you even suspect that there's something in your document that may look suspicious to a court, you should follow each of the tips in the list below, being especially sure to seek advice from separate lawyers.

2. Fair Process

Ultimately, *how* you negotiate your prenup could be even more important than what it actually says. Not only is an equitable process critical to making a prenup that's enforceable in court, but—probably much more important—negotiating fairly is what will leave the two of you with good feelings about each other and your agreement. We suggest that you stick to the following guidelines:

- Understand the property rights you would have in the event of a divorce or at death, without a premarital agreement (we'll discuss this in the next section).
- Understand every provision of the agreement before you sign it.
- Be impeccably honest in your negotiations, especially when it comes to disclosing information about your financial situation.
- Allow sufficient time for negotiating the terms of the agreement (as mentioned earlier, we think it's wise to allow at least two months for this part of the process).
- Have your document reviewed by separate lawyers before you sign it (see chapter 7).
- Don't sign the agreement under any kind of pressure, whether it be mental or emotional stress or a simple lack of time to consider and reflect upon what you're signing (remember, we suggest signing the agreement at least one month before your wedding). ■

Understanding Your State's Law

After you've considered your plan from the perspective of fairness, there's just one more step to take before you turn to the task of drafting your prenup: You'll want to compare your prenup plan to the laws of your state (and federal law, if necessary) to see how the two compare and to make a final decision about whether or not you need a prenup.

To see how your prenup compares to the law, you will need to consult a lawyer versed in these matters or do your own legal research—or both. The first thing this chapter does is help you determine which laws will govern your prenup. Then it provides an overview of the law itself and gives you more guidance on looking up the details.

A. Which Laws Apply to Your Prenup?

If you consult a lawyer at this stage, the lawyer can tell you when state law applies to your prenup provisions and when to turn to federal law. If you will be doing your own legal research, then you will need to make sure you are looking at state law when appropriate and at federal law when it applies. And because laws vary from state to state, you will also want to make sure you decide which state's laws are going to govern your prenup.

1. State or Federal Law?

When investigating the law that applies to your prenup, you will usually be referring to state law, which covers most aspects of family and estate planning law. Federal law comes up only if a federal benefit or federal program is involved. For example, pension and retirement benefits for federal workers and members of the military are regulated by federal law, which puts certain restrictions on what can be done with those benefits in the case of a divorce or death. And private sector retirement plans that are approved for favorable federal tax treatment, such as 401(k)s, are also subject to federal regulation that may affect what you want to accomplish in your prenup.

Social Security and Medicare benefits are also regulated by federal law, as are most matters related to bankruptcy.

So if you are thinking of making agreements about such matters in your prenup, you will need to consult both federal and state law to make sure you are aware of any extra federal requirements.

2. Which State's Law Applies to Your Prenup?

As for which state's laws to consider, start with the laws of the state where you maintain your permanent residence, called your "domicile" in legal jargon. Your domicile is typically the state where you live and work most of the time, own or rent your home, and vote.

If you know you will be moving to a different state after you marry, or even if you think a future move is a possibility, you may want to compare the laws of the different states you will live in to see which one provides you with the best options. Then you can include in your agreement a "choice of law" clause designating the state whose laws will govern your prenup no matter where you reside. (We provide an example of such a clause in Chapter 5.) For example, if you now live in New York and you plan to move to California, you would compare the laws of the two states and then designate the one that best supports your prenup in a "choice of law" clause.

B. Preparing to Review the Law

To prepare for a meeting with your lawyer or for doing your own research, refer to the prenup topics listed on Worksheet 5, "The Basics of Our Prenup." For each item on Worksheet 5, you will be asking the following questions:

1. What does the law say about this item?
2. Will the law allow us to create a different result in our premarital agreement?
3. Is there any special legal restriction, procedure, or consideration that applies to this item?

You can use Worksheet 6 (in Appendix B and on the CD-ROM) to record your answers to these questions.

Russ and Karen

Russ and Karen want Karen's veterinary practice to be considered her separate property. If the practice grows in value during their marriage, however, they want to come up with an equitable formula for sharing the increase between Karen and Russ. When Russ volunteers to do some research on the subject, he discovers these answers to his three questions about the veterinary practice:

How does the law cover this item? State law provides that a business owned before marriage is the separate property of the spouse who started it. If the value of the business increases during the marriage, then a portion of the increase in value may be considered jointly owned community property.

Will the law allow us to come up with a different result in our premarital agreement? Yes. State law will honor a written premarital agreement providing that some, all, or none of the value of the veterinary practice is to be considered jointly owned community property. If there is to be partially shared ownership, the prenup may specify a formula to be used in determining the shared portion.

Is there any special legal restriction, procedure, or consideration that applies to this item? Yes. If Karen and Russ divorce or when one of them dies, there is likely to be an expensive and complicated court procedure (with dueling experts) to determine the community share of Karen's veterinary practice—unless Karen and Russ have already specified their own approach in a written premarital agreement.

C. An Overview of State Law

When learning about the law, with or without a lawyer's help, one of your tasks is to gain some understanding of how your state regulates the property of married people who don't make written agreements. It may turn out that in your circumstances, state law takes care of some or all matters just as well as a prenup would.

Short of compiling a fifty-volume treatise, it would be impossible for us to cover every complexity and nuance of marital property law for every state. This section will give you some fundamental information as a place to start. (You can find more detailed information for your state in Appendix D.) If you have a question about state law that isn't answered in this book, you'll need to ask your lawyer or do some more research on your own. (See Section D, below, for more information about doing your own legal research.)

When to skim or skip this material. If you're already working with a lawyer, you may prefer to have the lawyer tell you how your prenup plan compares to state law. In that case, you can quickly review this section for general information—or skip it altogether and turn to Chapter 5 to begin drafting your agreement.

There are three main issues to consider when learning how your state governs marital property. This chapter covers:

- who owns property that either of you acquire while you are married
- what property one spouse is entitled to claim from the other's estate at death, and
- what will happen if you divorce, including how property and debts will be divided and whether or not alimony must be paid.

1. Community Property vs. Common Law States

Before turning to the specifics of how state law will treat your property, it's necessary to say a bit about the two major types of marital property law systems in the United States. A handful of states follow "community property" laws, while most states use a "common law" system. You'll need to understand the basics of your state's system before investigating the details.

Community Property and Common Law States	
Community Property	**Common Law**
Alaska*	All other states and the
Arizona	District of Columbia
California	
Idaho	
Louisiana	
New Mexico	
Nevada	
Texas	
Washington	
Wisconsin	

* Only if both spouses agree in writing.

a. Community Property States

A number of states, mostly in the West, use what's known as a "community property" system to govern marital property. (These laws originated with ancient Europeans and came to the Western United States through Spanish and French explorers and settlers.) The community property states are Arizona, California, Idaho, Louisiana, Nevada, New Mexico, Texas, and Washington. Wisconsin follows a system so similar that it is usually considered a community property state, though its laws use the term "marital property" instead. And in Alaska, a couple can elect to have their property treated as community property if they make a written agreement to that effect.

The basic rule of community property law is simple: During a marriage, all property earned or acquired by either spouse is owned 50-50 by each spouse, except for property received by only one of them through gift or inheritance.

More specifically, community property usually includes:

- All income received by either spouse from employment or any other source (except gifts to or inheritance by just one spouse)—for example, wages, stock options, pensions and other employment compensation, and business profits.

This rule generally applies only to the period when the couple lives together as husband and wife. Most community property states consider income and property acquired after the spouses permanently separate to be the separate property of the spouse who receives it.

- All property acquired with community property income during the marriage.
- All separate property that is transformed into community property under state law. This transformation can occur in several ways, including when one spouse makes a gift of separate property to both of them or when property is so mixed together that it's no longer possible to tell what property is separate (lawyers call this "commingling").
- In a few community property states, income earned during marriage from separate property—for example, rent, interest, or dividends—is community property. Most community property states consider such income to be separate property, however.

EXAMPLE: Beth and Daniel live in Idaho, one of the few community property states where income earned from separate property belongs to the community. Beth inherits 22 head of Angus cattle from her father. Those cattle go on to breed a herd of more than 100 cattle. All the descendants of the original 22 animals are considered income from Beth's separate property and are included in the couple's community property estate.

b. Common Law States

States that have not adopted a community property system are typically called "common law states." Common law principles are derived from English law, where in feudal times the husband owned all marital property; a wife had few property ownership rights and couldn't even leave any property by will. In the common law states today, the spouse who earns money or acquires property during the marriage owns it separately, unless it is transferred into a form of joint ownership such as joint tenancy, tenancy by the entirety, or tenancy in common. (See "Ways to Own Property Together," below.)

What Is Separate Property?

In community property states, a married person is permitted to treat certain types of earnings and assets as separate property. This means that the spouse can do what he or she wants with the property—for example, borrow against it, sell it, give it away, or leave it in a will—without the consent of the other spouse. The following property qualifies as separate property in virtually all community property states:

- property that a spouse owns before marriage
- property that a spouse receives after marriage by gift or inheritance
- property that a spouse purchases entirely with his or her separate property, and
- property that a spouse earns or accumulates after permanent separation.

In some states, additional types of property—such as personal injury awards received by one spouse during marriage—may also qualify as separate property.

As mentioned above, states differ in how they treat income earned from separate property. Most community property states hold that such income is separate. But a number of states take the opposite approach, treating income from separate property as community property.

Normally, separate property stays separate as long as it is not:

- so mixed with marital property that it is impossible to tell what is separate and what is not, or
- transferred in writing by the separate property owner into a form of shared ownership.

Just as separate property can be transformed into shared property, community property can be turned into separate property by a gift from one spouse to the other. The rules differ somewhat from state to state, but generally speaking, gifts made to transform one type of property into another must be made with a signed document.

Ways to Own Property Together

When two or more people are the legal owners of a piece of property, they are generally called "joint owners." There are several different ways that spouses can own property together. Here are the most common:

Joint tenancy. This type of property is held with a written ownership document identifying the owners either as "joint tenants" or "joint tenants with right of survivorship" (some states require minor variations to this language to make a joint tenancy legal). Each joint tenant owns an equal share of the property. The share of the first tenant to die must go to the survivors —that's what's meant by "right of survivorship."

Tenancy by the entirety. This form of ownership, limited to married couples, is recognized in about half the states. It is almost identical to joint tenancy and creates a right of survivorship between the spouses. Like a joint tenancy, it must be created in writing.

Community property. In the community property states (listed in Section C1, above), any property spouses earn or acquire during marriage is shared community property. This is true even if only one spouse's name is on the title document.

Community property with right of survivorship. This form of community property functions just like joint tenancy—the surviving spouse automatically inherits the property when the other spouse dies. It is available only in Alaska, Arizona, California, Nevada, and Wisconsin.

Tenancy in common. Any jointly owned property that doesn't fall into one of the categories listed above is held as tenants in common. This usually includes much of the property spouses own together in common law states. Owners' shares don't have to be equal, as they must be for joint tenancy property. You can own any percentage of tenancy in common property—for example, 5% or 95%. And unlike joint tenancy, at your death you can leave your portion of property held as tenants in common to anyone you choose, unless you are either restricted by an agreement or your spouse defeats the gift by exercising his or her inheritance rights. (See Section C3, below.)

The twist here is that even though common law states technically allow spouses to own and accumulate more separate property than spouses in community property states, they don't get to keep all of that property in the event of a divorce—or leave it without restrictions at death. Most property acquired during marriage is considered marital property, which means that the property is subject to division in the event of a divorce even if just one spouse owns the property on paper. (We discuss this in Section C4, below.) In this limited way, marital property functions very much like community property. And for inheritance purposes, even though a spouse is permitted to leave property held in his or her name to anyone at all, there are rules that guarantee that a surviving spouse will receive a portion of a deceased spouse's property, no matter what that spouse's will or other estate plan says. (See Section C3, below.)

2. Managing and Controlling Property During Marriage

During your marriage, you probably won't spend much time worrying about who owns a particular asset or item of property. When a marriage is going well, the issue rarely arises. It usually comes up only if there's a question or disagreement about who gets to control an asset—for example, if one spouse wants to sell or give away property and the other spouse objects, or if one person wants to manage money or other property in a way the other doesn't agree with. Though a couple can negotiate and choose to handle property however they wish, this section will give you an idea of who is legally entitled to control property in situations like this, when there is no written agreement covering the matter.

a. Community Property States

In almost all community property states, either spouse has the right to manage, control, or dispose of community property. But most states have created exceptions to this general rule. For example, in California (the most populous community property state), spouses must act together to sell, convey, or mortgage real estate—or to lease it for more than one year. (Cal. Fam. Code § 1102(c).) And one spouse is not permitted to give away community property without the written consent of the other. (Cal. Fam. Code § 1102(b).) Other states have similar laws restricting one spouse's ability to dispose of certain types of community property without the consent of the other spouse.

In addition, while spouses can usually share in the management and control of community property, many states impose restrictions on the management of certain assets. For instance, in many states, if just one spouse operates a business that consists mostly of community property, that spouse has primary management rights over the business property. (Cal. Fam. Code § 1100(d); Nev. Rev. Stat. § 123.230(6); N.M. Stat. Ann. § 40-3-14(B); Wash. Rev. Code Ann. § 26.16.030(6).)

EXAMPLE: Alicia and Sam live in California. When they got married in 1989, they each put all the money they brought to the marriage (which wasn't all that much) into joint bank accounts. Since then, they have continued to mix all of their property together—including $250,000 that Alicia inherited from a wealthy aunt—so that everything they own now is considered community property. In 2004, Sam decides to open a small retail business specializing in fine local wines, something he knows a great deal about. With Alicia's blessing, he funds the new venture by withdrawing money from a brokerage account that contains a mix of Alicia's inheritance and his own savings. Even though the business is funded with community property—much of which was formerly Alicia's separate inheritance—Sam is entitled to run the business on his own; he doesn't have to consult Alicia about day-to-day business matters. However, if Sam takes a significant action such as selling the business or pledging its assets as security for a loan, he must get Alicia's written consent.

Texas has taken a somewhat unique approach to community property management, calling certain assets "sole management community property." This is defined as all property that a spouse would have owned if single, including job earnings, income from separate property, and personal injury awards. (Tex. Fam. Code § 3.102(a).) Each spouse has the exclusive right to manage, control, and dispose of his or her sole management community property. All other community property in Texas is known as "joint community property," meaning that both spouses are entitled to participate in its management, control, and disposition. (Tex. Fam. Code § 3.102(c).)

EXAMPLE: Elena and Paul live in Texas. Elena deposits part of her monthly pay into a money market savings account in her name only. The money in this account is part of her sole management community property. When her sister needs help, Elena decides to lend her most of the money she's saved. She can do so even if Paul objects.

Wisconsin, too, takes a different approach. Even though it is considered a community property state, the management and control of marital property (Wisconsin's term for community property) usually depends on whose name is on the title document. For example, let's say that one spouse acquires a boat with money earned during marriage (so the boat is considered marital property) and takes title to it in his own name. The boat-owning spouse is permitted to manage and control the boat; the other spouse has a say over that property only in very limited circumstances. On the other hand, if the marital property doesn't have a title document—and much does not—either spouse may manage or control it.

Wisconsin law imposes restrictions on gifts of marital property by just one spouse, but doesn't impose any other restrictions on disposing of marital property.

The one thing that all community property states absolutely agree about is that spouses are required to act ethically with regard to community property. In other words, one spouse is never permitted to defraud the other of his or her interest in their shared assets.

Get help with questions about management or control of community property. Clearly, this is a complicated issue in every state. If you're unsure about your rights to buy, sell, give away, or invest community property, talk with your lawyer.

b. Common Law States

Most common law states give both spouses the right to manage and control their own shares of jointly owned property. This means that either spouse can sell, borrow against, give away, or invest the portion that they own. But there are exceptions to this rule in most states. One common exception is for property held in tenancy by the entirety (defined above in Section C1b): Neither spouse is permitted to sell or encumber his or her own half of the property without the written consent of the other.

Each spouse usually has complete control of his or her separate property, even though some of that property may be deemed marital property and divided between the spouses in the event of a divorce. A handful of states have created an exception to this rule for the family home, which may not be sold or used as collateral for a loan without the consent of both spouses, no matter whose name is on the deed.

The Duty to Treat Each Other Fairly

As we discussed in Chapter 3, if you make a prenup, you must approach your negotiations with the utmost good faith and honesty. But once married, whether or not you've made a written agreement, you've entered into what's called a "confidential relationship" with your spouse. People in confidential relationships have a duty to act fairly toward each other—sometimes termed a "fiduciary duty." This means that you may not conceal or misappropriate property from one another, or incur debts holding the other liable without authorization—and it means that you must be open and honest with each other even during divorce. If a spouse breaches any of these duties, that spouse will most likely be awarded less than his or her share of marital property in the event of a divorce.

HE DECIDED TO TAKE IT WITH HIM.

3. Property Rights at Death

As we discussed in Chapter 2, many couples make a prenup to specify how they will leave property at death. Usually, this amounts to making sure that children from a prior marriage receive their intended inheritance and that valuable property remains in the family. Without a prenup and some basic estate planning documents such as a will or trust, it's possible that state law could defeat these wishes.

In all states, spouses are guaranteed an inheritance when the other spouse dies. These laws are often called "election" laws because under them, the surviving spouse "elects" to take property other than what was left under the deceased spouse's will or other property transfer documents. Below, we explain in general terms what election laws are and how they work. We also discuss the rules that you must follow if you want to waive any or all election rights in your prenup. State lawmakers justly consider inheritance rights to be important protections for surviving spouses, so many states are quite particular about the requirements you must meet to waive them.

If You Die Without a Will

Every state has laws setting out what a surviving spouse and other family members will inherit if someone dies without a will or other valid estate plan. These are called "intestate succession" laws. This book doesn't discuss intestate succession laws for one important reason: We assume that in addition to preparing a prenup, you'll each make a will and any other documents necessary to plan for what happens at death. As we've discussed, prenups go hand-in-hand with estate planning. It wouldn't make sense to make a prenup and overlook your wills.

---

a. Spouses' Election Rights

For couples without prenups, how much property one spouse is entitled to when the other spouse dies depends in part on whether the state follows a community property or common law system. (See Section C1, above, for a list of community property and common law states.)

i. Community Property States

When one spouse dies, what happens to assets in a community property state is fairly straightforward: One-half of all community property belongs to the surviving spouse. Each spouse is free to leave his or her half of the community property—and all of his or her separate property—to whomever he or she chooses.

In a few states—and under limited circumstances—a surviving spouse may elect to take a portion of the deceased spouse's community or separate property. These laws are designed to prevent spouses from being either accidentally overlooked—for example, if one spouse makes a will before marriage and forgets to change it to include the new spouse—or deliberately deprived of their fair share of property. These spousal protections are available only in California, Idaho, and Wisconsin, and are detailed in the summaries for those states in Appendix D.

ii. Common Law States

Common law states give a surviving spouse legal rights to claim a certain portion—usually one-third to one-half—of the other's estate, no matter what the will or other estate planning documents say. As mentioned, these rights are usually known as a spouse's "election" rights, because the spouse can elect to take property other than what's offered by the will or other estate plan.

A Bit of History: Dower and Curtesy

The methods that common law states use to protect surviving spouses were developed hundreds of years ago by English courts. These courts crafted legal concepts called "dower" and "curtesy." "Dower" refers to the property rights of a surviving wife; "curtesy" is the share received by a surviving husband. Most of the states in this country originally adopted these concepts, and you may find dower and curtesy mentioned in your state's laws. However, most states have dropped the old terminology and now provide for "spousal election rights," "spousal inheritance rights," or something similar.

When determining the total value of the deceased spouse's estate—that is, the amount from which the surviving spouse's share will be calculated—some states provide that all of the deceased spouse's property, including any that was transferred by means other than a will, is subject to the surviving spouse's claim. Other states take a different approach: They include not only all of the deceased spouse's property, but some or all of the separate property owned by the surviving spouse as well. (The total amount of property used to calculate the surviving spouse's share is called the "augmented estate.")

A surviving spouse does not automatically inherit the share that's guaranteed by law; he or she must go to court and ask for it. So if a person leaves nothing to a spouse or leaves less than the spouse is entitled to under state law, the surviving spouse has a choice of either taking what the will or other transfer documents provide or rejecting the gift and instead claiming the minimum share allowed by state law. Taking the share permitted by state law is often called "taking against the will."

For details about your state's spousal election law, see Appendix D.

Allowances

In all states—community property and common law alike—surviving spouses are entitled to ask a court for certain benefits, known as allowances, after the death of a mate. Allowances typically fall into three categories: homestead, personal property, and family allowances (individual states may use different names). As with other spousal inheritance rights, the right to allowances can be waived in a prenup.

Homestead allowance. In most states, the surviving spouse has a homestead right of some sort. Often, the spouse is permitted to remain in the family home during the probate proceedings—and sometimes longer—even if the deceased spouse left the home to somebody else. In many states, the spouse can take a sum of money from the estate instead of the homestead right.

Personal property allowance. In the majority of states, a surviving spouse is entitled to claim a certain amount—often about $10,000 worth—of the deceased spouse's personal property, such as household furniture, appliances, and other items.

Family allowance. Most states allow a surviving spouse to ask a court for money to support the spouse and any children while the deceased spouse's affairs are being settled. Some states put a cap on this amount—for example, $1,000 per month or a lump sum of $18,000—but most leave it up to a judge to decide whether an allowance will be paid and how large it will be.

b. Waiving Election Rights

When a surviving spouse uses a spousal protection law to take more property than the deceased spouse left in a will or other estate planning document, the property comes out of what was left to others. In other words, other beneficiaries will get less. As we've discussed, preserving the deceased spouse's estate for beneficiaries other than the surviving spouse—usually children from an earlier marriage—is a primary goal of many couples who make prenups. To accomplish this, one or both spouses may explicitly waive (forgo) any or all rights to inherit the other's property. But because inheritance rights are so important, a number of states have explicit rules for waiving them.

Some states simply require that any waiver of inheritance rights be written down and signed by the person who is giving up the rights. Other states have more complex rules. Florida, for example, requires that a waiver of inheritance rights be signed in front of two witnesses who must also sign the waiver agreement. And California has a rather elaborate law governing waivers of inheritance rights. In California, even if a waiver is written and signed (as it must be), it is not valid if the surviving spouse can prove that either:

- the surviving spouse did not receive fair disclosure of the deceased spouse's finances (unless the surviving spouse waived disclosure after receiving advice from his or her own lawyer), or
- the surviving spouse was not represented by his or her own lawyer when the waiver was signed.

But the law does not end there. Even if the surviving spouse can prove that the waiver isn't valid for one of the reasons listed above, a court may go ahead and enforce the waiver if it determines that either:

- at the time it was signed, the waiver was fair to the surviving spouse, or
- the surviving spouse had, or reasonably should have had, adequate knowledge of the deceased spouse's finances—and the deceased spouse did not mislead the surviving spouse in any way.

You can see that if one or both of you will waive inheritance rights in your prenup, it is important to familiarize yourself with the requirements of your state's law. Otherwise, your waiver may not be valid and a court may refuse to enforce it. The state summaries in Appendix D list all waiver rules that were in effect at the time this book was published.

4. Property Rights If You Divorce

You may or may not want your prenup to cover what will happen to your property in the event of a divorce. Either way, it may help to know some basics about how states handle the property of divorcing couples who haven't made written agreements. Here, we discuss:

- how property is divided at divorce
- how states handle alimony payments, and

- when spouses may be liable for each other's debts.

When to skip this section. Some couples are quite sure that they don't want to spend time before their marriage contemplating the details of divorce. If that's true for you, go ahead and skip this section. You can jump to Section D to learn more about researching your state's law, or turn to Chapter 5 to begin drafting your prenup.

a. Community Property States

While there are many similarities in divorce procedures among the 50 states, a number of rules depend on whether the state follows community or common law principles. (See Section C1, above.) Here are the basics for spouses in community property states.

i. Dividing Property at Divorce

In any state, when a couple divorces, they are free to decide together how to divide their property, rather than leaving it up to a judge. But if a couple hasn't already set out their intentions in a premarital agreement and can't work things out during the breakup, they can submit their property dispute to a court, which will divide the property according to state law.

Courts usually divide community property equally between divorcing spouses. A spouse who contributed separate property to a community asset may be entitled to reimbursement for that contribution. On the other hand, the community estate may be reimbursed for community property contributions to a spouse's separate property. For example, the community may be entitled to compensation if the spouses use community money to fix up a house that one spouse owns separately. Or, the community might be reimbursed for something less tangible—such as using community property to fund an education that greatly increases the earning capacity of one spouse.

EXAMPLE: Meg and Gordon married in Wisconsin in 1993. Gordon started medical school while Meg got a job as an elementary school teacher. Though they never wrote anything down, they agreed that Meg would work so that Gordon could go to school. After Gordon finished school, Meg would stop working for a while so they could start a family. For the first four years of their marriage, Meg entirely supported the couple except for student loans that Gordon obtained to cover his education expenses. She also took care of all the household chores. Shortly after Gordon completed his residency and began practicing medicine, the couple separated and filed for divorce. When dividing the couple's community property, the court found that it would be unfair to deny Meg a share of the education's benefits while Gordon prospered from the degree and all its advantages. Meg was therefore awarded 80% of the couple's community assets and Gordon was required to make support payments to her for several years.

In most community property states, if the court thinks that dividing community property equally would result in unfairness to one party, the court may distribute the property in whatever proportion it thinks is right.

EXAMPLE: After a brief courtship, Than and Li get married in Washington state. Than doesn't have much property when they marry, but Li is financially comfortable because of a large inheritance from her grandfather. Certain that their marriage will succeed, they mix whatever property they have in joint accounts, but the marriage lasts only five years. When the court divides the couple's property, Li receives a much larger share to compensate her for contributing all of her inheritance money to the community.

That said, one thing courts generally are not permitted to do is award all or part of one spouse's separate property to the other spouse.

Several community property states—including California, Louisiana, and New Mexico—require courts to adhere to the standard of equal division of community property, with very limited exceptions. Even in these states where property division appears to be simple, however, thorny questions may arise when attempting to determine what is and what is not community property or how much certain property is worth. Life insurance, retirement benefits, and business interests are examples of property that can be particularly difficult to characterize and divide.

EXAMPLE: Greta owns and runs a successful art dealership in Santa Fe. After she marries Jim, her business continues to thrive and she opens a number of galleries throughout New Mexico. The assets of Greta's business are separate property because she began the business before she married Jim and he has never been involved with it. But what about all the work that Greta puts into the business during the marriage? Without a written agreement specifying otherwise, the benefits of Greta's labor belong to the community. Valuing and allocating such intangibles can be extremely complicated in the event of a divorce.

Quasi-Community Property

Quasi means "like." In some community property states, including California, Idaho, and Washington, the term "quasi-community property" refers to property accumulated by a married couple while living in a noncommunity property state. If a couple moves to a community property state that recognizes quasi-community property, the property acquired in the noncommunity property state is treated exactly like community property in the event of death or divorce.

Wisconsin recognizes a similar type of property, but calls it "deferred marital property."

ii. Alimony

Alimony (also called maintenance or spousal support) is money paid by one ex-spouse to the other during or after divorce for ongoing support. Without a prenup stating whether or not a spouse is entitled to alimony (and how much) alimony provisions are typically spelled out in a court order or property settlement agreement following a divorce. In all states—community property and common law—courts can order either spouse to pay alimony to the other after considering a long list of factors. (See "Factors Used to Establish Alimony Payments," below).

Factors Used to Determine Alimony Payments

When determining whether to award alimony and, if so, how much and for how long, courts may consider a great number of factors. The exact rules vary from state to state, but in most states the court may take into account the factors listed here:

- the earnings and earning capacities of both spouses
- the ages and the physical, mental, and emotional health of both spouses
- the sources of income of both spouses, which may include retirement, insurance, or other benefits
- any property that either spouse expects to receive by gift or inheritance
- the length of the marriage
- any contributions by one spouse to the education, training, or increased earning power of the other
- the extent to which the earning power, expenses, or financial obligations of one spouse will be affected by the need to care for children
- the standard of living that the spouses established while married
- the relative education of the parties and the time necessary to acquire sufficient education or training to enable the spouse seeking alimony to find appropriate employment
- the relative assets and liabilities of the spouses
- the property brought to the marriage by either spouse
- the contribution of a spouse as homemaker
- the relative needs of the spouses
- the marital misconduct of either of the spouses during the marriage (about half of the states no longer consider this factor when determining alimony)
- the tax consequences of the alimony award, and
- any other factors the court considers appropriate.

When determining the amount and duration of permanent alimony, courts are not supposed to be governed by the amount of temporary alimony payments. In practice, however—and despite the long list of factors judges are supposed to consider—a permanent alimony award often looks much like the temporary award that preceded it.

Traditionally, alimony was granted in most divorce cases: Ex-husbands were usually expected to provide their ex-wives with some form of permanent support. But those days are gone in many states—and quickly disappearing in others. Now, in some states, alimony is awarded in a minority of divorces. And in all states, either husband or wife may be ordered to pay alimony (though in practice, when alimony is awarded, it usually goes to the wife).

Since the 1980s, the trend in state divorce laws has been to favor short-term support awards over traditional permanent alimony. The idea behind this is that alimony should continue only until the recipient spouse can become self-supporting. Some courts also use property allocation to offset the need for alimony, giving more property to the spouse who would otherwise be entitled to short- or long-term support payments.

EXAMPLE: Jesse and Cindy have a volatile marriage that lasts just two years. At the time of their divorce, Jesse is earning about twice as much as Cindy. Rather than order Jesse to make short-term, monthly support payments to Cindy to help her make the transition to self-sufficiency, the court gives her the family car and the moderate amount of money in their shared savings account, dividing the rest of their property equally between them.

Of course, courts are also free to order long-term alimony payments, and sometimes they do—particularly when there has been a lasting traditional marriage or when a recipient spouse has little hope of supporting herself due to health concerns, childcare obligations, or other factors.

There are two basic types of alimony payments—temporary and permanent.

a. Temporary Alimony

When a couple separates or files for divorce, the spouses often need the immediate intervention of a court to establish support obligations, especially to help determine who pays the bills and lives in the family home while the divorce proceedings are underway. One spouse may also need temporary support to cover the costs of the divorce proceedings. Either spouse may request a hearing before the judge to have these issues temporarily resolved.

In some states or counties, courts calculate temporary alimony payments using a narrow formula based primarily on each spouse's income. If the parties cannot agree on an amount for temporary payments, a judge will most likely impose this formula-driven amount at a preliminary hearing. The payment amount may be changed later, when the court has a better understanding of what will be best in the long run. As a practical matter, however, courts may be strongly influenced by the amount of the temporary alimony award when setting the amount of permanent alimony.

b. Permanent Alimony

Permanent alimony is usually established in the court order that finalizes the divorce. It is intended to continue at the same payment rate until a time specified in the order—or until the ex-spouses' circumstances change significantly. Most states have laws that clearly establish when permanent alimony payments may be changed or terminated—for example, if the recipient spouse remarries (or moves in with someone, in a handful of states); or if the paying spouse loses a job or has a new child. Of course, permanent alimony may also be modified if both parties agree to the change.

The only time alimony cannot be modified is when the divorce decree or an agreement between the spouses specifically states that it may not be modified, or when it is part of a property settlement where alimony is paid as a part of the property division.

If a spouse fails to make alimony payments, the recipient spouse has many options for collecting them, including asking a court to garnish a spouse's wages. Federal and state laws make it very difficult to shirk alimony payments, and alimony debts will stick with the spouse who owes them; you can't get rid of alimony you owe by filing for bankruptcy.

iii. Debts

For divorcing couples, responsibility for paying a debt may depend on several things:

- whether the debt was incurred before, during, or after marriage
- the state in which the couple lives
- who agreed to the debt, and
- what the money was used for.

Here, to make our discussion easier to follow, we'll categorize debts according to when they were incurred.

a. Debts Incurred Before Marriage

Debts incurred by a spouse before marriage are primarily the responsibility of that spouse. However, creditors may turn to the couple's community property to collect a spouse's premarital debt. The spouse who did not incur the debt would then have to ask the other spouse for reimbursement.

All states place some restrictions on the type and amount of community property that can be taken to satisfy one spouse's premarital debts—or provide spouses with a method to protect a share of the community property. For instance, in California, the community property earnings of a nondebtor spouse may be shielded from the other spouse's premarital debts if the earnings are kept in a separate bank account and not mixed with other community property.

> **EXAMPLE:** When Marie and Pierre marry in California, Marie has a student loan debt of $45,000. She defaults on four payments of $250 each, and then continues not to pay. During the marriage, Pierre deposits his paycheck into a separate bank account in his own name. When the bank that lent Marie the money sues her for repayment, it can go after Marie's separate property, and most of Marie and Pierre's community property—but Pierre's separate savings account can't be touched.

In no case is the separate property of one spouse liable for debts incurred by the other spouse before marriage.

b. Debts Incurred During Marriage

In community property states, debts incurred during marriage by either spouse are considered "community debts." Usually, community property plus the separate property of the spouse who incurs the debt is liable for community property debts. In other words, if just one spouse binds the community to a debt, the separate property of the other spouse is normally protected. (There is usually an exception if the debt is for "necessaries of life" of either spouse—for example, food, housing, clothing, or medical care.) But if both spouses enter into a community debt, the separate property of each spouse is liable for that debt.

c. Debts Incurred Between Separation and Divorce

Community property states take different approaches when assigning liability for debts incurred after a couple separates but before a divorce is final. Often, a court's determination of whether such a debt is community or separate depends on whether the debt was incurred for a purpose that is related to the community, which is not formally dissolved until a divorce is finalized. For example, the community may be held responsible when debts are incurred for necessaries of life for one of the spouses—or, especially, for their children. The community is unlikely to be held responsible for debts that are more clearly separate, such as a debt related to one spouse's gambling losses or the purchase of nonessential property.

d. Dividing Debts at Divorce

If a couple divorces, community property debts (like other community property) are usually divided equally. However, if equal division isn't "equitable"—that is, if it isn't fair to both parties—the court will often divide debts according to who is better able to pay them. If a couple has many debts but also has a lot of property, a common result is for the spouse who is better able to pay the debts to assume their payment and also to receive a larger share of the property to even things up.

> **EXAMPLE:** Scott and Lyn divorce after almost 30 years together. Scott is a partner in a large law firm and Lyn is a successful freelance graphic designer. Their only child has recently graduated from college and is embarking on a career of her own. At the time of their separation, Scott and Lyn are quite wealthy. They own three homes—their primary residence in California and vacation homes in Hawaii and Colorado. They also have many secure investments. While Scott intends to continue with his law practice, Lyn wants to scale back a bit. Taking all these factors into consideration, the court orders that Lyn take ownership of the house in Colorado, which is paid for. Scott is ordered to take the more valuable homes in California and Hawaii, and assume responsibility for the mortgages. The rest of their investments are divided pretty much equally between them.

b. Common Law States

If you live in a common law state, the following rules generally apply to divorce proceedings.

i. Dividing Property at Divorce

As mentioned earlier, couples in all states are free to divide their own property if they divorce, rather than leaving the matter up to a judge. There is no requirement that a couple follow their state's laws when making the division. But if they can't reach an agreement, they may submit their dispute to a court, which will use state laws to determine what property should be considered marital property and how that property should be divided between them.

a. What Is Marital Property?

As you may remember from our discussion earlier in this chapter, marital property comes into being only if a couple in a common law state decides to divorce. If there's no divorce, all property is simply owned separately or jointly, depending on whose name is on the title document. But when a judge must step in to divide property, the concept of marital property is used give each spouse a fair share of property and leave neither at a disadvantage.

What constitutes marital property differs from state to state. Some states include all property and earnings obtained during marriage, though most exclude certain types of property such as gifts and inheritances. For the most part, when it comes to dividing property at divorce, marital property and community property are very much alike. (See Section C1a for a discussion of community property.)

Finding specific information for your state. If you have questions about whether a particular asset would be considered marital or separate property in the case of a divorce, ask your lawyer. Though he or she may not be able to tell you for certain how an asset will be classified if you divorce (not even a crystal ball can predict what a judge will do in all cases), you should be able to get a good idea of how the property will be treated. If you want to do your own research to learn more about what constitutes marital property in your state, be forewarned—it's a complicated subject. Section D, below, provides some research tips to get you started.

b. How Courts Divide Marital Property

In common law states, courts use a method called "equitable distribution" to allocate marital property at divorce. Under an equitable distribution system, assets and earnings accumulated during marriage are to be divided fairly—that is, "equitably." In theory, equitable means equal, or nearly so. In practice, however, equitable division of property varies—for example, a court may award two-thirds of the marital property to the higher wage earner and one-third to the lower wage earner, or any other proportion that the court believes to be fair.

> **EXAMPLE:** Maureen and Frank, who live in New York, are divorcing after ten years of marriage. During their marriage, they bought a house, some furniture, and a car with their earnings, and they made investments. Maureen earns substantially more than Frank; they shared the work around the house. Upon divorce, a court is likely to divide the property in a way that takes into account the money and work put into the marriage and property as well as the economic realities of the parties. Maureen, because of her higher earnings, will probably keep the house (and its mortgage), the furniture will be divided, the party who needs the car more will get it, and Maureen will pay Frank a sum of money equal to his portion of the house—probably near half.

Here are some of the factors most courts consider when deciding what's fair in the absence of an agreement between the spouses:

Separate property. If one spouse owns a great deal of separate, nonmarital property while the other spouse has little, the court may give more marital property to the less wealthy spouse.

Earning capacity. Similarly, if one spouse has an obvious capacity to earn more money than the other spouse, the court may award more marital property to the spouse that is in the more difficult position.

Effort. The court may consider whether one spouse worked harder or invested more than the other to acquire or maintain property. In the case of a business, it is common for a court to award all or most of the business ownership to the spouse who operates it. (The other spouse may, of course, be compensated with an award of other marital property.)

Nonmonetary contributions. Most states now recognize that a spouse's nonmonetary contributions to a marriage should be valued in the event of a divorce. Nonmonetary contributions include work such as homemaking, childcare, or assisting without a salary in a spouse's business. The spouse who contributed these services is likely to be compensated from the couple's property for their value. (If a stay-at-home spouse's earning capacity has been impaired because of a lengthy absence from the income-earning world, that spouse may also be compensated by a large alimony award.)

Fault. Most states no longer consider fault—such as infidelity—when dividing property at divorce. But in some states, whether or not a spouse obtains a divorce based on fault, a "guilty" spouse may receive less than his or her equitable share of the marital property.

Duration of marriage. Though times have changed, if a marriage has been a long and traditional one, it is not unusual for a woman to find herself with diminished earning power and less wealth than her husband at the time of divorce. A judge is likely to take this into account, awarding more property to the spouse who will find it more difficult to earn enough to enjoy a standard of living comparable to the one established during the marriage.

Spouses' needs. If one spouse is significantly older than the other or has health problems, a court may grant that spouse more marital property.

Tax consequences. Dividing property at divorce can affect the taxes of both spouses—for better or for worse. A court may look at the various tax consequences when attempting to craft a fair property settlement. For example, if selling a house would result in large capital gains taxes, the court may avoid ordering the sale of the house and find another way to balance property between the spouses. A judge will likely consider only those tax consequences that are immediate and specific, rather than speculating about what might happen years down the road.

ii. Alimony

Rules for awarding alimony or spousal support in common law states are the same as those in community property states. See Section 4a(ii), above.

iii. Debts

As in community property states, who is responsible for paying a debt depends on a number of factors. One of the most important is when the debt was incurred.

a. Debts Incurred Before Marriage

A spouse is generally not responsible for paying the debts his or her mate incurred before marriage. These debts are considered separate debts, and creditors will look first to the debtor-spouse's separate property for payment. In no case can the separately owned property of one spouse be taken by a creditor to pay the pre-marital debts of the other spouse.

> **EXAMPLE:** Martin is having financial troubles at the time of his marriage to Ellen. Just before they married, he closed his small construction business after failing to pay several subcontractors who are now threatening to sue him. If Ellen keeps her property clearly separate from Martin's, it will be safe from any court judgments these subcontractors obtain against him. If Ellen and Martin buy property together, however, or mix their money together in joint accounts, Ellen's interest in that shared property will be at risk for Martin's debts if Martin's separate property is not sufficient to cover what he owes.

b. Debts Incurred During Marriage

In most states, a spouse is individually liable for only those debts that he or she incurs during marriage. In other words, a spouse can't be forced to pay bills that the other spouse runs up. However, both spouses are usually responsible for paying the following debts:

- debts incurred with joint accounts
- debts where the creditor considered both spouses' credit information (many debts incurred during marriage are likely to be this type)
- debts incurred for the necessities of either spouse or their children, such as food, clothing, housing, or medical care, and
- debts incurred for the care or education of the spouses' children.

Creditors will first look to jointly owned property to satisfy joint debts. But if there is not enough jointly owned property to cover what's due, the separate property of one spouse can be taken to pay debts that both spouses incur together. And of course, the separate property of one spouse is always liable for that spouse's separate debts.

> **EXAMPLE:** Clare and Saul purchase an expensive Lexus sedan and register it in both of their names. When they fail to make the payments, the car is repossessed. To cover the balance remaining on the car loan after it is sold at auction—as well as collection costs—the bank that holds the loan first looks to see whether it can reach any of the couple's joint assets for payment. When the bank discovers that nothing is available, it obtains an order to garnish Clare's wages for the amount due.

c. Debts Incurred Between Separation and Divorce

Usually, debts incurred after spouses separate but before the divorce is final are the responsibility of the spouse that incurred them and must be paid by that person. There is an exception, however: Both spouses are almost always responsible for paying debts for either spouse's necessities and the children's education, regardless of who incurred them.

d. Dividing Debts at Divorce

When a couple divorces, responsibility for joint debts is allocated in accordance with the property division laws of the state. This usually means that the debts are divided equally or equitably, especially if they were incurred for necessities (food, clothing, housing, or medical care). The court also considers who is better able to pay the debts—usually the spouse with the higher income and/or lower living expenses. If a couple has a lot of debt and also a lot of property, the spouse who is better able to pay the debts often assumes their payment in exchange for a larger share of the marital property.

Regardless of the court's assignment of responsibility for a joint debt, a creditor collecting on an unpaid debt may sue either or both spouses and will do so on the basis of who is more likely to pay. Although spouses may make an agreement about which of them will pay these debts, the agreement is not binding on creditors; it does, however, entitle a spouse to reimbursement if the other spouse does not honor the agreement.

> **EXAMPLE:** During their marriage, Meera and Don purchased a valuable painting for cash, bought a car on credit, and charged a cruise to Europe on their credit card. When they divorce, Meera agrees to pay off the car in exchange for keeping the painting, and Don agrees to pay off the credit card. If Meera doesn't make the car payments or if Don fails to pay for the vacation, the creditor can seek payment from the other; the two of them will then have to work out who must pay and who is entitled to reimbursement.

D. Researching State Law

In addition to the information this book provides, you may find yourself wanting to learn a little more about the laws that affect prenups, marital property, or inheritance in your state. Since you'll be working with at least one lawyer, you may well find that the easiest thing to do is ask your lawyer for information. (See Chapter 7 for more information about working with lawyers.) But learning how to do some of your own research can provide real benefits if you have the energy and the patience for it. Not only are you likely to save money on professional fees, you'll also gain a feeling of mastery over an area of law that concerns you.

- Once you understand some basic research techniques, it is not too difficult to look up certain types of law. For example, to confirm that the statutes listed in your state's summary in Appendix D are up to date, or to browse other parts of your state's code, all you'll need to do is look up the statutes on the Internet or in a local library. Below, we provide some simple instructions to help you do this.
- On the other hand, if you want to delve into more complex issues—say, looking up court decisions

governing prenups or marital property in your state—you will have a more complex task ahead of you. We can't guide you through all the nuances of legal research in this book, but we do give you some information that will help you get started.

- Finally, we list some good self-help resources from Nolo that cover other matters that may be of interest to you, particularly basic estate planning tasks. As we've stressed, estate planning is something that you'll want to take care of in conjunction with making your prenup.

1. Looking Up State Statutes

If you're drafting your own prenup, you should review the summary for your state in Appendix D that lists the basic rules governing your agreement—such as what your agreement can or cannot cover and what you must do to be sure your contract is valid and enforceable. But it's wise to take your research a step farther and make sure that those laws haven't changed since the publication of this book. Fortunately, it's fairly simple to research state statutes.

a. Finding Statutes in a Law Library

You can always find state statutes at a law library or, usually, at the main branch of a public library. Depending on the state, statutes are compiled in books called statutes, revised statutes, annotated statutes, codes, or compiled laws. For example, the Vermont statutes are found in a series called *Vermont Statutes Annotated*, while Michigan's laws are found in two separate sets of books: *Michigan Statutes* or an alternate series called *Michigan Compiled Laws*. (The term "annotated" means that the statutes are accompanied by information about their history and court decisions that have interpreted them.) The citations in your state summary will indicate what the books are called in your state.

Once you've located the books you need, search for the specific statute by the citation provided in the state summary or, if you wish to research another topic, by looking up keywords in the index.

After you find a law in the statute books, it's important to look at the update pamphlet in the back of the book (called the "pocket part") to make sure your statute hasn't changed or been repealed. Pocket parts are published only once per year, so brand new laws often have not yet made it to the pocket part. Law libraries subscribe to services and periodicals that update the statute books on a more frequent basis than the pocket parts. You can ask a law librarian to help you find the materials you need.

b. Finding Statutes Online

All states have made their statutes available on the Internet. You can find them by visiting the legal research area of Nolo's website at www.nolo.com/research/index.html. Click on "State Laws" and then choose your state to search or browse the statutes.

In addition, almost every state maintains its own website for pending and recently enacted legislation. If you hear about a proposed or new law that affects prenups and you want to look it up, you can use your state's website to find not only the most current version of a bill, but also its history. To find your state's website, open your browser and type in www.state.[your state's postal code].us. Your state's postal code is the two-letter abbreviation you use for mailing addresses. For example, NY is the postal code for New York, so to find New York's state website, type www.state.ny.us. When you open your state's home page, look for links under "government." All states have separate links to their legislatures and they offer many different ways to look up bills and laws. You can also find any state's legislature through the National Conference of State Legislatures at www.ncsl.org.

2. Looking Up Court Cases

Statutes alone won't tell you the whole story of your state's prenup laws. You may also want to look at court cases, which explain how courts have interpreted the statutes. The state summaries in Appendix D list some of the most important prenup cases for each state, including their citations—that is, the location of each case as specified by book title, volume number, and page number. If you want to read one of these cases, you can follow the instructions below to look it

up. If you want information about other cases affecting prenups in your state, you should consult your lawyer or use a more detailed legal research manual (see Section D4, below) to learn how to find cases on the topic that interests you.

a. Finding Cases in a Law Library

In the library, state cases are found in a series of books called reporters. For example, California cases are contained in the *California Reporter*. You can also find state cases in books known as "regional reporters." These volumes contain cases from several states in a geographical region. For example, the *Atlantic Reporter* contains cases from several eastern states, including Delaware and Maryland.

If you have a case citation (for example, 21 Cal.App.3d 446), locating the case should be easy. Follow these three steps:

- Find the correct series of books (in the above example, it would be the California Appellate Reports, 3rd Series).
- Select the appropriate volume (here it's Volume 21).
- Open the book to the appropriate page (in the example, page 446).

If you don't have a citation but know the name of one or both of the parties in a case—for instance, in the case named *Jones v. Smith*, Jones and Smith are the names of the parties—you can use a "case digest." Look for the parties' names in the digest's Table of Cases. If you don't know the name of the case or the citation, then it will be very difficult to find the case in the law library.

b. Finding Cases Online

If a case is recent (within the last few years), you may be able to find it for free on the Internet. A good place to start is FindLaw at www.findlaw.com. Also, many state websites now publish recent cases. (See Section D1b, above, for instructions on finding your state's website.)

If the case is older, you can still find it on the Internet, but you will probably have to pay a private company for access to its database. VersusLaw, at www.versuslaw.com, maintains an excellent library of older state court cases. You can do unlimited research on VersusLaw for a fee of $8.95 per month. You can also get state cases online through the Lexis and Westlaw databases, though these options are pricier. To find out more about these services, visit Westlaw at www.westlaw.com or Lexis at www.lexis.com.

3. Finding Other Information About Prenups

In addition to looking up a particular state statute or case, you may be interested in doing some background reading about certain aspects of premarital agreements. Such reading can give you an overview of the law applicable to your concerns, possibly provide some initial answers, and refer you to more specific sources.

There are many types of background books; we'll suggest just a couple of them here. Keep in mind that these resources are written by lawyers, for lawyers, and you may have to struggle through loads of legalese to get to the information you want.

a. Practice Guides

Some states have books for lawyers that discuss a broad range of family law topics, including prenups. For example, in California, the Rutter Group publishes the *California Practice Guide: Family Law*, which contains information about pre- and postmarital agreements, marital property law, and a wide variety of other family law topics. The best way to search for this type of book for your state is to ask a law librarian or look in a library catalogue under "Family Law," "Marital Property," "Premarital Agreements," or similar headings.

b. Journals and Law Reviews

Many legal organizations publish journals (magazines) that contain articles covering current legal issues, including premarital agreements. Law schools also produce journals, called "law reviews," which consist of scholarly articles written by law students, law professors, and practicing attorneys. While law reviews are notorious for their complex and confusing language, they often cover timely topics and can provide leads to relevant statutes and cases.

To locate articles on prenups, you can use the *Index to Legal Periodicals*, the *Current Law Index*, or a computerized index called LEGALTRAC, found in many law libraries.

4. More Legal Research Help From Nolo

Nolo offers many tools designed to help you with basic legal research. You may want to start by visiting Nolo's website at www.nolo.com, where you'll find an entire area of the website devoted to helping you look up the law. (You can find the legal research center at www.nolo.com/research/index.html.)

If you want to pursue more detailed legal research, Nolo offers a book that will show you the way. *Legal Research: How to Find & Understand the Law*, by

Stephen Elias and Susan Levinkind, is a hands-on guide to research on the Internet and in the law library. It addresses research methods in detail and should answer most questions that arise in your research. In particular, it contains a good discussion of how to read and analyze statutes and instructions for looking up court cases.

E. Do You Still Want a Prenup?

Once you've come this far, it's a good idea to stop and think about whether signing a premarital agreement still makes sense for you. For any number of reasons, you may conclude that it doesn't. Perhaps the benefits of a prenup are minor compared with the hassles and expense of completing the written agreement. Maybe you'll discover that you're better protected legally without a prenup. Whatever the reasons, stopping short of preparing and signing a written premarital agreement may be the right course of action for you. If that's the case, you can close this book with a clear sense that, together, you considered the options carefully and made the best decision for the two of you—not a bad foundation for making decisions in the future.

On the other hand, your work thus far may have reinforced your initial interest in making a prenup. If so, it's time to take the concepts outlined on Worksheets 5 and 6 and put them into a draft of a written agreement. So take a moment to congratulate yourselves on your progress; when you're ready, turn to the next chapter.

■

Assembling Your Draft Agreement

In this chapter, we show you how to put together the basics of your draft agreement. If you completed Worksheet 6 using the suggestions found in Chapter 3, you've already worked out the main terms of your prenup. Now it's time to put those terms into clear language that you can include in the written document you'll take to your lawyers.

A. The Structure of Your Prenup

Your prenup will consist of a title such as "Premarital Agreement" or "Prenuptial Contract" and ten basic sections (we call them "paragraphs"), plus any optional paragraphs that you want to add. Each paragraph will consist of one or more clauses. Some paragraphs are pretty much the same for all prenups, except for your personal information, like names and addresses. For other paragraphs, you will choose from several clauses that we provide or craft your own, depending on what best fits your circumstances. The ten basic paragraphs are:

1. **Introductory facts.** This paragraph includes information such as your names and addresses, when you plan to marry, whether you have children, and the general purpose of your agreement, plus other optional information about yourselves you might choose to mention.

2. **Effective date and term.** Here, you state that the agreement takes effect when you marry and continues indefinitely or until some specified date in the future.

3. **Legal representation.** In this paragraph, you either identify the lawyers who are helping you with the agreement or state that you are opting not to use lawyers.

4. **Disclosures.** In this paragraph, you state that you are making written disclosures of financial or other personal information. Typically, the actual disclosure statements are attached to the end of the agreement; this paragraph simply refers to them.

5. **Definitions.** As its name implies, this paragraph explains some commonly used terms contained in the agreement, such as "separate property" or "marital property."

6. **Ownership of premarital assets.** You will use this paragraph to state whether your premarital assets will be considered separate property or shared between you once you are married.

7. **Ownership of assets acquired during marriage.** In this paragraph, you can state your intentions about how you will share or keep separate any new acquisitions after you marry.

8. **Responsibility for debts or expenses.** This is where you say who is responsible for premarital debts as well as any new debts incurred during your marriage.

9. **Provisions regarding interpretation, modification, and enforcement of agreement.** This paragraph is the last one before the paragraph containing your signatures. (As mentioned, you may choose to include optional paragraphs in your prenup. Any optional paragraphs will appear after Paragraph 8 of your agreement and before this one. Optional paragraphs are discussed in detail in Chapter 6.) In this paragraph, we've included all the standard provisions that make for a clear and binding agreement (sometimes called "boilerplate"), plus some optional clauses dealing with reviewing the agreement over time and providing a mechanism for resolving any future disagreements about the prenup.

10. **Signatures, notarization, and attorneys' certificates.** This one's obvious; it's where you and your lawyers sign.

B. Choosing the Clauses for Your Prenup

This is where you begin to choose and complete the paragraphs and clauses that go in your prenup. We expect that you will do this together. It will probably take you a few hours.

You'll start by completing the ten basic paragraphs. Then, if you've covered everything you want in your prenup, you can go on to the next step—finalizing your agreement—which is discussed in Chapter 7. Or, if you want to include other matters in your agreement, you can expand your prenup by selecting paragraphs from the additional options we provide in Chapter 6.

If you completed Worksheet 6, have that in hand when you begin. You'll also need the complete text of the clauses themselves, which you can find on the CD-ROM that came with this book or in Appendix C.

Using a computer. We assume that most of you will use the CD-ROM to prepare your agreement. To do so, follow the instructions in "Using the CD-ROM to Create Your Prenup," below.

Working by hand. If you're using Appendix C to draft your agreement, rather than the CD-ROM, you'll want to work through it as you read through this chapter, which explains what each clause means and gives you examples for guidance. It will probably be easiest if you make a photocopy of the appendix, so that you can keep the appendix and chapter side-by-side as you work.

Starting with the Introductory Facts paragraph, go through the clauses and explanations for each successive paragraph. Select the clauses that apply to you. Replace the bracketed instructions in each clause with your own information and check off the clause when you're done. Paragraphs and clauses that are mandatory for all agreements are already marked with a ✔.When you've finished, you'll type up your agreement using the clauses you've completed.

Creating custom clauses. If you don't find a clause that's exactly right for your situation, try using one that's close to what you want as a springboard for writing your own. If you're working on paper, be sure to check off that clause so you don't overlook it when you assemble your draft agreement.

1. Giving Your Prenup a Title

Decide what you want to call your agreement and put the title at the top of the page. The most common titles are:

- Premarital Agreement
- Prenuptial Agreement
- Antenuptial Agreement.

Choosing the title is mostly a matter of custom and personal style, even among lawyers. If you want to know how the laws of your state refer to prenups, check your state's summary in Appendix D, but don't feel bound by what you find there. Pick a title you're comfortable with. You can even customize your title by including your names, as in "Premarital Agreement of Ted Beckford and Grace Nelsen."

2. The Ten Basic Paragraphs

The tips in this section will help you draft the ten basic paragraphs of your agreement described in Section A, above. Most paragraphs contain multiple parts, or clauses. For each clause, we provide an example showing how one of the couples introduced earlier in the book—Ted and Grace, Karen and Russ, or Steven and Freda—or sometimes another fictional couple, completed that paragraph.

Using the default clauses to create a simple agreement. If you intend to use a premarital agreement only to identify and keep separate your premarital assets and debts, while leaving everything else to state law, you can create a very simple prenup. If you are working on paper, using Appendix C, select only the paragraphs and clauses that are already marked with a ✔ Then add the clauses that are marked ✱; these indicate default selections when you need to choose between clauses. You can also find a simple prenup on the CD-ROM. Look for the file called Simple Prenuptial Agreement (SimplePrenup.rtf). All you need to do is fill in the requested information and your draft is complete. This is what Steven and Freda used to prepare their prenup. You can find their completed simple agreement at the end of this chapter.

Decide whose name comes first. To avoid confusion we suggest that you decide whose name—woman's or man's—will come first throughout the agreement. In keeping with this suggestion, we have taken the somewhat contrary approach of putting all references to the woman first, followed by the man. Feel free to switch the order in your own agreement. Just remember to be consistent.

Same sex couples: Watch for pronouns. No matter whose name you put first, you'll need to change the gender of the pronouns used for one of you as you go through the clauses. For example, in Bryan and Juan's agreement, Juan's name is second, so the pronouns referring to him must be changed from "she" to "he," "hers" to "his," and so on.

Paragraph 1: Introductory Facts

The clauses in the first paragraph of your prenup are pretty self-explanatory. This is where you identify

Using the CD-ROM to Create Your Prenup

The prenup clauses discussed in this chapter are in rich text format (RTF) files that can be copied into your word processor from the CD-ROM at the back of this book. You can use these files to draft your prenup. (If you need help installing the CD-ROM and copying the files onto your computer, see Appendix A.) If you use the CD-ROM, you'll still need to read through the rest of this chapter to learn about each clause and decide which clauses you need.

Finding the Clauses You Want

Windows users. Each prenup clause in this chapter is located in the Prenuptial Agreements\Custom Prenuptial subfolder in the \Program Files folder of your computer. Open a file by selecting its "shortcut" as follows: (1) click the Windows "Start" button; (2) open the "Programs" folder; (3) open the "Prenuptial Agreements" subfolder; (4) open the "Custom Prenuptial" subfolder; and (5) click on the shortcut to the clause you want to work with.

Mac users. Each prenup clause in this chapter is located in the "Custom Prenuptial" subfolder in the "Prenuptial Agreements" folder. Open a file as follows: (1) use the Finder to go to the "Custom Prenuptial" folder; (2) open it; and (3) double-click on the specific file you want to open.

All file names are listed in Appendix A, Section C.

Drafting Your Prenup

When you're ready to begin assembling your prenup, open the file Custom Prenuptial Agreement Outline (Outline.rtf), which contains the title and paragraph headings for every prenup. After filling in the preliminary information, you can start opening, copying, and pasting from the other clause files into the Prenuptial Agreement Outline file. When you open a clause file, you'll see that it contains blank lines, which show you where you need to add your own information. In most cases, the blanks contain bracketed instructions telling you what information is required. After pasting a clause into your prenup, fill in the appropriate information, following the instructions and examples in this chapter. *Be sure to delete any blank underlines*

and the bracketed instructions from your finished document.

Alternatives. For prenup clauses with two or more alternative versions, all alternatives are included in the same file. Alternative clauses are indicated by instructional text and are always preceded by a checkbox. (The information in this chapter will help you choose among alternatives.) *Be sure to delete from your prenup file any alternatives you don't want to include as well as the checkbox for the alternative you choose and the italicized instructional text.*

Optional clauses and text. As you choose the clauses for your prenup, you'll find that a number of provisions are optional—you can use them or not, as you wish. This text is clearly indicated by instructional text and optional clauses are always preceded by a checkbox. *Be sure to delete any optional language that you don't want to include in your agreement as well as the checkboxes for any options you include and the italicized instructional text.*

Because the formatting of the files has been simplified, the clauses may look slightly different from the samples in the book. If you want your final agreement to look just like the samples, you'll need to format it with your word processor.

The optional clauses in the files on the CD-ROM are not numbered. Blanks are provided for numbering the optional paragraphs and clauses in your final document.

To save your draft prenup, use your word processor's "Save As" command to save and rename the file. (Because all the files are "read-only," you will not be able to use the "Save" command.) *You must rename the file for your protection. If you save the file without renaming it, the underlines that indicate where you need to enter your information and the instructional text will be lost and you will not be able to create a new document with this file without recopying the original file from the CD-ROM.*

If you do not know how to use your word processor to save or edit a document, consult the manual for your word processing program. Nolo's technical support department cannot provide help with the use of your word processing program.

yourselves and give basic information, such as the planned date of your marriage, if you've selected a date.

A. Parties

Use this clause to identify yourselves as the "parties" to this agreement by inserting your first and last names in the appropriate spaces. You can also include middle initials or names as Karen and Russ do.

This agreement is between Karen A. Schonberg and Russell J. Kroger. We refer to ourselves by our first names in this agreement.

B. Purpose of Agreement

This is where you indicate the date you plan to marry and your general purposes in making a prenup. If you haven't set a date yet you should give some general time frame.

We plan to marry later this year.

After you indicate the date or time frame of your planned marriage, you should specify the general purposes of your prenup—that is, the topics you will cover. We give you the following options to choose from (you should select all that apply):

- to identify your premarital assets and debts
- to define your mutual rights and obligations regarding property and finances after you marry
- to support your estate plans through waiver of certain spousal rights, and
- to set forth your rights and obligations if you separate or divorce.

Here is what Ted and Grace include in their agreement:

We plan to marry on May 1, 2004. The purpose of this agreement is to identify our premarital assets and debts, to define our mutual rights and obligations regarding property and finances after we marry, and to support our estate plans through waiver of certain spousal rights.

You can also add your own topics. For example, you might want to describe how you will handle joint bank accounts or how you will establish and manage your monthly budget. Feel free to include any agreement you make about your finances or property, to document your mutual understanding for future reference.

This agreement also establishes our plan for setting up and maintaining a monthly budget.

C. Current Circumstances

Use this clause to include some basic information about each of you, such as where you live, your occupations, and the names and ages of any children. Making note of this kind of information is part of the disclosure process required by most state laws. You can also include special facts about yourselves, such as your ages and general state of health, your countries of citizenship, or any other information you consider important enough to include. For example, Karen and Russ both have children from previous marriages, so they make a note of this in their prenup:

Karen currently resides at 56 Bell Street, Sacramento, California. Her occupation is veterinarian. She has two children: Shawn, age 16, and Kyle, age 13.

Russ currently resides at 247 Stone Creek Drive, Sacramento, California. His occupation is book-keeper. He has one child: Tiffany, age 6.

D. Future Plans [OPTIONAL]

Here, you can insert any specific plans to relocate, change jobs, attend college, or make similar major moves that might affect the agreements contained in your prenup.

For example, Grace plans to quit her job as a county social worker after she and Ted marry, so that the two of them can travel. They want to mention this in their prenup. Later in the agreement, there are provisions for transfers to Grace during the marriage and for including Grace in Ted's estate plan if he predeceases her, to compensate for the future earnings and job security Grace is giving up.

> After we marry, Grace plans to resign from her current employment so that we can travel together. As a consequence, Grace will be giving up future job security and potential earnings. This has been taken into consideration in the provisions regarding estate planning matters and property transfers set forth in Paragraphs 9 and 10 of this agreement.

Paragraph 2: Effective Date and Term

This paragraph covers two more essential aspects of your prenup: when your agreement takes effect and when it ends.

A. Effective Date of Agreement

The first clause of Paragraph 2 states what should be obvious: the agreement takes effect only when and if you marry. This means that any obligations to take certain actions—such as transferring property, setting up bank accounts, or changing insurance beneficiaries—won't be binding until after your marriage. There are no choices to make or blanks to fill in for this clause. It is the same in every prenup.

> This agreement will be effective on the day we marry. If we do not marry, this agreement will be null and void.

B. Term of Agreement

You also need to specify how long your prenup will stay in effect. Ordinarily, a premarital agreement lasts as long as your marriage does. Under some circumstances, however, you may want your prenup to last for a specified period of time, possibly because the main purpose of the prenup is to protect property from debts that will be paid off at some point, or perhaps because you feel that if you stay married for a given length of time, certain waivers of marital property or alimony claims will no longer be appropriate. If so, you can choose a clause that terminates the agreement on a certain date or after a specified number of years. Lawyers call this a "sunset clause." We give you the following alternatives for Clause B.

Alternative 1: Prenup Continues Indefinitely

If you want your prenup to stay in effect for as long as you are married, you will choose this clause. It states that the agreement will remain in effect indefinitely, unless you later decide to modify or revoke it. This is what Karen and Russ elect to do.

> After we marry, this agreement will remain in full force and effect indefinitely, unless and until we sign a new written agreement revoking or modifying this agreement.

Alternative 2: Prenup Ends on a Specified Date (Retroactive)

In this sunset clause, you specify that your agreement will end on a certain date, and that termination of the agreement is retroactive—meaning that once the agreement ends, your rights will be the same as if you had never signed a prenup.

> EXAMPLE: Harry is remarrying after a costly divorce. He wants a prenup that protects his assets from any claims if he and Marta get divorced within five years of marrying. However, he and Marta agree that if they stay together longer, the prenup shouldn't apply at all, even to assets bought during the first five years. So they use Alternative 2, specifying that the agreement will terminate after five years of marriage, and their rights from then on will be the same as if they had never signed a prenup.

Alternative 3: Prenup Ends on a Specified Date (Not Retroactive)

If you want a sunset clause, but you don't want it to retroactively cancel any property rights you've established while the prenup is in effect, you can use Alternative 3.

> EXAMPLE: Alexa and Randy live in California, a community property state. They are about to get married. Alexa has eight years left to pay off the mortgage on her house. Under California law, if Alexa uses her earnings during marriage to pay the

mortgage, an increasing percentage of ownership in the house will be community property. Randy is writing a textbook and he has a contract to write another one. Both books are scheduled to be finished in six years. California law states that any book royalties derived from Randy's writing efforts during marriage would be community property.

To avoid the effect of California law until after Alexa has a chance to pay off the mortgage and Randy finishes his two books, they sign a prenup that states that all earnings and assets acquired during the first nine years of their marriage (including the house and the royalties) will be separate property and not community property. After that, they want to start building up community property together, but they don't want to undo the prenup's protection of their separate property ownership of the house and the royalties. So they include a nine-year sunset clause, using Alternative 3.

Using sunset clauses for individual provisions. You can adapt a sunset clause so that it applies only to specific issues in your prenup, rather than the entire agreement. For example, if Alexa and Randy want everything in their agreement to continue during their marriage except the clauses that cover ownership of Alexa's house and Randy's book royalties, they can limit the sunset clause to just those items by modifying Alternative 3 to refer only to the specific clauses rather than the entire agreement.

Paragraph 3: Legal Representation

We've said it before and we'll say it again: If you go to all the trouble of preparing a premarital agreement, you should make sure that each of you is represented by a competent lawyer who can certify that you are fully informed at the time you sign the agreement. This paragraph is where you indicate the names of your representatives. Alternatively, if one or both of you choose not to heed our advice, this is where you make it clear that you thought about getting a lawyer and voluntarily decided against it.

In addition, this paragraph is where you'll state who has drafted your prenup—most likely, the two of you.

A and B. Representation of Each Party

You have two alternatives for Clauses A and B. You will most likely choose Alternative 1 for both clauses.

Alternative 1: Full Representation

This will clearly show that you each consulted a lawyer before signing your prenup. For example, Ted and Grace choose to be represented by lawyers. The clause designating Grace's lawyer is reprinted below. This clause in their prenup is followed by a similar provision naming Ted's lawyer.

Representation of Grace

Grace has been represented by Howard Greene in the negotiation and drafting of this agreement. Grace has fully discussed the terms of this agreement with her attorney and is voluntarily choosing to sign this agreement.

Alternative 2: Waiver of Independent Advice

If you decide against using a lawyer, choose Alternative 2, showing that one or both of you are waiving independent representation.

> **EXAMPLE:** Monica is working with an attorney to make a prenup. Her fiancé Kai does not want to hire an attorney. This is how their agreement reads:

Representation of Monica

Monica has been represented by Marianne Keig in the negotiation and drafting of this agreement. Monica has fully discussed the terms of this agreement with her attorney and is voluntarily choosing to sign this agreement.

Representation of Kai

Kai understands that he has a right to be represented by an independent attorney in the negotiation and drafting of this agreement. Kai does not want to be represented by an independent attorney, even though he has had ample time and has sufficient funds to hire an attorney. Kai understands the terms of this agreement and he is voluntarily choosing to sign this agreement without obtaining independent legal representation.

Check state requirements before waiving representation. The waiver clause in your prenup may need to meet certain standards imposed by the laws of your state. In California, for instance, a person who is not represented when signing a premarital agreement can have it set aside by a court later on, unless that person signed a separate waiver and was given a prior explanation of the terms of the agreement, written in language he or she could easily understand. If either of you decides not to hire a lawyer, check the legal requirements in your state to make sure your agreement will hold up in court.

C. Drafting of Agreement

This clause affects the way a court might interpret your prenup if there is ever a legal dispute about the meaning of any provision in the agreement. If it is clear that you have drafted your agreement together, the court is less likely to slant its interpretation of a particular clause for or against either of you.

Alternative 1: Prenup Drafted Together

This alternative allows you to document the fact that you've worked on your prenup together, as Karen and Russ did:

This agreement was drafted through the joint efforts of Karen and Russ.

Alternative 2: Prenup Not Drafted Together

Just in case your agreement has been written exclusively by one of you, we've given you an alternative clause that spells that out. But be aware that whoever writes up the agreement alone bears an extra responsibility for clear language. If there's a dispute and a court finds the language of a clause to be ambiguous, the confusion is likely to work against the person who wrote it.

Paragraph 4: Disclosures

In this paragraph, you specify the extent and form of the financial disclosures included in your prenup. Virtually every state requires couples signing a premarital agreement to exchange full written disclosures of their finances or to sign a written waiver of the right to a formal written disclosure. If you are thinking of waiving disclosures, see Alternative 2, below, and check your state's requirements in Appendix D.

Alternative 1: Formal Written Disclosure

Choose your clauses from the following options if one or both of you will be making formal written disclosures to the other.

A and B. Disclosures of Each Party

Disclosures usually consist of a complete list of assets and their values, the amount owed on any outstanding debts, and each person's annual or monthly income. You may also include a statement of each person's monthly or annual personal expenses, although this is less common. The disclosures themselves are usually listed on separate schedules attached to the end of the agreement. To avoid a question later on about whether each of you had enough time to consider the information in the disclosure before signing your prenup, we recommend that you exchange the disclosures in advance, and date and initial each schedule. (For an example of how your schedules might actually look, see Steven and Freda's completed prenup at the end of this chapter.)

A common question at this stage is just how much detail is necessary in the written disclosure, especially when it comes to assets. For instance, if you have a household full of furniture, do you really have to go to the trouble of listing and valuing every item?

When answering this question, it helps to understand that the reason disclosures are required is not only to ensure that you are both fully informed before signing the agreement, but also to make a record of your pre-marital assets for future reference. Your lists of assets should be specific enough to allow you (or your inheritors) to sort out your separate assets from your marital or community property if that question comes up at a later date. If you own items that you feel are so insignificant in value that you won't need to keep track of them separately, then you can group those items into one category rather than list and value each one.

For example, you can lump your household goods together as a group instead of separately listing them, except for pieces that are unique or especially valuable. Those items and their values can be listed separately. This is how Steven and Freda handle things in their prenup. (See the sample at the end of this chapter.)

Another approach is to set a minimum value for the assets included in the disclosure, and ignore items that are worth less than that amount. If you opt for this method, you will need to pick a dollar amount low enough to include items the two of you consider significant. For example, Karen and Russ decide to include only assets worth more than $1,500 in their prenup.

You can also combine these approaches. Ted and Grace take this route in their prenup. Ted attaches to his disclosure an inventory and estimated values of his antiques and family furnishings, which he had already prepared for insurance purposes, so those items can be easily identified and distributed among Grace and his children after his death. But for other assets, he and Grace decide it is unnecessary to include anything worth less than $3,000. Because neither of them has significant debts to disclose besides Ted's mortgages on commercial investment property, Grace's home mortgage, and one credit card of Grace's, they don't bother with a minimum for their debts. This is how the disclosures paragraph of their prenup reads. (Remember, the actual disclosures will be attached to the end of the document, on separate schedules.)

Grace's Disclosures

All of Grace's assets having a value greater than $3,000 and all of her debts are listed on Schedule 1, attached to this agreement. Grace's income for the calendar year 2003 is also listed on Schedule 1. Grace has provided the information on Schedule 1 in good faith. The values and other financial information on Schedule 1 are approximations and may not be exact, but they are intended to present a full, fair, and reasonable disclosure of Grace's assets, debts, income, and personal expenses as of the time they were presented to Ted.

Ted's Disclosures

All of Ted's assets having a value greater than $3,000 and all of his debts are listed on Schedule 2, attached to this agreement. All of Ted's antiques and family furnishings are listed on the appraisal dated June 16, 2000, attached to Schedule 2. Ted's income for the calendar year 2003 is also listed on Schedule 2. Ted has provided the information on Schedule 2 in good faith. The values and other financial information on Schedule 2 are approximations and may not be exact, but they are intended to present a full, fair, and reasonable disclosure of Ted's assets, debts, income, and personal expenses as of the time they were presented to Grace.

Be Specific When Listing Valuable Assets

Avoid later problems by listing any asset of significant value with enough precision so that it can be clearly identified. For example, Mary might list her "2002 Honda Accord," instead of the more generic "Mary's automobile." We recommend including at least the last four digits of bank account numbers, life insurance policies, or other assets that have account numbers.

For real estate, we recommend that in addition to listing the street address, you include or attach the legal description of the property. You can find it on the deed to the property; it consists of the county and state where the property is located, plus surveyor's language and any easements or restrictions relating to the property.

If you have retirement benefits, those should be listed by the official name of the retirement plan or account, such as "the ABC Brokerage Roth IRA, account number 555 1234," or "Retirement benefits with the Teachers' Retirement System of the State of Illinois."

C and D. Documents Provided [OPTIONAL]

Depending on how complex your finances are, you may also decide to include in your disclosure copies of tax returns, appraisals, financial statements, and other relevant documents. If you take this approach, it's a good idea to list the documents provided. For example, Ted's finances are complicated because he holds title to his commercial real estate investments through limited partnerships with others. He wants Grace and her lawyer to understand his situation in detail, so he gives Grace copies of numerous documents relating to the investments. Then he and Grace put the following clause in their prenup:

In addition to the information listed on Schedule 1, Ted has given Grace copies of the following documents:

1. Federal and State individual income tax returns filed by Ted for the years 2000 through 2003.

2. Tax returns for the years 2000 through 2003 for the following limited partnerships: Central 102, Blue Skies II, Park Place, and Boardwalk.

3. The following appraisals: 102 Central Avenue, September 3, 1998, by Acme Appraisal Co.; Clearwater Resort, May 5, 1995, by Appraisers Unlimited; Park Hotel, December 13, 2002, by Appraisal Monopoly Co.; Boardwalk, July 27, 1999, by Appraisal Monopoly Co.

E. Acknowledgment of Receipt of Disclosures

Some court cases about the validity of premarital agreements have turned on whether the written disclosures were received before or after the agreement was signed. To avoid trouble with this issue, we recommend that you date and initial the disclosures when you prepare and receive them, and that you include this clause in your prenup. In fact, as we mention elsewhere in this book, it's a good idea to exchange disclosures—together with any additional documents mentioned in the preceding clause—several days, if not weeks, before you sign your prenup. For example, Ted and Grace sign their prenuptial agreement on April 20, 2004. They exchanged the written disclosures (and Ted's financial documents) about a month earlier. Their agreement contains this clause:

Ted received a copy of Schedule 1 on March 15, 2004. Ted reviewed this information before signing this agreement.

Grace received a copy of Schedule 2 and the documents described in Paragraph 4C on March 12, 2004. Grace reviewed this information before signing this agreement.

F. Mutual Waiver of Further Disclosure [OPTIONAL]

This clause might be called the "gilding the lily clause." It probably isn't necessary, but if your disclosure includes estimates and approximations, you can use this provision to ward off any future arguments over whether your disclosures were complete and accurate enough. (Of course, a clause like this one won't save a prenup based on false or deliberately misleading disclosures, but we trust that no one using this book would stoop to such measures.)

This clause is mutual—that is, it applies to both of you, even if one of you provides more precise information than the other. For example, Karen decides to use her accountant's estimate of the value of her veterinary practice for the disclosure of her assets rather than pay for a formal appraisal. But both she and Russ use recent appraisals of their homes (and the office building housing Karen's business), because all three properties were appraised in connection with recent refinances. They include this mutual waiver of further disclosure in their agreement:

Each of us understands that certain values and other information on Schedules 1 and 2 are approximate. We consider this information sufficient and each of us voluntarily waives the right to be given any additional information.

Alternative 2: Waiver of Formal Written Disclosure

Use the following clauses if one or both of you will waive the right to receive full written information about the other's finances.

A and B. Waiver of Each Party

Let's say one or both of you feel you know enough about the other person's finances and you've decided—after checking your state's legal requirements—that it's not necessary to receive a written disclosure from your future mate. This pair of clauses gives you general language for waiving formal disclosure.

Note that this is not set up as a mutual waiver. Instead, there is a separate clause for each person. We've done it this way in case only one of you has decided to forgo a written disclosure. And even if you both waive the disclosures, we recommend separate clauses to make it clear that this was a decision each of you considered carefully.

EXAMPLE: Marisa and Alonso are marrying after living together for eight years. They both work for the same company. They own a house together and they have other mutual assets such as cars and bank accounts. Marisa owns some inherited property with her siblings. Marisa and Alonso decide to have a prenup to support Marisa's estate plan that leaves her share of the inherited property to her nieces and nephews. The prenup refers specifically to Marisa's inherited property, but she and Alonso decide they don't need to bother with formal disclosures. They include these clauses waiving formal disclosures:

Marisa's Waiver of Formal Written Disclosure.

Marisa is aware of Alonso's financial circumstances. She voluntarily waives the right to be given a formal written disclosure or any other information about Alonso's finances.

Alonso's Waiver of Formal Written Disclosure.

Alonso is aware of Marisa's financial circumstances. He voluntarily waives the right to be given a formal written disclosure or any other information about Marisa's finances.

⚠ **Think carefully before waiving disclosure.** Formal disclosures create a record of what each of you knew about the other person's financial situation before signing the agreement. This could avoid a later disagreement about whether you did or didn't know what you were agreeing to. If you decide to go forward without formal disclosures, your prenup should at least clearly state that you thought about it and concluded disclosures weren't needed. Depending on your state's requirements, you may also need to certify that you had an opportunity to consult an independent attorney before waiving disclosure. You may even need to make the waiver a separate document instead of including it as a part of the prenup. Be sure to check your state's legal requirements. If necessary, consult a qualified lawyer about what goes into the waiver.

Paragraph 5: Definitions

This paragraph defines some of the most common terms that will be used in your prenup. Including these definitions in your agreement will help avoid later misunderstandings. It will also save you the trouble of repeating the same definitions over and over in the document.

⚠ **Modify with care.** These definitions are coordinated with the terminology used in the rest of this book's prenup clauses. Therefore, use extreme caution if you decide to modify them in any way. If you do make changes, you'll need to make sure your use of these terms in other parts of your prenup is consistent with your new definitions.

A. This Agreement

Your prenup will contain many references to "this agreement." While this term obviously applies to the premarital agreement that you actually sign, the definition extends to any written modifications you make to the agreement later on.

This Agreement

The term "this agreement" refers to the provisions of this document, once signed by us, as modified by any subsequent amendments in writing signed by us.

B. Separate Property

As we explain in Chapter 4, there are two basic property systems used in the United States: the "community property" system and the "common law" system. In a community property state, married people own certain assets (generally those acquired during marriage) jointly as community property and other assets individually as separate property, regardless of whose name is on the title document. In common law states, ownership is determined according to title, so any asset held in the name of one spouse alone is that person's separate property. However, common law states also treat some assets acquired during marriage as "marital property" no matter whose name is on the title. Marital property can be divided in a divorce or set aside for a surviving spouse after the other spouse dies.

Our definition of separate property assumes that your agreement will designate certain assets (such as items you own before you marry) as separate property that won't be divided between you in a divorce, but will instead belong to whichever spouse is the designated owner. This definition spells out that intention.

Because most states require a separate waiver of inheritance rights by a surviving spouse, our definition of separate property does not rule out a claim by a surviving spouse unless your prenup also includes the separate waiver. (See the optional paragraph on estate planning matters in Chapter 6, Optional Paragraph 1.)

Separate Property

Any asset designated as one person's separate property in this agreement belongs exclusively to that person. A spouse has the sole right to manage and dispose of his or her separate property assets. Separate property is not subject to division between us if we divorce. However, if the owner of separate property dies, the surviving spouse may have a legal claim to it, unless he or she has signed a valid written waiver in this agreement or in another document.

C. Marital Property or Community Property

In addition to the separate property definition, you should choose a definition for marital property or community property, depending on which system your state uses. (If you live in Alaska or Wisconsin, see the end of this section for a note that applies to your choice.)

Alternative 1: Marital Property

If you are in a common law state, use the definition for marital property. It states that any asset designated as marital property in your prenup will be subject to division between you if you ever divorce. This form also includes an optional provision that spells out your rights to manage and control jointly and solely held marital property. For example, Ted and Grace live in New York, which is a common law state, so they choose the marital property definition, including the optional part about management and control.

Marital Property

An asset designated as marital property in this agreement may be subject to division between us by a court if we divorce, unless we provide otherwise in this agreement or in another document. Any asset designated as marital property may be subject to a claim by a surviving spouse, unless he or she has signed a valid written waiver of such claims in this agreement or in another document.

We will both have equal rights to manage and dispose of any marital property held in our joint names. If an asset designated as marital property is held in only one of our names, the sole title holder will have the exclusive right to manage, control, transfer, or sell that property, to the extent allowed by state law.

Alternative 2: Community Property

Use the community property definition if you live in a community property state. Unlike marital property, community property is jointly owned by spouses, and not just potentially subject to being divided up on divorce or death. So the first part of the community property definition differs from the first part of the marital property definition.

Ownership of community property also includes the right to manage and control the property. We give you a couple of different options for specifying how you will share management of your community property. You can pick one of our options or insert your own if what we've written doesn't address your situation. Or you can research state laws regarding management and control of community property: If what's there works for you, you can leave out this part of the definition.

EXAMPLE: Tara and Spike live in a community property state. Spike owns a restaurant that will remain his separate property. He and Tara plan to start up a new restaurant, "Tara's Bistro," after they marry, and they agree that it will be community property. However, Spike will run the restaurant. They insert this definition of community property in their prenup:

Community Property

Any asset designated as community property in this agreement belongs to both of us equally. Our community property will be subject to division between us by a court if we divorce, taking into account any requirements for division spelled out in this agreement.

We will have equal rights to manage and control any community property, subject to any exceptions provided by state law. However, if an asset designated as community property is held in only one of our names, the sole title holder will have the exclusive right to manage, control, transfer, or sell that property, to the extent allowed by state law. In addition, Spike will have the exclusive right to manage and control the community property restaurant business known as Tara's Bistro; provided that he cannot sell the business or substantially all of its assets without Tara's consent.

Special note for Alaska and Wisconsin readers. If you live in Alaska, you can make a written agreement specifying that you want your property to be treated as community property. If that's what you prefer, you should check the legal requirements for making that election and modify the community property definition to reflect your choice. If you do not want to opt for community property, then you should use the marital property definition.

Wisconsin residents face a different issue. Wisconsin's system is so similar to a community property system that it is considered a community property state. However, the term used in Wisconsin is "marital property." So if you're drafting a prenup in Wisconsin, you should use the community property definition, but substitute the word "marital" for the word "community," both in the definition and in references throughout the agreement. Wisconsin residents also have the option of using a form called the "Statutory Terminable Marital Property Classification Agreement Form." (You can find it in the Wisconsin Statutes at Section 766.588.) For couples that want to share everything 50/50, this form allows spouses (or future spouses) to have all of their existing solely owned property and their acquisitions during marriage treated as marital property. The statutory agreement stays in effect for only three years unless the spouses provide each other with complete financial disclosures. In addition, either spouse can terminate the agreement at any time by giving 30 days notice to the other spouse. (Terminating the agreement doesn't change the character of property already affected by the agreement; it affects only property acquired after the termination. Thus, ending the agreement probably won't amount to much of a change, since most property acquired after marriage in Wisconsin will be treated as marital property under the state's law.) If you think this type of agreement might be right for you, be sure to discuss it with your lawyer.

D. Divorce

Even if your prenup doesn't directly deal with divorce or separation issues, such as how your marital or community property will be divided or whether alimony will be paid, there are references to divorce in some of the standard clauses we've included, such as the definitions of marital property and community property discussed above. For that reason, you should include in your prenup a definition of divorce that covers the variety of legal names that could apply to a court proceeding that ends a marriage. You can also apply the term "divorce" to annulment, if you want the same rules to apply in that context.

Divorce

The term "divorce" in this agreement refers to any legal proceeding to end or alter a marital relationship, including a proceeding for divorce, dissolution of marriage, legal separation or separate maintenance, or annulment.

For more discussion of divorce-related clauses, see the optional paragraph, "Provisions Related to Divorce," in Chapter 6, Optional Paragraph 3.

Paragraph 6: Ownership of Premarital Assets

The clauses contained in this paragraph deal with the property you own before you get married—your "premarital assets." Here, you'll specifically address issues such as:

- whether or not your premarital assets will continue to be separate property after you marry
- what happens if you sell your premarital assets or if they appreciate in value during your marriage, and
- what happens if you use marital funds to pay off the mortgage on separate property real estate.

A. Your General Rule for Premarital Assets

Every state recognizes premarital assets as separate property, unless there is a valid written agreement converting those assets to marital or community property. You should use one of the following three alternatives to state your general intentions regarding premarital assets:

- Alternative 1 states that all premarital assets and any property traceable to those assets—that is, profits from them or increases in their value— remain separate property.
- Alternative 2 provides that all premarital assets remain separate property but any profits or increases in value will be marital or community property.
- Alternative 3 states simply that all premarital assets will be considered marital or community property.

After establishing your general rule, you'll have an opportunity to make exceptions to it for particular assets, if you choose to do so. Here's a little more detail about each of your choices.

Alternative 1: All Premarital Assets and Property Traceable to Them Remain Separate Property

This alternative states that premarital assets will remain each spouse's separate property after marriage. It also provides that any appreciation in value, profits (such as dividends or interest), or sales proceeds of premarital assets will continue to be separate property.

As discussed in Chapter 4, state laws differ in how they treat the profits and increases in value of premarital separate property. Some states consider profits and value increases to be property acquired during marriage and classify them as marital or community property. Other states say all property that's traceable to separate property remains separate.

To further complicate the question, some states distinguish between profits or value enhancement resulting from a spouse's efforts to build up the asset versus passive profits such as interest, dividends, or market-driven increases in value. In those states, passive profits are separate property, but profits or increased value due to spousal efforts are marital or community property. For example, in California, any profits or increase in the value of Karen's veterinary practice could be considered community property to the extent she devotes her time to the practice, unless Karen and Russ sign a prenup stating otherwise. Alternative 1 gives you the opportunity to address this issue by including—or omitting—in the definition of separate property any profits and increases that result from spousal efforts.

Alternative 1 also states that any assets acquired with (or in exchange for) premarital assets will be separate property. You can limit separate property to only those new assets that are held in one spouse's sole name or you can include assets held in joint names.

To show you how the optional parts might play out, we'll show you three different examples of Alternative 1. There's one for each of our fictional couples: Steven and Freda, Karen and Russ, and Ted and Grace.

Steven and Freda's version of Alternative 1 states that profits or enhancement in value resulting from a spouse's efforts during marriage are not included as separate property. Any asset acquired by selling a pre-

marital asset will still be considered separate property, but only if the new asset is kept in the spouse's sole name.

All Premarital Assets and Property Traceable to Them Remain Separate Property

Except as specified elsewhere in this agreement, Freda's premarital assets, which are listed on Schedule 1, and all property traceable to those assets, shall continue to be her separate property after we marry. "All property traceable to those assets" means any profits from or growth in value of those assets, not including profits or growth in value arising as a direct or indirect result of the efforts of one or both of us during our marriage. It also means any sales proceeds of those assets, any asset purchased with the sales proceeds, or any asset(s) acquired in exchange for those assets, as long as the sales proceeds or any such new asset is held in the sole name of Freda.

Except as specified elsewhere in this agreement, Steven's premarital assets, which are listed on Schedule 2, and all property traceable to those assets, shall continue to be his separate property after we marry. "All property traceable to those assets" means any profits from or growth in value of those assets, not including profits or growth in value arising as a direct or indirect result of the efforts of one or both of us during our marriage. It also means any sales proceeds of those assets, any asset purchased with the sales proceeds, or any asset(s) acquired in exchange for those assets, as long as the sales proceeds or any such new asset is held in the sole name of Steven.

Karen and Russ come to a different conclusion regarding profits. Their version of Alternative 1 provides for all profits to be separate property, even if they result from spousal efforts. The rest of their clause is the same as Steven and Freda's, including the requirement that any new asset derived from a premarital asset must be in the spouse's sole name in order to be considered separate. Later in Paragraph 6 of their prenup, they add clauses dealing with specific assets—their homes and Karen's veterinary practice—that customize the approach to profits and sales proceeds for those particular assets. (You can find the complete Paragraph 6 of their prenup with the sample documents at the end of this chapter.)

Ted and Grace, like Karen and Russ, decide that profits from spousal efforts will be separate property, but they want new assets derived from premarital assets to be separate property even if held in joint names instead of the sole name of one spouse. Their version of Alternative 1 looks like this:

All Premarital Assets and Property Traceable to Them Remain Separate Property

Except as specified elsewhere in this agreement, Grace's premarital assets, which are listed on Schedule 1, and all property traceable to those assets, shall continue to be her separate property after we marry. "All property traceable to those assets" means any profits from or growth in value of those assets, including profits or growth in value arising as a direct or indirect result of the efforts of one or both of us during our marriage. It also means any sales proceeds of those assets, any asset purchased with the sales proceeds, or any asset(s) acquired in exchange for those assets, as long as the sales proceeds or any such new asset is held in the sole name of Grace, or if held in joint names, as long as it is traceable to the premarital asset.

Except as specified elsewhere in this agreement, Ted's premarital assets, which are listed on Schedule 2, and all property traceable to those assets, shall continue to be his separate property after we marry. "All property traceable to those assets" means any profits from or growth in value of those assets, including profits or growth in value arising as a direct or indirect result of the efforts of one or both of us during our marriage. It also means any sales proceeds of those assets, any asset purchased with the sales proceeds, or any asset(s) acquired in exchange for those assets, as long as the sales proceeds or any such new asset is held in the sole name of Ted, or if held in joint names, as long as it is traceable to the premarital asset.

⚠️ **Tracing separate property through joint-title assets can be tricky.** Think carefully before agreeing that assets held in joint names can be treated as separate property. It may turn out to be quite difficult to identify the separate property portion of a jointly held asset. This is especially true if the asset in question is at all liquid, such as a bank account or a brokerage account, and if you combine separate and marital funds in the account. Unless you keep meticulous records of every transaction (as Ted and Grace plan to do), it can be nearly impossible to trace commingled separate property funds and marital property funds through years or even months of transactions. You'll make your lives easier if you agree up front that you will keep separate property assets in separate names and not try to trace them through jointly held assets. If on occasion you decide to contribute separate property to a joint-title asset, you can sign a separate agreement stating that a specified portion will be considered separate property, or that the spouse who contributed separate property will be entitled to reimbursement. You can even include a mechanism for this in Paragraph 7 of your prenup. (See the next section of this chapter for some examples.)

Alternative 2: All Premarital Assets Remain Separate Property But Not Property Traceable to Them

Alternative 2 for Clause A provides that—barring exceptions included later in the agreement—all premarital assets will continue to be a spouse's separate property. Unlike Alternative 1, however, this version designates as marital or community property all profits and increases in value, together with sales proceeds or new assets derived from premarital assets. Use this alternative if you want to consider everything but the original premarital assets to be marital or community property. You can of course adapt this alternative to apply only to certain categories of profits or gains if the blanket approach is too broad for your needs.

> **EXAMPLE:** Rick and Marian each own rental property that they intend to keep separate after they marry. They decide that any profits from the rental properties, including rental income, will be marital property. To minimize accounting and administrative burdens they also agree that if either of them sells their rental property during the marriage, they will throw the proceeds into the marital pot. (Their

lawyers have advised them that if either of them does decide to sell during marriage, and they decide that they want to keep all or some of the sales proceeds separate, they can enter into a separate agreement at that time.) If they don't sell the property and later divorce—or if one of them dies— they want to be sure that the property, including any increase in the property's value, will be considered separate property. They adapt Alternative 2 in this way:

All Premarital Assets Remain Separate Property but Not Property Traceable to Them

Except as specified elsewhere in this agreement, Marian's premarital assets, which are listed on Schedule 1, shall continue to be her separate property after we marry. However, all property traceable to those assets shall be considered marital property. "All property traceable to those assets" means any profits from those assets, including profits arising as a direct or indirect result of the efforts of one or both of us during our marriage. It also means any sales proceeds of those assets, any asset purchased with the sales proceeds, or any asset(s) acquired in exchange for those assets, even if the sales proceeds or any such new asset is held in the sole name of Marian. However, any increase in the value of Marian's premarital assets shall be her separate property.

Except as specified elsewhere in this agreement, Rick's premarital assets, which are listed on Schedule 2, shall continue to be his separate property after we marry. However, all property traceable to those assets shall be considered marital property. "All property traceable to those assets" means any profits from those assets, including profits arising as a direct or indirect result of the efforts of one or both of us during our marriage. It also means any sales proceeds of those assets, any asset purchased with the sales proceeds, or any asset(s) acquired in exchange for those assets, even if the sales proceeds or any such new asset is held in the sole name of Rick. However, any increase in the value of Rick's premarital assets shall be his separate property.

Alternative 3: All Premarital Assets Will Be Considered Marital or Community Property

If you want your premarital assets converted to marital property (if you are in a common law state) or to community property, use Alternative 3, inserting "marital" or "community" as applicable.

EXAMPLE: Gail and Frank have lived together (in a common law state) for several years. When they first moved in together, neither of them had much property. They now own a house together and each of them has a car, some savings, and a small retirement plan. They have decided that once they marry, they want all of their assets to be considered marital property, as if they had been married the whole time. So they use this clause:

All Premarital Assets Will Be Considered Marital Property

Except as specified elsewhere in this agreement, all of our premarital assets, which are listed on Schedules 1 and 2, and all property traceable to those assets, will be considered marital property as soon as we marry. "All property traceable to those assets" means any profits from or growth in value of those assets, including profits or growth in value arising as a direct or indirect result of the efforts of one or both of us during our marriage. It also means any sales proceeds of those assets, any asset purchased with the sales proceeds, or any asset(s) acquired in exchange for those assets, even if the sales proceeds or any such new asset is held in the sole name of one of us.

B. Other Clauses Affecting Specific Premarital Assets [OPTIONAL]

In this section, we provide optional clauses dealing with ownership of three types of premarital assets that tend to concern couples who make prenups: real estate, businesses, and retirement benefits.

We also offer a catchall clause you can use for other types of premarital assets. If none of the clauses in this section fit your situation exactly, feel free to modify them. But be sure to assign sequential letters to them if you add more than one clause. (To see how to do this, take a look at the excerpt from Karen and Russ's prenup at the end of this chapter.)

If you want all assets treated as you've described in Clause A, above, you needn't bother with these additional clauses. However, you will need to reformat your agreement to take out the "A," because you won't have a Clause B, Clause C, and so on. Leaving in the "A" could make it look like you accidentally forgot to include the subsequently lettered material. (For an example, see Steven and Freda's prenup in Section D, below.)

➡ **When to skip this section.** If you want to treat all assets acquired during your marriage as you've specified in the clause just above, Paragraph 6 of your prenup is complete. Skip ahead to Paragraph 7.

1. Premarital Real Estate [OPTIONAL]

If one or both of you own a home or other real estate when you marry, you might want to include a specific clause spelling out your agreement concerning the property. State marital property laws usually protect a spouse's premarital interest in real estate, but if you make mortgage payments with marital earnings, the property might someday be subject to a marital property claim in an estate or divorce proceeding—or even in a debt collection action. To avoid any unintended surprises, think through what you want to have happen in these circumstances and include a corresponding clause in your prenup.

We give you four alternatives to choose from:
- Alternative 1 states that the real estate will remain entirely separate even if you use marital funds to make payments, repairs, or improvements to the property.
- Alternative 2 allows you to specify a formula for apportioning the equity between separate property and marital or community property.
- Alternative 3 provides for reimbursement of any marital or community property funds used for the property.
- Alternative 4 makes the home or other real estate marital or community property after a certain date or event.

Alternative 1: Real Estate Will Remain Separate Property

Use this clause if you want the property to remain completely separate, even if you put marital funds into it. For example, Karen and Russ plan to live together in Karen's house. She will make the house payments from her community property earnings. Russ's condo will be rented out, and he will use the rents, supplemented by his earnings, to pay the mortgage and other expenses. They agree that each person's home—including any appreciation or sales proceeds—will remain entirely separate property without any reimbursement or community property claim, even if community property earnings are used for house payments, repairs, or improvements. (Again, see the end of this chapter for an excerpt from their prenup.)

Alternative 2: Real Estate Will Be Apportioned Between Separate Property and Marital or Community Property

Use this clause if you want to apportion ownership between separate property and marital or community property according to a formula you've agreed on.

EXAMPLE: Aaron and Laurie plan to live together and raise a family in Aaron's premarital home, which is located in a community property state. Aaron will make the house payments from his salary as an engineer and Laurie will be a stay-at-home mom. They agree that an increasing percentage of equity will be considered community property, as follows:

Equity in Aaron's Home Will Be Apportioned Between Separate Property and Community Property

The equity in Aaron's home located at 555 Serenity Lane will be apportioned between Aaron's separate property and community property as follows: beginning on our first anniversary and on each subsequent anniversary during our marriage, 5% of the equity in the home will be converted to community property, up to a maximum of 90% total community property equity, and the balance of the equity will be Aaron's separate property. For example, at the end of one year of marriage, 5% of the equity will be community property. After five years, 25% of the equity will be community property, and so forth until the maximum of 90% community property is reached on our eighteenth anniversary. The above provisions will apply to any sales proceeds or assets acquired in exchange for the home during our marriage.

Alternative 3: Marital or Community Property Contributions to Real Estate Will Be Reimbursed

Instead of apportioning the equity, you might prefer the clause that keeps the equity separate but provides for reimbursement of any marital or community property funds used to pay for the mortgage, capital improvements, or other property-related expenses. If you use this clause it is important to specify which types of payments qualify for reimbursement and under what circumstances the reimbursement becomes due and payable.

EXAMPLE: Nadia and Sami intend to continue living together in Nadia's home after they marry. They hope someday to remodel the kitchen. They will most likely use marital property funds for the remodel as well as for house payments. They agree that the home will remain Nadia's separate property and that house payments will not be reimbursed. However, any marital property funds used for capital improvements such as the kitchen remodel will be reimbursed and added to marital property

funds if Nadia receives a gift or inheritance, or if they get divorced. This is the clause they add to their prenup:

Marital Property Contributions to Nadia's Home Will Be Reimbursed

If marital property funds are used to pay for certain expenses related to Nadia's home located at 2020 Hindsight Avenue (referred to here as "Hindsight"), Hindsight will remain Nadia's separate property, but the marital property payments will be reimbursed as follows: if Nadia receives a gift or inheritance of more than $2,500, or if we divorce, Nadia shall reimburse to our marital property savings account the total amount of marital property funds used, plus simple interest of 3% per year, minus any amount already reimbursed. In the case of a gift or inheritance, the reimbursement from any single gift or inheritance shall not exceed the amount of the gift or inheritance, less $2,500. The reimbursable expenses referred to in this clause shall include only payments for costs and materials actually paid with marital property funds for the improvement or remodeling of Hindsight. Funds expended for ordinary maintenance, mortgage payments, property taxes and assessments, casualty insurance, or other incidental expenses not directly incurred in remodeling or improving Hindsight shall not be reimbursed.

Alternative 4: Real Estate Will Become Marital or Community Property

If you want to convert premarital real estate to marital or community property—perhaps in exchange for some other provision in the prenup or after a specified length of time—you can use this clause.

EXAMPLE: Kim owns a townhouse. Her fiancé Derek owns a parcel of undeveloped property in the mountains. Both properties are about equal in value. They are planning to sell the townhouse. With the proceeds, they will buy a bigger home that they will own together. Eventually, they will build a cabin on the mountain lot. In their prenup, they include a clause stating that once they get married, both the townhouse and the mountain property will be converted to marital property.

Real Estate Will Become Marital Property

Kim's real estate located at 345 Towne Court will become marital property as soon as we marry. Derek's real estate (unimproved lot) located in Soda Springs will become marital property as soon as we marry.

---

2. Premarital Businesses [OPTIONAL]

If either of you owns all or a share of a business or a professional practice that you intend to operate while you are married, you may want to use your prenup to state whether the business will remain entirely separate property. If you don't address the issue, the business— or any increase in its value—could later be subject to a marital or community property claim because of the work devoted to the business during marriage. (Remember, any value resulting from the efforts of either spouse during marriage is generally considered marital or community property.)

In this section, we give you two clauses that address rights in a premarital business. Alternative 1 provides that the business will remain separate property regardless of any time either spouse spends on the business after marriage. Alternative 2 allows you to specify a formula for determining any marital or community property interest in the business. Pick the one that matches your intentions, adapting it as needed.

Alternative 1: The Business or Professional Practice Will Remain Separate Property

Use this clause if you want a premarital business or professional practice to remain entirely the separate property of the spouse who owns it before marriage, regardless of how much time either one of you devotes to the business.

> EXAMPLE: Nick and Susan are in their early sixties. Nick owns a printing business that he plans to continue to run after his marriage to Susan, a college

professor. In a few years, Nick hopes to sell the printing business and retire on the proceeds. Susan will have a substantial monthly pension benefit when she retires from teaching. In their prenup, they insert the following clause regarding the printing business. (They also include a clause making Susan's pension—even the part earned during marriage— her separate property in a separate paragraph dealing with retirement benefits.)

Nick's Premarital Business Will Remain Separate Property

During our marriage, Nick plans to continue to operate his printing business, known as In the Nick of Time. The business shall continue to be Nick's separate property after we marry. Any increase in its value shall also be Nick's separate property, regardless of how we refer to it or how much time either or both of us devotes to it. If Nick sells the business or exchanges it for another asset, any sales proceeds or asset acquired in exchange will be his separate property.

Alternative 2: The Business or Professional Practice Will Be Subject to Apportionment Between Separate and Marital or Community Property

Some couples expect a premarital business to eventually have a marital property component to it, but they want to spell out an apportionment formula in their prenup to avoid any debate about how that component will be calculated.

This is what Russ and Karen decide to do. Since both Karen and Russ will be working in Karen's veterinary practice, they want a simple and fair way to calculate the marital property portion of any increase in the value of the practice if Karen were to die before Russ, or if they divorce. You can read their clause in the excerpt from their prenup at the end of this section.

3. Premarital Retirement Benefits [OPTIONAL]

If you want your premarital retirement benefits to remain separate property and if you have already provided in

Paragraph 6A that all premarital assets are to be separate property, you don't have to include a specific clause covering premarital retirement benefits. However, if you want to make a point of excluding your premarital retirement benefits from marital or community property claims or if you want to treat them as marital or community property, you can use one of the following clauses.

Alternative 1: Premarital Retirement Benefits Will Be Separate Property

Use this alternative if you want to make it clear that each person's retirement benefits—be they in the form of a pension, 401(k), IRA, or other type of retirement account—are to be that person's separate property, rather than marital or community property.

You must sign a waiver after you marry. Stating in your prenup that you want your retirement benefits to be separate property is important, but it's not enough. For most retirement plans, the law requires a married person to obtain his or her spouse's written waiver of benefits. Usually, you must sign the waiver after you are married, not when you sign your prenup. This clause makes it clear that you agree to sign any needed documents, including written waivers, after you are married. To minimize problems that could arise if one of you dies before you sign the necessary waivers, we recommend that you list each retirement plan by its full name on the schedule of premarital assets attached to your prenup—for example, "John's benefits with the Acme Company Pension and Profit Sharing Plan," rather than "John's 401(k) plan." Then be sure to have your signatures on the prenup notarized. (This is discussed in Chapter 7, along with other suggestions for finalizing your prenup.) While there are no guarantees that this will suffice, some courts have approved waivers of retirement benefits in prenuptial agreements where the retirement plan was specifically listed and the parties' signatures were notarized.

Ted and Grace state (in Paragraph 6A of their prenuptial agreement) that all of their premarital property is to remain separate. Even so, their lawyers have suggested that they mention the retirement benefits specifically, to avoid any misunderstanding. They include this clause as well:

Premarital Retirement Benefits Will Be Separate Property

All retirement benefits earned by (or in the name of) one of us before we marry, as listed on Schedules 1 and 2, will be the separate property of the person who earned them or in whose name those benefits are vested. This applies to all benefits in all retirement, pension, deferred compensation, and other employee benefit or tax deferred plans, whether qualified according to IRS regulations or nonqualified.

Each of us hereby waives any legal claim he or she may have now or in the future regarding the other person's premarital retirement benefits referred to above. Each of us understands that this waiver may not be effective under applicable laws unless reaffirmed after we marry in a written waiver in a form approved by the retirement plan. Therefore we agree that after we marry, upon request by the other party, each of us will sign any document necessary to carry out the intent of this clause, including a written waiver in a form approved by the retirement plan.

Alternative 2: Premarital Retirement Benefits Will Be Marital or Community Property

If you want to convert premarital retirement benefits to marital or community property, we recommend that you say so specifically. Then, after you marry, you will have to sign forms to change the way you own your retirement benefits. This clause includes a provision stating that you will do so.

EXAMPLE: Marilyn began to accrue benefits in her company pension one year ago. Patrick has a small 401(k) retirement plan through his employer. They live in a community property state where retirement benefits earned during marriage are community property. They agree that the premarital portion of their retirement benefits will be considered community property, too, and they include this clause in their agreement:

Premarital Retirement Benefits Will Be Community Property

All retirement benefits earned by (or in the name of) one of us before we marry, as listed on Schedules 1 and 2, will be considered community property. This applies to all benefits in all retirement, pension, deferred compensation, and other employee benefit or tax deferred plans, whether qualified according to IRS regulations or nonqualified.

Each of us understands that under applicable laws title to any retirement account or benefit can be held in the name of only one person, and that the written consent of both spouses may be required prior to making any election of benefits under a retirement plan. We agree that after we marry, upon request by the other party, each of us will sign any document necessary to carry out the intent of this clause.

4. Other Premarital Assets [OPTIONAL]

If you want to include a specific provision relating to a premarital asset other than real estate, a business, or retirement plans, you can use or adapt one of the following alternatives:

- Alternative 1 states that the assets you list will remain separate property.
- Alternative 2 states that the listed assets will be apportioned between separate and marital or community property.
- Alternative 3 states that the listed assets will become marital or community property.

Alternative 1: Certain Premarital Assets Will Remain Separate Property

Use this alternative if you state in Paragraph 6A that all premarital assets are to become marital or community property once you marry, but you want to make an exception for one or more specific assets.

EXAMPLE: Paragraph 6A of Len and Donna's prenup states that all of their premarital assets will become community property as soon as they marry,

except as otherwise specified in the prenup. They want Donna's heirloom art and jewelry to remain her separate property. They also want Len's baseball card collection to remain his separate property. They use Alternative 1 to accomplish this.

Certain Premarital Asset(s) Will Remain Separate Property

The following premarital assets will remain the separate property of the spouse who owns the assets prior to marriage and will not be converted to community property when we marry: Donna's heirloom art from her paternal grandparents and her heirloom jewelry from her maternal grandmother, as more specifically listed on Schedule 1, and Len's baseball card collection.

Alternative 2: Certain Premarital Assets Will Be Apportioned Between Separate and Marital or Community Property

This clause allows you to divide ownership of a particular premarital asset (other than real estate, a business, or retirement benefits) between separate and community property, according to whatever formula you choose. Be sure to specify when the apportionment is to occur.

EXAMPLE: Dorian is a sculptor. At the time of his marriage to Rachel, he is about halfway through the process of completing a large sculpture. He and Rachel put this clause in their prenup:

Certain Premarital Asset(s) Will Be Apportioned Between Separate and Community Property

The following premarital asset will be apportioned between Dorian's separate property and community property as soon as we marry as follows: the unfinished sculpture tentatively titled "Postliteracy" will be 50% Dorian's separate property and 50% community property. If this sculpture is sold during our marriage, the above provisions will apply to apportionment of any sales proceeds.

Alternative 3: Certain Premarital Assets Will Become Marital or Community Property

If you have stated in Paragraph 6A that your premarital assets will remain separate property, but you want a premarital asset (other than real estate, a business, or retirement benefits) to become marital or community property when you marry (or at some other time you specify), you can use this clause.

> EXAMPLE: Antonio and Lydia provide in their pre-nup that, except as otherwise stated, all premarital assets are to continue as separate property. Lydia and Antonio each own a share of a limited partnership that Antonio's brother manages. They want their shares of the partnership to be treated as marital property once they marry, so they use Alternative 3 to state their intentions.

Certain Premarital Assets Will Become Marital Property

The following premarital assets will become marital property as soon as we marry: Lydia's one-tenth interest in the limited partnership known as CDE Ltd. and Antonio's one-tenth interest in the limited partnership known as CDE Ltd.

Paragraph 7: Rights in Assets Acquired During Marriage

Now that you've determined how you will handle property you each own before you get married, it's time to consider the assets you will acquire during your marriage. (To make the discussion simpler, we'll often call these "postmarital" acquisitions.) Will you keep new acquisitions entirely separate, as though you were not married? Will you pool everything, share and share alike? Will you let state laws determine your rights? The clauses in this paragraph are designed to give you some typical alternatives for answering these and other questions about postmarital acquisitions.

To help you choose the best clauses for your situation, let's review some basic marital property concepts. As we explain in Chapter 4, state laws dealing with married couples' rights in property acquired during marriage fall into two main categories: common law and community property.

In common law states, ownership of assets acquired during marriage is determined by who holds title. However, if a spouse dies, common law states allow the surviving spouse to claim a certain percentage of the deceased spouse's property. And if a couple divorces in a common law state, much (if not all) of the assets acquired during the marriage will be considered marital property to be divided between the divorcing spouses, regardless of whose name appears on the title document.

In community property states, each spouse owns a one-half share of any assets acquired during marriage. If one spouse dies, the survivor keeps his or her half of the community property. In a divorce, the community property will be divided between the spouses.

You can use the clauses in this paragraph to confirm that your rights to assets acquired during marriage are to be determined by state law or to substitute your own rules for dealing with those assets.

A. Your General Rule for Assets Acquired During Marriage

This clause states your basic approach to dealing with acquisitions during marriage. You can choose from one of the following five alternatives:

- Alternative 1 states that rights in assets acquired during marriage will be determined according to state law.
- Alternative 2 provides that rights in assets acquired during marriage will be determined according to how title is held.
- Alternative 3 allows you to keep all property separate—no marital or community property rights accrue.
- Alternative 4 states that all assets acquired during marriage will be marital or community property.
- Alternative 5 provides that all assets acquired during marriage will be owned proportionately, according to a formula you specify.

After selecting one of these alternatives, you'll be finished with Paragraph 7 unless you want to make an exception for a certain type of asset.

Alternative 1: Rights in Assets Acquired During Marriage Will Be Determined According to State Law

If you like the approach to marital assets taken by your state's law, you can choose the default clause stating that your rights in any assets acquired during your marriage will be determined by that law. For an example of this alternative, take a look at Freda and Steven's prenup at the end of this chapter.

Alternative 2: Rights in Assets Acquired During Marriage Will Be Determined According to How Title Is Held

If you want your rights in postmarital acquisitions to be dictated by how you hold title rather than by state marital property laws that would mandate a different result, use this alternative.

> **EXAMPLE:** John and Carol live in California, a community property state. Since they are both retired, they do not expect to have any marital earnings that would be considered community property under California law. However, they want to leave open the possibility that they might buy property together and take title as community property for estate planning purposes. This is what they put in their prenup:

Our Rights in Assets Acquired During Marriage Will Be Determined According to How Title Is Held

Except as specified elsewhere in this agreement, every asset acquired after we marry, and any profits or growth in value or any sales proceeds or asset acquired in exchange for those assets, will be owned as specified in the document of title. If an asset is tangible personal property that does not have a document of title, the person who paid for the asset will be the owner.

Each of us understands that if it were not for this agreement, certain assets acquired during our marriage might be considered community property despite the name in which title is held, and we knowingly agree to waive our community property rights in such assets and be bound by this agreement instead, unless a community property form of ownership is specified in the title.

Alternative 3: All Property to Be Separate—No Marital or Community Property Rights Accrue

Use this alternative if you want the assets you acquire during your marriage, including any assets you purchase together in joint names, to be considered separate property. This clause is similar to Alternative 2 in that any asset held in one person's name will be that person's separate property. But this version states that any property in joint names will be co-owned by the spouses as if they were not married, whereas under Alternative 2 spouses could co-own joint title property either as separate property or as marital or community property, depending on how the title reads.

> **EXAMPLE:** Ryan comes from a wealthy family. He has built up an extensive investment portfolio from gifts and inheritances, and he is expecting to receive more gifts and inheritances as time goes on. His fiancée Tricia owns a duplex and she is planning to purchase another rental property shortly after the wedding. They might purchase a house together at some point in time. They agree that all assets they acquire during marriage, even assets they put in joint names, will be separate property, and not marital property, just as if they were not married. This is the clause in their prenup:

All Property to Be Separate—No Marital Property Rights Accrue

We intend to own all property acquired during our marriage, including property acquired in joint names, as separate property and not as marital property, as if we were unmarried. Each of us understands that if it were not for this agreement, certain assets acquired during our marriage might be considered marital property despite the name in which title is held, and we knowingly agree to be bound by this agreement instead.

SEPARATE   PROPERTY

Alternative 4: Assets Acquired During Marriage Will Be Marital or Community Property

If you want every new asset you acquire during your marriage to be treated as marital or community property regardless of who acquires it or who holds title, use this clause.

> **EXAMPLE:** Barrett is a real estate agent and Leilani manages a clothing store. Barrett sometimes buys "fixer-uppers," renovates them, and resells them for a profit. He and Leilani agree that everything they buy during their marriage, including the houses that Barrett purchases, will be marital property. They put this clause in their prenup:

Assets Acquired During Marriage Will Be Marital Property

Except as specified elsewhere in this agreement, every asset acquired by one or both of us after we marry will be considered marital property, regardless of how title is held. Each of us understands that if it were not for this agreement, certain assets acquired in the name of only one person during our marriage might be considered separate property of the person in whose name it is held, and we knowingly agree to be bound by this agreement instead.

Alternative 5: Assets Acquired During Marriage Will Be Owned Proportionately

This clause allows you to specify certain percentages of each asset you acquire during your marriage as separate property or as marital or community property.

> **EXAMPLE:** Suppose Barrett and Leilani, the couple described in the previous example, agree that instead of considering all of their new acquisitions marital property, they will divide ownership so that Barrett owns 30% as his separate property and the other 70% is marital property. They would insert this clause in their prenup:

Our Rights in Assets Acquired During Marriage Will Be Apportioned

Except as specified elsewhere in this agreement, our rights in every asset acquired during our marriage in the name of one or both of us, and any profits or growth in value or any sales proceeds or asset acquired in exchange for that asset, will be apportioned between us, according to the following formula: thirty percent of each asset shall be Barrett's separate property and the other seventy percent shall be marital property.

B. Other Clauses Affecting Assets Acquired During Marriage [OPTIONAL]

If you want to single out certain assets or types of assets for special provisions, you can include as many of the following clauses that apply. The clauses discussed in this section cover:

- income
- inheritances
- gifts
- joint accounts, and
- any other assets you want to treat differently than described in Clause 7A, above.

If you choose more than one of the clauses in this section, be sure to assign sequential letters to the remaining clauses, starting with "B" and continuing alphabetically as necessary. If you want all assets treated as you've described in Clause 7A, above, you needn't bother with these additional clauses. However, as we explained for Clause 6, above, you will need to reformat your agreement to take out the "A," because you won't have any subsequent clauses. Leaving in the "A" could make it look like you accidentally forgot to include some material. (For an example, see Steven and Freda's prenup in Section D, below.)

➡️ **When to skip this section.** If you want to treat all assets acquired during your marriage as you've specified in the clause just above, Paragraph 7 of your prenup is complete. Skip ahead to Paragraph 8.

1. Income Earned During Marriage [OPTIONAL]

You may remember from Chapter 4 that state laws usually treat marital earnings as community or marital property. Depending on the state where you live, unearned income—that is, income from investments, interest, or other sources besides wages and other work—may also be considered marital or community property. If you want to ensure that your earnings or other income received during marriage will (or won't) be considered marital or community property, you can insert one of the following alternative clauses in your prenup.

COMMUNITY PROPERTY

Alternative 1: All Income Will Be Marital or Community Property

This alternative allows you to treat all income, whether earned or unearned, as marital or community property.

> **EXAMPLE:** Alveno and Sabra live in a community property state. Under state law their earnings will be community property but unearned income (such as dividends or interest) from separate property would be considered separate property even if received during marriage. Alveno and Sabra want all income they receive or earn during their marriage to be community property. They insert this clause in their prenup:

All Income Will Be Community Property

Except as specified elsewhere in this agreement, our wages and other earned or unearned income will be considered community property. This clause applies to wages or income earned during our marriage even if received at a later time. It also applies to unearned income such as dividends, interest, rents, and partnership distributions received during our marriage.

Alternative 2: All Income Will Be Separate Property

Use this alternative if you want all income, whether earned or unearned, to be considered separate property.

For example, Ted and Grace won't have much earned income, because Ted is retired and Grace will be quitting her job once they marry. They want all of their income, including any earnings and any unearned income from investments, to be separate property rather than marital property, so they use Alternative 2.

All Income Will Be Separate Property

Except as specified elsewhere in this agreement, our wages or other earned or unearned income will be considered the separate property of the person who earned or received the income. This clause applies to wages or income earned during our marriage even if received at a later time. It also applies to unearned income such as dividends, interest, rents, and partnership distributions received during our marriage.

Alternatives 3 and 4: Earned and Unearned Income Will Be Treated Differently

If you want to treat earned and unearned income differently, you can pick Alternative 3 or Alternative 4, depending on which type of income is to be separate property and which is to be marital or community property. Use Alternative 3 if earnings are to be marital or community property and unearned income will be separate property, adding the appropriate optional language about unearned income derived from jointly owned assets. Use Alternative 4 if earnings will be separate and unearned income will be marital or community property.

EXAMPLE: Doreen and Tom want their earned income to be marital property and their unearned income to be separate property, except for un-earned income derived from assets held jointly, which will be considered marital property. They include Alternative 3 in their prenup:

Earned Income Will Be Marital Property; Unearned Income Will Be Separate Property

Except as specified elsewhere in this agreement, our wages and other income earned during our marriage, even if received at a later time, will be considered marital property. Except as specified elsewhere in this agreement, all unearned income such as dividends, interest, rents, and partnership distributions received during our marriage will be considered the separate property of the person who received the income, provided that any unearned income derived from an asset held in our joint names shall be considered marital property.

---

2. Inheritances Received During Marriage [OPTIONAL]

The laws of your state may spell out ownership rights to inherited property in a way that works for you. (See Chapter 4.) If not, we give you two alternatives to choose from. One allows you to specify that inherited property will be separate property. The other makes inheritances marital or community property.

Alternative 1: Inheritances Received by One Party During Marriage Will Be Separate Property

Use this alternative if you want inherited assets to be the separate property of the person who receives the inheritance. You can choose to treat any profits, increase in value, sales proceeds, or assets received in exchange for inherited assets as separate property, or as community or marital property.

For example, Russ and Karen decide that all inherited property—and any property that can be traced to an inheritance—will be separate property. They use Alternative 1 to create the following clause:

Inheritances Received by One Party During Marriage Will Be Separate Property

If one of us receives an asset as an inheritance, bequest, trust distribution, or other death benefit during our marriage, that asset will be his or her separate property. Any profits or growth in value or any sales proceeds or assets acquired in exchange for a separate property inheritance described above will also be separate property.

Alternative 2: Inheritances Received by One Party During Marriage Will Be Marital or Community Property

This alternative states that your inheritances will be treated as marital or community property. We presume here that you want any profits or other property trace-able to inherited assets to also be treated as marital or community property. If you want to handle profits and other returns on inheritances differently, you will need to modify this clause.

EXAMPLE: Raj and Sasha live in a community property state whose laws provide that inheritances are separate property. But they prefer to treat any inheritances—as well as profits, growth in value, and sales or exchange proceeds—as community property, so they choose this alternative.

Inheritances Received by One Party During Marriage Will Be Community Property

If one of us receives an asset as an inheritance, bequest, trust distribution, or other death benefit during our marriage, that asset will be community property. Any profits or growth in value or any sales proceeds or assets acquired in exchange for that asset will also be community property.

---

3. Gifts Received During Marriage [OPTIONAL]

Gifts, like inheritances, often get special treatment under state laws. Many states treat gifts as separate property; others do not. If you don't want to follow your state's rule, you can select the clause in this section that most closely fits your situation and adapt it as needed.

The gift clauses work much the same way as those for inheritances, except that we've added two alternatives that allow you to have one rule for gifts you give to each other and a different rule for gifts from other people.

Alternative 1: Gifts Received During Marriage Will Be Separate Property

This one is straightforward: All gifts received during marriage are the separate property of the recipient. The only optional part concerns profits and other returns on gifts. You can treat those as separate property as well, or you can choose the option that makes any profits or increased value marital or community property.

Ted and Grace want to keep all gifts—and profits from gifts—separate. Here is the clause as it appears in their prenup:

Gifts Received During Marriage Will Be Separate Property

Except as specified elsewhere in this agreement, any asset received by one us during our marriage as a gift from a third party or from the other spouse will be the separate property of the spouse who receives the gift. Any gift given to both of us jointly will be owned by us jointly in equal separate property shares unless at the time of making the gift the person making the gift specifies in writing a different percentage of ownership. Any profits or growth in value or any sales proceeds or assets acquired in exchange for a separate property gift described above will also be separate property.

Alternative 2: Gifts Received During Marriage Will Be Marital or Community Property

This alternative also takes a uniform approach to gifts, treating them all as marital or community property, regardless of whether they are given by a third party or a spouse. Notice that this alternative does not offer the option of treating profits of gifts as separate property; that would not ordinarily be something couples would want if they don't consider the gifts themselves separate property.

EXAMPLE: Drew and Amy decide that they are going to share all gifts as marital property. They use Alternative 2 to spell out their intentions.

Gifts Received During Marriage Will Be Marital Property

Except as specified elsewhere in this agreement, any asset received by one of us during our marriage as a gift from a third party or from the other spouse, and any gift given to both of us jointly, will be marital property. Any profits or growth in value or any sales proceeds or assets acquired in exchange for that asset will also be marital property.

Alternative 3: Third-Party Gifts Will Be Separate Property; Interspousal Gifts Will Be Marital or Community Property

Use this alternative if you want gifts from third parties to be considered separate property while gifts between the two of you ("interspousal gifts") are marital property.

For example, Russ and Karen opt to make gifts from other people separate property, but not gifts they give each other, unless the one who makes the gift specifies in writing that the gift is intended to be the recipient's separate property. They also choose to treat the profits of any separate property gifts as separate property.

Third-Party Gifts Will Be Separate Property; Interspousal Gifts Will Be Community Property

Except as specified elsewhere in this agreement, any asset received by one of us during our marriage as a gift from a third party will be the separate property of the spouse who receives the gift. Any gift given to both of us jointly will be owned by us jointly in equal separate property shares unless at the time of the gift the person making the gift specifies in writing a different percentage of ownership.

Except as specified elsewhere in this agreement, any asset received by one of us during our marriage as a gift from the other spouse will be community property, unless at the time of the gift the spouse making the gift specifies in writing that the gift is intended to be the separate property of the receiving spouse.

Any profits or growth in value or any sales proceeds or assets acquired in exchange for a separate property gift described above will also be separate property.

Alternative 4: Third-Party Gifts Will Be Marital or Community Property; Interspousal Gifts Will Be Separate Property

This one's the reverse of Alternative 3: All gifts from other people are considered marital property, while gifts to each other are separate property. You also have a choice about how to treat profits of separate property gifts: as separate property or as marital or community property. As with the other alternatives, you can adapt this version to fit your particular situation.

EXAMPLE: Julio and Carla decide that anything given to one or both of them by third parties (such as family members or friends) will be considered community property, unless the gift is clothing or jewelry. Gifts between them, and gifts of clothing or jewelry from other people, will be the separate property of the recipient. But profits or other returns on a separate property gift will be community property. This is what they put in their agreement:

Third-Party Gifts Will Be Community Property; Interspousal Gifts Will Be Separate Property

Except as specified elsewhere in this agreement, any asset other than an article of clothing or jewelry received by one of us during our marriage as a gift from a third party, and any gift given to both of us jointly, will be community property. Any profits or growth in value or any sales proceeds or assets acquired in exchange for that asset will also be community property.

Except as specified elsewhere in this agreement, any asset received by of one us during our marriage as a gift from the other spouse and any article of clothing or jewelry received from a third party will be the separate property of the spouse who receives the gift. However, any profits or growth in value or any sales proceeds or asset acquired in exchange for a separate property gift described above will be considered community property.

4. Joint Accounts [OPTIONAL]

Many couples like the convenience of having one or more joint bank accounts from which they pay household bills or other expenses, or into which they deposit wages or other funds. If one or both spouses deposit separate property funds into the joint account, questions can arise later about whether or not the separate funds should be repaid. And if an asset is purchased with the funds in the joint account, there may be an issue about whether and to what extent the asset was purchased with separate property.

One solution to this problem is to avoid depositing separate funds into joint accounts—or to refrain from having joint accounts in the first place. But if you want the flexibility of maintaining joint accounts and perhaps putting separate funds into them, we suggest you use one of the two alternative clauses in this section to establish some simple guidelines for keeping track of who owns what. The first alternative states that all money in a joint account will be marital or community property, while the second says that joint accounts will be made up of separate property shares. Use the alternative that most closely matches what you have in mind, and adapt the wording as needed.

Alternative 1: Joint Accounts Will Be Marital or Community Property

This alternative states that all funds in any joint account will be marital property—with or without potential reimbursement of separate property funds at some specified time. If you opt for reimbursement, you will need spell out when and under what circumstances reimbursement will be due.

> **EXAMPLE:** Marina and Anthony intend to open joint checking and savings accounts into which they plan to deposit only earnings. But since each of them has some separate property investments, they figure there may be times when they might want to deposit separate funds into a joint account. So they decide that all funds in the joint accounts will be considered marital property and that once a year they will review their bank records and reimburse any large deposits of separate property.

Joint Accounts Will Be Marital Property

Any funds deposited into a joint bank or other deposit account established by and between us will be considered marital property, even if one or both of us deposits separate property funds into the account. Whoever deposits $500 or more in a single deposit of separate property funds into a joint account will have a right of reimbursement for the amount of the funds contributed unless he or she signs a written waiver of the right to be reimbursed. Any reimbursement owed shall be payable as follows: Between January 1 and January 31 of each year, we will review our records and determine whether either of us has made any separate property deposits of $500 or more into a joint account during the prior calendar year. If so, that person will be repaid from available marital property funds the total amount of those deposits, without interest. If we are both entitled to reimbursement and insufficient funds are available to pay the full amount, each person shall receive a pro rata share from the available funds. Any reimbursement owed in excess of available marital property funds will be carried over to the following year.

Alternative 2: Joint Accounts Will Consist of Shares of Separate Property

This alternative provides that joint accounts will consist of specified percentage shares of separate property—with a choice about whether to require reimbursement of any marital funds deposited into the account. If you use this clause, you'll need to spell out the percentages of ownership or a formula for determining the percentages. If marital funds will be reimbursed, you'll need to say when and how the reimbursement is to be made.

Ted and Grace don't expect to have any marital property, but they might decide to open a joint checking or savings account after they're married. They agree that the funds in a joint account will retain their separate property character—proportionate to what each party deposits in the account—and if by chance any marital property funds get deposited in the account, each party will receive credit for half of the marital property funds when calculating their percentages. To make sure that they don't leave their heirs with a big accounting headache, they also agree that once a year they will review the account records and sign a memo specifying each person's share of the balance in the account at the end of the year. In case they don't get around to the annual review, they agree that the funds on deposit will be deemed to consist of equal shares of separate property. They adapt Alternative 2 as follows:

Joint Accounts Will Consist of Shares of Separate Property

If a bank or other deposit account is acquired by us jointly (in both of our names), each of us will own an undivided share of the funds in the account as separate property and not as marital property, as follows:

1. Each spouse's share of the funds on deposit at any date shall be in proportion to the total amount of separate property contributed by that spouse to the account during the calendar year in which the shares are determined;

2. Each spouse's contributions to a joint account in a given year shall consist of all separate property funds of that spouse plus one-half of any marital property funds deposited into the account during that year, plus that spouse's share of the balance in the account on December 31 of the preceding calendar year;

3. In January of each year, we will review the account records and determine each spouse's share of the funds on deposit in each joint account, and our determination shall be evidenced by a memorandum signed by both of us. If for any reason we do not complete this process in a given year, our respective shares of the funds on deposit for the year-end in question shall be conclusively deemed to be equal.

This clause shall apply to any joint account, even if we deposit marital property funds into the account, unless we sign a separate written agreement expressly specifying a different form or percentage of ownership regarding a particular account. There will be no right of reimbursement for deposits of any marital property funds unless we expressly agree in writing to a right of reimbursement regarding a particular account or a specific deposit.

5. Retirement Benefits [OPTIONAL]

Use one of the following clauses to state your expectations regarding retirement benefits earned after you marry. You can either make it clear that the general rule set out in Paragraph 7A of your agreement also applies to retirement benefits, or you can make an exception to that general rule.

Alternative 1: Retirement Benefits Earned During Marriage Will Be Separate Property

Select this alternative if you want to keep your retirement benefits separate—that is, not subject to marital or community property claims. As we explained in the discussion of premarital retirement benefits, above, you will need to sign waivers of spousal rights after you marry, so this clause requires each of you to sign any necessary documents later.

Ted and Grace have already provided in Paragraph 6 that their premarital retirement benefits are separate property. Even though Ted is already retired and doesn't expect to build up additional retirement benefits, Grace will be earning retirement through her job until she resigns shortly after the wedding. They use the following clause to specify that any retirement benefits earned after they marry will be separate property:

Retirement Benefits Earned During Marriage Will Be Separate Property

All retirement benefits earned by (or in the name of) one of us during our marriage will be the separate property of the person in whose name those benefits are vested. This applies to all benefits in all retirement, pension, deferred compensation, and other employee benefit or tax deferred plans, whether qualified according to IRS regulations or nonqualified.

Each of us hereby waives any legal claim he or she would otherwise have to the other person's retirement benefits referred to above. Each of us understands that this waiver may not be effective under applicable laws unless reaffirmed after we marry in a written waiver in a form approved by the retirement plan. We agree that after we marry, upon request by the other party, each of us will sign any document necessary to carry out the intent of this clause, including a written waiver in a form approved by the retirement plan.

Alternative 2: Retirement Benefits Earned During Marriage Will Be Marital or Community Property

If you want to make it clear that you will treat any retirement benefits accumulated during marriage as marital or community property, you can insert this clause in your premarital agreement.

This is what Russ and Karen decide to do. There are so many specific clauses in their agreement about other assets that they want to spell out their agreement about postmarital retirement benefits just to avoid any possible confusion. This is the clause as it appears in their prenup:

Retirement Benefits Earned During Marriage Will Be Community Property

All retirement benefits earned by (or in the name of) one of us during our marriage will be considered community property. This applies to all benefits in all retirement, pension, deferred compensation, and other employee benefit or tax deferred plans, whether qualified according to IRS regulations or nonqualified.

Each of us understands that under applicable laws title to any retirement account or benefit can be held in the name of only one person, and that the written consent of both spouses may be required prior to making any election of benefits under a retirement plan. We agree that after we marry, upon request by the other party, each of us will sign any document necessary to carry out the intent of this clause.

6. Other Assets Acquired During Marriage [OPTIONAL]

In Clause A of Paragraph 7, you specified the general rule regarding assets acquired during your marriage. If you want to make an exception for certain assets or categories of assets not covered in the clauses we've already discussed, such as specific investments you plan to purchase, you can use one of the next two alternatives to lay out your intentions for those specific assets. One alternative says the property you name will be kept separate; the other states that the assets will be marital or community property.

Alternative 1: Certain Assets Will Be Separate Property

You can use this alternative if you expect the assets you acquire during your marriage to be marital or community property but you want to carve out an exception for certain items.

For example, Karen knows another veterinarian who is talking about putting together a group practice emergency veterinary clinic. She and Russ agree that if Karen joins the group, her interest in the group practice (or in some other veterinary business venture that Karen might become involved in later) will be her separate property and not community property, and that if they divorce or if Karen predeceases Russ, he will receive a payment in lieu of his community property share using a formula as follows:

New Veterinary Business Ventures Will Be Separate Property

After we marry, Karen may acquire an interest in a group practice emergency veterinary clinic or other veterinary business venture. Any such veterinary business venture might otherwise be community property, but instead will be Karen's separate property. This also applies to any profits or increase in value or any sales proceeds or assets acquired in exchange for any such veterinary business venture. If Karen predeceases Russ or if we divorce, Russ shall be entitled to a payment equal to one-half of any community property funds invested in any such veterinary business venture, plus for each year of marriage, an amount equal to one percent of Karen's separate property investment in the business venture up to a maximum of $10,000 for the duration of the marriage.

Alternative 2: Certain Assets Will Be Marital or Community Property

If your prenup states that all assets acquired during your marriage will be separate property rather than marital or community property, this alternative allows you to make an exception for specific assets or categories of assets.

EXAMPLE: Alina and George have agreed that each person's postmarital assets will be treated as separate property, not marital property. But they plan to buy a house together. They agree to use separate property money to pay the down payment and to make house payments. All the equity in the house will be considered marital property. Their version of Alternative 2 reads like this:

Residence Will Be Marital Property

After we marry, we plan to acquire a residence in our joint names, using separate property funds for the down payment, mortgage payments, and all other expenses related to the residence. The residence might otherwise be separate property but instead will be considered equally owned marital property. This also applies to any profits or increase in value or any sales proceeds or assets acquired in exchange for the residence.

---

7. Contributions to Post Marital Acquisitions [OPTIONAL]

If one or both of you will use separate property funds to pay for the purchase or improvement of any marital or community property, you may want to spell out how the separate property will be treated. We give you three choices here:

- Alternative 1 apportions the separate property contributions between marital or community property and separate property.
- Alternative 2 provides that separate property funds will be reimbursed.
- Alternative 3 treats the contribution as a gift and waives any right to apportionment or reimbursement the laws of your state might otherwise give you.

Select the alternative clause that best fits your situation and adapt it as necessary.

Alternative 1: Contributions of Separate Property to Marital or Community Property: Ownership Will Be Apportioned

Use this alternative if you want to allocate separate property contributions between marital or community property and separate property. You will need to be clear about how you will determine the percentages. You will also need to decide whether or not to give credit to separate property funds spent on expenses other than direct purchase or improvement costs.

EXAMPLE: Salman and Jana want to be able pool separate property and community property if an investment opportunity comes along. They settle on this version of Alternative 1:

Contributions of Separate Property to Community Property: Ownership Will Be Apportioned

During our marriage, one or both of us may contribute separate property funds to the acquisition or improvement of community property. If so, ownership of any such property will be apportioned between separate property and community property as follows: 1) if separate property is contributed to a purchase, ownership shall be apportioned between separate property and community property based on the ratio of separate property funds to community property funds contributed to the purchase price, with any financed funds credited to community property; 2) if separate property is contributed to an improvement, the separate property share will be a percentage based on the ratio of separate property funds to community property equity immediately prior to the improvement, as determined by deducting from the market value of the property the total balance then outstanding on any liens against the property. There will be no apportionment for separate property funds paid for expenses related to community property other than for acquisition or improvement of the property.

Alternative 2: Separate Property Contributions to Marital or Community Property Will Be Reimbursed

If separate property funds are to be reimbursed, you'll use this alternative. Be sure to specify the amount, timing, and other conditions that apply to the reimbursement, or refer to some other clause of your prenup where those particulars are set forth.

EXAMPLE: Leila expects to receive a large distribution from a family trust during her marriage to Wayne. She might use some of these separate property funds for a down payment on a house for herself and Wayne, or to pay for fix-up or remodeling expenses. The house would be jointly owned marital property, but they agree that if they divorce, Leila would be reimbursed for any separate property funds used for the down payment, plus interest. They use Alternative 2 to state their intent to do this, and insert a cross-reference to a later section of their prenup, covering divorce, where the specifics are discussed.

Separate Property Contributions to Marital Property Residence Will Be Reimbursed

During our marriage, one or both of us may contribute separate property funds to acquire or improve a marital property residence. In the absence of a contrary written agreement, we will consider any such contribution to be subject to a right of reimbursement payable as set forth in Section 11G of this agreement. The reimbursable contributions referred to in this clause shall include only a down payment or other payments directly applied to the purchase of such a residence or payments for remodeling or other improvements to the residence, not payment of any other expenses for the residence such as mortgage payments, property taxes, insurance, assessments, or ordinary repairs.

Alternative 3: Waiver of Reimbursement for Separate Property Contributions

If you simply want any separate property contributions to be considered a gift to your marital or community property holdings, use Alternative 3. You can also adapt this clause to apply only to certain contributions, using it in combination with Alternative 1 or 2.

EXAMPLE: After Leila and Wayne use Alternative 2 to provide for reimbursement of Leila's separate property contributions to the purchase or improvement of a residence, they modify Alternative 3 to

state that all other separate property contributions will be considered gifts and not apportioned or reimbursed.

Waiver of Reimbursement for Other Separate Property Contributions

During our marriage, one or both of us may contribute separate property funds to acquire or improve marital property or to pay other expenses related to marital property. Except for contributions to acquire or improve a residence as provided in Sections 7D and 11G of this agreement, and in the absence of a contrary written agreement, we will consider any such contribution to be a gift of separate property. Neither of us shall be entitled to reimbursement for any such contribution, and each of us hereby waives any right to reimbursement otherwise granted by law.

Paragraph 8: Responsibility for Debts and Expenses

This paragraph contains clauses that spell out each spouse's responsibility for debts—debts that predate the marriage and, if you choose to address them, debts and expenses that come up after the wedding day.

As we explain in Chapter 4, every state considers the premarital debts of a married person to be that spouse's primary responsibility. The other spouse won't be held liable for them, nor will a creditor be able to collect from the other spouse's separate property to pay the debt. State laws differ on whether creditors can go after marital or community property for premarital debts and on the treatment of debts incurred during marriage. It's a good idea to review the applicable sections of Chapter 4 and the summary of your state's laws in Appendix D before selecting the appropriate clauses for this paragraph. Then choose as many of the clauses that apply and adapt them as needed.

⚠ **The clauses in this section may not provide complete protection.** Any agreement between just the two of you may not prevent a creditor from going after any available funds to collect a debt—even if your prenup states that the debt will be repaid from another source. In addition, any agreement to shift assets between you in order to avoid payment of debts could subject you to serious penalties. Take care when drafting any clauses relating to debts, and if you are at all in doubt, ask your lawyer for guidance before making a final decision.

A. Each Person Solely Responsible for Own Premarital Debts

This clause begins by stating the general rule that each person's premarital debts are his or her sole responsibility, and the other spouse will not be liable for those debts. You can also state your intent that the nondebtor spouse's share of marital or community property may not be used to pay a premarital debt, and you can add a requirement that each of you will pay the expenses of ("indemnify") the other spouse if a creditor nevertheless attempts to collect from the nondebtor spouse.

It's a good idea to include some form of this clause in your prenup, even if you don't select any of the optional clauses that follow.

Ted and Grace include this clause in their agreement. This is what it looks like:

Each Person Solely Responsible for Own Premarital Debts

Grace's debts listed on Schedule 1 are her sole and separate debts. Ted will not be responsible for them, nor may his separate property be used to pay them without his written consent. Grace will indemnify and hold Ted harmless from any proceeding to collect on Grace's debts from Ted's property, and she will be solely responsible for any expenses, including attorney's fees, incurred by Ted in connection with such a proceeding.

Ted's debts listed on Schedule 1 are his sole and separate debts. Grace will not be responsible for them, nor may her separate property be used to pay them without her written consent. Ted will indemnify and hold Grace harmless from any proceeding to collect on Ted's debts from Grace's property, and he will be solely responsible for any expenses, including attorney's fees, incurred by Grace in connection with such a proceeding.

B. Optional Clauses Related to Debts and Expenses Incurred During Marriage

The remaining clauses in this paragraph focus on responsibility for debts and expenses that arise after you marry. You can skip the rest of this section if you don't feel the need to pin down each person's responsibility for postmarital debts, or if you are satisfied that the laws of your state provide adequate clarity and protection for each of you.

If you're not sure whether you need to include any of the optional clauses that follow, we suggest you peruse them, compare them to state law, and then decide whether you want to put any or all of them in your agreement. As with the other clauses in this book, adapt them to your particular circumstances as needed. And don't forget to use sequential letters for each clause if you decide to use more than one. As for Paragraphs 6 and 7, if you don't include any optional clauses, you should remove the letter "A" from your first clause, above. This is so it won't appear that you've accidentally left out subsequent information. (For an example, see Steven and Freda's prenup in Section D, below.)

1. Each Spouse Solely Responsible for Debts Incurred By That Spouse During Marriage

Include this clause if, as a general rule, you don't want either of you to be responsible for the other person's sole debts incurred during marriage. Bear in mind that you could still be jointly liable to a creditor for any debt you take on together—such as a credit card or promissory note in both names—no matter who runs up the actual charges or what you put in your agreement. Nevertheless, a clause like this can be binding between the two of you unless the debt is one that the law of your state imposes on both of you, such as a debt for "necessaries of life," like food or medical bills.

EXAMPLE: Tkat and Han agree not to incur any joint debts. They plan to pay all household bills in cash or by separate checks, and they decide not to open any joint credit cards. They use this clause in their agreement:

Each Spouse Solely Responsible for Debts Incurred by That Spouse During Marriage

Except as specified elsewhere in this agreement, all debts incurred by Han in her sole name during our marriage will be her sole and separate debts. Tkat will not be responsible for them, nor may his separate property or his share of any community property be used to pay them without his written consent. Han will indemnify and hold Tkat harmless from any proceeding to collect on Han's debts from Tkat's property, and she will be solely responsible for any expenses, including attorney's fees, incurred by Tkat in connection with such a proceeding.

Except as specified elsewhere in this agreement, all debts incurred by Tkat in his sole name during our marriage will be his sole and separate debts. Han will not be responsible for them, nor may her separate property or her share of any community property be used to pay them without her written consent. Tkat will indemnify and hold Han harmless from any proceeding to collect on Tkat's debts from Han's property, and he will be solely responsible for any expenses, including attorney's fees, incurred by Han in connection with such a proceeding.

---

2. Debts Incurred During Marriage for Mutual Benefit Will Be Marital or Community Debts

Even if you intend that each person will be responsible for his or her own postmarital debts—whether or not you use the clause above—you may want to make an exception for debts related to purchases that clearly benefit both of you, from basics such as groceries and utility bills to discretionary expenses like the cost of a romantic vacation together. If so, you can add this clause to your agreement.

EXAMPLE: After inserting in their prenup the general clause discussed in the preceding section, Han and Tkat add this clause to their agreement:

Debts Incurred During Marriage for Mutual Benefit Will Be Community Debts

Any debt incurred by either or both of us for our mutual benefit during our marriage will be considered a community debt and will be paid from community property funds. A debt will be considered incurred for our mutual benefit if it covers any of the following expenses: our necessaries of life (housing, utilities, telephone, automobile or other transportation, food, and medical and dental care), household furnishings and appliances, any joint entertainment or travel, and any jointly made gifts or contributions; but not the following expenses: clothing, cosmetics and personal hygiene, separate entertainment and travel, or separate gifts. If one of us uses his or her separate property funds to pay all or part of the debt, he or she will not be entitled to be reimbursed from community property funds.

---

3. Taxes

This optional clause is designed to establish some basic ground rules for deciding whether to file joint income tax returns, exchanging tax information, and allocating tax-related benefits and responsibilities—for example, joint income and deductions, tax liabilities, tax refunds, and expenses for preparing tax returns.

After you marry, you will have a choice of whether to file your federal income tax returns as married people filing jointly or married filing separately. (You may also have this choice for state income tax returns, depending on state tax laws.) There can be tax or other advantages to filing jointly or separately, depending on your circumstances during the year in question. This will require you to analyze your particular tax situation, possibly with the help of a competent tax adviser.

Once you decide whether or not to file jointly, you will need to decide how to share the taxes or refund on a joint return, or how to divide up joint income and deductions if you file separately.

You may prefer to address these questions each year as they come up, or you may simply figure you'll file jointly every year and share all liability and refunds. In either of these cases, you can skip this clause.

Grace and Ted have been advised by their accountant that there may be advantages to filing separately in some years, depending on Ted's investment income and deductions. They include this clause in their prenup:

Taxes

We agree to confer each year prior to the deadline for filing federal and state income tax returns for the preceding year in order to determine whether it is to our mutual advantage to file joint or separate returns. We will determine this by preparing draft joint and separate returns and then comparing the overall taxes that would be due on the joint and separate draft returns. Each of us will provide all information necessary to prepare the draft returns.

If we agree that it is to our mutual benefit to file joint returns, we will do so. Any taxes owed on joint returns, and any accountant's fees or other expenses incurred in preparing the draft and final returns, will be paid by Ted. Any refund received shall be paid to Ted.

If we file separately:

1. Our income and deductions will be allocated as follows:

   a. Any unearned income, gain, loss, or credit from any investment in joint names will be allocated between us according to our percentage of ownership;

   b. Any earned income together with any unearned income from separate investments will be allocated to the person who earned the income or whose separate investment produced the unearned income;

   c. Any deductible expense paid from joint funds will be allocated between us according to our percentage of ownership;

   d. Any deductible expense paid from separate funds will be allocated to the person from whose funds they were paid.

2. Any taxes owed on any separate return will be paid by the person filing the separate return. Any refund on any separate return will be paid to the person filing the separate return. Any accountant's fees or other expenses incurred in preparing the draft and final returns will be paid by Ted.

---

4. Business Debts

Like other debts incurred during marriage, state laws dictate who is responsible for business debts. And as with other debts, there are legal limits to your ability to change the rules when it comes to the rights of creditors who are not parties to your prenuptial agreement. But if you want to do what you can to limit your liability for each other's business debts, or if you want to spell out between the two of you who pays what, you can include a clause to that effect in your agreement.

The following clause is designed to apply to both of you—if you are both in business for yourselves—or to just one of you, if that's more appropriate.

For example, Russ and Karen are both self-employed, so they insert the necessary language to cover both of them. Here is what this clause looks like in their agreement:

Each Spouse Solely Responsible for Own Business Debts

All debts incurred by Karen in connection with her veterinary practice or related business before or during our marriage will be her sole and separate debts. Russ will not be responsible for them, nor may his separate property or his share of any community property be used to pay them without his written consent. Karen will indemnify and hold Russ harmless from any proceeding to collect on Karen's debts from Russ's property, and she will be solely responsible for any expenses, including attorney's fees, incurred by Russ in connection with such a proceeding.

All debts incurred by Russ in connection with his bookkeeping business before or during our marriage will be his sole and separate debts. Karen will not be responsible for them, nor may her separate property or her share of any community property be used to pay them without her written consent. Russ will indemnify and hold Karen harmless from any proceeding to collect on Russ's debts from Karen's property, and he will be solely responsible for any expenses, including attorney's fees, incurred by Karen in connection with such a proceeding.

5. Household Expenses

The next two alternative clauses give you a chance to spell out any agreement you have about paying household expenses. They are set up to cover the most common aspects of such arrangements, including responsibility for children's expenses, if that's a concern. Pick one of the alternatives and adapt it as appropriate, or skip this clause altogether if you would rather not commit yourselves to a specific arrangement.

For each alternative, we give you a place to list the kinds of expenses that you want to include, such as housing costs, telephone, food, automobile expenses, and so forth, and to identify any expenses that are not covered, such as personal jewelry, separate hobbies, or other items you want to treat differently.

Keep in mind that a clause dealing with your day-to-day arrangements is unlikely to be enforced by a court, so its purpose is mostly to clarify your expectations rather than to create legally enforceable rights. Include it only if you find it helpful.

Alternative 1: Household Expenses Will Be Paid by One Spouse

Use this clause if only one of you will pay household expenses. Adapt it as necessary to fit your circumstances.

For example, Grace has been a little apprehensive about how to pay for her personal expenses after she and Ted marry, because she will be quitting her job. After talking things through, they agree that they will open a joint checking account into which Ted will deposit enough to cover all the household bills, including Grace's personal expenses and incidentals. They insert this clause in their premarital agreement:

Household Expenses Will Be Paid by Ted

Ted will be responsible for paying all reasonable household expenses from his separate funds. Household expenses will include all necessaries of life (housing, utilities, transportation, food, and medical and dental care), household furnishings and appliances, any entertainment or travel, any jointly made gifts, clothing, and personal hygiene and incidentals.

For convenience, we will establish a joint checking account into which Ted will deposit sufficient funds per month to cover the regular household expenses, plus additional amounts as necessary to cover extraordinary household expenses. Either one of us may write checks on the joint account to pay for household expenses. Ted will be responsible for balancing and reconciling the joint account on a regular basis.

Alternative 2: Household Expenses Will Be Shared

Use this alternative if you plan to share responsibility for household bills and you want to clarify how you will do that.

Russ and Karen choose this option. Because they both have children who will be in their home at times, they include the optional language about children's expenses.

Household Expenses Will Be Shared

We will be responsible for paying all reasonable household expenses on an equal basis, using community property earnings. Household expenses will include all ordinary expenses and any necessary extraordinary expenses incurred in furnishing and maintaining our home and our joint lifestyle, but will not include expenses incurred in maintaining either party's separate property.

For convenience, we will establish a joint checking account into which we will each deposit our earnings plus additional equal amounts of separate property if necessary to cover household expenses. Either one of us may write checks on the joint account to pay for household expenses. Russ will be responsible for balancing and reconciling the joint account on a regular basis.

The household expenses listed above include reasonable living expenses for Karen's children, Shawn and Kyle, and for Russ's child, Tiffany, while they are living with us. Each of us will deposit all of any child support payments received into the account established for payment of household expenses.

Paragraph 9: Interpretation, Modification, Review, and Enforcement of Your Agreement

This is the next-to-last paragraph of your prenup. If you decide to include any of the optional paragraphs discussed in Chapter 6, you should insert them before this paragraph and renumber it so it remains in sequence (just before the signatures).

As we mentioned at the beginning of this chapter, this paragraph includes all the standard provisions that make for a clear and enforceable agreement (sometimes called "boilerplate"). We also give you some options for setting up periodic reviews of the agreement and providing a mechanism for resolving any future disagreements about the prenup.

Because the clauses in this agreement are for the most part standard to all agreements, we will focus our discussion on those aspects of the clauses that either require some explanation or present you with choices.

A. Entire Agreement

This clause (sometimes referred to by lawyers as an "integration clause") provides that all aspects of your agreements with each other have been included in the prenup. By requiring everything to be in one written document, it prevents confusion down the road.

If you live together before you marry, it's a good idea to include in your prenup any matters you agreed on previously that you want to carry forward into your marriage. Then you'll want to include the optional language in this clause specifying that except for what's specifically stated in your prenup, any prior agreements between you are superseded.

> **EXAMPLE:** Trevor and Rebecca have lived together for five years. They put this clause in their agreement:

Entire Agreement

This agreement contains our entire agreement on the matters covered. Any oral representations made concerning this agreement shall be of no force or effect. This agreement supersedes any written or oral agreements or understandings between us prior to the date of this agreement. Each of us hereby waives any and all claims we may have against the other arising out of our cohabitation prior to the date of our marriage.

B. Binding Effect of Agreement

This clause makes it clear that you expect your premarital agreement—after you sign it—to be legally binding on you and on anyone benefiting from or carrying out your estate plan.

Once we sign this agreement, it shall be binding on us and our respective inheritors and estate representatives.

C. Commitment to Carry Out the Agreement

After you marry, you will probably need to take some steps to fulfill the terms of your prenup. For example, if you have agreed to set up a joint bank account for paying bills, you'll need to go to the bank and open up the account. Or if your prenup says you'll transfer property into both of your names, or that one of you will be added as a beneficiary of life insurance or retirement benefits, you'll have to take care of those things. This clause makes it clear that you expect to do what is necessary to implement the agreement once you are married.

Each of us shall take any steps that are reasonably necessary to carry out the terms and intent of this agreement, including signing, notarizing, and delivering any necessary documents, upon request by the other party.

D. Modification of this Agreement

To make it less likely that something you do or say could be interpreted incorrectly as modifying your agreement, we recommend including this clause:

This agreement may be modified only by a subsequent written agreement signed by both of us. Any oral or written statements made by us (other than express representations in a subsequent written agreement), including but not limited to statements referring to separate property as "ours" or to marital property as "mine," "yours," "his," or "hers" will be only for convenience and will not be deemed to modify this agreement in any way. The filing of joint or separate tax returns during our marriage will not be deemed to modify this agreement in any way.

E. Voluntary Transfers and Restoration of Rights

This clause is intended to prevent an inadvertent modification of your agreement by providing that either of you can be more generous to the other than the prenup requires, without changing the agreement. We recommend that you include it.

Nothing in this agreement prevents either of us from making a voluntary transfer of an interest in property to the other party, and any such transfer, once completed, shall be deemed a gift.

During our marriage, or upon death, either of us is free to restore to the other party any legal right waived in this agreement.

Absent an express written agreement modifying this agreement, any voluntary transfer or restoration of a right will not be deemed an amendment of this agreement nor a waiver of the terms of this agreement.

F. Interpretation and Choice of Law

This clause accomplishes three things. First, it states your intent to have your agreement interpreted in a fair and straightforward manner. Second, it points to the state law to be followed when interpreting or enforcing your agreement. In our mobile society, it's wise to specify that the laws you consider applicable when you make your agreement are the laws that apply no matter where you end up living. Finally, it provides that you can use a copy of the signed agreement to establish the terms of the agreement in any future legal proceeding. Hopefully, you won't misplace the signed original of your prenup, but in case you do, this allows you to use a copy in court without jumping through a lot of legal hoops.

This agreement has been drafted and entered into in the State of California. It shall be interpreted fairly and simply, and enforced according to the laws of California. A copy of the signed agreement may be submitted to the court and admitted into evidence in place of the original in any proceeding to enforce or interpret this agreement.

G. Severability

As we mention elsewhere in this book, courts sometimes refuse to enforce certain aspects of premarital agreements. To prevent a court from tossing out your whole agreement if one clause is found unenforceable, we recommend that you include this clause:

If any part of this agreement is determined by a court to be invalid, illegal, or unenforceable, the validity and enforceability of the remaining parts of this agreement shall not be affected.

H. Attorneys' Fees

We hope, as you do, that you never get near a courthouse with your agreement, and that it happily gathers dust among your important papers. But if you do end up in a legal dispute over the matters covered by your prenuptial agreement, this clause can discourage ill-founded legal arguments by requiring the losing party to pay the winning party's legal expenses.

In any proceeding to enforce or interpret the terms of this agreement, the prevailing party shall be entitled to recover his or her reasonable expenses incurred in connection with the proceeding, including reasonable attorneys' fees.

I. Optional Clauses Regarding Periodic Reviews and Dispute Resolution

Here, we give you three optional clauses: one requiring regular reviews of the agreement, and two containing provisions for resolving future disagreements. We suggest you read through them and then pick any or all that suit you, adapting them to your circumstances as you see fit.

Alternative 1: Periodic Reviews

The future is bound to bring changes, and it's smart to review your premarital agreement from time to time. You'll want to make sure the provisions still make sense to you and tweak any clauses that might need updating.

While you don't have to include a requirement that you review your prenup, doing so may make it more likely you'll actually get to it. If you add this clause to your agreement, be sure to specify a reasonable time frame for the reviews. Somewhere between every other year to every seven years is probably right. For example, Karen and Russ agree to look over their prenup every five years.

We agree to review the terms of this agreement every five years during the month of January, beginning in January 2009.

Alternative 2: Mediation of Disputes

Mediation is a private, voluntary way to work through a disagreement. In mediation, you and your spouse would meet with a mediator, a neutral third party whose job is to help you reach an agreement. The mediator has no authority to impose a decision on you, but is there to facilitate a productive, solution-oriented conversation. More and more people are recognizing the advantage of using mediation to work out disagreements between spouses rather than taking those agreements to court. Of course, there's no guarantee that mediation will be successful. Still, because it's both private and informal, it's almost always worth a try. If you want to commit to giving mediation a try, you can include this clause in your prenup, as do our fictional couples Ted and Grace, and Karen and Russ.

If any dispute arises between us concerning terms of this agreement, we will first try to resolve the dispute in mediation with a qualified mediator acceptable to both of us. The expenses of mediation shall be equally shared between us. The mediation sessions shall be confidential, and neither of us may subpoena the records of the mediator or call the mediator as a witness in any arbitration or other legal proceeding between us.

Alternative 3: Arbitration of Disputes

Use this clause if you want to submit any dispute over your prenup to private arbitration, either instead of mediation or if mediation is unsuccessful. There are pros and cons to arbitration. Submitting a disagreement to arbitration is much like having it decided by a judge: In both instances, the case is heard by a neutral third party who listens to the evidence and the arguments and then decides who's right and who's wrong. However, an arbitrator is selected and paid by the disputing parties, whereas a judge is paid and appointed by the state. This gives you more choice over who decides your case but it can also make it more expensive, because you are footing the bill. Arbitration is usually (but not always) a faster process than trial in a court. Arbitration is also private, so you may be able to protect sensitive information if you go that route. In most states, the decision of an arbitrator can be appealed only in very limited circumstances, which can provide quick closure; on the other hand, there may be no way to overturn an arbitrator's decision even if it is clearly wrong.

In short, arbitration is just what's needed in some circumstances, while for others it's the wrong choice. Think carefully, and consider getting some good legal advice before deciding whether to include this provision in your premarital agreement.

For example, Karen and Russ decide that arbitration makes sense for them because it is private. They hope not to have any dispute that would need to be decided by a third party, but if it happens, they would prefer to avoid any gossip that could affect their business reputations. So they include the arbitration clause in their prenup:

If a dispute between us concerning this agreement cannot be resolved in mediation, then we agree to submit the dispute to binding arbitration within fifteen (15) days after either of us makes a written demand. If we cannot agree on an arbitrator, each of us shall appoint one person and the persons so appointed shall select the arbitrator. Participation in arbitration or a waiver of arbitration by both of us shall be a prerequisite to any legal action brought by either of us concerning the matters covered by this agreement, unless applicable law prohibits arbitration of the disputed issue(s).

Paragraph 10: Signatures, Acknowledgments, and Attorneys' Certifications

This is the very last paragraph of your prenup. Its contents are simple and essential. This is where you and your lawyers sign and date the agreement.

We start with a place for the date and your signatures. This is followed by a page in which each lawyer certifies that she or he has thoroughly reviewed the agreement with you. Your lawyers may want to modify or replace this part with their own forms. (See Chapter 7 for more on working with lawyers.) If you've decided against using lawyers, you should delete this page.

The next page contains notary certificates. Many states require prenups to be notarized. Legalities aside, it's a good idea to ensure the authenticity of your signatures by notarizing them. The form we've given you is pretty standard. Still, some states may have specific requirements for the notary form; the notary should be able to provide what you need.

You can find more information about signing your agreement in Chapter 7. For an example of Paragraph 10 as it would appear in an agreement, see Steven and Freda's prenup at the end of this chapter.

C. Assembling the Pages of Your Draft

After you have selected the clauses that go in each paragraph of your draft prenup—including any of the optional paragraphs discussed in Chapter 6—you should put them in order and attach to them copies of the schedules containing your written disclosures. A suggested format for the disclosure schedules is included after Paragraph 10 in Appendix C and on the CD-ROM. You can find an example of the completed schedules in Steven and Freda's agreement at the end of this chapter.

Make one copy of the whole packet for each of you, and then congratulate yourselves on a job well done. When you're ready, continue on to Chapter 7.

D. Sample Prenups

To give you an idea of what your completed prenup may look like, here are some samples. The first is an excerpt from Karen and Russ's agreement, showing in detail how they decided to handle property they each owned before their marriage. That's followed by the complete simple prenup made by Steven and Freda.

Excerpt from Karen & Russ's Prenup

Paragraph 6: Ownership of Premarital Assets

A. All Premarital Assets and Property Traceable to Them Remain Separate Property

Except as specified elsewhere in this agreement, Karen's premarital assets, which are listed on Schedule 1, and all property traceable to those assets, shall continue to be her separate property after we marry. "All property traceable to those assets" means any profits from or growth in value of those assets, including profits or growth in value arising as a direct or indirect result of the efforts of one or both of us during our marriage. It also means any sales proceeds of those assets, any asset purchased with the sales proceeds, or any asset(s) acquired in exchange for those assets, as long as the sales proceeds or any such new asset is held in the sole name of Karen.

Except as specified elsewhere in this agreement, Russ's premarital assets, which are listed on Schedule 2, and all property traceable to those assets, shall continue to be his separate property after we marry. "All property traceable to those assets" means any profits from or growth in value of those assets, including profits or growth in value arising as a direct or indirect result of the efforts of one or both of us during our marriage. It also means any sales proceeds of those assets, any asset purchased with the sales proceeds, or any asset(s) acquired in exchange for those assets, as long as the sales proceeds or any such new asset is held in the sole name of Russ.

B. Real Estate Will Remain Separate Property

During our marriage, we plan to reside in Karen's home located at 56 Bell Street, Sacramento, California. The home shall continue to be Karen's separate property after we marry, regardless of how we refer to it or how long we live there. Use of community property funds to pay any mortgage payments, property taxes, insurance, improvements, repairs, or other expenses for the property will not alter the separate property nature of the home. Such payments will not be reimbursable to the community property estate unless we sign a written agreement expressly providing otherwise. Any increase in the home's value shall also be Karen's separate property. If Karen sells the home or exchanges it for another asset, any sales proceeds or asset acquired in exchange will be her separate property.

Russ plans to rent out his home at 247 Stone Creek Drive, Sacramento, California, after we marry. The home shall continue to be Russ's separate property after we marry, regardless of how we refer to it or whether we ever live there. Use of community property funds to pay any mortgage payments, property taxes, insurance, improvements, repairs, or other expenses for the property will not alter the separate property nature of the home. Such payments will not be reimbursable to the community property estate unless we sign a written agreement expressly providing otherwise. Any increase in the home's value shall also be Russ's separate property. If Russ sells the home or exchanges it for another asset, any sales proceeds or asset acquired in exchange will be his separate property.

C. Premarital Professional Practice Will Be Subject to Apportionment Between Separate and Community Property

During our marriage, Karen plans to continue to operate the veterinary practice known as Valley Pet Hospital, and Russ will provide bookkeeping services to the practice. After we marry, the practice will

Excerpt from Karen & Russ's Prenup (continued)

be subject to apportionment between Karen's separate property and our community property as follows.

If Russ predeceases Karen, the practice, including any increase in its value during our marriage, will be entirely Karen's separate property.

If Karen predeceases Russ, or if we divorce, the practice shall be appraised as of the date of Karen's death or the date of our separation (whichever is applicable). The appraisal shall be performed by Faultless Business Appraisal Co., or by another appraiser jointly selected by us. From the appraised value, an amount equal to the value of the practice as of the date of our marriage (as set forth on Schedule 1, attached to this agreement), plus $10,000 for each of the first five years of our marriage, shall be apportioned to Karen's separate property. The excess value, if any, shall be apportioned to community property.

If the practice is sold during our marriage, the above provisions will apply to apportionment of the sales proceeds. However, instead of appraising the practice, the value at sale will be equal to the net sales proceeds after deducting costs of sale and any taxes due on the sale.

Freda and Steven's Prenup

Prenuptial Agreement
of
Freda Hoyle and Steven Kawamoto

Paragraph 1: Introductory Facts

A. Parties

This agreement is between Freda Hoyle and Steven Kawamoto. We refer to ourselves by our first names in this agreement.

B. Purpose of Agreement

We plan to marry on June 5, 2004. The purpose of this agreement is to identify our premarital assets and debts and to define our mutual rights and obligations regarding property and finances after we marry.

C. Current Circumstances

Freda currently resides at 123 Hightower Street, Chicago, Illinois. Her occupation is teacher. She has no children.

Steven currently resides at 6578 Maplethorne Avenue, Des Plaines, Illinois. His occupation is sales manager. He has no children.

Paragraph 2: Effective Date and Term

A. Effective Date of Agreement

This agreement will be effective on the day we marry. If we do not marry, this agreement will be null and void.

B. Term of Agreement

After we marry, this agreement will remain in full force and effect indefinitely, unless and until we sign a new written agreement revoking or modifying this agreement.

Paragraph 3: Legal Representation

A. Representation of Freda

Freda has been represented by Pat McNight, Esq., in the negotiation and drafting of this agreement. Freda has fully discussed the terms of this agreement with her attorney and is voluntarily choosing to sign this agreement.

Freda and Steven's Prenup (continued)

B. Representation of Steven

Steven has been represented by Martine Neilsen, Esq., in the negotiation and drafting of this agreement. Steven has fully discussed the terms of this agreement with his attorney and is voluntarily choosing to sign this agreement.

C. Drafting of Agreement

This agreement was drafted through the joint efforts of Steven and Freda and their attorneys.

Paragraph 4: Disclosures

A. Freda's Disclosures

All of Freda's assets and all of her debts are listed on Schedule 1, attached to this agreement. Freda's income for the calendar year 2003 is also listed on Schedule 1. Freda has provided the information on Schedule 1 in good faith. The values and other financial information on Schedule 1 are approximations and may not be exact, but they are intended to present a full, fair, and reasonable disclosure of Freda's assets, debts, income, and personal expenses as of the time they were presented to Steven.

B. Steven's Disclosures

All of Steven's assets and all of his debts are listed on Schedule 2, attached to this agreement. Steven's income for the calendar year 2003 is also listed on Schedule 2. Steven has provided the information on Schedule 2 in good faith. The values and other financial information on Schedule 2 are approximations and may not be exact, but they are intended to present a full, fair, and reasonable disclosure of Steven's assets, debts, income, and personal expenses as of the time they were presented to Freda.

C. Acknowledgment of Receipt of Disclosures

Freda received a copy of Schedule 2 on February 22, 2004. Freda reviewed this information before signing this agreement.

Steven received a copy of Schedule 1 on February 25, 2004. Steven reviewed this information before signing this agreement.

Paragraph 5: Definitions

A. This Agreement

The term "this agreement" refers to the provisions of this document, once signed by us, as modified by any subsequent amendments in writing signed by us.

B. Separate Property

Any asset designated as one person's separate property in this agreement belongs exclusively to that person. A spouse has the sole right to manage and dispose of his or her separate property assets.

Freda and Steven's Prenup (continued)

Separate property is not subject to division between us if we divorce. However, if the owner of separate property dies, the surviving spouse may have a legal claim to it, unless he or she has signed a valid written waiver in this agreement or in another document.

C. Marital Property

An asset designated as marital property in this agreement may be subject to division between us by a court if we divorce, and the surviving spouse may have a legal claim to it, unless he or she has signed a valid written waiver in this agreement or in another document.

D. Divorce

The term "divorce" in this agreement refers to any legal proceeding to end or alter a marital relationship, including a proceeding for divorce, dissolution of marriage, legal separation, or separate maintenance.

Paragraph 6: Ownership of Premarital Assets

All Premarital Assets and Property Traceable to Them Remain Separate Property

Except as specified elsewhere in this agreement, Freda's premarital assets (which are listed on Schedule 1), and all property traceable to those assets, shall continue to be her separate property after we marry. "All property traceable to those assets" means any profits from or growth in value of those assets, not including profits or growth in value arising as a direct or indirect result of the efforts of one or both of us during our marriage. It also means any sales proceeds of those assets, any asset purchased with the sales proceeds, or any asset(s) acquired in exchange for those assets, as long as the sales proceeds or any such new asset is held in the sole name of Freda.

Except as specified elsewhere in this agreement, Steven's premarital assets (which are listed on Schedule 2), and all property traceable to those assets, shall continue to be his separate property after we marry. "All property traceable to those assets" means any profits from or growth in value of those assets, not including profits or growth in value arising as a direct or indirect result of the efforts of one or both of us during our marriage. It also means any sales proceeds of those assets, any asset purchased with the sales proceeds, or any asset(s) acquired in exchange for those assets, as long as the sales proceeds or any such new asset is held in the sole name of Steven.

Paragraph 7: Ownership of Assets Acquired During Marriage

Ownership of Assets Acquired During Marriage Will Be Determined According to State Law

Except as specified elsewhere in this agreement, our rights in every asset acquired after we marry and in any profits or growth in value or any sales proceeds or asset acquired in exchange for those assets, will be determined in accordance with the laws of Illinois.

Freda and Steven's Prenup (continued)

Paragraph 8: Responsibility for Debts and Expenses

Each Person Solely Responsible for Own Premarital Debts

Freda's debts listed on Schedule 1 are her sole and separate debts. Steven will not be responsible for them, nor may his separate property or his share of any marital property be used to pay them without his written consent. Freda will indemnify and hold Steven harmless from any proceeding to collect on Freda's debts from Steven's property, and she will be solely responsible for any expenses, including attorney's fees, incurred by Steven in connection with such a proceeding.

Steven's debts listed on Schedule 2 are his sole and separate debts. Freda will not be responsible for them, nor may her separate property or her share of any marital property be used to pay them without her written consent. Steven will indemnify and hold Freda harmless from any proceeding to collect on Steven's debts from Freda's property, and he will be solely responsible for any expenses, including attorney's fees, incurred by Freda in connection with such a proceeding.

Paragraph 9: Interpretation, Modification, Review, and Enforcement of This Agreement

A. Entire Agreement

This agreement contains our entire agreement on the matters covered. Any oral representations made concerning this agreement shall be of no force or effect.

B. Binding Effect

Once we sign this agreement, it shall be binding on us and our respective inheritors and estate representatives.

C. Commitment to Carry Out This Agreement

Each of us shall take any steps that are reasonably necessary to carry out the terms and intent of this agreement, including signing, notarizing, and delivering any necessary documents, upon request by the other party.

D. Modification of This Agreement

This agreement may be modified only by a subsequent written agreement signed by both of us. Any oral or written statements made by us (other than express representations in a subsequent written agreement), including but not limited to statements referring to separate property as "ours" or to marital property as "mine," "yours," "his," or "hers" will be only for convenience and will not be deemed to modify this agreement in any way. The filing of joint or separate tax returns during our marriage will not be deemed to modify this agreement in any way.

Freda and Steven's Prenup (continued)

E. Voluntary Transfers and Restoration of Rights

Nothing in this agreement prevents either of us from making a voluntary transfer of an interest in property to the other party, and any such transfer, once completed, shall be deemed a gift.

During our marriage, or upon death, either of us is free to restore to the other party any legal right waived in this agreement.

Absent an express written agreement, any voluntary transfer or restoration of a right will not be deemed an amendment of this agreement nor a waiver of the terms of this agreement.

F. Interpretation and Choice of Law

This agreement has been drafted and entered into in the State of Illinois. It shall be interpreted fairly and simply, and enforced according to the laws of Illinois. A copy of the signed agreement may be submitted to the court and admitted into evidence in place of the original in any proceeding to enforce or interpret this agreement.

G. Severability

If any part of this agreement is determined by a court to be invalid, illegal, or unenforceable, the validity and enforceability of the remaining parts of this agreement shall not be affected.

H. Attorneys' Fees

In any proceeding to enforce or interpret the terms of this agreement, the prevailing party shall be entitled to recover his or her reasonable expenses incurred in connection with the proceeding, including reasonable attorneys' fees.

Paragraph 10: Signatures, Acknowledgments, and Attorneys' Certifications

Each of us has read this agreement carefully and is signing it freely after obtaining all advice he or she considers appropriate.

Dated: _March 30, 2004_   _Freda Hoyle_
Freda Hoyle

Dated: _March 30, 2004_   _Steven Kawamoto_
Steven Kawamoto

Freda and Steven's Prenup (continued)

Certificate of Attorney for Freda Hoyle

I certify, as attorney for Freda Hoyle only, that she has freely and voluntarily signed the attached premarital agreement. I have advised her about the legal effects of the terms of this agreement, and she has had a full opportunity to discuss it with me and with any other advisors of her own choosing. I believe that she has been fully advised and that she is aware of all the legal effects of this agreement.

Dated: _March 30, 2004_   _Pat McNight_
_____
Pat McNight, Esq.

Certificate of Attorney for Steven Kawamoto

I certify, as attorney for Steven Kawamoto only, that he has freely and voluntarily signed the attached premarital agreement. I have advised him about the legal effects of the terms of this agreement, and he has had a full opportunity to discuss it with me and with any other advisors of his own choosing. I believe that he has been fully advised and that he is aware of all the legal effects of this agreement.

Dated: _March 30, 2004_   _Martine Neilsen_
_____
Martine Neilsen, Esq

Freda and Steven's Prenup (continued)

Certificate of Acknowledgment of Notary Public

State of Illinois

} ss

County of Cook

On ___March 30, 2004___, before me, ___Roger Glenfield___, personally appeared ___Freda Hoyle___, personally known to me or proved to me on the basis of satisfactory evidence to be the person whose name is subscribed to the within instrument, and acknowledged to me that he/she executed the same and that by his/her signature on the instrument he/she executed the instrument.

WITNESS my hand and official seal.

[NOTARIAL SEAL]   ___Roger Glenfield___

Notary Public for the state of Illinois

My commission expires ___April 1, 2006___

Certificate of Acknowledgment of Notary Public

State of Illinois

} ss

County of Cook

On ___March 30, 2004___, before me, ___Roger Glenfield___, personally appeared ___Steven Kawamoto___, personally known to me or proved to me on the basis of satisfactory evidence to be the person whose name is subscribed to the within instrument, and acknowledged to me that he/she executed the same and that by his/her signature on the instrument he/she executed the instrument.

WITNESS my hand and official seal.

[NOTARIAL SEAL]   ___Roger Glenfield___

Notary Public for the state of Illinois

My commission expires ___April 1, 2006___

Freda and Steven's Prenup (continued)

Schedule 1—Freda's Disclosures

Premarital Assets

Description	Approximate Value
Household furnishings	$3,500
Personal computer & software	$5,000
Diamond ring and other jewelry	$6,000
2003 Lexus SC 430	$60,000
Retirement benefits with the Teachers' Retirement System of the State of Illinois	$70,000
ABC Brokerage, Account # xxx 3492	$50,000

Premarital Debts

To Whom Owed	Approximate Balance
None	

Freda's Annual Income (Calendar Year 2003): $45,000

February 17, 2004	*FH*
Date Prepared	Initials

February 17, 2004	*SK*
Date Received	Initials

Freda and Steven's Prenup (continued)

Schedule 2—Steven's Disclosures

Premarital Assets

Description	Approximate Value
Furnishings	$4,000
Entertainment Center	$5,000
Bluemeadow Tennis Club Membership	$20,000
2003 Honda CrX	$16,000
Benefits with the Employee Profit Sharing Plan and Trust of XYZ Sales, Inc.	$130,000

Premarital Debts

To Whom Owed	Approximate Balance
Bank of Illinois Visa, Account # xxxx xxxx xxxx 1234	$1,800

Steven's Annual Income (Calendar Year 2003): $50,000

February 17, 2004	_SK_
Date Prepared	Initials

February 17, 2004	_FH_
Date Received	Initials

Additional Provisions for Your Prenup

n the previous chapter, you drafted the basic paragraphs and clauses for your prenuptial agreement.

If you want to go beyond those fundamentals, you can select additional provisions from the paragraphs and clauses we provide here. This chapter includes information and sample language on the following issues:

- whether you will retain your rights to inherit property from one another and whether you will leave specific gifts to one another when you die
- whether either of you will transfer property—for example, real estate, life insurance, cash, or securities—to the other, either after or at the time of your marriage
- whether either of you will purchase an annuity or a new life insurance policy for the other person's benefit
- how you want property, debts, and alimony to be handled in the event of a divorce, and
- any other matters you consider important for your agreement.

As with the basic provisions discussed in Chapter 5, all of the paragraphs and clauses in this chapter are available in Appendix C and on the CD-ROM that

accompanies this book. If you select any of the paragraphs from this chapter, you should insert them into your draft agreement before Paragraph 9: Interpretation, Modification, Review, and Enforcement of This Agreement. Then be sure to renumber the paragraphs as necessary, so that they remain in sequence. If you need more help, Chapter 5, Section B, provides general instructions on how to fill in clauses and add them to your agreement, either by hand or using a computer.

When your draft is complete, turn to Chapter 7 to learn how to finalize your prenup.

Optional Paragraph 1: Estate Planning Matters

This paragraph contains clauses that address what happens if one of you dies while the prenup is in effect. These clauses are intended to support and supplement your estate plans. As we've stressed, your prenup is not a substitute for a good estate plan. After you get married, it is important to follow through by completing your wills and other estate planning documents. (Chapter 9 gives you some suggestions for this.)

A. Waiver of Inheritance Rights

The clauses in this section ensure that state laws regarding spousal inheritance rights will not interfere with your estate plans. It can be especially important to include one of these clauses if you expect to provide for someone other than—or in addition to—each other in your will or other estate planning documents. For example, you may want to make sure that your children from a prior marriage receive the inheritance you intend, or that certain property stays in your family when you die. As we discuss in Chapters 2 and 4, without a prenup and some basic estate planning documents such as a will or trust, it's possible that state law could defeat these wishes.

The clauses below allow you to waive some or all of your inheritance rights as a surviving spouse. You'll choose Alternative 1 if you want to waive all surviving spouse rights, or Alternative 2 if you want to waive only some of them. Waiving all inheritance rights is an extreme measure. Carefully read the rest of this section—and consult your lawyer, if one is helping you with the prenup—before you make this important decision.

In most states, a surviving spouse has some or all of these rights:

- to claim a portion of the deceased spouse's estate under "dower" or "curtesy" laws, or any similar state laws (see Chapter 4, Section C3, for a definition of dower and curtesy)
- to take property of the deceased spouse other than what is left under a will or other estate planning document
- to claim a share of the deceased spouse's separate property if he or she dies without a will
- to act as administrator or executor of the deceased spouse's estate
- to claim a homestead allowance, and
- to claim a family allowance or personal property allowance.

The first three of these rights are "election" rights. As you may remember from Chapter 4, all states guarantee a surviving spouse an inheritance when the other spouse dies. These laws are often called "election" laws because under them, the surviving spouse elects to take property —often as much as one-third to one-half of the deceased spouse's estate—instead of what was left under the deceased spouse's will or other property transfer documents. In community property states, a surviving spouse already owns half of the community property. Even so, a few community property states give a surviving spouse the right to take a portion of the deceased spouse's community or separate property, in some circumstances.

In addition to election rights, a surviving spouse may also ask to be appointed executor (or administrator) of the deceased spouse's estate and may request "allowances." Allowances typically fall into three categories: homestead, personal property, and family allowances (though individual states may use different names). An allowance may give the surviving spouse the right to stay in the family home, to receive support payments from the estate, or to claim a certain amount of the household goods and other personal property that belonged to the deceased spouse. Depending on your situation, you may decide that it makes sense to waive some or all of these additional rights.

One final note: These clauses are set up to be mutual—that is, both of you waive and retain the same rights. If you want your choices about waivers to be different for each of you, you'll need to adapt the appropriate clause to apply to only one of you at a time.

Think carefully before waiving surviving spouse rights. Waiving your legal right to something is a big step. Be sure you understand what you might be entitled to and think through whether you really need a waiver to help you carry out your estate plans. For a more thorough explanation of your rights, see Chapter 4, Section C3. Then check the summary of your state's laws found in Appendix D. If you are at all in doubt about what's involved, get some advice on the subject from a qualified lawyer. Finally, make sure you follow your state's legal requirements for a waiver. As we note in Chapter 4, state requirements can be quite complex. While we've tried to give you a comprehensive waiver clause, it may need some tweaking to pass muster in your state.

Alternative 1: Mutual Waiver of Rights in Each Other's Estate—Complete Waiver

Use this clause if you want to waive all of your surviving spouse rights. Typically, you would use a complete waiver if your estate plans cover everything that needs to be addressed if one of you dies, and if you want to be sure there won't be a glitch in those plans due to the spousal rights conferred by state law.

Ted and Grace, for example, choose this alternative. They have already written up detailed estate plans that they will be signing as soon as they marry. Ted's plan leaves the bulk of his estate, including family heirlooms, to his children, and also makes provisions for Grace, since she will be giving up her job to marry Ted. Grace's estate, which is much smaller and includes a share of a family farm, will go to Grace's sister. Ted is naming one of his adult children as executor of his estate. Grace's sister is designated to handle her estate. The couple decides that a complete waiver is the best way to assure that their plans will be carried out and that state spousal protection laws will not cause any delays or uncertainty in settling their estates. This is the clause they put in their prenuptial agreement:

Mutual Waiver of Rights in Each Other's Estate—Complete Waiver

Each of us waives and forever gives up any and all right or claim that he or she may acquire in the separate property of the other person due to our marriage, including but not limited to:

1. Rights or claims of dower, curtesy, or any substitute for those rights or claims provided by any applicable state statute at the time of the other person's death;

2. The right of election to take against the will of the other;

3. The right to a share in the separate property estate of the other person if he or she dies without a will;

4. The right to act as administrator of the estate of the other;

5. The right to a probate homestead or homestead allowance;

6. The right to a family allowance and to a personal property allowance.

Nothing in this agreement shall be deemed to constitute a waiver by either of us of any gift that the other person might choose to make to him or her by will or other estate planning document, or to act as executor designated in the will of the other. However, we acknowledge that no promises of any kind have been made by either of us to the other person regarding any such gift or designation, except for any specific provisions included in this agreement.

Alternative 2: Mutual Waiver of Rights in Each Other's Estate—Partial Waiver

This clause allows you to waive certain surviving spouse rights while retaining others. For example, Karen and Russ know that they want to waive their rights to claim a share of each other's property when one of them dies, so that property earmarked for their respective children will go to the children without a hitch. But they decide not to waive the right to be ex-

ecutors of each other's estates, or to request allowances. Russ in particular decides against waiving allowances, because he and Karen plan to live in Karen's home. He wants to be sure he can ask for the right to stay in the home if Karen dies, and for an allowance to help with the mortgage if necessary. So they opt for a partial waiver, using the following version of Alternative 1:

Mutual Waiver of Rights in Each Other's Estate—Partial Waiver

Each of us waives and forever gives up the following rights or claims that he or she may acquire in the separate property of the other person due to our marriage:

1. Rights or claims of dower, curtesy, or any substitute for those rights or claims provided by any applicable state statute at the time of the other person's death;

2. The right of election to take against the will of the other;

3. The right to a share in the separate property estate of the other person if he or she dies without a will.

Nothing in this agreement shall be deemed to constitute a waiver by either of us of any gift that the other person might choose to make to him or her by will or other estate planning document, or to act as executor designated in the will of the other. However, we acknowledge that no promises of any kind have been made by either of us to the other person regarding any such gift or designation, except for any specific provisions included in this agreement.

B. Leaving Property to Each Other at Death

This clause is for couples who want to make a binding agreement to provide for each other in their estate plans. In general, state laws allow you to change your will whenever you feel like it. In fact, you are not legally required to have a will (or any other estate planning document) at all. And other than legal protections for surviving spouses and children, you are free to leave your estate to anyone you choose. In most states, however, you can voluntarily bind yourself to include certain provisions in a will or other estate planning document by signing a written agreement to that effect. This is what is often referred to as an "agreement to make a will" or a "contract to make a will." The clause below is intended to constitute such an agreement. It is binding unless you are in the process of legally separating, divorcing, or getting an annulment when one of you dies.

Ted and Grace choose this clause for their prenup. Ted's assets are such that he knows he will be well off even if Grace predeceases him. Grace, on the other hand, expects to need some support from Ted's estate, especially since her retirement benefits from the county will be less as a result of her decision to stop working after she and Ted marry. If Ted dies, Grace also wants to be able to stay for a while in Ted's house (where she and Ted plan to live) before moving back into her own house (which will be rented out while they are married). After talking about various options, they decide that Ted should include in his estate plan a provision that gives Grace the right to stay in Ted's house rent free for up to one year, plus $3,000 per month for her living expenses for one year, and a distribution of $250,000 from Ted's estate. This is how the clause looks:

Provision for Grace Upon Ted's Death

Upon Ted's death, if no proceeding for divorce, dissolution, legal separation, or annulment is pending at the date of death, Grace shall be entitled to receive the following distribution from Ted's estate:

A lump sum payment of $250,000.

In addition, Grace shall be entitled to occupy (rent free) the residence in which we have been residing at the date of Ted's death, for a period of up to one year after Ted's death, and she shall be entitled to receive the monthly sum of $3,000, payable from Ted's estate for a period of one year after Ted's death.

At all times during our marriage, Ted shall maintain in full force and effect a valid will, trust, or other estate planning document that includes the foregoing provisions.

State laws may differ. The requirements for an agreement to make a will can vary from state to state, so you will need to check the laws of your state before including a clause like this in your prenup. You should also be sure to coordinate what you say here with your actual estate plan. Be sure to have your draft of this clause reviewed by your lawyer.

C. Making Consistent Estate Plans

If you are waiving some or all of your surviving spouse rights or if you have agreed to provide for each other after death, it is especially important to make a binding commitment to follow through with your estate plans as soon as you marry. This clause does that. Here is how it looks in Ted and Grace's agreement:

Estate Plans to Be Consistent With This Agreement

We acknowledge the importance of making valid estate plans that are consistent with this agreement. Therefore, as soon as possible after our marriage, each of us will establish and maintain in effect a valid will, trust, and/or other estate planning document or combination of documents that will be consistent with, and carry out the terms of, this agreement. We further agree to review our estate plans periodically to ensure that our estate planning documents remain consistent with this agreement and to modify our estate planning documents if necessary to keep them consistent with this agreement.

Optional Paragraph 2: Property Transfers or Purchases of Insurance Upon Marriage

Use one or more of the clauses in this paragraph to set forth an agreement that one of you will:

- give property or cash to the other person after you are married, or

• set up a life insurance policy or annuity for the benefit of the other person.

We give you several common scenarios to choose from. If none of them fits exactly, pick the one that's closest and adapt it to your situation.

Be aware of possible tax consequences. Gifts between spouses are usually exempt from gift taxes, while gifts between unmarried people may not be. Making the transfer after marriage may make the transfer a nontaxable gift between married people, even though a prenup signed before marriage requires the transfer. However, the tax consequences can differ, depending on the circumstances. Avoid unpleasant surprises by familiarizing yourself with the tax rules that will apply to your agreement; ask your tax adviser or lawyer if you need help.

A. Transferring Real Estate

Use this clause to set forth an agreement to transfer ownership of real estate following your wedding.

EXAMPLE: Rodney owns land where he and Tina plan to build a house together. They agree that after three months of marriage, Rodney will transfer a one-half interest in the land to Tina. The title will be in joint tenancy with right of survivorship, which means that if one of them dies after the transfer, the surviving spouse will own the entire property. This is the clause as it appears in their prenup:

Transfer of Real Estate

Within 90 days after our marriage, Rodney will sign, deliver, and record a deed granting to Tina a 50% interest, as joint tenants with right of survivorship, in the following real estate: unimproved real property located in the state of Maine, more specifically described on Schedule 1 attached to this agreement. Each of us will pay for one-half of any expenses related to the transfer, including the cost of obtaining title insurance on the property.

B. Transferring Cash, Securities, or Other Personal Property

This clause provides for the payment of cash or transfer of property other than real estate following marriage. As with the other clauses in this section, it is worded to provide for a one-time payment or transfer, but you can adapt it to provide for multiple transfers.

EXAMPLE: Olga and Jorge are in their mid-twenties. Olga owns extensive investments inherited from her grandparents, plus her car and household goods. Jorge has only a small savings account, a car, and household goods. They want to be able to save and invest for their joint future on more equal footing. They agree that each year on their anniversary, Olga will transfer a share of her investments to a joint account so that over time, they will have more and more joint investments. This is how they adapt this clause:

Transfer of Cash, Securities, or Other Personal Property

Within 30 days after our marriage, and each year within 30 days after our wedding anniversary for nine additional years, Olga will deliver and assign to a joint securities account to be established by us, ownership of the following property: $10,000 in funds and/or investments selected by Olga, for a total of $100,000 over the first ten years of our marriage. Olga will pay all expenses related each transfer.

C. Assigning Life Insurance

Use this clause if one of you has agreed to transfer ("assign") ownership of a life insurance policy to the other person after marriage. Assigning ownership of life insurance is usually done by people whose estates might be subject to estate taxes in order to reduce the overall value of their estate and therefore avoid taxes. Typically, the insured person is also the "owner" of the life insurance policy, meaning that the insured person has the right to designate beneficiaries and to control all other aspects of the policy. If the insured person dies, the proceeds of the life insurance policy will be counted as part of the estate that is subject to estate tax. But if the insured person assigned ownership of the policy to someone else and therefore did not own it at the time of death, the proceeds won't be subject to tax. (For a further explanation of estate taxes and ways to reduce or avoid them, see the resources listed in Chapter 9.)

Changing ownership of life insurance is normally part of an overall estate plan. It also gives complete control of the policy to the new owner: If you transfer ownership of a life insurance policy to your spouse and you later divorce, you can't cancel the policy or get it back. So be sure to consider your plans carefully before including this clause. If you decide that it meets your needs, you can go ahead and use it.

> **EXAMPLE:** Michael and Evelyn are in their late forties and marrying, each for the second time. Michael owns a home, investments, retirement accounts, and miscellaneous other assets. Evelyn is much less wealthy. Michael owns life insurance on his life with a death benefit of $750,000. He and Evelyn agree that she should be designated the beneficiary of the policy; they also want to get the policy out of his taxable estate. They decide to use this clause to transfer ownership of the policy to Evelyn. She can then designate herself as beneficiary.

Assignment of Life Insurance

Within 15 days after our marriage, Michael will deliver and assign to Evelyn ownership of the following fully paid life insurance policy on Michael's life: XYZ Insurance Company policy number 222333, face amount $750,000. Michael will pay any expenses related to the assignment.

D. Purchasing an Annuity or Life Insurance

Some people include in their prenups a clause requiring one of them to buy an annuity or life insurance policy for the benefit of the other person. To decide whether to include such a clause, you'll need to know something about the potential benefits and costs of annuities and life insurance. A comprehensive analysis of these matters is beyond the scope of this book, but here are some basic considerations to keep in mind.

Typically, you purchase an annuity by paying a certain amount of money up front or at regular intervals. In exchange, the annuity provider agrees to make specified monthly, quarterly, or annual payments to a beneficiary that you designate. Payments begin at a specified time and continue for the beneficiary's lifetime. An annuity is used to provide cash flow for the beneficiary, and there can be income tax benefits involved in setting up some types of annuities.

Life insurance is similar to an annuity, except that the payments don't begin until the death of the insured person, and the payment to the beneficiary is usually a lump sum. Obviously, the main purpose of life insurance is to provide cash when the insured person dies. As noted above in Section C, the proceeds may be subject to estate tax.

As with all of the clauses in this paragraph, you should be sure to think through all the implications—including tax consequences—before using one or both of the following clauses in your agreement.

Here are two examples of the completed clauses, one involving an annuity and one providing for life insurance.

> **EXAMPLE:** Beatriz and Arnolfo plan to have children after they marry. They agree that Beatriz will take time off from her job until their children reach school age. To make up for any reduction in Beatriz's retirement benefits, they agree that Arnolfo will buy an annuity that Beatriz can start to draw on after age 50.

Purchase of Annuity

Within 60 days after our marriage, Arnolfo will purchase an annuity contract that will pay at least $30,000 per year beginning on Beatriz's 50th birthday, and continuing until the death of Beatriz, who shall be designated as sole primary beneficiary of the annuity. Arnolfo will pay all of the costs of purchasing and maintaining the annuity.

EXAMPLE: Dirk is quitting his job and relocating in order to marry Maxine. Maxine plans to support the two of them until Dirk reestablishes himself in a new job. Dirk is concerned about how he will pay his expenses if something happens to Maxine before he is fully self-supporting again. They agree to take out life insurance on Maxine's life for Dirk's benefit, so that Dirk will have funds to live on if Maxine dies unexpectedly.

Purchase of Life Insurance Policy

Within 90 days after our marriage, Maxine will purchase a life insurance policy that will pay at least $300,000 upon her death. Dirk shall be designated as sole primary beneficiary of the policy. Maxine and Dirk will each pay one-half of the costs of purchasing and maintaining the policy.

Optional Paragraph 3: Provisions Applicable to Divorce

This paragraph contains clauses that allow you to spell out in advance how various financial and property matters will be handled if you divorce. (If in Paragraph 5 of your prenup you have defined the term "divorce" to include other legal proceedings, such as legal separation or annulment, this paragraph will apply to those events too.)

Before you decide whether or not to include a paragraph on divorce matters, we suggest that you review the general information on divorce in Chapter 4, Section C4. Then check the summary of your state's laws found in Appendix D, and follow up if you need to so that you clearly understand what's likely to happen to your property and finances if you say nothing about divorce in your prenup.

You may conclude that you don't need to include this paragraph at all. If you have specified what is separate property and what is marital or community property in the preceding paragraphs of your prenup, you can leave the details of how the marital assets and debts get allocated to later negotiation or court decision. But if you want to dictate some specific results in advance, this is where you should do that.

A court may not enforce some terms regarding divorce. All states allow you to make a binding agreement about how some financial matters will be handled if you divorce. However, there can be exceptions in some areas, especially when it comes to child support and alimony. For example, no state will allow you to waive child support in advance. Some states don't allow advance waivers of alimony, either, while others impose certain requirements for a valid alimony waiver. Even some property division agreements can be set aside, if a court finds that the provisions violate public policy. Read Chapter 4, Section C4, and review the summary of your state's laws in Appendix D for more information. Be sure you understand any legal limits on what you can include in this paragraph before using any of the clauses that follow.

A. Making Sure Your Prenup Applies If You Divorce

If you decide to include a paragraph dealing with divorce matters, you should start with this clause. It requires you to file your prenup with the divorce court at the beginning of the case, and directs that any dispute about the agreement be resolved before any decisions about property or other financial matters can be made.

Karen and Russ include a paragraph about divorce in their prenup, so they start the paragraph with this clause:

Terms of This Agreement to Control

In the unhappy event that our marriage ends in divorce, as that term is defined in Paragraph 5 of this agreement, we want to resolve all issues as amicably and efficiently as possible. Therefore, if we divorce, we agree to the following:

1. This agreement will control all issues addressed by this agreement.

2. As soon as possible after the case is filed, we will file this agreement (or a true copy of it) in court and we will sign and file a stipulation acknowledging the validity of this agreement.

3. Any dispute about the validity or interpretation of this agreement will be separated from all other issues in the case and submitted to the court for determination before any issues addressed in this agreement are decided.

B. Dividing and Distributing Property

Chances are good that your paragraph addressing divorce issues will include one or more of the optional clauses in this section. We'll discuss them separately, so that you can decide which of them are right for your situation. If you don't see exactly what you need, pick one that's close and adapt it to your requirements.

1. Distribution of Separate Property Assets

This clause ensures that each spouse ends up with his or her separate property in a divorce. If you like, you can also include language providing for any separate property held in joint names to be divided into two shares (if possible) or else sold, with the proceeds divided according to each person's ownership share.

Russ and Karen include this clause in their prenup. Even though they live in California, a community property state, they leave in the optional part about dividing any assets made up of separate property that they hold in a form of joint ownership, such as joint tenancy. Though California law presumes that any joint ownership property acquired during marriage is community property, they could opt out of the community property system for a particular asset by making a written agreement to hold it as separate property in a joint ownership form. They include the full clause because they want to keep all of their options open.

Distribution of Separate Property Assets

In any divorce proceeding, our separate property assets will be distributed as follows:

1. Each party's separate property assets, as defined in this agreement, shall be confirmed to him or her absolutely, without being included in any division of community property.

2. Each jointly owned separate asset shall be divided between us in proportion to our respective ownership interests in the asset ("in kind"), if that is possible without making us co-owners of the same asset after the asset is divided. If an in-kind division of any asset is not possible, the asset shall be sold and the net proceeds divided in proportion to our respective ownership interests in the asset.

2. Distribution of Marital Property Assets

Even if your prenup clearly identifies what is to be considered marital or community property, you will have to divide that property between you if you divorce. If you don't spell out a method of division, you'll have to make that decision later, in settlement negotiations— or a judge will make the decision for you in court. To limit uncertainty, or to establish a different standard for accomplishing the division of marital or community property than the one your state provides, you can include a clause setting forth your intent.

We give you two alternative clauses, one dictating an equal division of the assets and one allowing for an "equitable" (not necessarily equal) division. There are many other possibilities. For example, you might want the property to be divided in some specified proportion (such as 60/40 or 70/30), or you might want to exclude certain categories of assets. Pick one of the alternatives we give you as a starting point and adapt it to meet your needs.

If you want to provide for special treatment of a particular asset, there's a place to do that further on in this paragraph.

Alternative 1: Equal Distribution of Marital or Community Property Assets

This clause assumes that the marital or community property assets will be divided so that you each wind up with assets of equal value. The division may occur by:

- literally dividing individual assets in half—for example, splitting the money in bank accounts
- selling assets and dividing the proceeds, or
- agreeing to give certain assets to one person and other assets to the other.

It also allows for exceptions, so you can use this clause to set out a general approach and then insert a separate clause to designate any assets you'd like to treat differently. And it provides that you can agree later to a different way of dividing things, as long as you put your new agreement in writing.

In most states, the law allows the judge in a divorce case to divide marital property unequally unless the divorcing spouses make their own settlement agreement stating otherwise. This is true in all equitable distribution states and a number of community property states as well. (See Appendix D for information on how property is divided in your state.) If you live in one of these states and you want your property to be divided equally even if you don't reach a settlement, then you may want to consider including this clause or some variation of it that accomplishes what you have in mind.

EXAMPLE: Chan and Mara live in New Jersey, an equitable distribution state. They feel that an equal

division of their marital property would be more fair than leaving open the possibility that one of them might end up with less than half if they were unable to agree. They add the following clause to their prenup:

Equal Distribution of Marital Property Assets

In any divorce proceeding, except as provided elsewhere in this agreement or in a written agreement signed by both of us at the time of the divorce, any marital property assets shall be distributed between us in such a way as to achieve a monetarily equal division of the aggregate net value of the marital property assets. If we so agree, certain assets may be distributed to one of us in exchange for a distribution of offsetting assets to the other party. Otherwise, each asset will be divided between us equally ("in kind"), if that is possible without making us co-owners of the same asset after the asset is divided. If an asset cannot be divided in kind and there is no agreement to assign the asset to one party, it shall be sold and the net proceeds divided so as to accomplish an equal division of all the assets. In determining whether the assets have been equally divided, any asset not sold will be valued at its fair market value as of the date the assets are divided.

Even if you live in a state where the law requires a judge to divide the property equally unless you reach a settlement agreeing to an unequal division (this is the case in a few community property states), you might still use this clause to specify how the equal division of the property will be accomplished or to confirm your intent to divide things equally. For example,

Russ and Karen live in California, a state where equal division of property is almost always required unless a couple agrees otherwise. They use this alternative to state their general intent that their community property will be divided equally, but they don't include any details of how that will be accomplished. This is the clause as it appears in their agreement:

Equal Distribution of Community Property Assets

In any divorce proceeding, except as provided elsewhere in this agreement or in a written agreement signed by both of us at the time of the divorce, any community property assets shall be distributed between us in such a way as to achieve a monetarily equal division of the aggregate net value of the community property assets.

Alternative 2: Equitable Distribution of Marital or Community Property Assets

As mentioned just above, most states don't require that marital or community property be divided equally at the time of divorce. Unless a couple agrees otherwise, the divorce judge can divide the assets in whatever proportion seems fair ("equitable") to the judge.

If you are in one of the few states that require equal division of common property and you prefer the equitable distribution approach, you can use this clause to say so.

If you live in a state where common assets will be divided equitably and you are comfortable with that approach, you can use this clause to confirm your position or you can skip it and allow property to be divided according to a settlement agreement or state law.

Note that this alternative, like the first one, allows you to create exceptions for specific assets and to make a later agreement that divides your common property in some other way.

EXAMPLE: Lupe and Ike live in an equitable distribution state. They might someday move to a community property state where equal division is required. They like the equitable distribution concept, but they want to provide some guidelines. They decide to include this version of Alternative 2 in their prenup:

Equitable Distribution of Marital or Community Property Assets

In any divorce proceeding, except as provided elsewhere in this agreement or in a written agreement signed by both of us at the time of the divorce, any marital or community property assets shall be distributed between us in such a way as to achieve an equitable division of the aggregate net value of the marital or community property assets, as determined by written agreement signed by both of us or by the court in the divorce case. If we so agree, certain assets may be distributed to one of us in exchange for a distribution of offsetting assets to the other. Otherwise, each asset will be divided between us ("in kind"), if that is possible without making us co-owners of the same asset after the asset is divided. If an asset cannot be divided in kind and there is no agreement to assign the asset to one party, it shall be sold and the net proceeds divided so as to accomplish an equitable division of all the assets. In determining whether the assets have been equitably divided, any asset not sold will be valued at its fair market value as of the date the assets are divided.

---

3. Dividing Retirement Benefits

If you want to spell out what will happen to any marital or community property share of retirement benefits in the event of a divorce, you can include one of the clauses in this section.

We give you four alternatives for this clause:

- Alternative 1 states that the retirement benefits are allocated to the person whose name is on them. The other spouse gets some other property or a payout in exchange (as part of either an equal division or an equitable distribution, depending on which general approach you are using).
- Alternative 2 provides that any marital or community property interest in retirement benefits will be divided up, with each spouse getting a percentage of the benefits.
- Alternative 3 states that each person keeps his or her own retirement benefits, without including

them in any division of marital or community property.

- Alternative 4 states that you will decide how to distribute any marital or community property share of a spouse's retirement benefits if and when you divorce.

Read through the alternative clauses and pick the one that most closely fits the way you want to handle retirement benefits. As always, adapt a clause if necessary.

Alternative 1: Retirement Benefits Are Divided by the Offset Method

Use this alternative if you want to make sure that any retirement benefits will be assigned to the person who earned or accumulated them, with some other asset or payment given to the other party in exchange. This is called the "offset method" because what one spouse gives up is "offset" (compensated) by an award of other property.

EXAMPLE: Kyle and Hannah both have retirement plans through their jobs. Both of them have been working only a short time, so most of their retirement benefits will be considered marital property because it will have been earned while they are married. They agree that if they ever divorce, each of them will keep his or her own retirement benefits. If one person's benefits are worth more, the other will receive some other property to even things up. They use this clause in their prenup:

Retirement Benefits to Be Divided— Offset Method

If we divorce, the terms of the divorce decree or judgment shall provide that any marital property interest in retirement, pension, deferred compensation, and other employee benefit or tax deferred plans, whether qualified according to IRS regulations or nonqualified, shall be divided so that the person who earned the benefits or in whose name those benefits are held receives all of the benefits and the other person receives other property or funds as an offset in the equitable division of the marital property.

Alternative 2: Retirement Benefits Are Divided in Kind

This alternative provides that any marital or community property share of retirement benefits will be divided between you, regardless of whose name they are in. This is usually called an "in kind" division. Dividing a retirement asset in kind is often accomplished through a qualified domestic relations order ("QDRO"), which provides for each spouse to receive a share of the benefits directly from the retirement plan. The clause states that the spouses will cooperate in preparing the necessary order.

EXAMPLE: Bal expects to make major contributions to his 401(k) plan during his marriage to Xenia. They hope to have a family together and the plan is for Xenia to be a stay-at-home mom. They agree that if there is a divorce, the community property share of Bal's 401(k) will be divided in kind between them. This is the clause they use:

Retirement Benefits to Be Divided— In-Kind Method

If we divorce, the terms of the divorce decree or judgment shall provide that any community property interest in retirement, pension, deferred compensation, and other employee benefit or tax deferred plans, whether qualified according to IRS regulations or nonqualified, shall be divided so that each of us receives a share of the benefits payable, with each person's share calculated in a manner consistent with equitable division of the community property. Each of us will cooperate in preparing any court order for division of the benefits required by the plan or as provided by applicable law.

Alternative 3: Retirement Benefits Are Not Divided

You should use this alternative if you want each of you to keep your own retirement benefits, without including them in the division of other marital or community property assets.

EXAMPLE: Maxine and David want any retirement benefits they earn while they're married to be considered community property if one of them dies. If they divorce, however, they want to keep their retirement benefits completely separate. They decide to accomplish this by including the following clause in their prenup:

No Division of Retirement Benefits

If we divorce, the terms of the divorce decree or judgment shall provide that any community property interest in retirement, pension, deferred compensation, and other employee benefit or tax deferred plans, whether qualified according to IRS regulations or nonqualified, shall be confirmed to the person who earned the benefits or in whose name those benefits are vested and shall not be included in the equal division of the community property.

Alternative 4: Method of Dividing Retirement Benefits to Be Determined at Time of Divorce

Most people who want to defer the question of how to divide up retirement benefits won't need to add this clause; anything left out of the prenup will be decided at the time of a divorce anyway. But if you are including specific instructions on everything else and the issue of retirement benefits is the only issue you haven't addressed, you can use this alternative.

EXAMPLE: Andres and Lara are providing in their prenup for equal division of their personal property and any liquid assets if they divorce. They aren't sure what to do with their retirement benefits, so they decide to make it clear that this issue will be decided when and if they divorce. They use this clause:

Retirement Benefits to Be Divided—Method to Be Determined

If we divorce, the terms of the divorce decree or judgment shall provide that any marital property interest in retirement, pension, deferred compensation, and other employee benefit or tax deferred plans, whether qualified according to IRS regulations or nonqualified, shall be divided in a manner consistent with the equitable division of the marital property, as determined by a written agreement signed by both of us or by the court in the divorce case.

4. Dividing Other Assets

Once you've laid out your general approach to dividing your marital or community property assets and dealt with any issue relating to retirement benefits, there may still be one or more assets that require special treatment. For example, you may be planning to buy a house together and want to allow one of you to buy out the other person's share if you divorce. Or you may have a similar agreement regarding a business you plan to start up.

This is where you would put such a clause. Use the same format we've given you for other clauses, give your clause a title, and insert it in your prenup. Here is an example.

EXAMPLE: Kamlesh and Bhavana plan to buy a house together after they marry. They agree that if they ever divorce, Kamlesh can buy out Bhavana's share on certain prearranged terms. Here is what they put in their prenuptial agreement:

Right to Purchase Residence

We plan to purchase a residence in which we will live together during our marriage. The residence will be considered marital property. If we ever divorce, Kamlesh will have the right to buy out Bhavana's share of the equity in the residence as follows: The fair market value of the residence shall be determined by a mutually approved appraiser. If we cannot agree on an appraiser, each of us will select a licensed appraiser, and those appraisers shall select a licensed appraiser to perform the appraisal. The amount owing on any mortgages or liens shall then be deducted from the fair market value to determine the equity in the residence. Kamlesh shall pay Bhavana cash in an amount equal to one-half of the equity. Kamlesh may refinance the property to obtain the funds for the buyout, and Bhavana agrees to cooperate with such a refinance. The buyout must be completed within 60 days after the divorce decree or judgment, unless we agree in writing to extend the time. If Kamlesh does not buy Bhavana out by that time, Bhavana shall have 60 days to buy out Kamlesh on the same terms and conditions. If neither of us buys out the other person's share, the house shall be listed for sale and sold as soon as possible, and the net proceeds shall be divided equally between us.

C. Responsibility for Outstanding Debts

The next few clauses contain provisions for dealing with outstanding debts in the event of a divorce. Ordinarily, state laws give divorce judges the power to divide up responsibility for debts incurred by one or both spouses during marriage. (See Chapter 4, Section C4, for a review of this issue.) Often, a judge will have fairly broad discretion to allocate debts, depending on the circumstances at the time of the divorce. If you want to provide a more predictable outcome, you can use one or more of these clauses to do so.

1. Premarital Debts

Though state law usually dictates that one spouse is not responsible for the other's premarital debts, you can include this clause to ensure this result. This guarantees that a divorce judge can't order one of you to pay the other person's premarital debts.

Here's the clause that Karen and Russ add to their agreement:

Responsibility for Premarital Debts

If we divorce, the terms of the divorce decree or judgment shall provide that any outstanding premarital debt will be allocated to the person who incurred the debt, and he or she shall be required to pay the debt and to hold the other person harmless from the debt and all costs related to it.

2. Debts Incurred During Marriage— General Rule

In the absence of an agreement between the spouses, state law gives divorce judges a lot of latitude to divide debts incurred during marriage. You may want to eliminate this uncertainty by establishing your own guidelines in case you ever need them. We give you a couple of alternatives to select or adapt as needed. The first requires that debts be divided equally between you. The second allows debts to be divided in a manner that's fair at the time you divorce, either by agreement between the two of you or, if you can't agree, according to the divorce judge's decision.

Alternative 1: Equal Responsibility for Debts Incurred During Marriage

You'll probably want to use this clause if you stated that you want your assets to be divided equally in the event of a divorce. You'll want to make sure that provision is not undermined by an unequal division of debts. Because it's not always practical to equally divide debts—for example, one spouse may be a homemaker and not able to make debt payments—this clause allows for an unequal division of debts to be balanced out in the division of property. Note that this clause states a general rule, leaving room for exceptions to be addressed in other clauses of the prenup.

EXAMPLE: Chan and Mara, who opted for an equal division of their marital property in a previous clause of their agreement, include this clause requiring equal division of any mutual debts:

Equal Responsibility for Debts Incurred During Marriage—General Rule

Except as provided elsewhere in this agreement, if we divorce, the terms of the divorce decree or judgment shall provide that any outstanding debts incurred by one or both of us during our marriage will be paid and allocated between us equally, to the extent an equal allocation is practical, as specifically determined by written agreement signed by both of us, or by the court in the divorce case. If the allocation is unequal, there shall be a corresponding offset in the division of our marital property assets, in order to equalize the overall division of assets and debts.

If a debt is allocated to one of us in accordance with this clause, the person to whom it is allocated shall be required to hold the other person harmless from the debt and all costs related to it.

Alternative 2: Equitable Allocation of Debts Incurred During Marriage

This alternative says that debts incurred while you are married will be divided between you if you divorce, but leaves the exact method of division to be determined according to a flexible "equitable" standard. If you have opted for equitable division of your property, you will probably want to stick with an equitable division of debts, too. As with Alternative 1, this clause allows for exceptions to the general rule.

EXAMPLE: Ike and Lupe have opted for equitable division of their marital property, so they include this clause to deal with debts incurred while they are married:

Equitable Allocation of Responsibility for Debts Incurred During Marriage—General Rule

Except as provided elsewhere in this agreement, if we divorce, the terms of the divorce decree or judgment shall provide that any outstanding debt incurred by one or both of us during our marriage will be paid and allocated between us equitably, as determined by written agreement signed by both of us or by the court in the divorce case.

If a debt is allocated to one of us in accordance with this clause, the person to whom it is allocated shall be required to hold the other person harmless from the debt and all costs related to it.

3. Student Loans

If one of you takes out a student loan while you are married and you get divorced before it's completely paid back, will the debt be the sole responsibility of the person who got the education or can it be allocated between you in the divorce? State laws vary on this point, so you may want to include your own clause here. We give you two alternatives to choose from. The first makes student loans the sole responsibility of the student, while the second allows them to be shared between the spouses.

Alternative 1: Sole Responsibility for Student Loans

This clause makes any balance due on a student loan the sole responsibility of the spouse who was the student.

EXAMPLE: Lamont plans to finish his bachelor's degree and get a teaching credential after he and Jetta marry. Lamont will take out student loans to cover his educational expenses. He and Jetta agree that the student loans will be their joint responsibility while they are married. But if they ever get divorced, Lamont will be solely responsible for anything still owing on the loans. Although it is unlikely that Jetta will go back to school, if she does, the same rules will apply to any student loans she takes out. They use this clause in their prenup:

Sole Responsibility for Student Loans

If we divorce, the terms of the divorce decree or judgment shall provide that any outstanding student loan debt will be allocated to the person whose education was financed by the loan, who shall be required to pay the debt and to hold the other person harmless from the debt and all costs related to it.

Alternative 2: Shared Responsibility for Student Loans

Use this alternative if you want to treat student loans as a shared responsibility.

> **EXAMPLE:** Ty plans to attend graduate school after he and Jen marry. Jen is already in medical school. Both of them will use student loans to help pay for their tuition and expenses. They agree that the loans will be their mutual responsibility while they are married and if they ever divorce. They insert this clause in their agreement:

Shared Responsibility for Student Loans

If we divorce, the terms of the divorce decree or judgment shall provide that any outstanding student loan debt will be allocated between us in the same manner as any other debts incurred during our marriage for which we are mutually responsible, and not solely to the person whose education was financed by the loan.

4. Sole Responsibility for Certain Debts Incurred by One Spouse During Marriage

Besides student loans, you may incur other types of debts during marriage that you want just one spouse to pay back. For example, one person's business debts might be allocated to him or her. Or perhaps one of you might plan to borrow money for an expensive hobby and you both agree that only the spouse who takes on the debt should pay it back. You may also want to provide for general contingencies, such as the possibility that one of you might run up a debt without

the other person's consent. If you want to provide this type of exception to the general approach used for allocating debts incurred during your marriage, this is the place to do it.

For example, Karen and Russ are both self-employed. If they divorce, they agree that each of them will be solely responsible for business debts incurred during their marriage.

Sole Responsibility for Certain Debts Incurred by One Party During Marriage

If we divorce, the terms of the divorce decree or judgment shall provide that any of the following outstanding debts incurred by one of us during our marriage will be allocated solely to the person who incurred the debt: 1) Debts incurred by Karen in the course of engaging in the practice of veterinary medicine or in any other business; 2) Debts incurred by Russ in the course of operating his bookkeeping business or any other business.

If a debt is allocated to one of us in accordance with this clause, the person to whom it is allocated shall be required to hold the other person harmless from the debt and all costs related to it.

D. Reimbursement for Debts or Expenses Paid

This clause addresses whether either of you will be reimbursed, if and when you divorce, for certain debts or expenses you paid for during marriage. There are two alternatives: one listing particular types of payments that will be reimbursed, the other providing for no reimbursement.

Alternative 1: Reimbursement for Debts or Expenses Paid

This alternative provides for reimbursement to a spouse who pays certain expenses of the other party. We give you a few different categories of expenses to select from, and a space to add others, as well as a cross-reference to any other provision for reimbursement that might be contained in other parts of your prenup, such as a provision for reimbursement of funds spent on separate property assets already covered in Paragraph 6 of the agreement. (See Chapter 5.) You can modify and add to this list as necessary. At the end, decide whether you want to limit possible reimbursement to just the items you list. If so, include the optional sentence providing for no reimbursement other than what you specify.

Be aware that if you use this clause, you'll need to keep good records of the reimbursable expenditures.

EXAMPLE: You may remember our discussion of Jetta and Lamont, who agree that each of them will be responsible for his or her own student loans if they divorce. They use this clause to require reimbursement for money spent on premarital debts and student loans during their marriage:

Reimbursement for Debts or Expenses Paid

In any divorce proceeding, each of us will be entitled to reimbursement from the other for:

1. Payments made during our marriage from separate property funds of one of us for premarital debts owed by the other;

2. One-half of payments of made during our marriage from marital property funds for premarital debts owed by the other;

3. Payments made from separate property funds of one of us for necessary expenses incurred by the other in connection with attendance at an accredited educational institution (including tuition, fees, books, and supplies but not including living expenses), whether paid directly or by payments on student loans incurred for those expenses;

4. One-half of payments made during our marriage from marital property funds for necessary expenses incurred by the other in connection with attendance at an accredited educational institution (including tuition, fees, books, and supplies but not including living expenses), whether paid directly or by payments on student loans incurred for those expenses;

5. Any other amounts expressly agreed to be reimbursable as provided elsewhere in this agreement.

Neither of us will be entitled to any reimbursement from the other for paying any debts or expenses except those listed above, whether paid from separate property funds or marital property funds or both.

Alternative 2: No Reimbursement for Debts or Expenses Paid

If you do not want to reimburse each other for payment of debts or expenses, other than what you may have stated in some other part of your prenup, you can include this clause in your agreement. This is what Karen and Russ do. They both have children that they expect to spend money on while they are married, and they don't want to go to the trouble of keeping track of those or other personal expenditures during their marriage. They use this clause:

No Reimbursement for Debts or Expenses Paid

In any divorce proceeding, neither of us will be entitled to any reimbursement from the other for paying the debts or expenses of the other during our marriage except as may be provided elsewhere in this agreement, whether paid from separate property funds or community property funds or both.

E. Alimony

As you may recall from reading Chapter 2, there are some subjects that are considered off-limits for premarital agreements. For example, all states prohibit agreements waiving the right to receive child support. As for alimony, state laws vary on the question of whether you can use a prenup to waive the right to receive it. Some states absolutely forbid such waivers. Some allow waiver of permanent alimony, but not of temporary alimony. Other states allow waivers but provide an exception if this means that the waiving spouse will be eligible for welfare. Still others allow a judge to set the waiver aside if it is "unconscionable" (extremely unfair) when the agreement is signed, or in some states, at the time of the divorce. Some states also impose requirements for independent attorney representation and the signing of separate waivers. (See Appendix D for information about whether or not you can waive the right to alimony in your state.)

Because of the many possible restrictions on agreements about alimony, you should check out the laws of your state very carefully before including an alimony clause in your prenup. This is one area where independent attorney representation in the making of your prenup is especially important. Your attorneys may also have suggestions for adapting one of the clauses we give you so that it meets the legal requirements in your state.

We give you two alternatives for this clause, one consisting of a complete waiver and the other providing for alimony with specific limits on the amount or length of time. If it suits your situation, you can use a different alternative for each of you. For example, you might agree that one of you will waive the right to alimony using Alternative 1 while the other is entitled to alimony payments as specified using Alternative 2.

Consider carefully before waiving alimony. There is a reason state laws are tough on alimony waivers. Unless you are already well established in a secure career or retired with a sure and steady source of support for your lifetime, your economic future may be hard to predict. You may find yourself needing some help from your spouse in order to make ends meet.

Alternative 1: Waiver of Alimony

Use this alternative if you want to completely waive the right to ask for alimony if you divorce. If the laws of your state don't allow for a total waiver, you can change the clause to waive what you can. If both of you will waive alimony, include a separate clause for each of you.

For example, Karen and Russ both have established careers, Karen as a veterinarian and Russ as a bookkeeper. Neither one of them wants to be in a position of paying or receiving alimony (called "spousal support" in California, where they live). They check California law and discover that in order to include a valid waiver of spousal support in their premarital agreement, each of them must be represented by an independent attorney (they are) and the waiver cannot be "unconscionable" at the time of a divorce. To ensure that the waiver won't be considered unconscionable later, they include a limited exception for spousal support payments if one of them becomes disabled and can't support himself or herself. Following is the clause in which Russ waives spousal support. (The agreement contains an identical clause for Karen.)

Waiver of Alimony (Spousal Support) by Russ

Russ expects to have sufficient earning capacity, income, and assets to provide for his reasonable needs if we divorce. Therefore, Russ hereby waives absolutely any and all rights to request temporary and permanent alimony from Karen, except in the following limited circumstances only: If at the time we divorce, Russ is disabled and unable to fully provide for his own support, he may request and receive temporary or permanent spousal support in a reasonable amount determined by taking into consideration all relevant circumstances, including Karen's reasonable ability to pay without impairing her own standard of living, for a period not to exceed one-half the length of our marriage. Russ understands that this waiver could later result in a hardship, and has taken that risk into account in making this waiver.

Alternative 2: Specified Alimony Payments

Instead of waiving alimony, you may want to provide for limited payments in a certain amount or for a specified period of time. This clause lets you do so. To the extent that it ties the hands of a divorce judge to make a different order, it will have to comply with state laws regarding alimony waivers, so be sure to check on any legal limitations in your state before using this alternative.

Ted and Grace use this clause to provide for alimony payments to Grace if they divorce, because she is giving up her job as a social worker in order to marry Ted. (As for Ted, his assets and income are such that he will have no need for alimony, so he waives his right to alimony in their prenuptial agreement.) This is the clause that applies to Grace:

Specified Alimony to Grace

If we divorce, Grace shall be entitled to temporary or permanent alimony payments of $3,000 per month from Ted, beginning on the date when we stop living together and ending absolutely on the date of Grace's remarriage, the death of either party, or when Grace reaches the age of 62, whichever occurs first. This clause may not be modified except by a written agreement signed by both of us. Grace hereby waives absolutely any and all rights to request temporary and permanent alimony from Ted except as provided in this clause. Grace understands that this waiver could later result in a hardship, and has taken that risk into account in making this waiver.

F. Other Provisions Related to Divorce

This is a place for you to insert any other provisions that will apply if you divorce. The possible topics are numerous, depending on your individual circumstances. For example, you might agree that one of you will have the right to occupy the family residence during the time you are separated, or that one or both of you will make contributions to a college education fund, or that you will share custody of (and financial responsibility for) your pets. Agreements involving custody of children, such as where the children will live or how much child support you will pay, are generally off-limits for prenups as a matter of state law, but some parenting issues, such as whether to educate children in certain schools or to provide lessons in certain activities, may be okay to include. Below are a couple of examples.

EXAMPLE: After they marry, Enrique and Lashana will move into the house leased by Enrique. There are three years left on the lease. They decide that if they divorce before the lease is up, Enrique will have the right to stay in the house and Lashana will move out. This is the clause they put in their agreement:

Occupancy of Rental

We plan to reside together in a home leased by Enrique. If during the remaining lease term, we separate and divorce, Lashana will move from the home within 60 days after the filing and service of a complaint for divorce, and from that date on Enrique shall have the sole right to occupy the home, the sole obligation to pay all expenses related to the home, including lease payments, and the sole right to receive any refund of the security deposit paid to the landlord.

EXAMPLE: Diane and Brad share a love of purebred Chesapeake Retriever dogs. They are planning to breed and show Chesapeake Retrievers together after they marry. They agree on the following arrangement for sharing their dogs if they ever get divorced. This is what they include in their prenup:

Agreement Regarding Dogs

If we divorce, we agree to share possession and responsibility for any dogs we own as follows: We will share possession of our dogs on an alternating weekly basis. The dogs shall be kept together and not separated from each other. Each of us will be responsible for one-half of any expenses for the dogs, including food and veterinary expenses. We will equally share any profits from breeding the dogs. Any dispute about the welfare of a dog will be submitted for binding decision to the dog's veterinarian. In addition, each of us shall have the right to sole ownership of up to two of the next available purebred puppies born to or sired by the dogs. We will flip a coin to determine who has first pick of the puppies and then alternate between us.

Optional Paragraph 4:
Other Matters

If there are other issues you want to address in your prenup and they don't fit in any of the other paragraphs, you can use this paragraph for those matters. For example, if you have agreed to put each other through college or graduate school, you might insert a clause on that subject here.

You may be tempted to include nonmonetary provisions in this paragraph, such as responsibility for household chores or upbringing of children. As we caution you in Chapter 2, however, agreements on such subjects probably aren't enforceable, and they may cause a judge to take the rest of your prenup less seriously. Our advice is to leave those subjects out of your official prenup, although you can certainly include them in a separate and nonbinding private agreement, if you find that helpful.

You may also be thinking of including a so-called "bad boy" (or girl) clause in your agreement. This is a provision that imposes a financial penalty on a spouse who is caught being unfaithful. Such a clause is problematic at best. First, consider the effect on a marriage of planning for infidelity in this way; it's almost surely enough to provide in the preceding paragraph for the possibility of divorce if things don't work out despite your best efforts. Aside from those concerns, the clause may be unenforceable, especially in states where there is no-fault divorce. If you are considering including such a clause, you should definitely investigate the legal and emotional consequences of doing so.

Here are a couple of examples of clauses that would be appropriate to include in this paragraph. One addresses a couple's agreement to support each other through graduate school; the other concerns a couple's plans to save money.

> EXAMPLE: Neal and Jana are both college graduates. They are planning to buy a house together, using equal amounts of premarital savings for the down payment. Neal is planning to attend a two-year Masters program in business administration. Jana will work to support them during that time and then she hopes to attend architecture school. Neal will support her while she is in school. They also agree to take out a home equity loan to pay the

tuition for both of them. They include this clause in their agreement:

Graduate Education

After we marry, Jana's employment will support us for two years while Neal obtains a Masters degree in business administration at Temple University. After Neal completes the program, he will support us through employment while Jana attends an accredited program leading to a degree in architecture, for up to two years. The tuition and fees for both programs shall be paid from a home equity loan to be obtained by us after we marry and purchase the home we plan to acquire together. The home equity loan will not be used for any other purpose without our joint written approval. The terms of this clause shall apply even if we divorce.

> EXAMPLE: Antoine and Natasha agree that they will each contribute a percentage of their monthly earnings to a savings account that will be earmarked for a down payment on a house or for other joint investments. This is what they put in their prenup:

Contributions to Savings

During our marriage, each of us will deposit each month an amount equal to 2.5% of his or her gross monthly income into a savings account in our joint names. The account shall require two signatures for any withdrawal and the funds deposited shall be used only for a down payment on a residence in our joint names or for other investments we both agree upon.

Congratulations! You've now worked through all the clauses you need for your draft prenup. If you still need help putting together your draft, Chapter 5, Section B, provides general instructions on how to assemble your agreement, either by hand or using a computer.

If your draft is complete, turn to the next chapter to learn how to finalize your agreement. ■

Turning Your Draft Into a Binding Agreement

After you select the clauses for your prenup and assemble them in a draft, you are ready to turn the draft into a legally binding document. To begin, you'll take the draft to separate lawyers (unless you've decided to throw caution to the wind and proceed without them). Then, you or your lawyers will make any final changes to the draft to ensure that it is clear and legally sound. Finally, you'll arrange for one last review of the written agreement before signing it and tucking it safely away prior to the big day. This chapter takes you through each of these steps.

Finishing Up: A Checklist

- Interview and select lawyers. (See Section B.)
- Give your draft prenup to the lawyers for review. (See Section C.)
- Make any changes necessary to finalize your document. (See Section C.)
- Review your prenup one last time to be sure it says exactly what you want it to say and that you understand every part of it. (See Section C.)
- Sign the final agreement in the manner required by the laws of your state. (See Section F.)

A. Planning Ahead

As we discussed in Chapter 1, you should give yourselves at least three months to complete your premarital agreement. Unless you've already hired lawyers, finding and selecting a good representative for each of you may take some time. It is not uncommon to be told that you'll have to wait several weeks for an initial appointment with a lawyer. And after you choose lawyers, you'll need enough time to discuss any changes they suggest, plus time to prepare and review the final document. Realistically, this means that you should start the process of contacting and meeting with lawyers several months prior to the wedding.

B. Finding Good Lawyers

When to skip this section. If you already know and are working with good lawyers, you can skip ahead to Section C. But if you need help locating and selecting a lawyer, or if you want tips for dealing with lawyers, read on.

We cannot emphasize strongly enough the importance of finding a competent lawyer for each of you—one who will carefully review your prenup and sign the document to indicate that he or she has advised you about the document.

The ideal lawyer to consult in connection with a prenup is one who is experienced in preparing prenuptial agreements and who has expertise in the area of family law, including property issues and divorce. It's a plus, although less common, to find a lawyer who also has some experience with estate planning issues. You want a lawyer who has good communication skills and who can advise you about your best interests while working with your fiancé's lawyer collaboratively—that is, without becoming adversarial in the process.

Be prepared. Minimize the risk that involving lawyers might make the process unnecessarily adversarial by putting down in writing the basics of your prenup *before* asking your lawyers to draft or finalize the specifics of the agreement. Stick with what you've agreed on unless there's a really good reason to make a change.

A Note About Lawyers' Fees

Look for a lawyer who will charge you by the hour without demanding a big payment in advance—called a "retainer." But be prepared for the hourly fee to range as high as $250 to $500, especially in major metropolitan areas.

When you do find a lawyer who charges by the hour without requiring a retainer, it's a good idea to confirm the fee arrangement in writing.

1. Making a List of Lawyers to Interview

One of the first steps in finding a good lawyer is making a list of candidates—at least three or four—to interview and choose from. This is a step the two of you can take together.

a. Getting Referrals

The best way to find names for your list is through referrals. Here are some good places to start:

- If one of you already has a lawyer to work with on the prenup, that lawyer can probably give you names of others who are qualified.
- If one of you has a good working relationship with a lawyer whose expertise does not include prenups, that lawyer may still be a good source of referrals.
- If you are planning a religious wedding, your priest, rabbi, or minister may be able to give you a list of qualified lawyers.
- If you are working with a counselor, or financial or other advisor, you may be able to obtain referrals that way.
- You might get names from friends, family, and acquaintances, especially if they have been through the process of making a prenup themselves.

In addition to personal referrals, you can contact your local bar association and ask if it offers a lawyer referral service. If you have group legal services benefits through your job or membership in an organization, you might have access to a qualified lawyer at a reduced rate. Finally, you can get listings of lawyers by geographical area and field of expertise through Martindale-Hubbell, a national lawyer directory available in many public libraries, law libraries, and on the Internet at www.martindale.com.

b. Coordinating Your Lists

When you have a list of names to choose from, the two of you should divide the list between you so that you don't create a conflict of interest for any of the lawyers. (This could happen if both of you call the same lawyer—or even lawyers at the same firm, because conflict of interest rules prevent lawyers in the same firm from representing both sides to a contract or a dispute.) If one of you already has a lawyer, then the other person can select names from the entire list.

If there's enough time, you can take turns finding a lawyer: After one of you finds a good lawyer, that lawyer may be the best way to locate a lawyer for the other person. If there is not time to do this, both of you will be interviewing lawyers at the same time. In that case, you may want to compare notes as you go.

It's also a good idea to decide in advance which person's lawyer will take the lead in preparing the final document. As a matter of logistics and cost-savings, it usually makes more sense to have all drafts prepared by one office even when both sides are contributing ideas and wording. As the use of scanners and email increases, this may change, but you should start with the assumption that one lawyer will do the paperwork. Deciding who that will be is arbitrary—you can even flip a coin to settle it. The key is to avoid costly duplication of efforts at the outset by designating one lawyer to write up the agreement. Be open to a different arrangement if your lawyers suggest it; there may be reasons why your situation calls for a different approach.

2. Interviewing and Selecting a Lawyer

After dividing the list of potential lawyers between you, you're ready to set up interviews and select the lawyers who will represent each of you. This is something you'll each do separately, either in sequence (as discussed just above) or simultaneously.

a. Making Appointments

With your list in front of you, decide how many appointments you will start with. The number of initial appointments you make may be dictated by what you can afford. It's rare to find a lawyer with any experience who will agree to meet with you for free, so be prepared to pay for the lawyer's time.

If your budget allows, consider making appointments with two or three candidates before making your selection. Or simply start at the top of the list and make one appointment at a time until you meet someone who seems like a good fit.

When you call to make an appointment, be prepared to give some basic information, including your name and the name of your fiancé (for conflict of interest screening), your address, and so forth. Tell the person who answers that you want an appointment to discuss possible representation regarding a prenuptial agreement. You may be put through to the lawyer directly—some lawyers take calls from prospective clients. More likely you will speak with a receptionist or secretary, who will schedule you for an in-person appointment.

Remember to ask about the lawyer's fee for the initial appointment so there will be no surprises later on.

b. Interviewing Prospective Lawyers

Your initial appointment is an opportunity to find out whether you are comfortable with the lawyer. You should prepare for the appointment by making a list of questions about the lawyer's experience and qualifications. (We've made a list of suggested questions to get you stared; see below.) Then review your draft prenup and any notes you have made about the draft. Jot down any questions you have about your prenup and the process of finalizing and signing it.

SO MUCH FOR THE SMALL TALK! HOW MUCH DO YOU CHARGE?

Questions to Ask a Prospective Prenup Lawyer

The following questions cover the basics of the lawyer's qualifications and approach to writing up a prenup. Feel free to omit, modify, or add to them as you see fit.

- What is your experience and expertise in:
  - advising clients who want prenups
  - drafting prenups
  - divorce and separation issues, and
  - estate planning?
- If the lawyer does not have estate planning expertise: How do you handle estate planning issues that come up in prenups?
- What is your attitude toward prenups? Do you think they are a good idea or not?
- Are you willing to take the draft we've worked out together and help us turn it into a binding agreement?
- If so, how would you go about this?
- How long do you think it will take to review and finalize the agreement?
- How much do you think it will cost, and what would be the arrangement for payment?

Take your notes and the draft of your prenup with you to the appointment. Tell the lawyer a little about yourself and your situation. Then let the lawyer know you have some questions. Start with any questions about the lawyer's qualifications and approach; then, if you still feel comfortable with the lawyer, show the lawyer your draft and move on to your questions about it. Refer to your notes as you go along and check them again at the end of your meeting, to make sure you've covered everything.

You should receive direct answers to your questions about the lawyer's qualifications and experience and some general information about the process of finalizing the agreement. You will probably not get answers to all your questions about the specifics of your prenup until the attorney has had a chance to review your draft. But bringing up your questions at the first appointment will let the lawyer know what your concerns are. That will make for a more meaningful conversation during your initial meeting and it will give the lawyer a focus for reviewing your draft prenup later.

After the appointment, reflect on your experience. Were your questions answered clearly? Were you treated respectfully? Do you feel that the lawyer understood your concerns? If you can answer yes to these questions, and if you are satisfied with the lawyer's qualifications, you may not need to look any farther. If you are uncertain or uncomfortable with how things went in the appointment, interview other candidates. You will be spending both money and time on a lawyer—and your future happiness and security may be affected by the advice you get about the prenup—so it's important to find someone you feel good about.

C. Preparing the Final Agreement

After you choose the lawyers who will help you finish your prenuptial agreement, the process of drawing up the final document begins in earnest. The lawyers will probably start by thoroughly reviewing your draft prenup. What happens next depends on how the lawyers divide up the job of preparing the final agreement, and on whether any new provisions or changes need to be worked out before putting the agreement in final form. This section offers some suggestions for working with your lawyers to make this part of the experience as constructive and efficient as possible.

1. Provide a Written Draft or Outline

You will make the best use of your lawyer's time if the two of you have carefully considered and agreed on the contents of your prenup. To avoid unnecessary misunderstandings, it's best to put your plan in writing, either in a draft containing actual clauses or in a detailed written outline. (Even if your fiancé's lawyer is the one who will prepare the final draft, it is a good idea to provide your own lawyer with a draft or outline of what the two of you have in mind. This will give your lawyer a sense of what to expect from the other lawyer and it will help your lawyer alert you to potential problems so you can deal with them before the final draft is prepared.)

If you've already made a draft or outline, all you need to do is give a copy to your lawyer and you'll be on your way. If you haven't yet prepared a draft, you can use Chapters 5 and 6 to develop one.

When reviewing your draft or outline, your lawyer may have questions about why you chose certain clauses and may ask for additional information about your financial situation. Normally, the lawyer will meet with you after reviewing the draft to advise you of any suggestions or concerns and to answer any questions you have.

2. Be Flexible

Every lawyer has an individual approach to advising clients and drafting legal documents, so what happens in your case depends to some extent on how your lawyer does things. And your situation is even more unique because you will be dealing with the styles of two different lawyers. Not to worry. Good lawyers are used to working with other lawyers and their clients on collaborative drafting projects, so the whole process should go smoothly. Just know that not every step can be predicted in advance and be prepared to adapt as needed.

For example, you should be prepared for your draft to undergo a significant transformation before you sign it. Most lawyers have their own forms containing standard clauses that they have drafted with state law in mind. The lawyer preparing the final agreement may be reluctant to use the organization and clauses contained in your draft if they vary too greatly from the lawyer's preferred format. It is also possible that it will not be cost effective to have the lawyer take the extra time necessary to revise your draft to conform to state law rather than simply using a form familiar to the lawyer. As long as the agreement still says what you intend it to say, be open to a document that looks quite different from what you started with.

3. Keep the Lines of Communication Open

Even though each of you will work with your own lawyer, it's important to keep each other abreast of the discussions you are having with your lawyers. Stay on top of things by asking your lawyer to give you an estimated date for completion of each step. Then write the date down in your datebook or calendar and follow up if the date passes without any word from your lawyer. Let each other know the projected timeline and advise each other of any changes or delays.

If your lawyer tells you that something you've already agreed upon should be changed, make sure you understand the advice and the reasons for it. Then sit down with your fiancé and talk about it. See if the proposed change makes sense to the two of you. Have your fiancé run the idea by her or his lawyer. If either of you still has questions about the proposed change, consider scheduling a four-way meeting with the two of you and your lawyers present.

Successfully finalizing a prenup is a joint effort. Whatever you do, don't keep each other in the dark about what you're each hearing from your lawyers. (If you get stuck and need help communicating with each other about your prenup, see Chapter 8.)

Keeping things confidential. Conversations between you and your lawyer are usually private; your lawyer can't disclose the details later—even if asked to testify in court—unless you consent. But if you tell someone else (even your fiancé) about what was said, the rule of confidentiality no longer applies to that conversation. We think the value of staying in close communication about your prenup outweighs the loss of confidentiality. But if you find yourself in a special situation where you need to insulate sensitive information from potential disclosure to others, talk to your lawyer about how to proceed without losing the legal protection afforded by lawyer-client confidentiality rules.

4. Read Each Draft Carefully

Be sure to read each version of the proposed final agreement carefully and thoroughly. This is especially important if each lawyer is making revisions as the document goes back and forth, but it is good practice even when just one office is generating all the drafts.

Make your own copy of each draft as you receive it, and write the date you receive it on your copy. If you get a later version, you can compare the two to look for any changes that were supposed to be made and to check for typographical errors. Let your lawyer (and each other) know if you find anything amiss.

5. Guidelines for Working With Your Lawyer

Beyond the specific steps outlined above, here are some general points to keep in mind when working with your lawyer. Most important is to remember that, like all relationships, your relationship with your lawyer is a two-way street: There are some basic things you can expect from your lawyer and some actions you can take to make the most of both your time and your money.

a. Communication

Your lawyer should communicate with you clearly and in plain language. By the same token, you'll need to take responsibility for your end of the communication. If you don't understand something, say so. Be persistent. Ask questions until you're sure you get it. Your lawyer should be open to your questions.

b. Responsiveness

Expect your lawyer to respond to your telephone calls or letters within a reasonable time, usually two or three days for nonurgent phone messages and a week or so for letters. You are not the lawyer's only client, so there will be times when you can't reach your lawyer right away. You can and should expect to hear back soon, however. If there is special urgency, be sure to say so when you leave a message. If you don't get a return call or a letter within the times we've suggested, call and find out the reason for the delay.

c. Questions

Before meeting with your lawyer each time, write down your questions and concerns. Leave room to jot down your lawyer's answers and notes about what you plan to do next.

Bring your list with you to the appointment. Tell your lawyer that you have a list of questions and double check the list at the end of the meeting. Write down notes of your lawyer's answers as you go along. Go as slowly as you need to.

d. Support People

If you're having trouble focusing and find it difficult to remember your questions or the answers, consider bringing along a support person—a friend or family member—when you meet with the lawyer. Be sure to clear this with your lawyer ahead of time, and consider whether there is any need to maintain the legal privilege of lawyer-client confidentiality. As we mention above, the rule of confidentiality no longer applies if another person learns the details of a conversation with a lawyer. Normally, this won't be a concern. If it is, discuss with your lawyer how to best handle the situation. For example, you might decide to have a support person present for some but not all of the discussions with your lawyer.

If you bring a support person, ask him or her to take notes for you during the meeting. Some people also find it helpful to tape-record their meetings with their lawyer. If you think this would be useful, be sure to discuss it with your lawyer in advance.

e. Summing Up Meetings

Before you end a meeting with your lawyer, review what's been discussed and ask your lawyer to summarize the next steps to be taken, and to give a time frame for each one. Make notes of the steps and the timetable.

f. Using the Lawyer's Advice

Take seriously the advice you get. You a paying a professional to give you advice you wouldn't think of on your own. Make sure you understand the advice and the reasons for it. Consider it carefully before accepting or rejecting it.

D. Preparing an Abstract of the Agreement

If you own separate property real estate that you intend to sell, lease, or borrow against during your marriage, and you want to be able to carry out these transactions without obtaining your spouse's consent each time, you can prepare what's called an "abstract" of your prenup and put it on file in the local land records office.

The abstract summarizes the parts of your prenup that contain your agreements about the real estate. You both must sign it in front of a notary public, after you are married. Then, you can record the abstract in the county where the real estate is located so that it becomes part of the official county records, just as a deed would be. You could always record your entire prenup as proof of your ownership agreements, but then your prenup would be a public record, available for anyone to see. The advantage of recording an abstract instead of the whole agreement is that you can keep the other parts of your agreement private.

It's convenient to prepare the abstract when the prenup is prepared, but you don't have to do them together. If you're not sure whether you'll need an abstract, you can always prepare and record one later on.

For more explanation and an example of an abstract, see Chapter 9, Section B. A form for an abstract is included at the end of Appendix C.

E. If Problems Arise

Hopefully, completing the final agreement will go smoothly and you won't need to refer to this next section at all. If you do hit a snag, chances are it will fall into one of two categories:

- you have a problem with your lawyer, or
- there's trouble between you and your fiancé.

We'll address each of those situations in turn.

1. Problems With Your Lawyer

Three of the most common problems that can arise when working with a lawyer are:

- communication problems

- unhappiness with the lawyer's work, or
- fee disputes.

a. Communication Problems

A communication problem between you and your lawyer might be solved with a little constructive attention. If the problem is a lack of responsiveness—for example, your lawyer isn't returning your phone calls or hasn't communicated with you for an extended period of time—try sending a polite letter setting out your concerns. In your letter, ask for an appointment to go over your questions and concerns together. Let your lawyer know you'll be calling for an appointment, then follow up.

If the problem lies in the actual communications—your lawyer says things you don't understand or doesn't seem to get what you are talking about—start by letting your lawyer know there's a problem. Say you're having trouble following what you're being told and ask your lawyer to rephrase the information. Or explain that you aren't sure your questions or concerns are being heard. Your lawyer may be unaware there is a problem. Once you bring it up, your lawyer will probably work harder to communicate well.

If these suggestions don't work, consider suggesting mediation to work on your communication problems if you still want this lawyer to represent you. A bad deskside manner doesn't mean that the lawyer doesn't do excellent legal work. If all else fails, you can look for a new lawyer whose style of communication is more consistent with your own.

b. Unhappiness With the Lawyer's Work

You might find yourself unhappy with the advice you are getting from your lawyer or you may be dissatisfied with the format or content of documents prepared by your lawyer.

If you are confused by the advice you're getting or if you disagree with it, talk with your lawyer. Ask what the advice is based on, and what other options might be available to you. Then decide for yourself whether you want to follow the advice, disregard it, or get a second opinion.

A different but related problem arises if your lawyer tells you something about the law that seems to contradict the legal advice your fiancé is getting. Ask your lawyer to help you sort out the reason for the discrepancy. If there really seems to be a disagreement about the law, ask the two lawyers to talk to each other and determine whether there really is a difference of opinion, or whether the law itself is not as black and white as it seems. If all else fails, consider getting another lawyer's opinion.

EXAMPLE: Simon's lawyer tells him that his separate property investment in real estate would remain entirely his separate property if he and Elena divorce, even without a prenup to spell that out. Elena's lawyer tells her that the investment would be partly community property in a divorce, unless the prenup makes it separate property. What's going on? Perhaps the legal guidelines aren't clear and the two lawyers interpret them differently. Maybe they are using different factual information in forming their opinions. Or one of them might be wrong about the law.

Simon and Elena ask their lawyers to talk about the problem. As a result, the lawyers learn that they agree on the general legal principles, but each has been making a different factual assumption about the extent of Simon's involvement in the managing the asset. After talking, the lawyers agree that it would be impossible to say whether a divorce court would find a partial community property interest in the investment. On their lawyers' advice, Simon and Elena then insert a specific provision on the subject in their prenup, so that there will be no uncertainty if they divorce later on.

If you find what you think is a mistake in any document prepared by your lawyer, bring this to the lawyer's attention. Give the lawyer a copy of the document with the mistakes noted and keep a copy for yourself so you can double check that the errors have been fixed. Keep a sense of perspective when it comes to typographical errors. Lawyers and their staff are only human; a typo here and there shouldn't be cause for concern if steps are taken to correct them. Repeated or multiple errors may be indications of a bigger problem, however, and at some point you may decide to take your business elsewhere.

Unhappiness with the actual terms of a document drafted by your lawyer probably derives from a communication problem: Either you weren't clear about what you intended or your lawyer misunderstood what you meant, or perhaps a bit of both. Try talking it through with your lawyer. That will usually take care of the problem.

c. Fee Disputes

Avoid problems about fees at the outset by making sure you have a written agreement with your lawyer covering how fees will be charged, when you will be billed, and other details. If you do not pay as you go, ask for a detailed monthly bill and address any problems as soon as they arise.

Maintain your perspective when it comes to fees. Many a great working relationship has been poisoned by disagreements over relatively minor fee amounts. If you are otherwise pleased with your lawyer's performance, consider cutting your lawyer some slack when it comes to the fees.

If you end up with a significant dispute about fees and if talking about it doesn't resolve the problem, you may be able to get help from your local or state bar association. Often, there is a panel of volunteer lawyers available to review the situation and give an advisory opinion about the fee dispute.

 Visit Nolo's website for more information. You can find more information about working with your lawyer, including what to do when problems arise, in the Lawsuits & Mediation section of Nolo's free Legal Encyclopedia at www.nolo.com.

2. Problems Between the Two of You

If a difficulty arises between you and your fiancé while you are finalizing your agreement, try to figure out what's at the bottom of it. Consider first whether you're reacting to the stress of getting ready for the big day. If that's the case, maybe you need to take a vacation from the whole topic for a day or two, or even longer. Do something fun and relaxing together. The whole thing may look different after you've had a break from it.

If what's going on between you is not just a reaction to pressure, and if you seem to be communicating reasonably well about the subject, you may have a real disagreement about some provision of the prenup. In that case you will need to find a way to resolve the disagreement before you can move on, either on your own, or with the help of your lawyers or another qualified person (such as a counselor or a mediator). For more on how to deal with disagreements, see Chapter 8.

F. Signing the Agreement: Formalities and Fun

When the final draft of your premarital agreement has been read, re-read, and approved, it's time for you and your lawyers to sign it. You can make separate trips to your respective lawyers' offices and sign the agreement there. Logistically, this may be the simplest way to get the necessary signatures, because you'll need to coordinate the schedules of only two people at a time.

If you want to make more of an occasion out of signing the agreement, consider asking for an appointment when the two of you—and both lawyers—can all meet and sign at one time. Or you could have a private signing ceremony of your own, just the two of you, either before or after the lawyers sign their part of the agreement. If you like the idea of signing without your lawyers present, be sure to clear this with your lawyers. They may have reservations about this approach, because there would be no witnesses to call if a question later arises about whether you voluntarily signed the document. Some lawyers even like to videotape the signing as additional insurance against a claim that one of you did not sign voluntarily. If so, you may want to dress up for the occasion, even though the video may not be one you'll keep on the shelf next to your wedding album.

Another potential barrier to a completely private signing ceremony is that state law may require you to sign the document in front of others. Although some states simply require that your signatures be acknowledged—that is, authenticated—by a notary public (not necessarily at the time you sign), other states require that you sign in front of the notary or other witnesses. At least one state, Georgia, requires that you sign your prenup in front of two witnesses as well as a notary. If witnesses other than a notary are required, ask if signing in the presence of your lawyers will do. (See the state summaries in Appendix D for the requirements in your state; be sure to confirm these with your lawyer.)

If witnesses are not legally required in your state, it is still a good idea to have your signatures notarized so that there won't be any doubt about the fact that you actually signed the agreement. If your agreement will be notarized, ask ahead of time whether your lawyer will provide the notary.

A note for New Yorkers. If you live in New York, you'll see from your state's information sheet that your agreement must be notarized. But New York has recently passed a law allowing anyone who is authorized to conduct a marriage ceremony to acknowledge a prenup. We're not suggesting that you sign your agreement at the altar, but you might feel more comfortable asking the person who will solemnize the marriage, rather than a notary public, to be present when you sign the agreement and to acknowledge your signatures.

Even if you decide not to make an event out of the signing, consider making a point of acknowledging together the completion of this big and important project. It could be a toast over dinner at your favorite restaurant, a weekend trip to a favorite getaway, or maybe something as simple as a high-five or a handshake. Whatever you do, think of some way to congratulate yourselves and to mark this accomplishment before you put the signed agreement away in a safe place and turn your attention to the other details of preparing for your wedding. ■

Working Together

Ideally, working together on your prenup will be a positive and constructive experience. But even couples who communicate well may run into some difficult issues when discussing property and money matters. This chapter contains ideas and suggestions that will help the process go smoothly.

Every stage of putting together a prenup involves working together, so you may find yourselves referring to this chapter more than once as you go along. You can read it to get a general understanding of ways to avoid problems, and you can turn to it for tips to help you deal with any challenges that do arise.

A. Five Keys to Working Together Successfully

If you keep the following tips in mind, you'll probably find it easier to work together and negotiate at every step of the process. You may even be able to head off problems before they come up.

1. Know Yourself

Understanding yourselves—including your financial goals, your general attitude toward money, your spending and saving habits, and your approach to communicating about those issues—is essential to a healthy and productive partnership in the making of your prenup. If both of you maintain self-awareness as you go, each will always know where the other stands.

The steps outlined in Chapter 3 of this book give you a chance to better understand how you approach financial issues. If you want to expand your self-knowledge beyond the financial realm, you might consider doing an inventory of your individual approach to a variety of life experiences. (See "Using a Premarital Inventory," just below.). Regardless of whether you limit your self-examination to financial issues or broaden your inquiry, the key is to hone your self-knowledge so that you can deal with each other more clearly.

Using a Premarital Inventory

There are a variety of ways to investigate what makes you tick—your strengths and weaknesses, your likes and dislikes, your preferences and pet peeves. Many premarital counseling programs offered by churches, temples, and other religious communities include this kind of inventory. You can also do this work with the help of a licensed counselor.

To learn about a variety of inventory programs, you can use the Internet. Simply type the term "premarital inventory" into your computer search engine and browse the many offerings that come up.

If you prefer to work on your own, without seeking assistance from a premarital counselor, you can take a more general personality inventory using one of the many books available on the market. A classic is *Please Understand Me: Character and Temperament Types*, by David Keirsey and Marilyn Bates (Prometheus Nemesis Book Co.), which offers a simplified version of the Myers-Briggs personality inventory. Other choices include *Discovering Your Personality Type: The Essential Introduction to the Enneagram, Revised and Expanded*, by Don Richard Riso and Russ Hudson (Houghton Mifflin Co.), and *The 16 Personality Types: Descriptions for Self-Discovery*, by Linda V. Berens and Dario Nardi (Telos Publications).

As long as you don't take tests like these too seriously, they can be a useful, informative, and often entertaining way to focus on some of the differences and similarities between the two of you.

---

2. Accept Your Differences

Being able to accept and appreciate the ways in which the two of you are different is the second key to successfully negotiating and drafting your prenup. It's pretty easy to agree on terms when you see eye to eye. The challenge is in finding ways to accommodate your differences. Start with the premise that differences can be a good thing in a relationship—in moderation, of course. Then be prepared to learn about and accept the ways in which you see things differently. You can practice doing this as you work through the material in Chapter 3.

3. Communicate Effectively

Creating a prenup that works for both of you depends on clear communication between you. We will have lots more to say about how to communicate effectively in Section C of this chapter. For now, take our word for it that good communication is a key ingredient.

4. Negotiate Lovingly

It is unlikely that you will agree on every detail of your prenup, at least in the beginning. You are two different people, with different financial circumstances and backgrounds, and there are bound to be some issues that you will need to negotiate to a satisfactory conclusion. This does not mean that the negotiation needs to be adversarial. On the contrary, your mutual love and respect will give you a foundation from which to negotiate with each other's best interests at heart. We call this negotiating lovingly, and Section D of this chapter offers more suggestions on how to proceed.

5. Accentuate the Positive

Last, but not least, maintain a positive outlook. The whole point of your prenup is to support each other and your relationship by agreeing in advance to clear financial guidelines that will carry you for many years to come. Experts who study marriage conclude that maintaining a positive attitude toward each other and the relationship is a critical factor in the health of a marriage. By maintaining a open and constructive outlook toward the experience of making your prenup, you will not only enhance the chances of ending up with a solid agreement, you will also be practicing a life skill that will support your marriage.

B. A Suggested Approach to Working Together

Here are some simple points to remember each time you prepare to work together on some aspect of your prenup.

1. Before You Begin

- **Think through your concerns.** Be aware not just of what you want, but why you want it.
- **Prepare to listen.** As you decide what goes into your prenup, try to really hear and understand each other's concerns. You may find that what seemed like a disagreement is actually a simple miscommunication.
- **Be open to new ideas.** It often happens that the solution that best addresses your mutual concerns is different from what was first proposed. Being ready to accept fresh ideas will enhance your chances of finding the right approach for your prenup.
- **Set the stage.** Pay attention to when and how you discuss your prenup. Pick a time and place that are conducive to a thoughtful conversation about your agreement. Consider setting a reasonable time limit in advance, so that you aren't tempted to bite off more than you can chew at one time.

2. While You Are Talking

- **Speak clearly.** Say what you mean. Be specific and accurate in communicating what's on your mind.
- **Listen to understand.** Pay attention to what you are being told, and check to be sure you've heard correctly.
- **Don't interrupt.** Let your fiancé finish his or her thought before you respond.

For more on communicating effectively, see Section C of this chapter.

3. If You Run Into Trouble

- **Check your communications so far.** Have you said something unclear? Did you misunderstand each other? (See Section C, below, for suggestions on resolving miscommunications.)

- **Look for options that work for both of you.** If you seem to disagree about some aspect of the prenup, think about whether you're considering the needs of both of you in the matter. Try to come up with a solution that takes both sides into account. (For more on how to do this, see Section D, below.)

- **Get help if you need it.** There are times when you are just too close to a situation to understand exactly what's going on, and what you can do to move things forward. If you've tried the suggestions in this chapter and you're still having trouble working through an issue, maybe a little help from an outsider—your clergyperson, a wise elder, or a qualified counselor—is what you need. (For tips on finding the right help, see Section E5, below.)

C. Communicating Effectively

Good communication is at the heart of creating a successful premarital agreement. You'll need to be able to communicate clearly and effectively with each other, with your lawyers, and perhaps with interested family members throughout the process. Here are some suggestions for enhancing your communication skills.

1. What Is Communication?

There are undoubtedly many ways to define communication. Because we are talking here about communication leading to a legally binding agreement, we define communication as an oral statement made by one person (the speaker) that imparts information to another person (the listener).

Using this definition, here are three examples of communication:

"Waiter, there's a fly in my soup."

"Dave, we're giving you a raise of 50 cents an hour starting the first of next month."

"I can't come to your party because I'll be out of town that day."

In each of these examples, the speaker makes a statement containing information for the listener. Our everyday lives are made up of hundreds of communications like these. In most of our daily communications, the information is accurately expressed by the speaker and understood by the listener. The waiter now knows that there is a fly in the customer's soup; Dave has learned that he will get a raise next month; and the party host knows not to expect the friend who will be out of town.

For a communication to go smoothly, the speaker's statement needs to be clear and the listener must hear what is actually being said.

2. Tips for Speakers

The first part of any communication is the speaker's statement. When you are the one speaking, your job is to clearly and accurately convey the information you want to get across. Here are some tips that may help you.

- **Be clear about what you want to say.** Ask yourself what you intend to communicate. Are you expecting to impart factual information? Do you want to convey your opinion or your feelings about something? Is it your intention to state a preference for one option over others? Are you making a proposal? Knowing what you want to say will help you figure out the best way to say it.

- **Say what you mean.** Once you are sure about what you want to say, put your statement in words that will be easy for your listener to understand. When conveying factual information, be as specific and accurate as possible. If you have a purpose beyond imparting factual information, begin with a phrase that will clue your listener in to your purpose. For example, "I think we should do x, y, or z" or "What I want is thus and such."

3. Tips for Listeners

The listener's attitude and approach have as much to do with quality of the communication as does the speaker's delivery.

Listen attentively. When you are the one listening, one of the most important things you can do is pay attention to what the speaker is saying. Listen to the whole statement and don't interrupt. This sounds simple, but we all know how difficult it can be. Do all you can to avoid being distracted by your own thoughts. Maintain eye contact with the speaker until he or she finishes. This will help focus your attention on what is being said. (If direct eye contact is considered rude and inappropriate in your culture, adapt your behavior to maintain a respectful listening posture.)

Pay attention to your body language. If you are fidgeting with papers, looking away, or frowning, you are probably not listening and you may be distracting the speaker. Whether you intend to or not, you are also conveying a lack of interest in what the speaker is saying, which can stop any conversation in its tracks.

Confirm the communication. Make sure there is no misunderstanding by confirming the communication using a simple feedback technique: state your understanding of the speaker's statement, in your own words.

Even if you're sure you know what the speaker means, you can put your feedback into the form of a question by starting with something like "Are you saying ...?" or "Do you mean ...?" You might be surprised to discover you missed something, and even if you got it right, you'll send the message that you're listening and sincerely wanting to understand.

Steven and Freda

Steven says to Freda, "I'll meet you at Starbucks at 8:00 a.m. tomorrow morning." Freda assumes Steven is referring to the Starbucks across from Steven's office, whereas Steven is thinking of the one down the street from the art museum. If they don't clear this up, they will be waiting in dif-

ferent cafes at opposite ends of town the following morning. But if Freda says, "So I'll see you at 8:00 a.m. tomorrow morning at the Starbucks across from your office, right?" Steven can say, "No, I meant the one next to the art museum." By using feedback, Freda has averted a potential mishap.

4. Pay Attention to Emotions

Make sure the emotions accompanying a communication are handled appropriately so they don't derail your efforts. Not every communication includes an emotional component. When emotions run high, however, it is important to recognize the emotion to avoid getting thrown off course.

The emotional content of a communication is like an ocean current at the beach. If it is recognized and well marked, swimmers can safely enjoy the surf. They can even use the current to swim farther and faster. But if the emotion in the communication is ignored, it can be like an undertow pulling unwitting swimmers out to sea.

Depending on whether you are the speaker or the listener, you can "swim" with the emotional currents in the communication by following these guidelines.

When you are speaking, alert your listener to your emotional state. If you feel strongly enough about something, you will probably express how you feel nonverbally. If your words don't include some acknowledgment of your emotional state, you risk confusing or alarming your listener into a reaction that prevents true listening. So take a moment to tune in to how you are feeling before speaking. Check for physical signs. Is your jaw clenched? Are you fidgeting in your chair? Is your face flushed and hot? Are you fighting back tears? These are just a few examples of the nonverbal signals (body language) you send to yourself and your listener when you are in the grip of a strong emotion.

You may not feel comfortable at the moment saying how you feel. If that's the case, take a little time to breathe and calm down. See if your feelings subside before you speak. If not, try to let your listener know, in words, that the subject under discussion evokes some strong feelings for you. You don't have to talk about your feelings if you don't want to. But because your body language is bound to be sending a signal that something is going on, you'll keep the communication clear by making your verbal statement consistent with your nonverbal one. If even this is impossible, take a break before you continue your discussion.

If you find that your emotional reactions consistently interfere with your communications, you'll probably benefit from spending some time working with a professional counselor. (See Section E5, below.)

When listening to a statement, be attentive to any emotional content. Just as it's important to check your understanding of the informational content of a statement, it is also critical to verify your assessment of the emotions being communicated. Including your understanding of the emotional content of a statement in your feedback is what communication specialists call reflective listening. Reflective listening has a dual benefit. It ensures that there is no misunderstanding in the communication and it promotes respectful and constructive dialogue by demonstrating an understanding of the speaker's feelings.

Reflective listening should be done carefully and it takes some practice. Here are three points to remember:

1. **Put your feedback about the emotion in the form of a question.** Putting your feedback in the form of question lets the speaker know what you heard and saw while allowing for the possibility that you got it wrong.

2. **Pick a word you think will accurately describe the emotion being expressed without understating or exaggerating it.** Sticking to a word that accurately describes the emotion shows respect for the speaker and allows him or her to offer a correction that will clear up any misunderstanding. If you under- or overstate what you perceive, the conversation is likely to turn to your poor perception skills, rather than the speaker's feelings.

3. **Accept any correction by the speaker without argument.** The speaker has the final word on how she or he feels and what she or he is trying to express. If the speaker corrects your feedback, accept the correction without argument. Otherwise, you will turn a good communication into an unproductive debate.

Resources for Increasing Your Communication Competence

There is a lot more that can be said about communicating, and fortunately there are plenty of resources available to help you improve your skills. If you want to go farther, here are a few suggestions to get you started:

Messages: The Communication Skills Book, by Patrick Fanning, Matthew McKay, and Martha Davis (New Harbinger Publications). This book describes in detail the basic skills involved in communicating, including expressing, self-disclosure, and listening.

Nonviolent Communication: A Language of Compassion, by Marshall B. Rosenberg (Philadelphia Press), describes a system of communication based on empathic listening.

You'll find an excellent chapter on communication in *The Tao of Negotiation*, by Joel Edelman (Harper-Business). And finally, for an interesting take on gender differences in communication, see *You Just Don't Understand: Women and Men in Conversation*, by Deborah Tannen (Ballantine Books).

D. Negotiating Lovingly

If at any point in the process of making a premarital agreement you find that the two of you see things differently, you will probably need to negotiate those differences to decide how to address them in your prenup.

Negotiating the terms of a prenup is different from many other kinds of negotiation. For you, the goal of the negotiation is to find a solution that meets the needs of both of you and that provides a solid foundation for your marital partnership. So the two of you will want your negotiations to be caring. In this section, we take general negotiating techniques and show you how to use them to negotiate in a loving way.

1. Everyone Negotiates

We all negotiate in our daily lives. Any time we ask someone to cooperate with us in accomplishing something we can't (or don't want to) do on our own, we are negotiating. When we respond to another person's request for our cooperation by stating the conditions under which we will participate, we are also negotiating. Almost all of us have negotiated some major issue in our lives, perhaps buying a house or a car, taking on a new job, or asking for a raise. We also conduct personal negotiations on a regular basis. For example, we might negotiate with friends about what movie to go see Saturday night or where to meet for dinner. For the most part, we conduct these daily negotiations with overall success and without a great deal of thought about how we are negotiating.

When negotiating with each other about your prenup, you will use the same basic techniques you've developed in your daily negotiations. You'll have the advantage of your love for one another and your strong motivation to make things work. So negotiating in this context will mostly be a question of staying focused on your ultimate goal: a prenup that represents your common interests and your individual aspirations.

2. How to Negotiate Successfully

Not only do you want to want to end up with a premarital agreement that works for you both; you also want the process of making the agreement to be mutually supportive and caring. You have an excellent chance of success if you keep these four basic guidelines in mind:

- be patient
- be clear about your interests
- balance assertiveness and attentiveness
- look for solutions that meet both persons' interests.

Be patient. One of the best ways to doom a negotiation is to push for a resolution without fully exploring each person's concerns and all of the possible solutions. Conversely, the route to a successful negotiation is to allow enough time to fully understand the dimensions of the problem, how each person views it, and the pros and cons of all potential solutions.

Be sure to allow yourselves enough time to hear each other out, ponder the options, and negotiate an outcome that will be lasting and fair.

Be clear about your interests. An effective negotiation results in an agreement that meets the interests of both people. What is an interest? An interest is someone's need, goal, concern, or dream that the agreement must address to be acceptable to that person.

Ted and Grace

Ted's interests include passing a significant portion of his estate, (including family heirlooms) to his children, providing for Grace if he dies before her, and living a lifestyle that includes travel with Grace. Among Grace's interests are leaving her share of a family farm to her sister, traveling with Ted, and financial security (including owning her own home) if she and Ted divorce or if she outlives Ted. They need to address each of these interests in the terms of their prenup.

Typical negotiations begin with each party promoting a position (solution) that meets that person's interests, often at the expense of the other person's interests. If there is never any discussion of each person's interests, the negotiation will—at best—result in a compromise that is not entirely satisfactory to either person. At worst, the negotiators will reach an impasse.

If the focus of the negotiation shifts from your stated positions to your underlying interests, you can try to come up with options that satisfy the interests of both of you. This is often referred to as "interest-based negotiation."

In order to focus on your interests, you first need to be very clear about what they are. To do this, try asking yourself the following questions about the issue being negotiated.

- What do I want the prenup to say about this?
- Why do I want the prenup to say this?
- What concerns of mine would be addressed by this solution?
- How will this meet my needs?
- What dreams or aspirations of mine are furthered by the position I am taking?

Balance assertiveness and attentiveness. Another essential component of a successful negotiation is maintaining a healthy balance between asserting what's important to you (your interests) and attending to what is important to your fiancé (your fiancé's interests). This requires you to build on the communication skills we discussed earlier in this chapter.

Assertiveness is a two-part process. First, you must get very clear about what is important to you about the issue you are negotiating (see above). Second, you must speak up about your interests during the negotiation. This means being specific and accurate about your interests, and it may mean being persistent in standing up for them.

Attentiveness also involves a two-part process. First, you must listen carefully to what your fiancé says about his or her interests. Then, you must be open to considering options that address your fiancé's interests as well as your own.

Maintaining the proper balance between these two modes—asserting your interests and attending to your fiancé's interests—isn't always easy. At times, it can be very tempting to either give up on your own desires or close your ears to the needs of your fiancé. Try to resist the temptation. If you can stay the course, chances are good that the two of you will find some way to accommodate the most important points on both sides.

The best way to make sure you balance these modes as you negotiate is to pay attention. Make a mental inventory from time to time: Am I asserting my important interests? Is something being overlooked? Do I understand what's important to my fiancé? Am I considering my fiancé's interests?

If you pay attention, and if you resist the urge to either abandon your own interests or to ignore your fiancé's, you'll find the right balance. The result will be well worth the effort: a premarital agreement that truly addresses each person's needs and concerns.

Look for solutions that meet both persons' interests. Once both of you have identified and clearly expressed your interests, you can shift your attention to exploring the options that are most likely to address them. Have faith that you will find some way to support each other in what you want. Then, commit yourselves to considering all possible options before rejecting any of them. Here is a step-by-step approach to finding the optimum solution.

1. **Gather your ideas.** Take out a blank piece of paper and, working together, brainstorm a complete list of all conceivable options. Write down each idea as it comes, without stopping to evaluate it.

2. **Rank your options.** When your list is as complete as you can make it, make a copy of the list for each of you. Then separately rank the options, based on their ability to satisfy the most important needs of both of you on a sliding scale of one to five (one being the most desirable and five being the least desirable).

3. **Compare results.** When you are finished ranking each option, compare your results. This will highlight the most promising options. Look for the options that ranked high for both of you, starting with any that received a combined rank of one/one, then one/two, then two/two, and so forth.

4. **Choose the best approach.** Talk about whether these options seem to work for both of you and why. Which interests do they address? Are any important interests not addressed by an option? Can the option be improved? As you do this, you may find that some compromises are in order. That's okay as long as you're still taking into account the most important concerns you each have. Before you know it, you'll probably zero in on an agreeable solution to the issue at hand.

E. What to Do When Problems Arise

What should you do if you hit a snag while putting together your prenup? If the problem is between the two of you, you need to diagnose it and figure out the best way to address it. This section outlines the steps you can take.

1. Diagnosing the Problem

The problem is likely to be either a communication problem or a negotiation problem—or a combination of both. Start by figuring out which kind of problem confronts you. Then you can tailor your approach to resolving it.

a. Where Are You Stuck?

Whether the problem derives from a communication failure or a negotiation difficulty will depend in large part on where you are in the process of making your prenup. There are four possible places where you can have trouble.

1. The first time you discuss the possibility of having a prenup is one place where you can get off

track. If so, your problem primarily concerns communication.

2. Another place you can run into difficulties is when sharing your financial information, goals, and ideas, following the steps outlined in Chapter 3. If you get stuck at this stage, you are likely to have encountered a communication problem.

3. Some couples run into trouble when working through the clauses of the draft agreement using Chapter 5 or Chapter 6. If you have trouble at this point, you probably have a negotiation issue— perhaps compounded by a communication problem.

4. You may have difficulties putting together the final draft. This is likely to involve both communications and negotiation.

b. Deciding on Your Approach

If you're having communication trouble, follow the suggestions for resolving communication problems in Section 2, just below. If you are hung up at the negotiation stage, see if you can fix the problem using the tips in Section 3, below. If you're not sure what the problem is, or if you know you've got problems with communicating *and* negotiating (don't worry—you won't be the only ones), cover your bases by reading through Sections 2 and 3, and implementing all the suggestions that seem to apply.

2. Resolving Communication Problems

To address a communication problem, begin by revisiting the conversation in which you had trouble. Discuss the issue again, making sure each of you clearly understands what the other person intends to say.

Agree to take as long as you need to do this and set aside a time when there is no pressure to finish quickly. Pick a comfortable place to have the conversation. Make sure you are both rested and refreshed before you begin. Review the guidelines for effective communication in Section C, above.

When you are ready, start at the beginning of the discussion. Don't try to repeat the exact conversation you had before, and don't try to analyze where you went wrong. Just focus on taking turns expressing yourselves and listening attentively. Use feedback (reflective listening) to make sure that you truly understand what each of you is trying to say. Go as slowly as you need to. If you get tired, take a break. Don't rush it. Remember: The goal of communicating is to understand each other, determine who's right or wrong.

If you're still having trouble after trying this approach, consider getting some help. (Section E5, below.)

3. Resolving Negotiation Problems

To work through a negotiation difficulty, begin by checking your communications. Much of the time what seem to be a problematic negotiation has its roots in a miscommunication.

If you are satisfied that your communications have been clear and that each of you understands the other person's point of view, then you'll need to take a similar approach to solving the negotiation problem that we described for addressing communication problems, above.

First, set aside a comfortable time and place so that you can take as long as you need to resolve the problem.

Next, review the tips for negotiating discussed in Section D, above. The problem may be that one or both of you isn't entirely clear about what's most important to you in the negotiation—in other words, what your interests are. Look carefully at the position each of you is taking. What are your reasons for taking those positions? What are you hoping to accomplish? What concerns do you have that would be addressed by adopting your position? These and similar questions will help you uncover your true interests in the matter.

When you feel sure that you know what your interests are, try making a list of them: List one person's interests on the left-hand side of a piece of paper, and the other person's interests on the right-hand side. Double check to be sure the list of each person's interests is accurate and that both of you understand each interest. Then take a few moments, silently, to prioritize your own list. On a scale of one to five, which interests are most important to you? Which are less important? Write the number for each interest's priority next to it. This will help you evaluate whether a particular solution is going to meet your most important interests.

Now both of you should try to think of as many different ways as possible to structure your prenup so that it satisfies the interests you've listed. Use the brainstorming and ranking techniques described above, in Section D.

If you follow this approach, you'll likely work the kinks out of the negotiation and find some promising alternatives for shaping your prenup. If you try the method described here and find you're still hung up, consider getting some help. (See Section E5, below.)

4. Dealing With Serious Roadblocks

There are a couple of situations that deserve special attention, beyond simply focusing on your communication and your negotiating skills. If you seem to reach an impasse, there are particular steps you can take to keep things moving forward. Similarly, if you find yourselves in a take-it-or-leave-it situation, there may be a unique way to address the problem.

a. Breaking an Impasse

What happens if you reach a point where you seem to be stuck? Each of you is clear about what you want and no compromise seems possible. There are two possibilities here. First, it could be that you have come up against a truly irreconcilable difference. For example, if your discussions have led you to discover that one of you wants to have children and the other doesn't, you may simply need to acknowledge a difference that cannot be reconciled. You will then have to decide whether the issue is one that you can simply agree to disagree about (at least for now) or whether it is more fundamental. You may wish to consider getting help from a qualified counselor to help you consider and decide on the consequences for your relationship.

The other possibility is that the impasse stems from an incomplete consideration of each person's interests. Even if you think you have identified your interests regarding the issue in question, try looking a little more deeply to see whether that helps you break the log jam.

b. Avoiding the Take-It-or-Leave-It Syndrome

It is unlikely that you will encounter this problem if the two of you have worked together to draft your prenup. But if just one of you has prepared the draft, or worse yet, a lawyer representing one of you has prepared a draft without any input from the other party, you may find yourselves in what appears to be a take-it-or-leave-it situation.

Obviously, it's best to avoid this problem by working together from the outset. If you don't have that luxury, the next best option is to agree to set aside the proposed draft and go back to the drawing board. Start by examining your individual situations. Share your information with each other, discuss your goals and concerns, and work together to create the outlines of an agreement that will be acceptable to both of you. Use the clauses offered in Chapters 5 and 6 to put your outline into written form and use the resulting draft as a basis for making revisions to what was presented as a one-sided offering.

5. Working With Advisers

If you're stuck and need some help, there are a number of options open to you, depending on what you need and who is available. For example, one or both of you could work with a counselor to improve your communication skills. Or, if you want help negotiating a particular issue, you might find it more useful to seek advice from your lawyers or financial advisers. You could also hire a mediator to help you work out the terms of your prenup.

In this section, we review some of the most common options for getting help and suggest ways to make the experience of working with an adviser as productive as possible.

a. Guidelines for Working With Advisers

Whatever type of adviser you choose, following these general guidelines will help you get the most from your experience.

Check out qualifications such as licensing and years of experience. Make sure you pick someone who is

Karen and Russ: Breaking an Impasse

Karen and Russ run into a stumbling block when talking about potential community property rights in Karen's veterinary practice and the emergency clinic she's thinking of buying into. They resolve the question of what to do with the practice fairly easily, but the issue of the emergency clinic has them stumped. Here's how it happens:

Karen has been approached by some other veterinarians who are starting a limited liability company to operate an emergency clinic. They plan to have a group practice and have invited Karen to join. Each member will be required to be on-call for a certain number of hours per month and to contribute a percentage of the start-up costs. Profits from the company will be shared according to the partners' percentages. Karen is still mulling over whether to get involved, but if she does, she will be putting $10,000 of her own premarital savings into it, and she feels that it should be her separate property. She is unwilling to use the same approach they have come up with for her practice—allocating a share of any increase in value to community property—because she considers the clinic primarily an investment opportunity. She will be paid a salary for her on-call time and Russ will not work in the business (as he will in her regular practice), so it makes no sense to her to consider the return on her investment to be community property.

Russ feels equally strongly that the clinic should be considered at least part community property. If Karen decides to go forward, everything will take place while they are married, and the time she spends on the clinic during their marriage is time she won't spend on other community property endeavors. Russ suggests they agree to give Karen a right of reimbursement for any premarital funds she puts in and call the whole investment community property. This is completely unacceptable to Karen.

After several tense conversations about the clinic, Karen and Russ seem no closer to agreement than before. They realize they are stuck. They decide to try looking again at what each of them has at stake regarding this issue—that is, to examine their interests more closely. They agree that Russ will start by talking about his interests. Karen will listen and then feed back to Russ what she's heard. Then Karen will talk and Russ will listen and give feedback. They agree to keep taking turns like this until both of them feel they have said everything that's on their minds. Then, and only then, they will see if they can come up with a solution that works for both of them.

Russ starts by saying that he feels it is important for Karen's investment of time in the marriage to be fully compensated. He is also concerned that if the emergency clinic partners are required to contribute more money, those funds will have to come from community property, which would mean a community property investment in the business. Karen makes sure she's understood these concerns by telling Russ in her own words what she's heard.

Karen then says that in addition to the fact that the investment in this clinic will be funded with her separate property, she's worried about the potential for problems if her partners must cooperate in appraising the practice if she and Russ divorce or if she dies before he does. Russ hears her out, and feeds back what she's said. Then it's Russ's, turn to speak again. He tells Karen how important it is to him to feel that they are building something together.

Slowly, it becomes clear that the main concerns for Russ are reimbursing any community property funds spent on additional contributions to the emergency clinic, and building up a community property investment together. Adequate compensation for Karen's work at the clinic is not such a big deal to Russ, especially once Karen explains she will receive overtime pay for extra hours, in addition to salary.

On Karen's part, she realizes that in addition to her interest in avoiding a valuation hassle, her biggest concern is making sure she can be free to deal with the clinic partners in making business decisions about the clinic without having to consult Russ.

Based on this new understanding of each other's interests, they agree that the clinic (and any other new veterinary business opportunity that comes up) will be Karen's separate property, but that if they divorce or if Karen dies before Russ, he will be entitled to one-half of any community property funds invested in the business, plus an amount equal to 1% of the amount of Karen's original separate property investment in the business multiplied by the number of years of the marriage, up to a maximum of $10,000.

Clearly identifying the clinic as Karen's separate property will give her the discretion she needs to make business decisions, while determining (and capping) the amount Karen or her estate would have to pay Russ meets her interest in avoiding valuation hassles and keeping the buyout affordable. Providing for reimbursement of community property funds plus an increasing share of equity addresses Russ's interest in getting back a share of community property funds and building up some equity together.

qualified to help you. Ask about licenses, credentials, or certifications. Find out about the adviser's specialties. Ask how long the adviser has been in practice. If possible, get personal references from satisfied clients or other professionals.

Consider interviewing more than one candidate. If you can afford it—or if free interviews are an option—meet with two or more potential advisers before settling on one. Regardless of a professional's qualifications, his or her style and personality can make a difference. See how comfortable you feel with two or three different candidates. Then pick one who is qualified and who seems easy to work with.

Be clear about what you expect from your adviser. Let your adviser know what you want help with. Make sure that this is something your adviser is able and willing to offer.

Agree in advance about fees—preferably in writing. Avoid unpleasant surprises or misunderstandings by finding out about fees at the beginning. Does the adviser charge by the hour? If so, what is the rate? Does he or she charge for time spent on the phone or consulting other professionals on your behalf? Will you be expected to pay at the time of each meeting or will you be billed? Is an advance deposit required? Can you pay by credit card? Can you make monthly payments? Ask your adviser to put the fee arrangement in writing, or prepare a memo summarizing your understanding of the arrangement and ask your adviser to look it over and approve it.

Prepare for each meeting with your adviser. Prior to each meeting with your adviser, think about what you want to accomplish at the meeting. Jot down some notes to refer to. If you have questions you want to raise, write them down, too. Take your notes with you to the meeting and check them occasionally to make sure you've covered everything.

Follow through. Working with advisers can involve "homework" on your part. If you agree to assemble information or to practice a skill in between meetings, make a point of following through. You'll get the most out of the advice you're paying for only if you hold up your end.

Take seriously the advice you receive. If your adviser makes a suggestion, consider it carefully. If you don't understand the advice, say so, and ask for clarification. If you disagree with the advice, share your reservations

with your adviser. Perhaps there is an angle you have overlooked, or maybe there is some piece of information your adviser is unaware of that would make a difference. You are spending good money on your adviser, so take the time to try to fully understand his or her opinion rather than rejecting it out of hand.

b. Licensed Marriage and Family Counselors

One option available to you, especially if you need help with communication, is a licensed marriage and family counselor. These counselors may go by various names, depending on where you live. Typically they include licensed clinical psychologists, psychiatrists, marriage and family counselors, and licensed social workers. Generally, the fees of a marriage and family counselor or social worker will be lower than those of psychiatrists and clinical psychologists. Some insurance companies will cover part of the expense of counseling; check with your health insurance provider to find out.

The best way to find a counselor is through personal referrals from friends, neighbors, family, and other trusted sources. Follow the guidelines outlined at the beginning of this section to get the most out of using a counselor.

c. Premarital Counselors

Another choice open to you—again, especially for help with communication problems—is to work with a premarital counselor. Many churches, temples, and other religious communities offer premarital counseling. There are also secular counselors who offer premarital counseling. (In at least one state (Minnesota), the fee for a marriage license is reduced if the couple attends premarital counseling with an approved counselor.) If you are already working with a premarital counselor whom you like and trust, he or she might be the right person to help one or both of you improve your communication skills or even negotiate the terms of your prenup.

If you aren't working with a premarital counselor but are interested in doing so, the best way to find one is through personal referrals from friends, family, business associates, or other people whose opinion you trust. You may also be able to locate a premarital counselor through a church, synagogue, or other religious community, or even through a search of premarital counseling programs using an Internet search engine.

Whether or not you already have a relationship with a premarital counselor, follow the guidelines outlined above to ensure that you get the most out of the experience.

d. Attorneys or Financial Advisers

If you are looking for help with negotiating the terms of your prenup, you might want to consider getting help from a lawyer or a financial adviser. Before you do, be sure to look for someone who is willing to be nonadversarial when advising you. Adversarial advice focuses exclusively on what is to your best advantage, regardless of the potential disadvantages to your fiancé and your relationship. Instead, your adviser should be prepared to help you find ways to negotiate a premarital agreement that supports the needs and interests of both of you.

Unless you have already selected a lawyer to work with, refer to Chapter 7 for help finding a good one. If you do not have a financial adviser, use personal referrals to find a qualified person.

Whether you opt for help from a lawyer, a financial adviser, or both, follow the guidelines outlined at the beginning of this section for working with any legal or financial adviser you select.

e. Mediators

Because it is nonadversarial—the mediator is neutral and has no power to decide for or against a party—mediation can be an ideal way to hammer out the details of a prenup.

Historically, mediation has been used to resolve labor disputes and international disagreements. The last 20 years have seen an expansion of the use of mediation to resolve various interpersonal and community disagreements. There are more and more professionals—in fields ranging from law to psychology to accounting to business—who are becoming trained to mediate disputes in their fields. Mediating premarital agreements is a relatively new option for couples.

If the mediator is also a lawyer or has other expertise in the legal and financial aspects of preparing premarital agreements, she or he can draft the final agreement from a neutral point of view, so that your advising lawyers will only have to review the document to ensure its clarity and thoroughness. When choosing a mediator, try to find someone who has experience with prenups. Look for referrals from family, friends, colleagues, and other trusted sources. Then follow the approach outlined at the beginning of this section to ensure a successful mediation experience. ■

9

After You've Made a Prenup

The process of making a prenup doesn't end when you sign on the dotted line. Although you've finished the hardest part, there are still a few things you'll need to do to make sure that your agreement has its intended effect.

In this chapter, we discuss the various steps you might take in the months and years to come, from such basics as storing the original document to occasionally reviewing and changing your agreement.

A. Storing the Original Agreement and Copies

The first thing you should do with your prenup is agree on a safe place to store the original document, in case you ever need to present it to a judge, county clerk, or other official. Typically, an original prenuptial agreement will be stored with other important family papers, such as real estate deeds, certificates of title for vehicles or other assets, and birth certificates. A good storage place might be a safe deposit box or a filing cabinet in your home. Whatever location you choose, make sure that both of you know where to find the original agreement if and when you need it. It is also a good idea to keep at least one photocopy of the agreement in some other location, in case the original is ever misplaced or destroyed.

B. Recording an Abstract of the Agreement

Occasionally, a couple signing a prenup also prepares and signs what is known as an "abstract" of the agreement, to file with the public land records office. The abstract is shorter than the agreement and usually summarizes only the provisions relating to real estate. The purpose of the abstract is to enable one or both spouses to buy and sell separate property real estate without having to obtain the other spouse's signature.

If you prepare an abstract, you will record (file) it in the county where one or both of you owns separate property real estate. The land records office is called the county recorder's office in most places, but in some states it may go by another name, such as the registry of deeds. Because any document that is recorded in the county's

official records is available to the public, using an abstract instead of the entire prenuptial agreement allows you to keep the details of your prenup private.

EXAMPLE: Barry is a licensed real estate broker. In the course of his business, he occasionally buys and sells real estate in his own name, and he owns several rental properties. Barry and Chantelle have signed a prenup providing that Barry's rental properties, and any new real estate he purchases, will be his separate property. To avoid having to obtain Chantelle's signature on the deed every time he sells a property or borrows against it, Barry and Chantelle prepare and sign an abstract of their prenuptial agreement summarizing just the clauses relating to Barry's separate property real estate. They record the abstract in each county where Barry owns real estate so that title companies, lenders, and potential purchasers will know that Barry has the right to sell or borrow against the property without Chantelle's involvement. Because the abstract contains only provisions relating to real estate, the rest of their prenup can be kept private. You can find a sample of their abstract at the end of this section.

If you decide to make an abstract, you may want to ask your lawyers to help you draw it up at the time you prepare your final agreement. Otherwise, you can make one later, with help or on your own.

The abstract must be signed and notarized. This is usually done after the wedding, so that the abstract can include a provision stating that the prenup is in effect. If you own real estate in more than one county or expect to in the future, you should sign enough originals of the abstract so that you can record one in each county.

After you record the abstract, the land records office will return the original to you, stamped to show that they've recorded the document. You should store the recorded original abstract with your original prenup.

Check the laws in your location. Laws and procedures dealing with title to real estate vary from state to state and even from county to county within a given state. If you think you need an abstract, it's best to check the legal requirements before preparing the document and taking it to the land records office.

RECORDING REQUESTED BY
AND WHEN RECORDED RETURN TO

Barry Agha
123 Main St.
Hayesville, NC 28904

[LEAVE THIS SPACE BLANK
FOR RECORDER'S STAMP]

Abstract of Prenuptial Agreement

We, Barry Agha (Barry) and Chantelle Agha (Chantelle), declare:

1. We were married on December 20, 2003 and are now husband and wife.

2. We entered into a prenuptial agreement on November 12, 2003.

3. The prenuptial agreement became effective on the date of our marriage and it remains in full force and effect as of the date of execution of this abstract.

4. Among the provisions of the prenuptial agreement are the provisions that follow:

   a. Paragraph 6A provides that the real property described on Exhibit A to this abstract, which is incorporated by reference, is and shall be Barry's separate property, and Barry's has the sole right to manage and dispose of the property described on Exhibit A.

   b. Paragraph 7E provides that any real property acquired by Barry in his sole name during our marriage shall be considered Barry's separate property, and Barry has the sole right to manage and dispose of any such property.

   c. Paragraph 2B provides that the prenuptial agreement will remain in full force and effect indefinitely.

We sign this abstract on January 20, 2004 at Hayesville, North Carolina.

Barry Agha
_____
Barry Agha

Chantelle Agha
_____
Chantelle Agha

Certificate of Acknowledgment of Notary Public

State of _North Carolina_

County of _Clay_ }} ss

On _January 20, 2004_, before me, _Melinda Washington_
personally appeared _Barry Agha_ ,
personally known to me or proved to me on the basis of satisfactory evidence to be the person whose
name is subscribed to the within instrument, and acknowledged to me that he/she executed the same
and that by his/her signature on the instrument he/she executed the instrument.

WITNESS my hand and official seal.

[NOTARIAL SEAL]   _Melinda Washington_

Notary Public for the state of _North Carolina_

My commission expires _November 6, 2005_

Certificate of Acknowledgment of Notary Public

State of _North Carolina_

County of _Clay_ }} ss

On _January 20, 2004_, before me, _Melinda Washington_
personally appeared _Chantelle Agha_ ,
personally known to me or proved to me on the basis of satisfactory evidence to be the person whose
name is subscribed to the within instrument, and acknowledged to me that he/she executed the same
and that by his/her signature on the instrument he/she executed the instrument.

WITNESS my hand and official seal.

[NOTARIAL SEAL]   _Melinda Washington_

Notary Public for the state of _North Carolina_

My commission expires _November 6, 2005_

C. Following Your Own Rules

Once you have made a prenup, it is important to avoid doing anything that would be inconsistent with the terms of your agreement. Otherwise, you could find yourselves in a position later on where your agreement says one thing and your actions point to something different. At best this creates confusion, and it could even lead to genuine disagreement over the meaning and validity of your prenup.

Even the simplest prenup requires consistent follow-through. For example, the prenup signed by Steven and Freda (see Chapter 5) states that the premarital assets listed on their disclosure schedules will remain their separate property after they marry. Their prenup does not attempt to carve out special rules regarding new property or debts incurred during their marriage. Nevertheless, to ensure that their premarital assets continue to be considered separate property, Steven and Frieda need to keep those assets in separate names and not mix them together with marital assets. And if one of them decides to contribute separate property funds to a marital asset, they should consider writing up a separate loan agreement unless the one contributing the funds intends to convert them to marital property.

In addition to acting in a way that is consistent with your prenup, you may need to follow through on specific steps you've agreed to take. If so, it's a good idea to make a list of those steps and a plan for completing them. Again, not doing so could create confusion and could even lead to a result you do not intend.

For example, Ted and Grace have agreed to several provisions that require them to take action after they marry, including writing up their estate plans (see Section D, below), and signing waivers of surviving spouse rights to each other's retirement benefits. Before putting their prenup away in a safe place, they make a list of all the steps they need to take. When they get back from their honeymoon, they will refer to the list and agree upon a timetable for completing everything.

Finally, if you have agreed in your prenup that you will do certain things on a regular basis, such as putting money away for your children's college education or paying certain recurring expenses, it is important to continue to follow through with those items. For instance, the premarital agreement signed by Ted and Grace contains two such provisions in Paragraph 8. One clause sets up a process for deciding whether or not to file joint income tax returns each year and allocating their incomes, deductions, and taxes or refunds. They also include a clause stating that Ted will pay the household expenses, by contributing the necessary amount each month to a joint bank account. If Ted and Grace decide to deal with the income taxes or household expenses in a different way, they should renegotiate that part of their prenup and sign an addendum or modification (see Section F of this chapter). Otherwise, they should be sure to follow the process they have laid out for each of these items as time goes by.

D. Completing Your Estate Plan

You may have used your prenup to set out some of the ways you want to leave your property when you die. In addition, you may have waived some or all of the rights you would otherwise have to receive property from each other's estates. If your prenup touches on estate planning issues such as these, it's critically important that you prepare the necessary documents—wills, trusts, or other paperwork—that will actually transfer your property as you intend. Your prenup doesn't take the place of these important transfer documents, and if you neglect to complete them, it could lead to much confusion and extra work for your inheritors after your death.

For instance, if one or both of you has agreed in the prenup to leave some money or property to the other when you die—perhaps in exchange for giving up some spousal inheritance rights—you'll need to follow up by making wills (and perhaps trusts) soon after you marry. Depending on the complexity of your plan and the size of your estate, you may want to enlist your lawyers to help you choose the best estate planning devices and draw up your papers. If your needs are simple—for example, you don't have significant assets and want to make a moderate gift to your spouse—you can probably prepare your own will or living trust with a good self-help book or software.

Whether you decide to enlist your lawyers for this part of the process or not, there are many resources available to help you learn more about estate planning and perhaps handle some of the necessary tasks on your own.

⚠️ **More information about estate planning.** Nolo offers many tools designed to help with your estate planning tasks. You may want to start by visiting Nolo's website at www.nolo.com, where you'll find lots of helpful (and free) information about estate planning in our legal encyclopedia.

Quicken WillMaker Plus (software for Windows) allows you to prepare a comprehensive will, living trust, health care directive, and durable power of attorney for finances using your computer. It also enables you to prepare a document setting out your wishes for final arrangements and many other useful forms.

Plan Your Estate, by Denis Clifford and Cora Jordan, offers in-depth coverage of all significant elements of estate planning, from simple wills to probate avoidance and complex tax-saving trusts.

Estate Planning Basics, by Denis Clifford, is a short course in estate planning, providing straightforward explanations that help you learn just what you need to know to complete your plan.

Nolo's Simple Will Book, by Denis Clifford, shows you how to prepare a will that meets your needs, including basic trusts for minor children. Will forms are available as tear-outs or on a CD-ROM included with the book.

Make Your Own Living Trust, by Denis Clifford, provides a complete explanation of how to prepare a living trust. The book contains forms (tear-out and on CD-ROM) allowing you to create a probate avoidance living trust and, for married couples, a tax-saving "AB" trust.

8 Ways to Avoid Probate, by Mary Randolph, offers a thorough discussion of all the major ways to avoid probate by transferring property at death outside of a will.

E. Reviewing the Agreement

It's a good idea to take a look at your prenup from time to time to be sure it still works for you. Someday you may find that it needs some tweaking or even a major overhaul. If your prenup includes a clause requiring review at specified intervals, then you already have a plan in place and you just need to

remember to do it. If you have a "sunset clause" that automatically terminates your prenup after a specified period of time, you will certainly want to review the prenup prior to the expiration date and decide whether you want to extend your agreement or to let it lapse.

Even if you haven't provided for a formal review or termination date, we recommend that you revisit the provisions of your prenup every so often. An ideal time to do this is whenever you update your estate plans— for example, if the two of you have kids of your own or if there are other major changes in your family or your assets. Often, the terms of your estate plans will need to be coordinated with those of your prenup, because a change made in one can affect the other.

Just as you did when you first began to discuss the terms of your prenup, be sure to choose a time and place for your review that will be free of distractions and conducive to a relaxed conversation. Prepare separately for your discussion by reading through the agreement with a fresh attitude and writing down notes of any thoughts or questions that come to mind.

The reviewing process might result in a mutual affirmation of the terms of your prenup. If so, put the agreement away until the next review and just remember to follow its terms.

If the review leads you to conclude that some changes to the agreement are in order, you'll need to make those changes in a separate document. For more on how to do this, read on.

F. Changing Your Prenup: Postnuptial Agreements

During a review of your prenup you may find something that needs to be changed. A major change in your circumstances might also prompt some revisions.

In either situation, you will probably need a new written agreement to bring your agreement up to date.

An agreement changing the terms of a prenuptial agreement may be called an amendment or addendum to the agreement. Because it is signed *during* marriage, it is governed by state laws that apply to postnuptial (sometimes called "postmarital" or even just "marital") agreements, rather than by laws that apply to prenups. After you are married, the laws of your state may hold you to a higher standard in your dealings with each other than you had before you were married. In many states, spouses are considered to have a "confidential" or "fiduciary" relationship to one another. Each spouse is expected to have the other person's interests at heart in dealing with financial matters, and any agreement that appears to be to only one person's advantage can be set aside.

Get help with a postnup. An examination of state laws relating to postnuptial agreements (including those modifying prenups) is beyond the scope of this book. Suffice it to say that you should check the legal requirements of your state carefully before attempting to amend your prenup. In all likelihood, you will each need the assistance of a competent lawyer to ensure that the amendment will be binding, just as you did with the prenup itself. In fact, if you were happy with the lawyers who represented you in making your prenup, it may be a very simple matter to go back to them for help with drawing up and signing an amendment.

G. Closing Thoughts

Making a prenup can be a lot of work. It can be stressful and scary at times. It can also be very satisfying and even exciting to find that you can work together as partners in your financial affairs. Even if your prenup does little more than identify your premarital assets, by dealing directly and respectfully with each other about some tough financial and legal issues, you will have laid a firm foundation for your future relationship as life partners.

We hope that this book plays a part in building that foundation, and that your marriage will be stronger and more secure as a result. ■

How to Use the CD-ROM

The forms in Appendix C, as well as the worksheets in Appendix B, are included on a CD-ROM in the back of the book. This CD-ROM, which can be used with Windows computers, installs files that can be opened, printed, and edited using a word processor or other software. It is *not* a stand-alone software program. Please read this Appendix and the README.TXT file included on the CD-ROM for instructions on using the Forms CD.

Note to Mac users: This CD-ROM and its files should also work on Macintosh computers. Please note, however, that Nolo cannot provide technical support for non-Windows users.

How to View the README File

If you do not know how to view the file README.TXT, insert the Forms CD-ROM into your computer's CD-ROM drive and follow these instructions:

- **Windows 9x, 2000, Me, and XP:** (1) On your PC's desktop, double click the My Computer icon; and (2) double click the icon for the CD-ROM drive into which the Form2s CD-ROM was inserted; and (3) double click the file README.TXT.
- **Macintosh:** (1) On your Mac desktop, double click the icon for the CD-ROM that you inserted; and (2) double click on the file README.TXT.

While the README file is open, print it out by using the Print command in the File menu.

A. Installing the Form Files Onto Your Computer

Word processing forms that you can open, complete, print, and save with your word processing program (see Section B, below) are contained on the CD-ROM. Before you can do anything with the files on the CD-ROM, you need to install them onto your hard disk. In accordance with U.S. copyright laws, remember that copies of the CD-ROM and its files are for your personal use only.

Insert the Forms CD and do the following:

1. Windows 9x, 2000, Me, and XP Users

Follow the instructions that appear on the screen. (If nothing happens when you insert the Forms CD-ROM, then (1) double click the My Computer icon; (2) double click the icon for the CD-ROM drive into which the Forms CD-ROM was inserted; and (3) double click the file WELCOME.EXE.)

By default, all the files are installed to the \Prenuptial Agreements folder in the \Program Files folder of your computer. A folder called "Prenuptial Agreements" is added to the "Programs" folder of the Start menu.

2. Macintosh Users

Step 1: If the "Prenuptial Agreements CD" window is not open, open it by double clicking the "Prenuptial Agreements CD" icon.

Step 2: Select the "Prenuptial Agreements" folder icon.

Step 3: Drag and drop the folder icon onto the icon of your hard disk.

B. Using the Word Processing Files to Create Documents

This section concerns the files for forms that can be opened and edited with your word processing program.

All word processing forms come in rich text format. These files have the extension ".RTF." For example, the form for the Simple Prenuptial Agreement discussed in Chapter 5 is on the file SimplePrenup.rtf. All forms and their filenames are listed in Section C, below.

RTF files can be read by most recent word processing programs, including all versions of MS Word for Windows and Macintosh, WordPad for Windows, and recent versions of WordPerfect for Windows and Macintosh.

To use a form from the CD to create your documents you must: (1) open a file in your word processor or text editor; (2) edit the form by filling in the required information; (3) print it out; and (4) rename and save your revised file.

The following are general instructions on how to do this. However, each word processor uses different commands to open, format, save, and print documents. Please read your word processor's manual for specific instructions on performing these tasks.

For specific instructions on how to create either a simple prenuptial agreement or a custom prenuptial agreement, please refer to the instructions in Chapter 5.

Do not call Nolo's technical support if you have questions on how to use your word processor.

Step 1: Opening a File

There are three ways to open the word processing files included on the CD-ROM after you have installed them onto your computer.

- Windows users can open a file by selecting its "shortcut" as follows: (1) Click the Windows "Start" button; (2) open the "Programs" folder; (3) open the "Prenuptial Agreements" subfolder; (4) open either the "Custom Prenuptial" or "Worksheets" subfolder, if applicable; and (5) click on the shortcut to the form you want to work with.
- Both Windows and Macintosh users can open a file directly by double clicking on it. Use My Computer or Windows Explorer (Windows 9x, 2000, Me, or XP) or the Finder (Macintosh) to go to the folder you installed or copied the CD-ROM's files to. Then, double click on the specific file you want to open.
- You can also open a file from within your word processor. To do this, you must first start your word processor. Then, go to the File menu and choose the Open command. This opens a dialog box where you will tell the program (1) the type of file you want to open (*.RTF); and (2) the location and name of the file (you will need to navigate through the directory tree to get to the

folder on your hard disk where the CD's files have been installed). If these directions are unclear, you will need to look through the manual for your word processing program—Nolo's technical support department will *not* be able to help you with the use of your word processing program.

Where Are the Files Installed?

Windows Users
- RTF files are installed by default to a folder named \Prenuptial Agreements in the \Program Files folder of your computer.

Macintosh Users
- RTF files are located in the "Prenuptial Agreements" folder.

Step 2: Editing Your Document

Fill in the appropriate information according to the instructions and sample agreements in the book. Underlines, frequently containing bracketed instructions, are used to indicate where you need to enter your information. *Be sure to delete the underlines and instructions from your edited document.* If you do not know how to use your word processor to edit a document, you will need to look through the manual for your word processing program. Nolo's technical support department will not be able to help you with the use of your word processing program.

Step 3: Printing Out the Document

Use your word processor's or text editor's "Print" command to print out your document. If you do not know how to use your word processor to print a document, you will need to look through the manual for your word processing program. Nolo's technical support department will not be able to help you with the use of your word processing program.

Step 4: Saving Your Document

After filling in the form, use the "Save As" command to save and rename the file. Because all the files are "read-only." you will not be able to use the "Save" command. This is for your protection. *If you save the file without renaming it, the underlines that indicate where you need to enter your information will be lost, and you will not be able to create a new document with this file without recopying the original file from the CD-ROM.*

If you do not know how to use your word processor to save a document, you will need to look through the manual for your word processing program. Nolo's technical support department will not be able to help you with the use of your word processing program.

C. Files Provided on the Forms CD-ROM

The following files are included in rich text format (RTF):

File Name	Form Title
Worksheet1.rtf	Worksheet 1: Financial Inventory
Worksheet2.rtf	Worksheet 2: Credit History and Spending Habits
Worksheet3.rtf	Worksheet 3: Financial Outlook
Worksheet4.rtf	Worksheet 4: Prenup Goals
Worksheet5.rtf	Worksheet 5: The Basics of Our Prenup
Worksheet6.rtf	Worksheet 6: Comparison of Prenup to Law
SimplePrenup.rtf	Simple Prenuptial Agreement
Outline.rtf	Prenuptial Agreement Outline
Introductory.rtf	1. Introductory Facts
Term.rtf	2. Effective Date and Term
Representation.rtf	3. Legal Representation
Disclosures.rtf	4. Disclosures
Definitions.rtf	5. Definitions
Ownership.rtf	6. Ownership of Premarital Assets
MarriageAssets.rtf	7. Rights in Assets Acquired During Marriage
Expenses.rtf	8. Responsibility for Debts and Expenses
Estate.rtf	9. Estate Planning Matters—Optional
Transfers.rtf	10. Property Transfers, Payments, or Purchases Upon Marriage—Optional
Divorce.rtf	11. Property Transfers, Payments, or Purchases Upon Marriage—Optional
Other.rtf	12. Other Matters—Optional
Interpretation.rtf	13. Interpretation, Modification, Review, and Enforcement of This Agreement
Signatures.rtf	14. Signatures, Acknowledgments, and Attorneys' Certifications
Abstract.rtf	Abstract of Prenup
Schedule1.rtf	Schedule 1—Financial Disclosures
Schedule2.rtf	Schedule 2—Financial Disclosures

B

Worksheets

_____   _____
Date Prepared   Your Name

Worksheet 1: Financial Inventory

1. Assets

Real Estate

Address or Description	Percentage Owned	Current Market Value
_____	_____ %	$_____
_____	_____ %	$_____
_____	_____ %	$_____

Cash and Bank Accounts (Checking, Savings, or Money Market Accounts, CDs)

Type of Account	Current Balance
_____	$_____
_____	$_____
_____	$_____

Other Investment Assets (Stocks and Stock Options, Bonds, Mutual Funds, Annuities, Life Insurance)

Description	Current Market Value
_____	$_____
_____	$_____
_____	$_____
_____	$_____

Retirement Assets (Pension, IRA, 401(k), Deferred Compensation Plans)

Description	Current Market Value
_____	$_____
_____	$_____

Personal Property (Vehicles, Household Goods, Art, Antiques, Jewelry, Tools, Equipment, Animals, Other Items)

Description	Current Market Value
_____	$_____
_____	$_____
_____	$_____
_____	$_____

Business Ownership

Business Name	Form (Corporation, LLC, Partnership, Sole Proprietorship)	Percentage Owned	Current Market Value
_____	_____	_____ %	$_____
_____	_____	_____ %	$_____
_____	_____	_____ %	$_____

Other Assets (Including Money Owed to You)

Description	Current Market Value
_____	$_____
_____	$_____
_____	$_____

Total Assets	$

2. Debts

Secured Loans (Mortgages, Auto Loans, Other Loans Secured by Assets)

Owed To	Secured by (Asset Description)	Current Balance	Date Due
		$	
		$	
		$	
		$	

Credit Card Debts

Owed To	Current Balance	Date Due
	$	
	$	
	$	
	$	

Bank Loan/Lines of Credit

Owed To	Current Balance	Date Due
	$	
	$	
	$	
	$	

Private Loans

Owed To	Current Balance	Date Due
	$	
	$	

Student Loans

Owed To	Current Balance	Date Due
	$	
	$	

Child Support/Alimony

Owed To	For	Current Balance	Date Due
		$	
		$	

Divorce Settlement or Other Judgment Debt

Owed To	For	Current Balance	Date Due
		$	
		$	

Other Debts

Owed To	For	Current Balance	Date Due
		$	
		$	
		$	

Total Debts $_____

3. Income

Type of Income	Annual Amount (Before Tax)
Salary/Wages	$_____
Business Income (Sole Proprietorship)	$_____
Dividends, Interest	$_____
Capital Gain (or Loss) Income	$_____
Pension or Annuity Income	$_____
Rental or Partnership, S-Corporation Income	$_____
Social Security Benefits	$_____
Tax-Free Income	$_____
Other (specify):	
_____	$_____
_____	$_____
_____	$_____
Total Income	$_____

4. Personal Expenses (indicate monthly or annual)

	Annual Expense	Monthly Expense
Housing Expenses		
Rent or Mortgage	$_____	$_____
Property Tax	$_____	$_____
Insurance	$_____	$_____
Utilities and Maintenace	$_____	$_____
Other Housing Expenses (specify):		
_____	$_____	$_____
_____	$_____	$_____
Transportation and Auto		
Auto Payment	$_____	$_____
Registration and Insurance	$_____	$_____
Repairs and Maintenace	$_____	$_____
Gas, Parking	$_____	$_____
Other Transportation Expenses (specify):		
_____	$_____	$_____
_____	$_____	$_____
Necessities		
Food and Supplies	$_____	$_____
Clothing	$_____	$_____
Medical/Dental	$_____	$_____
Personal Hygiene	$_____	$_____
Other Necessities (specify):		
_____	$_____	$_____
_____	$_____	$_____
_____	$_____	$_____
_____	$_____	$_____

	Annual Expense	Monthly Expense
D. Other		
Entertainment and Travel	$_____	$_____
Dues, Subscriptions, and Hobbies	$_____	$_____
Gifts and Donations	$_____	$_____
Insurance	$_____	$_____
Other (specify):		
_____	$_____	$_____
_____	$_____	$_____
_____	$_____	$_____
_____	$_____	$_____
_____	$_____	$_____
_____	$_____	$_____
Total Expenses	$_____	$_____

_____   _____
Date Prepared   Your Name

Worksheet 2: Credit History and Spending Habits

A. Credit History

    1. a. Have you ever been sued for failing to pay a debt? ☐ yes ☐ no

       b. If so, give details (when, by whom, what court, amount of the claim, and the outcome).

      _____

      _____

      _____

      _____

    2. a. Do you currently owe any debt that is more than 60 days overdue? ☐ yes ☐ no

       b. If so, specify the debt and the amount you owe.

      _____

      _____

      _____

      _____

    3. a. Have you been turned down for a loan or credit card in the last two years? ☐ yes ☐ no

       b. If so give details (when, by whom, and the reason given for the denial of credit).

      _____

      _____

      _____

      _____

B. Spending and Saving Habits

    1. How important is it to you to set aside savings on a regular basis? (circle one)

      Not important   1   2   3   4   5   Very important

    2. How comfortable are you with going into debt in order to take advantage an investment opportunity? (circle one)

      Not comfortable   1   2   3   4   5   Very comfortable

    3. Do you usually pay bills ☐ early ☐ on time ☐ a little late ☐ very late?

    4. Of the following methods, which ones do you use to pay bills and everyday expenses (check all that apply):

      ☐ Cash

      ☐ Check

      ☐ Automatic Transfer

      ☐ Credit Card

      ☐ Other (specify): _____

      _____

    5. How many credit cards do you currently have?   _____

6. Do you pay credit card bills in full each month?

☐ Always   ☐ Never   ☐ Sometimes   ☐ Occasionally

7. How often do you balance your checkbook?

☐ Always   ☐ Never   ☐ Sometimes   ☐ Occasionally

8. Do you participate in a voluntary savings program?   ☐ yes   ☐ no

9. Have you set aside money in a savings account or other investment in the past 12 months?   ☐ yes   ☐ no

10. How many secured loans have you obtained in the past 12 months? (Include details)

_____

_____

11. How many unsecured loans have you obtained in the past 12 months? (Include details)

_____

_____

12. Other information you consider significant:

_____

_____

_____

_____

_____

_____

_____

_____   _____
Date Prepared   Your Name

Worksheet 3: Financial Outlook

	Yes	No

1. a. Do you plan to make a major purchase or an investment of more than $5,000 in the next two years? ☐ ☐

   b. If so, give details.

_____

_____

_____

2. a. Are you planning a career change in the next two years? ☐ ☐

   b. If so, give details

_____

_____

_____

3. a. Are you planning to retire from your current occupation in the next five years? ☐ ☐

   b. If so, give details.

_____

_____

_____

4. a. Are you planning to enter a college, vocational, or professional school in the next two years? ☐ ☐

   b. If so, give details.

_____

_____

_____

5. a. Do you expect to receive a significant inheritance or gift in the next few years? ☐ ☐

   b. If so, give details.

_____

_____

_____

6. a. Do you know of any other approaching events that are likely to affect your financial status? ☐ ☐

   b. If so, give details.

_____

_____

_____

_____

_____

_____

_____
Date Prepared

_____
Your Name

Worksheet 4: Prenup Goals

(Check all that apply; highlight or mark those that are most important to you)

Keeping Property Separate

☐ 1. Keep my premarital assets separate

   Exceptions: _____

☐ 2. Have the following assets acquired during marriage considered separate property, marital property, or community property

	Separate	Marital Property	Community Property
☐ a. Real estate purchased during our marriage	☐	☐	☐
☐ b. Each person's salary earned during marriage	☐	☐	☐
☐ c. My retirement benefits earned during our marriage	☐	☐	☐
☐ d. Stock options and other employment benefits	☐	☐	☐
☐ e. Any increase in the value of a premarital business	☐	☐	☐
☐ f. Other investments made during our marriage	☐	☐	☐
☐ g. Joint bank accounts	☐	☐	☐
☐ h. Other: _____	☐	☐	☐

   Comments: _____

   _____

   _____

   _____

☐ 3. Include the following special provisions regarding assets acquired during marriage:

   _____

   _____

Debts

☐ 4. Protect one or both of us from the other person's premarital debts

☐ 5. Protect one or both of us from the other person's business debts or other debts incurred during marriage

Financial Responsibilities During Marriage

☐ 6. Specify a process for filing income tax returns each year

☐ 7. Specify each person's responsibility for household expenses while we're married

☐ 8. Other:

☐ 9. Provide for my children

☐ 10. Pass on family property

☐ 11. Avoid disagreements between my spouse and my other heirs after my death by including certain terms in my estate plan

Providing for Each Other

☐ 12. Provide for my support if my spouse dies

☐ 13. Provide for my spouse when I die

Divorce

☐ 14. Avoid an expensive and complicated divorce by deciding property issues in advance

☐ 15. Specify that I will/will not (circle one) receive alimony if we get divorced

Other Goals

☐ 16. _____

_____

_____

_____

_____

_____

_____

_____

_____

_____   _____
Date Prepared   Your Name

Worksheet 5: The Basics of Our Prenup

1. Premarital assets will be:

   ☐ Separate property

   ☐ Marital property

   ☐ Community property

   ☐ Exceptions or special provisions (specify): _____

2. Assets we acquire during our marriage will be:

	Separate	Marital Property	Community Property
a. Real estate purchased during our marriage	☐	☐	☐
b. Each person's salary earned during marriage	☐	☐	☐
c. Retirement benefits earned during our marriage	☐	☐	☐
d. Stock options and other employment benefits earned during our marriage	☐	☐	☐
e. Any increase in the value of a premarital business	☐	☐	☐
f. Other investments made during our marriage	☐	☐	☐
g. Joint bank accounts	☐	☐	☐
h. Other: _____	☐	☐	☐

3. Special provisions concerning assets acquired during marriage. Details:

   _____

   _____

   _____

4. Our prenup will provide the following regarding each person's premarital debts. Details:

   _____

   _____

   _____

5. Our prenup will provide the following regarding business debts or other debts incurred during marriage. Details:

   _____

   _____

   _____

6. Our prenup will spell out a process for deciding whether to file joint tax returns and how to allocate income, deductions, taxes, and refunds. Details:

   _____

   _____

   _____

7. Our prenup will define each person's responsibility for household expenses. Details:

_____

_____

_____

8. This is how our prenup will support our intended estate plans (this may require waivers of surviving spouse rights). Details:

_____

_____

_____

_____

_____

_____

_____

_____

_____

9. Our prenup will provide for our estate plans to include the following terms. Details:

_____

_____

_____

_____

10. Our prenup will provide for support of the surviving spouse. Details:

_____

_____

_____

_____

11. Our prenup will specify what should happen to our property if we separate and divorce. Details:

_____

_____

_____

12. Our prenup will limit, avoid, or provide for alimony if we separate and divorce. Details:

_____

_____

_____

13. Our prenup will include other agreements that apply if we divorce. Details:

_____

_____

_____

_____

14. Other provisions of our prenup. Details:

_____

_____

_____

_____

_____

_____

_____

_____

_____

_____

_____

_____

_____

_____

_____

Date Prepared   Your Name

Worksheet 6: Comparison of Prenup to Law
(use a separate sheet for each item identified on Worksheet 5)

Prenup Item Number and Description:

_____

_____

_____

_____

_____

_____

1. What does the law say about this item?

_____

_____

_____

_____

_____

_____

2. Will the law allow us to create a different result in our premarital agreement?

_____

_____

_____

_____

_____

_____

_____

3. Is there any special legal restriction, procedure, or consideration that applies to this item?

_____

_____

_____

_____

_____

_____

_____

_____

Clauses for Building Your Prenup

This appendix contains all of the clauses you'll need to assemble your prenup. The clauses are organized into ten basic paragraphs that should be included in every prenuptial agreement, followed by a series of optional paragraphs and clauses. After the clauses, you'll find suggested formats for the financial disclosures you will attach to the agreement. And at the end of the appendix, there is a template you can use to create an abstract of your prenup, as explained in Chapter 9.

 Use this appendix with Chapters 5 and 6. Refer to the detailed instructions and examples found in those chapters before attempting to create your prenup with the clauses in this appendix.

➡ **Creating a simple prenup.** To create a very simple prenup that identifies your premarital separate property assets and debts and leaves everything else to state law, use the clauses that have already been checked ☑ and those marked with a ✻. Making a simple prenup is discussed in Chapter 5, Section B2. You can also find a file containing a simple prenup template on the CD-ROM that accompanies this book. Look for the file Simple Prenuptial Agreement (SimplePrenup.rtf).

A. Your Prenup's Title

Choose one:

✻ ☐ | **Premarital Agreement**

☐ | **Prenuptial Agreement**

☐ | **Antenuptial Agreement**

☐ | **[Other]**

B. The Ten Basic Paragraphs (Mandatory for All Agreements)

☑ **Paragraph 1: Introductory Facts**

A. Parties

This agreement is between [woman's first and last name] and [man's first and last name]. We refer to ourselves by our first names in this agreement.

B. Purpose of Agreement

We plan to marry on [date]. The purpose of this agreement is: [insert all that apply, or insert your own provisions]

✻ ☐ | to identify our premarital assets and debts,

✻ ☐ | to define our mutual rights and obligations regarding property and finances after we marry,

☐ | to support our estate plans through waiver of certain spousal rights,

☐ | to set forth our rights and obligations if we separate or divorce.

☐ | This agreement also covers [specify].

☑ **C. Current Circumstances**

[Woman's name] currently resides at [address]. Her occupation is [occupation]. She has [number] children: [names and ages]. [OPTIONAL: She is [age] and in good health]. [Insert optional additional information.]

[Man's name] currently resides at [address]. His occupation is [occupation]. He has [number] children: [names and ages]. [OPTIONAL: He is [age] and in good health]. [Insert optional additional information].

* ☐ **D. Future Plans**

[Insert any specific plans to relocate, change jobs, attend college, or similar matters.]

☑ **Paragraph 2: Effective Date and Term**

A. Effective Date of Agreement

This agreement will be effective on the day we marry. If we do not marry, this agreement will be null and void.

Choose one:

Alternative 1: Prenup Continues Indefinitely

* ☐ **B. Term of Agreement**

After we marry, this agreement will remain in full force and effect indefinitely, unless and until we sign a new written agreement revoking or modifying this agreement.

Alternative 2: Prenup Ends on a Specified Date (Retroactive)

☐ **B. Term of Agreement**

After we marry, this agreement will remain in full force and effect until [date when agreement will no longer apply], unless prior to that date we sign a new written agreement revoking or modifying this agreement. On [date when agreement will no longer apply] this agreement will be automatically terminated and it will no longer have any force and effect, unless we sign a new written agreement extending this agreement. After the automatic termination of this agreement, our rights and obligations will be governed by applicable laws as if we had never signed this agreement.

Alternative 3: Prenup Ends on a Specified Date (Not Retroactive)

☐ **B. Term of Agreement**

After we marry, this agreement will remain in full force and effect until [date when agreement will no longer apply], unless prior to that date we sign a new written agreement revoking or modifying this agreement. On [date when agreement will no longer apply] this agreement will be automatically terminated and it will no longer have any force and effect, unless we sign a new written agreement extending this agreement. After the automatic termination of this agreement, our rights and obligations will be governed by applicable laws without regard to the terms of this agreement, except that whatever property rights and obligations we have accrued by that date will not be retroactively affected. That is, any property defined by this agreement as separate property and any debt defined by this agreement as a separate debt shall remain separate, and any property or debts defined by this agreement as [marital OR community] property and debts shall remain so.

☑ **Paragraph 3: Legal Representation**

Choose one:

Alternative 1: Woman's Representative

* ☐ **A. Representation of [Woman's Name]**

[Woman's name] has been represented by [name of woman's attorney] in the negotiation and drafting of this agreement. [Woman's name] has fully discussed the terms of this agreement with her attorney and is voluntarily choosing to sign this agreement.

Alternative 2: Woman's Waiver of Independent Advice

☐ **A. Representation of [Woman's Name]**

[Woman's name] understands that she has a right to be represented by an independent attorney in the negotiation and drafting of this agreement. [Woman's name] does not want to be represented by an independent attorney, even though she has had ample time and has sufficient funds to hire an attorney. [Woman's name] understands the terms of this agreement and she is voluntarily choosing to sign this agreement without obtaining independent legal representation.

Choose one:

Alternative 1: Man's Representative

✳ ☐ **B. Representation of [Man's Name]**

[Man's name] has been represented by [name of man's attorney] in the negotiation and drafting of this agreement. [Man's name] has fully discussed the terms of this agreement with his attorney and is voluntarily choosing to sign this agreement.

Alternative 2: Man's Waiver of Independent Advice

☐ **B. Representation of [Man's Name]**

[Man's name] understands that he has a right to be represented by an independent attorney in the negotiation and drafting of this agreement. [Man's name] does not want to be represented by an independent attorney, even though he has had ample time and has sufficient funds to hire an attorney. [Man's name] understands the terms of this agreement and he is voluntarily choosing to sign this agreement without obtaining independent legal representation.

Choose one:

Alternative 1: Prenup Drafted Together

✳ ☐ **C. Drafting of Agreement**

This agreement was drafted through the joint efforts of [names].

Alternative 2: Prenup Not Drafted Together

☐ **C. Drafting of Agreement**

This agreement was drafted by [name].

☑ **Paragraph 4: Disclosures**

Choose one:

Alternative 1: Formal Written Disclosure

✳ ☐ **A. [Woman's Name]'s Disclosures**

All of [woman's name]'s assets [OPTIONAL: having a value greater than $_____] and all of her debts [OPTIONAL: exceeding $_____] are listed on Schedule 1, attached to this agreement. [Woman's name]'s income for the calendar year [insert year] [OPTIONAL: and the approximate amount of her personal expenses for that year] [is OR are] also listed on Schedule 1. [Woman's name] has provided the information on Schedule 1 in good faith. The values and other financial information on Schedule 1 are approximations and may not be exact, but they are intended to present a full, fair, and reasonable disclosure of [woman's name]'s assets, debts, income, and personal expenses as of the time they were presented to [man's name].

✳ ☐ **B. [Man's Name]'s Disclosures**

All of [man's name]'s assets [OPTIONAL: having a value greater than $_____] and all of his debts [OPTIONAL: exceeding $_____] are listed on Schedule 2, attached to this agreement. [Man's name]'s income for the calendar year [insert year] [OPTIONAL: and the approximate amount of his personal expenses for that year] [is OR are] also listed on Schedule 2. [Man's name] has provided the information on Schedule 2 in good faith. The values and other financial information on Schedule 2 are approximations and may not be exact, but they are intended to present a full, fair, and reasonable disclosure of [man's name]'s assets, debts, income, and personal expenses as of the time they were presented to [woman's name].

☐ **C. Documents Provided by [*Woman's Name*]**

In addition to the information listed on Schedule 1, [*woman's name*] has given [*man's name*] copies of the following documents [*list all documents that apply*]:

☐   1. Federal and state individual income tax returns filed by [*woman's name*] for the year(s) [*insert year(s)*].

☐   2. The following appraisals: [*for each appraisal, specify property appraised, date, and appraiser*].

☐   3. [*List any additional documents provided.*]

☐ **D. Documents Provided by [*Man's Name*]**

In addition to the information listed on Schedule 2, [*man's name*] has given [*woman's name*] copies of the following documents [*list all documents that apply*]:

☐   1. Federal and state individual income tax returns filed by [*man's name*] for the year(s) [*insert year(s)*].

☐   2. The following appraisals: [*for each appraisal, specify property appraised, date, and appraiser*].

☐   *3. [List any additional documents provided.*]

* ☐ **E. Acknowledgment of Receipt of Disclosures**

[*Woman's name*] received a copy of Schedule 2 [*INSERT IF APPLICABLE:* and the documents described in Paragraph 4C] on [*date*]. [*Woman's name*] reviewed this information before signing this agreement.

[*Man's name*] received a copy of Schedule 1 [*INSERT IF APPLICABLE:* and the documents described in Paragraph 4D] on [*date*]. [*Man's name*] reviewed this information before signing this agreement.

☐ **F. Mutual Waiver of Further Disclosure**

Each of us understands that the values and other information on Schedules 1 and 2 are approximate. We consider this information [*INSERT IF APPLICABLE:* and the documents described in Paragraphs 4C and 4D] sufficient and each of us voluntarily waives the right to be given any additional information.

Alternative 2: Waiver of Formal Written Disclosure

☐ **A. [*Woman's Name*]'s Waiver of Formal Written Disclosure**

[*Woman's name*] is aware of [*man's name*]'s financial circumstances. She voluntarily waives the right to be given a formal written disclosure or any other information about [*man's name*]'s finances.

B. [Man's Name]'s Waiver of Formal Written Disclosure

[*Man's Name*] is aware of [*woman's name*]'s financial circumstances. He voluntarily waives the right to be given a formal written disclosure or any other information about [*woman's name*]'s finances.

☑ **Paragraph 5: Definitions**

A. This Agreement

The term "this agreement" refers to the provisions of this document, once signed by us, as modified by any subsequent amendments in writing signed by us.

B. Separate Property

Any asset designated as one person's separate property in this agreement belongs exclusively to that person. A spouse has the sole right to manage and dispose of his or her separate property assets. Separate property is not subject to division between us if we divorce. However, if the owner of separate property dies, the surviving spouse may have a legal claim to it, unless he or she has signed a valid written waiver in this agreement or in another document.

Choose one:

Alternative 1

* ☐ **C. Marital Property**

An asset designated as marital property in this agreement may be subject to division between us by a court if we divorce, unless we provide otherwise in this agreement or in another document. Any asset designated as marital property may be subject to a claim by a surviving spouse, unless he or she has signed a valid written waiver of such claims in this agreement or in another document.

Add if applicable:

☐ We will both have equal rights to manage and control any martial property held in our joint names. If an asset designated as marital property is held in only one of our names, the sole owner will have the exclusive right to manage, control, transfer, or sell that property, to the extent allowed by state law.

Alternative 2

* ☐ **C. Community Property**

Any asset designated as community property in this agreement belongs to both of us equally. Our community property will be subject to division between us by a court if we divorce, taking into account any requirements for division spelled out in this agreement.

We will both have equal rights to manage and control any community property, subject to any exceptions provided by state law. [*OPTIONAL*: If an asset designated as community property is held in only one of our names, the sole title holder will have the exclusive right to manage, control, transfer, or sell that property, to the extent allowed by state law.]

* ☐ **D. Divorce**

The term "divorce" in this agreement refers to any legal proceeding to end or alter a marital relationship, including a proceeding for divorce, dissolution of marriage, legal separation or separate maintenance [*OPTIONAL:* , or annulment].

☑ **Paragraph 6: Ownership of Premarital Assets**

Choose one:

Alternative 1

* ☐ **A. All Premarital Assets and Property Traceable to Them Remain Separate Property**

Except as specified elsewhere in this agreement, [*woman's name*]'s premarital assets (which are listed on Schedule 1), and all property traceable to those assets, shall continue to be her separate property after we marry. "All property traceable to those assets" means any profits from or growth in value of those assets [including *OR* not including] profits or growth in value arising as a direct or indirect result of the efforts of one or both of us during our marriage. It also means any sales proceeds of those assets, any asset purchased with the sales proceeds, or any asset(s) acquired in exchange for those assets, as long as the sales proceeds or any such new asset is held in the sole name of [*woman's name*] [*ADD IF APPLICABLE:* or if held in joint names, as long as it is traceable to the premarital asset].

Except as specified elsewhere in this agreement, [*man's name*]'s premarital assets (which are listed on Schedule 2), and all property traceable to those assets, shall continue to be his separate property after we marry. "All property traceable to those assets" means any profits from or growth in value of those assets [including *OR* not including] profits or growth in value arising as a direct or indirect result of the efforts of one or both of us during our marriage. It also means any sales proceeds of those assets, any asset purchased with the sales proceeds, or any asset(s) acquired in exchange for those assets, as long as the sales proceeds or any such new asset is held in the sole name of [*man's name*] [*ADD IF APPLICABLE:* or if held in joint names, as long as it is traceable to the premarital asset].

Alternative 2

☐ **A. All Premarital Assets Remain Separate Property but Not Property Traceable to Them**

Except as specified elsewhere in this agreement, [*woman's name*]'s premarital assets, which are listed on Schedule 1, shall continue to be her separate property after we marry. However, all property traceable to those assets shall be considered [marital *OR* community] property. "All property traceable to those assets" means any profits from or growth in value of those assets, including profits or growth in value arising as a direct or indirect result of the efforts of one or both of us during our marriage. It also means any sales proceeds of those assets, any asset purchased with the sales proceeds, or any asset(s) acquired in exchange for those assets, even if the sales proceeds or any such new asset is held in the sole name of [*woman's name*].

Except as specified elsewhere in this agreement, [*man's name*]'s premarital assets, which are listed on Schedule 2, shall continue to be his separate property after we marry. However, all property traceable to those assets shall be considered [marital *OR* community] property. "All property traceable to those assets" means any profits from or growth in value of those assets, including profits or growth in value arising as a direct or indirect result of the efforts of one or both of us during our marriage. It also means any sales proceeds of those assets, any asset purchased with the sales proceeds, or any asset(s) acquired in exchange for those assets, even if the sales proceeds or any such new asset is held in the sole name of [*man's name*].

Alternative 3

☐ **A. All Premarital Assets Will Be Considered [Marital *OR* Community] Property**

Except as specified elsewhere in this agreement, all of our premarital assets, which are listed on Schedules 1 and 2, and all property traceable to those assets, will be considered [marital *OR* community] property as soon as we marry. "All property traceable to those assets" means any profits from or growth in value of those assets, including profits or growth in value arising as a direct or indirect result of the efforts of one or both of us during our marriage. It also means any sales proceeds of those assets, any asset purchased with the sales proceeds, or any asset(s) acquired in exchange for those assets, even if the sales proceeds or any such new asset is held in the sole name of one of us.

Optional Clause for Premarital Real Estate

Choose one:

Alternative 1

☐ **__. [Real Estate *OR Specify Certain Real Estate*] Will Remain Separate Property**

During our marriage, [*name*]'s real estate located at [*address*] shall continue to be [*name*]'s separate property after we marry [*IF IT IS A HOME YOU WILL LIVE IN TOGETHER, ADD:* regardless of whether we refer to it as "our" home and no matter how long we live there]. Use of [marital *OR* community] property funds to pay any mortgage payments, property taxes, insurance, improvements, repairs, or other expenses for the property will not alter the separate property nature of the home. Such payments will not be reimbursable to the [marital *OR* community] property estate unless we sign a written agreement expressly providing otherwise. [*OPTIONAL:* Any increase in the property's value shall also be [*name*]'s separate property. If [*name*] sells the property or exchanges it for another asset, any sales proceeds or asset acquired in exchange will be [his *OR* her] separate property.]

Alternative 2

☐ **__. Equity in [Real Estate *OR Specify Certain Real Estate*] Will Be Apportioned Between Separate Property and [Marital *OR* Community] Property**

The equity in [*name*]'s real estate located at [*address*], will be apportioned between [*name*]'s separate property and [marital *OR* community] property as follows: [*specify the percentage that will be separate property and the percentage that will be marital or community property, or the method to be used to apport the asset]. [ADD IF APPLICABLE: The above provisions will apply to any sales proceeds or assets acquired in exchange for the property during our marriage.]*

Alternative 3

☐ __. [Marital *OR* Community] Property Contributions to [Real Estate *OR Specify Certain Real Estate*] Will Be Reimbursed

If [marital *OR* community] property funds are used to pay for certain expenses related to [name]'s real estate located at [address], the property will remain [name]'s separate property, but the [marital *OR* community] property payments will be reimbursed as follows: [*specify how and when the reimbursement would be payable, such as all or one-half of what was paid, with or without interest, to the estate or to the nonowner, upon death and/or upon divorce. If applicable, cross-refer to any paragraphs relating to estate planning or divorce].* The reimbursable expenses referred to in this clause shall include only payments for [*specify types of payments that qualify, such as payments reducing the principal balance owed on a mortgage, mortgage interest, property taxes, repairs, or capital improvements*].

Alternative 4

☐ __. [Real Estate *OR Specify Certain Real Estate*] Will Become [Marital *OR* Community] Property

[Name]'s real estate located at [address] will become [marital *OR* community] property [*specify when this will happen, such as on a certain date or "as soon as we marry"*].

Optional Clause for a Premarital Business

Choose one:

Alternative 1

☐ __. Premarital [Business *OR* Professional Practice] Will Remain Separate Property

During our marriage, [name] plans to continue to operate the [business *OR* professional practice] known as [name of business or professional practice]. The [business *OR* professional practice] shall continue to be [name]'s separate property after we marry. Any increase in its value shall also be [name]'s separate property, regardless of how we refer to it or how much time either or both of us devotes to it. If [name] sells the [business *OR* practice] or exchanges it for another asset, any sales proceeds or asset acquired in exchange will be [his *OR* her] separate property.

Alternative 2

☐ __. Premarital [Business *OR* Professional Practice] Will Be Subject to Apportionment Between Separate and [Marital *OR* Community] Property

During our marriage, [name] plans to continue to operate the [business *OR* professional practice] known as [name of business or professional practice]. After we marry, the [business *OR* practice] will be subject to apportionment between [name]'s separate property and [marital *OR* community] property as follows: [*specify the method to be used to apportion the asset*]. [ADD IF APPLICABLE: If the [business *OR* practice] is sold during our marriage, the above provisions will apply to apportionment of any sales proceeds.]

Optional Clause for Premarital Retirement Benefits

Choose one:

Alternative 1

☐ __. Premarital Retirement Benefits Will Be Separate Property

All retirement benefits earned by (or in the name of) one of us before we marry, as listed on Schedules 1 and 2, will be the separate property of the person who earned them or in whose name those benefits are vested. This applies to all benefits in all retirement, pension, deferred compensation, and other employee benefit or tax deferred plans, whether qualified according to IRS regulations or nonqualified.

Each of us hereby waives any legal claim he or she may have now or in the future regarding the other person's premarital retirement benefits referred to above. Each of us understands that this waiver may not be effective under applicable laws unless reaffirmed after we marry in a written waiver in a form approved by the retirement plan. Therefore we agree that after we marry, upon request by the other party, each of us will sign any document necessary to carry out the intent of this clause, including a written waiver in a form approved by the retirement plan.

Alternative 2

___. Premarital Retirement Benefits Will Be [Marital *OR* Community] Property

All retirement benefits earned by (or in the name of) one of us before we marry, as listed on Schedules 1 and 2, will be considered [marital *OR* community] property. This applies to all benefits in all retirement, pension, deferred compensation, and other employee benefit or tax deferred plans, whether qualified according to IRS regulations or nonqualified.

Each of us understands that under applicable laws title to any retirement account or benefit can be held in the name of only one person, and that the written consent of both spouses may be required prior to making any election of benefits under a retirement plan. We agree that after we marry, upon request by the other party, each of us will sign any document necessary to carry out the intent of this clause.

Optional Clauses for Other Premarital Assets

Choose all that apply:

Alternative 1

☐ ___. Certain Premarital Assets Will Remain Separate Property

The following premarital asset(s) will remain the separate property of the spouse who owns the asset(s) prior to marriage and will not be converted to [marital *OR* community] property when we marry: [*for each person, list each asset from Schedules 1 or 2 to which this applies*].

Alternative 2

☐ ___. Certain Premarital Assets Will Be Apportioned Between Separate and [Marital *OR* Community] Property

The following premarital asset(s) will be apportioned between [name]'s separate property and [marital *OR* community] property [*as soon as we marry OR specify when this will take effect*] as follows: [*for each person, list each asset from Schedules 1 or 2 to which this applies, and specify the method to be used to apportion the asset(s)*]. [*ADD IF APPLICABLE:* If any asset listed in this clause is sold during our marriage, the above provisions will apply to apportionment of any sales proceeds.]

Alternative 3

☐ ___. Certain Premarital Assets Will Become [Marital *OR* Community] Property

The following premarital assets will become [marital *OR* community] property [*as soon as we marry OR specify when this will take effect*]: [*list the assets from Schedules 1 or 2 to which this applies*].

☑ Paragraph 7: Rights in Assets Acquired During Marriage

Choose one:

Alternative 1

✳ ☐ A. Our Rights in Assets Acquired During Marriage Will Be Determined According to State Law

Except as specified elsewhere in this agreement, our rights in every asset acquired after we marry, and in any profits or growth in value or any sales proceeds or asset acquired in exchange for those assets, will be determined in accordance with the laws of [*name of state*].

Alternative 2

☐ **A. Our Rights in Assets Acquired During Marriage Will Be Determined According to How Title Is Held**

Except as specified elsewhere in this agreement, every asset acquired after we marry, and any profits or growth in value or any sales proceeds or asset acquired in exchange for those assets, will be owned as specified in the document of title. If an asset is tangible personal property that does not have a document of title, the person who paid for the asset will be the owner.

Each of us understands that if it were not for this agreement, certain assets acquired during our marriage might be considered [marital OR community] property despite the name in which title is held, and we knowingly agree to waive our [marital OR community] rights in such assets and be bound by this agreement instead, unless a [marital OR community] property form of ownership is specified in the title.

Alternative 3

☐ **A. All Property to Be Separate—No [Marital OR Community] Property Rights Accrue**

We intend to own all property acquired during our marriage, including property acquired in joint names, as separate property and not as [marital OR community] property, as if we were unmarried. Each of us understands that if it were not for this agreement, certain assets acquired during our marriage might be considered [marital OR community] property despite the name in which title is held, and we knowingly agree to be bound by this agreement instead.

Alternative 4

☐ **A. Assets Acquired During Marriage Will Be [Marital OR Community] Property**

Except as specified elsewhere in this agreement, every asset acquired by one or both of us after we marry will be considered [marital OR community] property, regardless of how title is held. Each of us understands that if it were not for this agreement, certain assets acquired in the name of only one person during our marriage might be considered separate property of the person in whose name it is held, and we knowingly agree to be bound by this agreement instead.

Alternative 5

☐ **A. Our Rights in Assets Acquired During Marriage Will Be Apportioned**

Except as specified elsewhere in this agreement, our rights in every asset acquired during our marriage in the name of one or both of us, and any profits or growth in value or any sales proceeds or asset acquired in exchange for that asset, will be apportioned between us, according to the following formula: [insert formula].

Optional Clause for Income

Choose one:

Alternative 1

☐ **___. All Income Will Be [Marital OR Community] Property**

Except as specified elsewhere in this agreement, our wages and other earned or unearned income will be considered [marital OR community] property. This clause applies to wages or income earned during our marriage even if received at a later time. It also applies to unearned income such as dividends, interest, rents, and partnership distributions received during our marriage.

Alternative 2

☐ **___. All Income Will Be Separate Property**

Except as specified elsewhere in this agreement, our wages and other earned or unearned income will be considered the separate property of the person who earned or received the income. This clause applies to wages or income earned during our marriage even if received at a later time. It also applies to unearned income such as dividends, interest, rents, and partnership distributions received during our marriage.

Alternative 3

☐ **__. Earned Income Will Be [Marital OR Community] Property; Unearned Income Will Be Separate Property**

Except as specified elsewhere in this agreement, our wages and other income earned during our marriage, even if received at a later time, will be considered [marital OR community] property. Except as specified elsewhere in this agreement, all unearned income such as dividends, interest, rents, and partnership distributions received during our marriage will be considered the separate property of the person who received the income,

Choose one:

☐ provided that any unearned income derived from an asset held in our joint names shall be owned by us in the same manner and proportions as the asset from which it is derived is owned.

OR ☐ provided that any unearned income derived from an asset held in our joint names shall be considered [marital OR community] property.

Alternative 4

☐ **__. Earned Income Will Be Separate Property; Unearned Income Will Be [Marital OR Community] Property**

Except as specified elsewhere in this agreement, our wages or other income earned during our marriage, even if received at a later time, will be considered the separate property of the person who earned or received the income. Except as specified elsewhere in this agreement, all unearned income such as dividends, interest, rents, and partnership distributions received during our marriage will be considered [marital OR community] property.

Optional Clause for Inheritances

Choose one:

Alternative 1

☐ **__. Inheritances Received by One Party During Marriage Will Be Separate Property**

If one of us receives an asset as an inheritance, bequest, trust distribution, or other death benefit during our marriage, that asset will be his or her separate property.

Choose one:

☐ Any profits or growth in value or any sales proceeds or assets acquired in exchange for a separate property inheritance described above will also be separate property.

OR ☐ However, any profits or growth in value or any sales proceeds or assets acquired in exchange for a separate property inheritance described above will be considered [marital OR community] property.

Alternative 2

☐ **__. Inheritances Received by One Party During Marriage Will Be [Marital OR Community] Property**

If one of us receives an asset as an inheritance, bequest, trust distribution, or other death benefit during our marriage, that asset will be [marital OR community] property. Any profits or growth in value, and any sales proceeds or assets acquired in exchange for that asset will also be [marital OR community] property.

Optional Clause for Gifts

Choose one:

Alternative 1

☐ **__. Gifts Received During Marriage Will Be Separate Property**

Except as specified elsewhere in this agreement, any asset received by one us during our marriage as a gift from a third party or from the other spouse will be the separate property of the spouse who receives the gift.

Any gift given to both of us jointly will be owned by us jointly in equal separate property shares unless at the time of making the gift the person making the gift specifies in writing a different percentage of ownership.

Choose one:

☐ Any profits or growth in value or any sales proceeds or assets acquired in exchange for a separate property gift described above will also be separate property.

OR ☐ However, any profits or growth in value or any sales proceeds or asset acquired in exchange for a separate property gift described above will be considered [marital OR community] property.

Alternative 2

☐ __. Gifts Received During Marriage Will Be [Marital OR Community] Property

Except as specified elsewhere in this agreement, any asset received by one of us during our marriage as a gift from a third party or from the other spouse, and any gift given to both of us jointly, will be [marital OR community] property. Any profits or growth in value or any sales proceeds or assets acquired in exchange for that asset will also be [marital OR community] property.

Alternative 3

☐ __. Third-Party Gifts Will Be Separate Property; Interspousal Gifts Will Be [Marital OR Community] Property

Except as specified elsewhere in this agreement, any asset received by one of us during our marriage as a gift from a third party will be the separate property of the spouse who receives the gift. Any gift given to both of us jointly will owned by us jointly in equal separate property shares unless at the time of the gift the person making the gift specifies in writing a different percentage of ownership.

Except as specified elsewhere in this agreement, any asset received by one of us during our marriage as a gift from the other spouse will be [marital OR community] property, unless at the time of the gift the spouse making the gift specifies in writing that the gift is intended to be the separate property of the receiving spouse.

Choose one:

☐ Any profits or growth in value or any sales proceeds or assets acquired in exchange for a separate property gift described above will also be separate property.

OR ☐ However, any profits or growth in value or any sales proceeds or asset acquired in exchange for a separate property gift described above will be considered [marital OR community] property.

Alternative 4

☐ __. Third-Party Gifts Will Be [Marital OR Community] Property; Interspousal Gifts Will Be Separate Property

Except as specified elsewhere in this agreement, any asset received by one of us during our marriage as a gift from a third party, and any gift given to both of us jointly, will be [marital OR community] property. Any profits or growth in value or any sales proceeds or assets acquired in exchange for that asset will also be [marital OR community] property.

Except as specified elsewhere in this agreement, any asset received by one of us during our marriage as a gift from the other spouse will be the separate property of the spouse who receives the gift.

Choose one:

☐ Any profits or growth in value or any sales proceeds or assets acquired in exchange for a separate property gift described above will also be separate property.

OR ☐ However, any profits or growth in value or any sales proceeds or asset acquired in exchange for a separate property gift described above will be considered [marital OR community] property.

Optional Clause for Joint Accounts

Choose one:

Alternative 1

☐ **___. Joint Accounts Will Be [Marital *OR* Community] Property**

Any funds deposited into a joint bank or other deposit account established by and between us will be considered [marital *OR* community] property, even if one or both of us deposits separate property funds into the account.

Choose one:

☐ There will be no right of reimbursement for any separate property funds deposited into a joint account unless we expressly agree in writing to a right of reimbursement regarding a particular account or specific deposit.

OR ☐ Whoever deposits separate property funds into a joint account will have a right of reimbursement for the amount of the funds contributed unless he or she signs a written waiver of the right to be reimbursed. Any reimbursement owed shall be payable as follows: [*specify how and when the reimbursement is payable— for example, at certain times of year, upon death or divorce, with or without interest; if applicable, cross-refer to paragraphs relating to estate planning or divorce*].

Alternative 2

☐ **___. Joint Accounts Will Consist of Shares of Separate Property**

If a bank or other deposit account is acquired by us jointly (in both of our names), each of us will own an undivided share of the funds in the account as separate property and not as [marital *OR* community] property, as follows: [*specify each person's percentage or the method to be used to determine percentages, such as equal shares or in proportion to the total amount contributed by each spouse to the account*].

This clause shall apply to any joint account, even if we deposit [marital *OR* community] property funds into the account, unless we sign a separate written agreement expressly specifying a different form or percentage of ownership regarding a particular account.

Choose one:

☐ There will be no right of reimbursement for deposits of any [marital *OR* community] property funds unless we expressly agree in writing to a right of reimbursement regarding a particular account or a specific deposit.

OR ☐ There will be a right of reimbursement for any deposit of [marital *OR* community] property funds unless the spouse who did not make the deposit of [marital *OR* community] property funds signs a written waiver of the right to be reimbursed. Any reimbursement owed shall be payable as follows: [*specify how and when the reimbursement is payable—for example, at certain times of year, upon death or upon divorce, with or without interest; if applicable, cross-refer to paragraphs relating to estate planning or divorce*].

Optional Clause for Retirement Benefits

Choose one:

Alternative 1

☐ **___. Retirement Benefits Earned During Marriage Will Be Separate Property**

All retirement benefits earned by (or in the name of) one of us during our marriage will be the separate property of the person in whose name those benefits are vested. This applies to all benefits in all retirement, pension, deferred compensation, and other employee benefit or tax deferred plans, whether qualified according to IRS regulations or nonqualified.

Each of us hereby waives any legal claim he or she would otherwise have to the other person's retirement benefits referred to above. Each of us understands that this waiver may not be effective under applicable laws unless reaffirmed after we marry in a written waiver in a form approved by the retirement plan. We agree that after we marry, upon request by the other party, each of us will sign any document necessary to carry out the intent of this clause, including a written waiver in a form approved by the retirement plan.

Alternative 2

☐ __. **Retirement Benefits Earned During Marriage Will Be [Marital *OR* Community] Property**

All retirement benefits earned by (or in the name of) one of us during our marriage will be considered [marital *OR* community] property. This applies to all benefits in all retirement, pension, deferred compensation, and other employee benefit or tax deferred plans, whether qualified according to IRS regulations or nonqualified.

Each of us understands that under applicable laws title to any retirement account or benefit can be held in the name of only one person, and that the written consent of both spouses may be required prior to making any election of benefits under a retirement plan. We agree that after we marry, upon request by the other party, each of us will sign any document necessary to carry out the intent of this clause.

Optional Clause for Certain Assets

Choose one:

Alternative 1

☐ __. **[Certain Assets *OR* Insert Name of Asset(s)] Will Be Separate Property**

After we marry, [*name*] [plans to *OR* may] acquire [certain assets or types of assets *OR* insert the name of the asset, such as "a home"]. [Any such asset *OR* asset name] might otherwise be [marital *OR* community] property, but instead will be [*name*]'s separate property. [*ADD IF APPLICABLE:* This also applies to any profits or increase in value or any sales proceeds or assets acquired in exchange for [any such asset *OR* asset name]. [*IF SPECIFIC ASSET COVERED IS NOT INSERTED ABOVE, ADD:* The assets or types of assets to which this applies are listed below:

[*Insert list of assets or types of assets that will be separate property and insert any additional conditions that apply.*]

Alternative 2

☐ __. **[Certain Assets *OR* Insert Name of Asset(s)] Will Be [Marital *OR* Community] Property**

After we marry, we [plan to *OR* may] acquire [certain assets or types of assets *OR* insert the name of the asset, such as "a home"]. [Any such asset *OR* asset name] might otherwise be separate property but instead will be considered [marital *OR* community] property. [*ADD IF APPLICABLE:* This also applies to any profits or increase in value or any sales proceeds or assets acquired in exchange for [any such asset *OR* asset name.] [*IF SPECIFIC ASSET COVERED IS NOT INSERTED ABOVE, ADD:* The assets or types of asset to which this applies are listed below:

[*Insert list of assets or types of assets that will be considered marital or community property and insert any additional conditions that apply.*]

Optional Clauses for Contributions of Separate Property to Marital Assets

Choose all that apply:

Alternative 1

☐ __. **Contributions of Separate Property to [Marital *OR* Community] Property: Ownership Will Be Apportioned**

During our marriage, one or both of us may contribute separate property funds to the acquisition or improvement of [*OPTIONAL:* or payment of other expenses related to] [marital *OR* community] property. If so, ownership of any such property will be apportioned between separate property and [marital *OR* community] property as follows: [*specify the percentages that will be separate property and marital or community property, or the method to be used to apportion the asset*]. [*ADD IF APPLICABLE:* There will be no apportionment for separate property funds paid for expenses related to community property other than for acquisition or improvement of the property.]

Alternative 2

☐ __. **Separate Property Contributions to [Marital *OR* Community] Property Will Be Reimbursed**

During our marriage, one or both of us may contribute separate property funds to acquire or improve [*OPTIONAL:* or to pay other expenses related to] [marital *OR* community] property. In the absence of a contrary written agreement, we will consider any such contribution to be subject to a right of reimbursement payable as follows: [*specify how and when the reimbursement would be payable—for example, at certain times of year, upon death or divorce, with or without interest; if applicable, cross-refer to paragraphs relating to estate planning or divorce*]. The reimbursable contributions referred to in this clause shall include only payments for [*specify types of payments that qualify, such as down payments, payments reducing the principal balance owed on a mortgage or other financing, interest and finance charges, property taxes, repairs, or capital improvements*].

Alternative 3

☐ __. **Waiver of Reimbursement for Separate Property Contributions**

During our marriage, one or both of us may contribute separate property funds to acquire or improve [*OPTIONAL:* or to pay other expenses related to] [marital *OR* community] property. In the absence of a contrary written agreement, we will consider any such contribution to be a gift of separate property. Neither of us shall be entitled to reimbursement for any such contribution, and each of us hereby waives any right to reimbursement otherwise granted by law.

☑ Paragraph 8: Responsibility for Debts and Expenses

Choose all that apply:

✳ ☐ __. **Each Person Solely Responsible for Own Premarital Debts**

[*Woman's name*]'s debts listed on Schedule 1 are her sole and separate debts. [*Man's name*] will not be responsible for them, nor may his separate property [*ADD IF APPLICABLE:* or his share of any [marital *OR* community] property] be used to pay them without his written consent. [*Woman's name*] will indemnify and hold [*man's name*] harmless from any proceeding to collect on [*woman's name*]'s debts from [*man's name*]'s property, and she will be solely responsible for any expenses, including attorney's fees, incurred by [*man's name*] in connection with such a proceeding.

[*Man's name*]'s debts listed on Schedule 2 are his sole and separate debts. [*Woman's name*] will not be responsible for them, nor may her separate property [*ADD IF APPLICABLE:* or her share of any [marital *OR* community] property] be used to pay them without her written consent. [*Man's name*] will indemnify and hold [*woman's name*] harmless from any proceeding to collect on [*man's name*]'s debts from [*woman's name*]'s property, and he will be solely responsible for any expenses, including attorney's fees, incurred by [*woman's name*] in connection with such a proceeding.

☐ __. **Each Spouse Solely Responsible for Debts Incurred by That Spouse During Marriage**

Except as specified elsewhere in this agreement, all debts incurred by [*woman's name*] in her sole name during our marriage will be her sole and separate debts. [*Man's name*] will not be responsible for them, nor may his separate property [*ADD IF APPLICABLE:* or his share of any [marital *OR* community] property] be used to pay them without his written consent. [*Woman's name*] will indemnify and hold [*man's name*] harmless from any proceeding to collect on [*woman's name*]'s debts from [*man's name*]'s property, and she will be solely responsible for any expenses, including attorney's fees, incurred by [man's name] in connection with such a proceeding.

Except as specified elsewhere in this agreement, all debts incurred by [man's name] in his sole name during our marriage will be his sole and separate debts. [Woman's name] will not be responsible for them, nor may her separate property [ADD IF APPLICABLE: or her share of any [marital OR community] property] be used to pay them without her written consent. [Man's name] will indemnify and hold [woman's name] harmless from any proceeding to collect on [man's name]'s debts from [woman's name]'s property, and he will be solely responsible for any expenses, including attorney's fees, incurred by [woman's name] in connection with such a proceeding.

☐ __. **Debts Incurred During Marriage for Mutual Benefit Will Be [Marital OR Community] Debts**

Any debt incurred by either or both of us for our mutual benefit during our marriage will be considered a [marital OR community] debt and will be paid from [marital OR community] property funds. A debt will be considered incurred for our mutual benefit if it covers any of the following expenses: [insert the types of expenses included]; but not the following expenses: [insert expenses not included]. If one of us uses his or her separate property funds to pay all or part of the debt, he or she [will OR will not] be entitled to be reimbursed from [marital OR community] property funds. [If separate property funds are to be reimbursed, specify how and when the reimbursement is to be made.]

☐ __. **Taxes**

We agree to confer each year prior to the deadline for filing federal [ADD IF APPLICABLE: and state] income tax returns for the preceding year in order to determine whether it is to our mutual advantage to file joint or separate returns. We will determine this by preparing draft joint and separate returns and then comparing the overall taxes that would be due on the joint and separate draft returns. Each of us will provide all information necessary to prepare the draft returns.

If we agree that it is to our mutual benefit to file joint returns, we will do so. Any taxes owed on joint returns, and any accountant's fees or other expenses incurred in preparing the draft and final returns, will be [paid from joint funds OR shared equally OR paid by [name] OR specify some other method for allocation]. Any refund received shall be [shared equally OR paid to [name] OR specify some other method for allocation].

If we file separately:

1. Our income and deductions will be allocated as follows [include all that apply; letter sequentially]:

☐ a. Any unearned income, gain, loss, or credit from any investment in joint names will be allocated between us according to our percentage of ownership;

☐ b. Any unearned income, gain, loss, or credit from any investment that is [marital OR community] property will be allocated equally;

☐ c. Any earned income together with any unearned income from separate investments will be allocated to the person who earned the income or whose separate investment produced the unearned income;

☐ d. Any deductible expense paid from [marital OR community] property funds will be allocated between us [equally OR specify allocation];

☐ e. Any deductible expense paid from separate funds will be allocated to the person from whose funds they were paid.

☐ 2. Any taxes owed on any separate return will be paid by the person filing the separate return. Any refund on any separate return will be paid to the person filing the separate return. Any accountant's fees or other expenses incurred in preparing the draft and final returns will be [paid by [*name*] *OR* shared equally *OR specify how the expenses will be paid or allocated*].

Add if applicable:

☐ 3. If one of us elects to file separate returns and the other does not, and if this results in greater taxes for the other person than he or she would have owed on a joint return for the same year, [the person who elected to file separately will pay the additional amount owed by the other party *OR* the additional amount owed will be paid from joint funds].

☐ **__. [*Name OR* Each Spouse] Solely Responsible for Own Business Debts**

Choose one or both:

☐ All debts incurred by [*woman's name*] in connection with [*name of her business*] before or during our marriage will be her sole and separate debts. [*Man's name*] will not be responsible for them, nor may his separate property [*ADD IF APPLICABLE:* or his share of any [marital *OR* community] property] be used to pay them without his written consent. [*Woman's name*] will indemnify and hold [*man's name*] harmless from any proceeding to collect on [*woman's name*]'s debts from [*man's name*]'s property, and she will be solely responsible for any expenses, including attorney's fees, incurred by [*man's name*] in connection with such a proceeding.

☐ All debts incurred by [*man's name*] in connection with [*name of his business*] before or during our marriage will be his sole and separate debts. [*Woman's name*] will not be responsible for them, nor may her separate property [*ADD IF APPLICABLE:* or her share of any [marital *OR* community] property] be used to pay them without her written consent. [*Man's name*] will indemnify and hold [*woman's name*] harmless from any proceeding to collect on [*man's name*]'s debts from [woman's name]'s property, and he will be solely responsible for any expenses, including attorney's fees, incurred by [*woman's name*] in connection with such a proceeding.

Optional Clause for Payment of Household Expenses

Choose one:

Alternative 1

☐ **__. Household Expenses Will Be Paid by [*Name*]**

[*Name*] will be responsible for paying all reasonable household expenses from [his *OR* her] [earnings *OR* separate funds]. Household expenses will include [*specify included expenses*], but will not include [*specify any excluded expenses*]. [*ADD IF APPLICABLE:* For convenience, we will establish a joint checking account into which [*name*] will deposit [sufficient funds *OR specify amount*] per month to cover the regular household expenses, plus additional amounts as necessary to cover extraordinary household expenses. Either one of us may write checks on the joint account to pay for household expenses. [*Name*] will be responsible for balancing and reconciling the joint account on a regular basis.] [*ADD IF APPLICABLE:* The household expenses listed above include reasonable living expenses for [*name*]'s children, [*names of children*], while they are living with us. [*Name*] will deposit [all *OR specify amount or percentage*] of any child support payments received into the account established for payment of household expenses.]

Alternative 2

☐ **__. Household Expenses Will Be Shared**

We will be responsible for paying all reasonable household expenses on [an equal *OR* a pro rata] basis. [*ADD IF PRO RATA:* [*Name*]'s share will be [*specify percentage*] and [*name*]'s share will be [*specify percentage.*] Household expenses will include [*specify included expenses*], but will not include [*specify excluded expenses*].

Add if applicable:

☐ For convenience, we will establish a joint checking account into which we will each deposit every month our share of [an amount we will agree upon from time to time OR specify amount] to cover the regular household expenses, plus additional amounts as necessary to cover extraordinary household expenses. Either one of us may write checks on the joint account to pay for household expenses. [Name] will be responsible for balancing the joint account on a regular basis.

Add if applicable:

☐ The household expenses listed above include reasonable living expenses for [name]'s children, [names of children], while they are living with us. [Name] will deposit [all OR specify an amount or percentage] of any child support payments received into the account established for payment of household expenses.

☑ **Paragraph __: Interpretation, Modification, Review, and Enforcement of This Agreement**

A. Entire Agreement

This agreement contains our entire agreement on the matters covered. Any oral representations made concerning this agreement shall be of no force or effect. [OPTIONAL: This agreement supersedes any written or oral agreements or understandings between us prior to the date of this agreement. Each of us hereby waives any and all claims we may have against the other arising out of our cohabitation prior to the date of our marriage.]

B. Binding Effect

Once we sign this agreement, it shall be binding on us and our respective inheritors and estate representatives.

C. Commitment to Carry Out This Agreement

Each of us shall take any steps that are reasonably necessary to carry out the terms and intent of this Agreement, including signing, notarizing, and delivering any necessary documents, upon request by the other party.

D. Modification of This Agreement

This agreement may be modified only by a subsequent written agreement signed by both of us. Any oral or written statements made by us (other than express representations in a subsequent written agreement), including but not limited to statements referring to separate property as "ours" or to [marital OR community] property as "mine," "yours," "his," or "hers" will be only for convenience and will not be deemed to modify this agreement in any way. The filing of joint or separate tax returns during our marriage will not be deemed to modify this agreement in any way.

E. Voluntary Transfers and Restoration of Rights

Nothing in this agreement prevents either of us from making a voluntary transfer of an interest in property to the other party, and any such transfer, once completed, shall be deemed a gift.

During our marriage, or upon death, either of us is free to restore to the other party any legal right waived in this agreement.

Absent an express written agreement modifying this agreement, any voluntary transfer or restoration of a right will not be deemed an amendment of this agreement nor a waiver of the terms of this agreement.

F. Interpretation and Choice of Law

This agreement has been drafted and entered into in the State of [*state name*]. It shall be interpreted fairly and simply, and enforced according to the laws of [*state name*]. A copy of the signed agreement may be submitted to the court and admitted into evidence in place of the original in any proceeding to enforce or interpret this agreement.

G. Severability

If any part of this agreement is determined by a court to be invalid, illegal, or unenforceable, the validity and enforceability of the remaining parts of this agreement shall not be affected.

H. Attorneys' Fees

In any proceeding to enforce or interpret the terms of this agreement, the prevailing party shall be entitled to recover his or her reasonable expenses incurred in connection with the proceeding, including reasonable attorneys' fees.

Optional Clauses for Periodic Reviews and Dispute Resolution

Choose all that apply:

☐ **__. Periodic Reviews**

We agree to review the terms of this agreement [*specify frequency*].

☐ **__. Mediation of Disputes**

If any dispute arises between us concerning terms of this agreement, we will first try to resolve the dispute in mediation with a qualified mediator acceptable to both of us. The expenses of mediation shall be equally shared between us. The mediation sessions shall be confidential, and neither of us may subpoena the records of the mediator or call the mediator as a witness in any arbitration or other legal proceeding between us.

☐ **__. Arbitration of Disputes**

[If any dispute arises between us concerning this agreement *OR* If a dispute between us concerning this agreement cannot be resolved in mediation], we agree to submit the dispute to [advisory *OR* binding] arbitration within fifteen (15) days after either of us makes a written demand. If we cannot agree upon an arbitrator, each of us shall appoint one person and the persons so appointed shall select the arbitrator. Participation in arbitration or a waiver of arbitration by both of us shall be a prerequisite to any legal action brought by either of us concerning the matters covered by this agreement, unless applicable law prohibits arbitration of the disputed issue(s).

☑ ## Paragraph __: Signatures, Attorneys' Certifications, and Acknowledgments

Each of us has read this agreement carefully and is signing it freely after obtaining all advice he or she considers appropriate.

Dated: _____   _____
                            [*Name*]

Dated: _____   _____
                            [*Name*]

* ☐

Certificate of Attorney for [*Woman's Name*]

I certify, as attorney for [wo*man's name*] only, that she has freely and voluntarily signed the attached premarital agreement. I have advised her about the legal effects of the terms of this agreement, and she has had a full opportunity to discuss it with me and with any other advisors of her own choosing. I believe that she has been fully advised and that she is aware of all the legal effects of this agreement.

Dated: _____   _____
                            [*Attorney's Name*]

* ☐

Certificate of Attorney for [*Man's Name*]

I certify, as attorney for [*man's name*] only, that he has freely and voluntarily signed the attached premarital agreement. I have advised him about the legal effects of the terms of this agreement, and he has had a full opportunity to discuss it with me and with any other advisors of his own choosing. I believe that he has been fully advised and that he is aware of all the legal effects of this agreement.

Dated: _____   _____
                            [*Attorney's Name*]

*　☐

Certificate of Acknowledgment of Notary Public

State of _____

County of _____ } ss

On _____, before me, _____,

personally appeared _____,

personally known to me or proved to me on the basis of satisfactory evidence to be the person whose name is subscribed to the within instrument, and acknowledged to me that he/she executed the same and that by his/her signature on the instrument he/she executed the instrument.

WITNESS my hand and official seal.

[NOTARIAL SEAL]

_____

Notary Public for the state of _____

My commission expires _____

Certificate of Acknowledgment of Notary Public

State of _____

County of _____ } ss

On _____, before me, _____,

personally appeared _____,

personally known to me or proved to me on the basis of satisfactory evidence to be the person whose name is subscribed to the within instrument, and acknowledged to me that he/she executed the same and that by his/her signature on the instrument he/she executed the instrument.

WITNESS my hand and official seal.

[NOTARIAL SEAL]

_____

Notary Public for the state of _____

My commission expires _____

C. Optional Paragraphs—Insert After Paragraph 8, Above

☐ **Paragraph __: Estate Planning Matters**

Optional Clause for Waiver of Surviving Spouse Rights

Choose one:

Alternative 1

☐ **__. Mutual Waiver of Rights in Each Other's Estate—Complete Waiver**

Each of us waives and forever gives up any and all right or claim that he or she may acquire in the separate property of the other person due to our marriage, including but not limited to:

1. Rights or claims of dower, curtesy, or any substitute for those rights or claims provided by any applicable state statute at the time of the other person's death;

2. The right of election to take against the will of the other;

3. The right to a share in the separate property estate of the other person if he or she dies without a will;

4. The right to act as administrator of the estate of the other;

5. The right to a probate homestead or homestead allowance;

6. The right to a family allowance and to a personal property allowance.

Nothing in this agreement shall be deemed to constitute a waiver by either of us of any gift that the other person might choose to make to him or her by will or other estate planning document, or to act as executor designated in the will of the other. However, we acknowledge that no promises of any kind have been made by either of us to the other person regarding any such gift or designation, except for any specific provisions included in this agreement.

Alternative 2

☐ **__. Mutual Waiver of Rights in Each Other's Estate—Partial Waiver**

Each of us waives and forever gives up the following rights or claims that he or she may acquire in the separate property of the other person due to our marriage:

Choose all that apply:

☐ 1. Rights or claims of dower, curtesy, or any substitute for those rights or claims provided by any applicable state statute at the time of the other person's death;

☐ 2. The right of election to take against the will of the other;

☐ 3. The right to a share in the separate property estate of the other person if he or she dies without a will;

☐ 4. The right to act as administrator of the estate of the other;

☐ 5. The right to a probate homestead or homestead allowance;

☐ 6. The right to a family allowance and to a personal property allowance.

Add if applicable:

☐ Nothing in this agreement shall be deemed to constitute a waiver by either of us of any gift that the other person might choose to make to him or her by will or other estate planning document, or to act as executor designated in the will of the other. However, we acknowledge that no promises of any kind have been made by either of us to the other person regarding any such gift or designation, except for any specific provisions included in this agreement.

Additional Estate Planning Clauses

Choose all that apply:

☐ __. **Provision for [*Name*] Upon [*Name*]'s Death**

Upon [*name*]'s death, if no proceeding for divorce, dissolution, legal separation, or annulment is pending at the date of death, [*name*] shall be entitled to receive the following distribution(s) from [*name*]'s estate:

Choose all that apply:

☐ A lump sum payment of $ [*insert amount*].

☐ An amount equal to [*percentage*]% of [*name*]'s gross estate. The term "gross estate" as used here does not include life insurance proceeds, retirement benefits, or other death benefits payable on the death of [*name*].

☐ An amount based on the following formula: [*insert formula*].

☐ An amount based on the following formula: [*insert formula*].

☐ The following described property: [*insert property description*].

Add if applicable:

☐ In addition, [*name*] shall be entitled to [*insert any other agreed provision, such as a life estate, payments for a certain period of time, or a right to use or occupy certain property*].

☐ At all times during our marriage, [*name of person whose estate is responsible*] shall maintain in full force and effect a valid will, trust, or other estate planning document that includes the foregoing provisions.

☐ __. **Estate Plans to Be Consistent With This Agreement**

We acknowledge the importance of making valid estate plans that are consistent with this agreement. Therefore, as soon as possible after our marriage, each of us will establish and maintain in effect a valid will, trust, or other estate planning document or combination of documents that will be consistent with, and will carry out the terms of, this agreement. We further agree to review our estate plans periodically to ensure that our estate planning documents remain consistent with this agreement and to modify our estate planning documents if necessary to keep them consistent with this agreement.

☐ **Paragraph __: Property Transfers, Payments, or Purchases Upon Marriage**

Choose all that apply:

☐ __. **Transfer of Real Estate**

Within [*number*] days after our marriage, [*name*] will sign, deliver, and record a deed granting to [*name*] a [*percentage*]% interest, as [*specify how title will be held, for example, tenants in common, joint tenants, or his or her sole and separate property*] in the following real estate: [*address and legal description of the property*]. [*Name(s)*] will pay [*specify share, such as all, half, or some other proportion*] of any expenses related to the transfer, including the cost of obtaining title insurance on the property.

☐ __. **Transfer of Cash, Securities, or Other Personal Property**

Within [*number*] days after our marriage, [*name*] will deliver and assign to [*name*] ownership of the following property: [*describe property or cash to be transferred*]. [*Name(s)*] will pay [*specify share, such as all, half, or some other proportion*] of any expenses related to the transfer.

☐ __. Assignment of Life Insurance

Within [number] days after our marriage, [name] will deliver and assign to [name] ownership of the following [OPTIONAL: fully paid] life insurance [policy OR policies] on [name]'s life: [insert insurance company name, policy number, and face amount]. [Name(s)] will pay [specify share, such as all, half, or some other proportion] of any expenses related to the assignment. [OPTIONAL: [Name(s)] will pay [specify share, such as all, half, or some other proportion of] of any premiums due on the policy after the assignment.]

☐ __. Purchase of Annuity

Within [number] days after our marriage, [name] will purchase an annuity contract that will pay at least $[annual amount] per year beginning [specify the event or date that will trigger payments to begin, such as a certain number of years following the purchase, or when the beneficiary reaches a certain age], and continuing until the death of [name], who shall be designated as sole primary beneficiary of the annuity. [Name(s)] will pay [specify share, such as all, half, or some other proportion] of the costs of purchasing and maintaining the annuity.

☐ __. Purchase of Life Insurance Policy

Within [number] days after our marriage, [name] will purchase a life insurance policy that will pay at least $[insert amount] on [his OR her] death. [Name] shall be designated as sole primary beneficiary of the policy. [Name(s)] will pay [specify share, such as all, half or some other proportion] of the costs of purchasing and maintaining the policy.

☐ Paragraph __: Provisions Applicable to Divorce

A. Terms of This Agreement to Control

In the unhappy event that our marriage ends in divorce, as that term is defined in Paragraph 5 of this agreement, we want to resolve all issues as amicably and efficiently as possible.

Therefore, if we divorce, we agree to the following:

1. This agreement will control all issues addressed by this agreement.

2. As soon as possible after the case is filed, we will file this agreement (or a true copy of it) in court and we will sign and file a stipulation acknowledging the validity of this agreement.

3. Any dispute about the validity or interpretation of this agreement will be separated from all other issues in the case and submitted to the court for determination before any issues addressed in this agreement are decided.

Optional Clause for Distribution of Marital or Community Property Assets

☐ __. Distribution of Separate Property Assets

In any divorce proceeding, our separate property assets will be distributed as follows:

1. Each party's separate property assets, as defined in this agreement, shall be confirmed to him or her absolutely, without being included in any division of [marital OR community] property.

Add if applicable:

☐ 2. Each jointly owned separate asset shall be divided between us in proportion to our respective ownership interests in the asset ("in kind"), if that is possible without making us co-owners of the same asset after the asset is divided. If an in-kind division of any asset is not possible, the asset shall be sold and the net proceeds divided in proportion to our respective ownership interests in the asset.

Optional Clause for Distribution of Marital or Community Property Assets

Choose one:

Alternative 1

☐ __. **Equal Distribution of [Marital *OR* Community] Property Assets**

In any divorce proceeding, except as provided elsewhere in this agreement or in a written agreement signed by both of us at the time of the divorce, any [marital *OR* community] property assets shall be distributed between us in such a way as to achieve a monetarily equal division of the aggregate net value of the [marital *OR* community] property assets. If we so agree, certain assets may be distributed to one of us in exchange for a distribution of offsetting assets to the other party. Otherwise, each asset will be divided between us equally ("in kind"), if that is possible without making us co-owners of the same asset after the asset is divided. If an asset cannot be divided in kind and there is no agreement to assign the asset to one party, it shall be sold and the net proceeds divided so as to accomplish an equal division of all the assets. In determining whether the assets have been equally divided, any asset not sold will be valued at its fair market value as of the date the assets are divided.

Alternative 2

☐ __. **Equitable Distribution of [Marital *OR* Community] Property Assets**

In any divorce proceeding, except as provided elsewhere in this agreement or in a written agreement signed by both of us at the time of the divorce, any [marital *OR* community] property assets shall be distributed between us in such a way as to achieve an equitable division of the aggregate net value of the [marital *OR* community] property assets, as determined by written agreement signed by both of us or by the court in the divorce case. If we so agree, certain assets may be distributed to one of us in exchange for a distribution of offsetting assets to the other. Otherwise, each asset will be divided between us ("in kind"), if that is possible without our ending up as co-owners of the same asset after the asset is divided. If an asset cannot be divided in kind and there is no agreement to assign the asset to one party, it shall be sold and the net proceeds divided so as to accomplish an equitable division of all the assets. In determining whether the assets have been equitably divided, any asset not sold will be valued at its fair market value as of the date the assets are divided.

Optional Clause for Division of Retirement Benefits

Choose one:

Alternative 1

☐ __. **Retirement Benefits to Be Divided—Offset Method**

If we divorce, the terms of the divorce decree or judgment shall provide that any [marital *OR* community] property interest in retirement, pension, deferred compensation, and other employee benefit or tax deferred plans, whether qualified according to IRS regulations or nonqualified, shall be divided so that the person who earned the benefits or in whose name those benefits are held receives all of the benefits and the other person receives other property or funds as an offset in the [equal *OR* equitable] division of the [marital *OR* community] property.

Alternative 2

☐ __. **Retirement Benefits to Be Divided—In-Kind Method**

If we divorce, the terms of the divorce decree or judgment shall provide that any [marital *OR* community] property interest in retirement, pension, deferred compensation, and other employee benefit or tax deferred plans, whether qualified according to IRS regulations or nonqualified, shall be divided so that each of us receives a share of the benefits payable, with each person's share calculated in a manner consistent with the [equal *OR* equitable] division of the [marital *OR* community] property. Each of us will cooperate in preparing any court order for division of the benefits required by the plan or as provided by applicable law.

Alternative 3

☐ __. **No Division of Retirement Benefits**

If we divorce, the terms of the divorce decree or judgment shall provide that any [marital OR community] property interest in retirement, pension, deferred compensation, and other employee benefit or tax deferred plans, whether qualified according to IRS regulations or nonqualified, shall be confirmed to the person who earned the benefits or in whose name those benefits are vested and shall not be included in the [equal OR equitable] division of the [marital OR community] property.

Alternative 4

☐ __. **Retirement Benefits to Be Divided—Method to Be Determined**

If we divorce, the terms of the divorce decree or judgment shall provide that any [marital OR community] property interest in retirement, pension, deferred compensation, and other employee benefit or tax deferred plans, whether qualified according to IRS regulations or nonqualified, shall be divided in a manner consistent with the [equal OR equitable] division of the [marital OR community] property, as determined by a written agreement signed by both of us or by the court in the divorce case.

Optional Clause for Division of Specific Assets

☐ __. [*Insert Title of Clause, such as Family Residence, Business, or Joint Securities*]

[*Insert applicable terms of clause.*]

Optional Clause for Division of Premarital Debts

☐ __. **Responsibility for Premarital Debts**

If we divorce, the terms of the divorce decree or judgment shall provide that any outstanding premarital debt will be allocated to the person who incurred the debt, and he or she shall be required to pay the debt and to hold the other person harmless from the debt and all costs related to it.

Optional Clause for Responsibility for Debts Incurred During Marriage

Choose one:

Alternative 1

☐ __. **Equal Responsibility for Debts Incurred During Marriage—General Rule**

Except as provided elsewhere in this agreement, if we divorce, the terms of the divorce decree or judgment shall provide that any outstanding debts incurred by one or both of us during our marriage will be paid and allocated between us equally, to the extent an equal allocation is practical, as specifically determined by written agreement signed by both of us, or by the court in the divorce case. If the allocation is unequal, there shall be a corresponding offset in the division of our [marital OR community] property assets, in order to equalize the overall division of assets and debts.

If a debt is allocated to one of us in accordance with this clause, the person to whom it is allocated shall be required to hold the other person harmless from the debt and all costs related to it.

Alternative 2

☐ __. **Equitable Allocation of Responsibility for Debts Incurred During Marriage—General Rule**

Except as provided elsewhere in this agreement, if we divorce, the terms of the divorce decree or judgment shall provide that any outstanding debt incurred by one or both of us during our marriage will be paid and allocated between us equitably, as determined by written agreement signed by both of us or by the court in the divorce case.

If a debt is allocated to one of us in accordance with this clause, the person to whom it is allocated shall be required to hold the other person harmless from the debt and all costs related to it.

Optional Clause for Student Loans

Choose one:

Alternative 1

☐ __. Sole Responsibility for Student Loans

If we divorce, the terms of the divorce decree or judgment shall provide that any outstanding student loan debt will be allocated to the person whose education was financed by the loan, who shall be required to pay the debt and to hold the other person harmless from the debt and all costs related to it.

Alternative 2

☐ __. Shared Responsibility for Student Loans

If we divorce, the terms of the divorce decree or judgment shall provide that any outstanding student loan debt will be allocated between us in the same manner as any other debts incurred during our marriage for which we are mutually responsible, and not solely to the person whose education was financed by the loan.

Optional Clause for Certain Debts Incurred During Marriage

☐ __. Sole Responsibility for Certain Debts Incurred by One Party During Marriage

If we divorce, the terms of the divorce decree or judgment shall provide that any of the following outstanding debts incurred by one of us during our marriage will be allocated solely to the person who incurred the debt: [*specify debt or type of debt to be allocated to one spouse, such as one spouse's business debts, any debt incurred without the knowledge and consent of the other party, or debts related to certain activities*].

If a debt is allocated to one of us in accordance with this clause, the person to whom it is allocated shall be required to hold the other person harmless from the debt and all costs related to it.

Optional Clause for Reimbursement for Debts or Expenses Paid

Choose one:

Alternative 1

☐ __. Reimbursement for Debts or Expenses Paid

In any divorce proceeding, each of us will be entitled to reimbursement from the other for:

Choose all that apply:

☐ 1. Payments made during our marriage from separate property funds of one of us for premarital debts [*OPTIONAL:* , including child support or alimony,] owed by the other;

☐ 2. One-half of payments made during our marriage from [marital *OR* community] property funds for premarital debts [*OPTIONAL:* or child support or alimony] owed by the other;

☐ 3. Payments made from separate property funds of one of us for necessary expenses incurred by the other in connection with attendance at an accredited educational institution (including tuition, fees, books, and supplies [but not including *OR* and] living expenses), whether paid directly or by payments on student loans incurred for those expenses;

☐ 4. One-half of payments made during our marriage from [marital *OR* community] property funds for necessary expenses incurred by the other in connection with attendance at an accredited educational institution (including tuition, fees, books, and supplies [but not including *OR* and] living expenses), whether paid directly or by payments on student loans incurred for those expenses;

☐ 5. [*Insert any additional reimbursements*];

☐ 6. Any other amounts expressly agreed to be reimbursable as provided elsewhere in this agreement.

Add if Applicable:

☐   Neither of us will be entitled to any reimbursement from the other for paying any debts or expenses except those listed above, whether paid from separate property funds or [marital *OR* community] property funds or both.

Alternative 2

☐   **__. No Reimbursement for Debts or Expenses Paid**

In any divorce proceeding, neither of us will be entitled to any reimbursement from the other for paying debts or expenses of the other during our marriage except as may be provided elsewhere in this agreement, whether paid from separate property funds or [marital *OR* community] property funds or both.

Optional Clauses for Alimony (Check State Law for Specific Requirements or Limitations)

Choose all that apply:

Alternative 1 (If Both Spouses Are Waiving Alimony, Include a Separate Clause for Each)

☐   **__. Waiver of Alimony by [*Name*]**

[*Name*] expects to have sufficient earning capacity, income, and assets to provide for [his *OR* her] reasonable needs if we divorce. Therefore, [*name*] hereby waives absolutely any and all rights to request [*OPTIONAL:* temporary and] permanent alimony from [*name*] [*ADD IF APPLICABLE:* , except in the following limited circumstances only: *specify circumstances—for example, if waiving spouse would be eligible for welfare without alimony*]. [*Name*] understands that this waiver could later result in a hardship, and has taken that risk into account in making this waiver.

Alternative 2 (Include a Separate Clause for Each Spouse to Whom This Applies)

☐   **__. Specified Alimony to [*Name*]**

If we divorce, [*name*] shall be entitled to [*OPTIONAL:* temporary or] permanent alimony payments of [*OPTIONAL:* no more than] $[*amount*] per month from [*name*] [*OPTIONAL:* for a period of *number of years or months*], beginning [*specify starting point, such as the date when we stop living together or the date the case is filed*] and ending absolutely on [*specify ending point, such as remarriage, death, or a certain date or number of months or years; if more than one event or date could end alimony payments, add "whichever occurs first" after listing the possible ending dates or events*]. This clause may not be modified except by a written agreement signed by both of us. [*Name*] hereby waives absolutely any and all rights to request [*OPTIONAL:* temporary and] permanent alimony from [*name*] except as provided in this clause. [*Name*] understands that this waiver could later result in a hardship, and has taken that risk into account in making this waiver.

Other Clauses for Divorce

☐   **__. [*Insert Title of Clause*]**

[*Insert applicable terms of clause.*]

☐   **Paragraph __: Other Matters**

[*Insert any clauses for matters not covered in other paragraphs; insert sequential letters if you use more than one, starting with letter A.*]

☐   **__. [*Insert Title of Clause*]**

[*Insert applicable terms of clause.*]

D. Financial Disclosures

☑

Schedule 1—[*Woman's Name*]'s Disclosures

ASSETS

Description   Approximate
                                                                                        Value

DEBTS

To Whom Owed   Approximate
                                                                                        Balance

[*Woman's name*]'s annual income (calendar year [*insert year*]): $ _____

[*OPTIONAL*] [*Woman's name*]'s annual personal expenses: $ _____

_____   _____
Date Prepared   Initials

_____   _____
Date Prepared   Initials

✓

Schedule 2—[*Man's Name*]'s Disclosures

ASSETS

Description   Approximate
                                                                               Value

DEBTS

To Whom Owed   Approximate
                                                                               Balance

[*Man's name*]'s annual income (calendar year [*insert year*]): $ _____

[*OPTIONAL*] [*Man's name*]'s annual personal expenses: $ _____

Date Prepared   Initials

Date Prepared   Initials

☑ E. Abstract of Prenup

RECORDING REQUESTED BY
AND WHEN RECORDED RETURN TO

[LEAVE THIS SPACE BLANK FOR
RECORDER'S STAMP]

[*Insert name and address of spouse whose
property is referred to*]

Abstract of [*Title of Prenup*] Agreement

We, [*man's name, followed by man's first name in parenthesis*] and [*woman's name, followed by woman's first name in parenthesis*], declare:

1. We were married on [*date*] and are now husband and wife.

2. We entered into a [*title of prenup*] on [*date*].

3. The [*title of prenup*] became effective on the date of our marriage and it remains in full force and effect as of the date of execution of this abstract.

4. Among the provisions of the [*title of prenup*] are the provisions that follow:

    a. [*Insert paragraph number and letter of clause*] provides that the real property described on Exhibit A to this abstract, which is incorporated by reference, is and shall be [*insert owner's first name*]'s separate property, and [*owner's first name*] has the sole right to manage and dispose of the property described on Exhibit A.

    b. [*Insert a summary of any additional clauses you want to include in the abstract, such as a clause providing for real estate acquired during marriage to be considered the separate property of a spouse.*]

    c. Paragraph [*number and letter of clause*] provides that the [*title of prenup*] will remain in full force and effect [indefinitely OR until *specify date*].

We sign this abstract on _____[*date*]_____ at _____[*place*]_____

_____   _____
[*Name*]   [*Name*]

APPENDIX

Summary of State Prenup Laws

The following pages contain basic information about each state's laws regarding prenuptial agreements. This information will help you decide whether or not you need a prenup and to draft your own agreement, if you choose to do so.

Each state summary is divided into three sections:

- **Prenuptial agreements.** This section tells you the rules you must follow when making a prenup in your state.
- **Inheritance**. This section explains what one spouse is entitled to claim from the other's estate at death.
- **Divorce.** Here, we give you an overview of how the state divides the property of divorcing couples who don't make prenuptial agreements.

In addition to setting out the basic rules in these areas, each section provides citations to state laws—both statutes (laws enacted by state legislatures) and cases (court decisions that set legal precedent in the state)—that you can use to do your own legal research, if you want or need to look at your state's rules in more detail. (See Chapter 4, Section D, to learn more about doing your own research.)

A. Prenuptial Agreements

The first section of each summary provides an overview of the state's laws governing prenuptial agreements. All states allow premarital agreements to a greater or lesser degree, but there are many important details you'll want to know. We start by giving you the term for a prenup that is most commonly used by the state's lawmakers and lawyers—for example, antenuptial agreement, premarital agreement, or marital property agreement—and we tell you whether the state has adopted the Uniform Premarital Agreement Act (UPAA), a law crafted to promote consistency in prenups from state to state.

What Is the UPAA?

As prenups became more common in the 1970s and '80s, states started passing new laws governing them. In so doing, they took many different approaches to questions such as what a prenup could include and what would render an agreement unenforceable. Eventually, to promote more uniformity and predictability between states in an increasingly mobile society, national lawmakers drafted and approved a model set of legal standards for prenups. The model law, called the "Uniform Premarital Agreement Act" (UPAA) was approved in 1983. Individual states are free to adopt or reject this act—or to adopt just parts of it.

As of the writing of this book, the following states have adopted the UPAA. Many states have adopted it without any changes. However, a significant number of states have modified some aspect of the law. So it is important that you refer to the summary for your state rather than rely on the text of the UPAA itself, even if your state has adopted it.

Arizona	Indiana	North Carolina
Arkansas	Iowa	North Dakota
California	Kansas	Oregon
Connecticut	Maine	Rhode Island
Delaware	Montana	South Dakota
Dist. of Columbia	Nebraska	Texas
Hawaii	Nevada	Utah
Idaho	New Jersey	Virginia
Illinois	New Mexico	Wisconsin*

* The Uniform Law Commissioners list Wisconsin as a state that has adopted the UPAA, even though its laws bear very little resemblance to the act.

To read the UPAA in its entirety—or if you want more general information about the law, including states that are considering adopting it—visit the Uniform Law Commissioners' website at www.nccusl.org/nccusl/desktopdefault.aspx. Select "Premarital Agreement Act" from the drop-down list and click "Search."

The first section of each state summary also describes the formalities necessary to make a prenup, such as whether the agreement needs to be in writing, signed by both parties, notarized, or recorded in the public records for your county. Virtually all states require prenups to be in writing. Although some states will recognize an oral prenup under certain limited circumstances, these are rare exceptions to the rule. To ensure that your prenup is enforceable and that you have proof of your agreement, you must put it in writing.

We also tell you what your premarital agreement can cover (such as property rights—that is, who owns, manages, and controls which items of property), how property is divided at divorce, alimony agreements, and so forth. Finally, we provide a list of the circumstances under which a premarital agreement will be considered unenforceable. This is an area where state laws can vary greatly, even in states that have adopted the UPAA.

B. Inheritance

In the inheritance section of each state's summary, you'll find information about the state's laws governing:

- the amount of property a surviving spouse is entitled to receive from a deceased spouse's estate (called the surviving spouse's "election rights") in the absence of a prenup or other written agreement between the spouses, and

- the state's requirements for waiving these rights in a prenup or other contract.

Before turning to your state's laws, however, you may find it helpful to read the overview of these topics in Chapter 4, Section C3, where we discuss in general terms what one spouse is entitled to inherit from the other if the couple doesn't make a prenup or other agreement about their property rights at death.

C. Divorce

The divorce section of each state's summary provides information about:

- how marital property is classified—that is, what system the state uses to determine who owns what if a couple divorces
- how property is divided at divorce
- how the state handles alimony payments, and
- how the state allocates debts.

To best understand the laws presented in the state summaries, you should first read the discussion in Chapter 4, Section C4. It will introduce you to the differences between community property and common law states, and provide you with general information about each of the subjects listed above.

D. State Summaries

The laws for each state are summarized below.

Alabama

Prenuptial Agreements

Legal term: Antenuptial Agreement

Has state adopted UPAA? No

State code sections: Ala. Code §§ 30-4-9, 43-8-72

Important court cases: *Kilborn v. Kilborn,* 628 So.2d 884 (1993); *Barnhill v. Barnhill,* 386 So.2d 749 (1980)

Required Formalities for Prenuptial Agreements

- In writing

Permitted Subjects of Prenuptial Agreements

- Property rights
- What happens to property at divorce or separation
- What happens to property upon death
- Alimony (spousal support or spousal maintenance)
- Any other matter that does not violate public policy or criminal laws

What Makes a Prenuptial Agreement Unenforceable?

- Agreement not made voluntarily
- Subject of agreement violates public policy or criminal laws
- Agreement not "fair, just and equitable," with full disclosure of finances and opportunity for independent advice

Inheritance

Election Rights

Ala. Code § 43-8-70

- Surviving spouse has the right to take one-third of deceased spouse's estate or all of the deceased spouse's estate minus the value of the surviving spouse's separate estate, whichever is less

Allowance Rights

- **Homestead.** Allowance of $6,000 (Ala. Code § 43-8-110)
- **Exempt property.** Up to $3,500 in household furniture, automobiles, furnishings, appliances, and personal effects (Ala. Code § 43-8-111)
- **Family allowance.** Reasonable maintenance while estate is being settled, but no longer than one year (Ala. Code § 43-8-112)
- Homestead and family allowance are in addition to elective share or any share passing to the surviving spouse by the will

Waiver of Inheritance Rights

Ala. Code § 43-8-72

- Spouse may waive right to statutory share of other spouse's estate or allowances by signing a written contract after fair disclosure
- A waiver of "all rights" presumes waiver of elective share, homestead allowance, exempt property, family allowance, and all benefits that would pass to surviving spouse by intestate succession or by the provisions of any will executed before the waiver

Divorce

Division of Property at Divorce

Ala. Code §§ 30-2-51 to -52

Property division method: Equitable distribution

Marital fault considered: Yes

Other factors affecting property division:

- Property, or income from it, must have been used regularly for the common benefit of the parties during the marriage
- Retirement benefits included in joint property only if acquired a during marriage that lasted at least ten years
- Court may award an extra portion of marital property to one spouse if that spouse has no separate property or property is insufficient for maintenance

Temporary Alimony

Ala. Code §§ 30-2-50

- Court may order either spouse to pay temporary alimony to the other while divorce is pending
- Award based on standard of living and value of marital property

Permanent Alimony Award

Ala. Code §§ 30-2-51 to -52

Marital fault considered? Yes

Other factors affecting award:

- Whether each spouse has sufficient separate property for maintenance
- Family conditions of spouse who will pay alimony

Circumstances That Terminate or Modify Alimony

Ala. Code § 30-2-55

- Remarriage or cohabitation by spouse receiving alimony

Debts

- Neither spouse is liable for the other's debts, whether incurred before, during, or after marriage (Ala. Code §§ 30-4-1 to 30-4-4, 30-4-6 to 30-4-7)

Alaska

Prenuptial Agreements

Legal term: Prenuptial Agreement
Has state adopted UPAA? No
State code sections: Alaska Stat. § 13.12.213
Important court cases: *Brooks v. Brooks*, 733 P.2d 1044 (1987); *Compton v. Compton*, 902 P.2d 805 (1995)

Required Formalities for Prenuptial Agreements

- In writing
- Signed by both parties

Permitted Subjects of Prenuptial Agreements

- Property rights
- What happens to property at divorce or separation
- What happens to property upon death
- Any other matter that does not violate public policy or criminal laws

What Makes a Prenuptial Agreement Unenforceable?

- Agreement not made voluntarily
- Waiver of surviving spouse rights unconscionable and prior to signing, party objecting to enforcement was not given fair and reasonable disclosure
- Agreement was not "legally procured and ostensibly fair in result"
- Facts and circumstances changed so as to make enforcement unfair and unreasonable

Inheritance

Election Rights

- **Non-community property.** Surviving spouse has the right to take one-third of the deceased spouse's augmented estate; if this amounts to less than $50,000, spouse is entitled to a supplemental share (Alaska Stat. § 13.12.202)
- **Community property.** If couple makes a community property agreement, one-half of the community property must go to the surviving spouse; deceased spouse may dispose of the other half as desired (Alaska Stat. § 13.41.015)

Allowance Rights

Surviving spouse entitled to:

- **Homestead.** Allowance of $27,000 (Alaska Stat. § 13.12.402)
- **Family allowance.** Reasonable support for up to one year while estate is being settled (Alaska Stat. § 13.12.404)
- **Exempt property.** $10,000 in household furniture, furnishings, automobiles, appliances, and personal effects; if property is worth less than $10,000, surviving spouse entitled to a supplemental share that has priority over all claims except homestead and family allowances (Alaska Stat. § 13.12.403)
- All allowances are in addition to elective share or any terms of the will

Waiver of Inheritance Rights

Alaska Stat. § 13.12.213

- All rights may be wholly or partially waived by written agreement or contract signed by waiving spouse
- Waiver is not enforceable if: 1) it was not made voluntarily; 2) person executing waiver was not given fair disclosure of decedent's property or financial obligations, did not expressly waive right to such disclosure, and did not have or could not have had knowledge of property or obligations; or 3) waiver was unconscionable (court must decide this issue)
- Waiver of "all rights" presumes waiver of right to elective share, homestead, property, and family allowance

Divorce

Division of Property at Divorce

Property division method: Equitable distribution, unless spouses make a community property agreement (see below)
Marital fault considered: No
Non-community property. (Alaska Stat. § 25.24.160(a)(4))
Factors affecting property division:

- Duration of marriage and standard of living established while married
- Age and health of each spouse
- Earning capacity of each spouse, including educational backgrounds, training, employment skills, work experiences, length of absence from the job market, and custodial parent responsibilities during marriage
- Financial condition of each spouse, including availability and cost of health insurance
- Conduct of each spouse after separation or during divorce proceedings, including unreasonable depletion of marital assets
- Desirability of awarding family home, or right to live in it, to spouse who has primary physical custody of children
- Circumstances and needs of each spouse

- How joint property was acquired, how long it took to acquire it, and the property's value and income-producing capacity

Community property. A couple can make a written agreement to turn any or all of their joint or separate property into community property (Alaska Stat. §§ 34.77.010 and following; Alaska Stat. § 25.24.160(e))

Factors affecting division of community property:

- Nature and extent of community property
- Nature and extent of separate property
- Duration of marriage
- Economic circumstances of each spouse, including desirability of awarding family home, or right to live in it, to spouse with whom the children reside most of the time

Temporary Alimony

Alaska Stat. § 25.24.140(a)(1),(a)(2)

- May be awarded to either spouse based on economic circumstances, need, and ability to pay; may cover reasonable costs and attorney fees that relate to the actual expenses of the divorce proceedings and reasonable support, including health insurance

Permanent Alimony Award

Alaska Stat. § 25.24.160(a)(2)

Marital fault considered? No

Factors affecting award:

- Share of marital property awarded
- Factors applied in non-community property division (above)

Circumstances That Terminate or Modify Alimony

Alaska Stat. § 25.24.170

- Financial change of circumstances

Debts

- Neither spouse is liable for the other's debts, whether incurred before or during marriage (Alaska Stat. § 25.15.050)
- Neither spouse's separate property is liable for the other's debts (Alaska Stat. § 25.15.010)

Arizona

Prenuptial Agreements

Legal term: Premarital Agreement

Has state adopted UPAA? Yes

State code sections: Ariz. Rev. Stat. Ann. §§ 25-201, 25-202; 14-2101

Required Formalities for Prenuptial Agreements

- In writing
- Signed by both parties

Permitted Subjects of Prenuptial Agreements

- Property rights
- Rights to sell, transfer, or control property
- What happens to property at divorce or separation
- What happens to property upon death
- Alimony (spousal support or spousal maintenance)
- Terms of wills, trusts, and other estate planning documents
- Life insurance ownership and arrangements
- Applicable state law
- Any other matter that does not violate public policy or criminal laws

What Makes a Prenuptial Agreement Unenforceable?

- Agreement not made voluntarily
- Agreement unconscionable when signed and prior to signing, party objecting to enforcement did not know other party's finances and was not given fair and reasonable disclosure
- Alimony waiver not enforceable if it would cause waiving spouse to be eligible for public assistance
- Annulment of marriage, unless result would be inequitable
- Subject of agreement violates public policy or criminal laws

Inheritance

Election Rights

- Surviving spouse is entitled to one-half of all community property; deceased spouse may leave the other half and all his or her separate property as desired (Ariz. Rev. Stat. § 14-3101(A))

Allowance Rights

Surviving spouse entitled to:

- **Homestead.** Allowance of $18,000 (Ariz. Rev. Stat. § 14-2402)
- **Exempt property.** Up to $7,000 in household furniture, furnishings, appliances, personal effects, and automobiles; if property is worth less than $7,000, spouse is entitled to a supplemental share that has priority over all claims except homestead and family allowances (Ariz. Rev. Stat. § 14-2403)
- **Family allowance.** Reasonable support for up to one year while estate is being settled; has priority over all claims except homestead allowance (Ariz. Rev. Stat. § 14-2404)
- All allowances will be charged against any benefit received from the will or nonprobate transfers

Waiver of Inheritance Rights

Ariz. Rev. Stat. § 14-2207

- May waive homestead, exempt property, and family allowance rights either before or after marriage by a written contract.
- Waiver is not enforceable if: 1) it was not made voluntarily; 2) person executing waiver was not given fair disclosure of decedent's property or financial obligations, did not expressly waive right to such disclosure, and did not know or could not have known of property or obligations; or 3) waiver was unconscionable (court must decide this issue)
- Waiver of "all rights" presumes waiver of right to elective share, homestead, property, and family allowance

Divorce

Division of Property at Divorce

Ariz. Rev. Stat. § 25-318(A)

Property division method: Community property

Marital fault considered: No

Factors affecting property division:

- Excessive or abnormal expenditures, destruction, concealment, or fraudulent disposition of community and other joint property
- Court divides community and other jointly owned property equitably
- Each spouse keeps his or her own separate property

Temporary Alimony

Ariz. Rev. Stat. § 25-315(E)

- Either spouse may be ordered to pay temporary maintenance or support
- Court may also make temporary division of property

Permanent Alimony Award

Ariz. Rev. Stat. § 25-319

Marital fault considered: No

Factors affecting award:

- Spouse seeking support lacks sufficient separate property, including share of joint property, to provide for own reasonable needs
- Spouse seeking support is unable to be self-sufficient through appropriate employment
- Spouse seeking support has custody of a child whose age or condition requires parent to be at home
- Spouse seeking support contributed to other spouse's educational opportunities and earning ability and reduced own income or career opportunities
- Spouse seeking support was in a marriage of long duration and is of an age that may preclude gaining adequate employment
- Age, employment history, earning ability, and physical and emotional condition of spouse seeking support
- Time necessary for spouse seeking support to acquire sufficient education or training to find appropriate employment and whether such education or training is readily available
- Duration of marriage and standard of living established while married
- Ability of the spouse from whom support is sought to meet own needs while meeting those of the spouse seeking alimony
- Comparative financial resources of both spouses, including earning abilities
- Ability of both parties to contribute to the future educational costs of their children after the divorce
- Excessive or abnormal expenditures, destruction, concealment, or fraudulent disposition of community and other joint property

- Health insurance costs

Circumstances That Terminate or Modify Alimony

Ariz. Rev. Stat. § 25-327

- Remarriage of spouse receiving alimony
- Death of either spouse
- Substantial and continuing change in economic circumstances
- Change in the availability of health insurance coverage

Debts

Ariz. Rev. Stat. § 25-215

- Separate property of one spouse is not liable for the separate debts of the other spouse
- If one spouse contributed property to the community that would have been separate property if single, the community property is liable for that spouse's pre-marital separate debts up to the value of the contributed property
- Community property is liable for a spouse's debts incurred outside Arizona after marriage, if the debts would have been community debts in Arizona
- Either spouse can incur a community debt during marriage; debt is paid first from community property, then from the separate property of the spouse contracting the debt
- Consent of both spouses required for any contract or debt that places a guarantee, mortgage, or other security on community property (Ariz. Rev. Stat. § 25-214(C))
- Upon divorce, the court may assign responsibility for payment of community debts to either spouse (Ariz. Rev. Stat. § 25-318)

Arkansas

Prenuptial Agreements

Legal term: Premarital Agreement

Has state adopted UPAA? Yes

State code sections: Ark. Code Ann. §§ 9-11-401 to 9-11-413

Important court cases: *Arnold v. Arnold*, 553 S.W.2d 251 (1997)

Required Formalities for Prenuptial Agreements

- In writing
- Signed by both parties
- Notarized

Permitted Subjects of Prenuptial Agreements

- Property rights
- Rights to sell, transfer, or control property
- What happens to property at divorce or separation
- What happens to property upon death
- Alimony (spousal support or spousal maintenance)
- Terms of wills, trusts, and other estate planning documents
- Life insurance ownership and arrangements
- Applicable state law
- Any other matter that does not violate public policy or criminal laws

What Makes a Prenuptial Agreement Unenforceable?

- Agreement not made voluntarily
- Agreement unconscionable when signed and prior to signing, party objecting to enforcement did not know other party's finances and was not given fair and reasonable disclosure
- Alimony waiver not enforceable if it would cause waiving spouse to be eligible for public assistance
- Annulment of marriage, unless result would be inequitable
- Subject of agreement violates public policy or criminal laws

Inheritance

Election Rights

- Surviving spouse not entitled to elective share unless married at least one year (Ark. Code Ann. § 28-39-401)
- If deceased spouse had children, surviving spouse entitled to one-third of deceased spouse's personal property and life interest in one-third of real estate (Ark. Code Ann. §§ 28-11-301 to 28-11-306)
- If deceased spouse had no children, surviving spouse entitled to one-half of real estate and personal property; if estate is also subject to creditors' claims, surviving spouse entitled to one-third (Ark. Code Ann. § 28-11-307)
- If deceased spouse's real estate is "ancestral," surviving spouse entitled to life interest in one-half the property, one-third if there are creditors (Ark. Code Ann. § 28-11-307)
- If deceased spouse had no children or other immediate relatives, surviving spouse entitled to any property remaining in the estate after all obligations and expenses are met and all property left by the will is distributed (Ark. Code Ann. § 28-39-401)

Allowance Rights

- **Homestead.** If deceased spouse had no children, surviving spouse entitled to homestead, unless owner of separate homestead (Ark. Code Ann. § 28-39-201). If deceased spouse had children, surviving spouse entitled to one-half of homestead rents and profits until last child is 21, then entitled to all rents and profits. Surviving spouse entitled to homestead rights only if married at least one year
- **Exempt property.** Surviving spouse entitled to $4,000 in personal property ($2,000 if estate has creditors) as well as household furniture, furnishings, and appliances (Ark. Code Ann. § 28-39-101(a), (b)). Right to exempt property is in addition to homestead and any other rights
- **Family allowance.** Surviving spouse entitled to allowance of up to $1,000 for a period of two months after the death (Ark. Code Ann. § 28-39-101(c))

Waiver of Inheritance Rights

- No statute

Divorce

Division of Property at Divorce

Ark. Code Ann. § 9-12-315

Property division method: Equitable distribution

Marital fault considered: No

General rule is to award each party their own separate property and one-half of the marital property; if that distribution is not equitable, the following factors are considered:

- Duration of marriage
- Age and health of each spouse
- Occupation, vocational skills, and employability of each spouse

- Amount and sources of income
- Estate, liabilities, and needs of each spouse
- Opportunity for further acquisition of capital assets and income by each spouse
- Contribution of each spouse to acquisition, preservation, or appreciation of marital property, including services as a homemaker
- Federal income tax consequences of the property division

Temporary Alimony

Ark. Code Ann. § 9-12-309(a)(1)

- Either party may be awarded support, reasonable attorney fees, and expert witness fees while divorce is pending

Permanent Alimony Award

Ark. Code Ann. § 9-12-312

Marital fault considered: May be considered if meaningfully relates to need or ability to pay [*Murphy v. Murphy,* 787 S.W.2d 684 (1990))

Other factors affecting award:

- Ability of one party to pay and need of the other party are primary factors (*Burns v. Burns,* 847 S.W.2d 23 (Ark. 1993))

Circumstances That Terminate or Modify Alimony

Ark. Code Ann. § 9-12-312

- Death of either spouse
- Remarriage of spouse receiving alimony
- If party receiving alimony has a child and either receives or is ordered to pay child support, this is considered the equivalent of remarriage and alimony will terminate

Debts

Ark. Code Ann. §§ 9-11-506 to 9-11–508

- Neither spouse is liable for the other's premarital debts, unless they agree otherwise in a written contract
- Neither spouse's separate property may be sold to pay for the other's premarital debts
- Neither spouse is liable for a contract the other spouse makes with his or her own separate property
- Wife's separate property acquired before or during marriage is not liable for husband's debts (Ark. Const. Art. 9, § 7)
- Credit card debt incurred during a legal separation is marital debt (*Schumacher v. Schumacher,* 986 S.W.2d 883 (1999))

California

Prenuptial Agreements

Legal term: Premarital Agreement
Has state adopted UPAA? Yes
State code sections: Cal. Fam. Code §§ 1600 to 1617

Required Formalities for Prenuptial Agreements

- In writing
- Signed by both parties

Permitted Subjects of Prenuptial Agreements

- Property rights
- Rights to sell, transfer, or control property
- What happens to property at divorce or separation
- What happens to property upon death
- Alimony (spousal support or spousal maintenance)
- Terms of wills, trusts, or other estate planning documents
- Life insurance ownership and arrangements
- Applicable state law
- Any other matter that does not violate public policy or criminal laws
- *Not permitted: child support restriction*

What Makes a Prenuptial Agreement Unenforceable?

- Agreement not made voluntarily (it is assumed that a prenuptial agreement was not made voluntarily unless the court finds all of the following to be true: (1) the party against whom enforcement is sought was represented by a lawyer when the agreement was signed, or the party signed a document expressly waiving the right to a lawyer's advice; (2) the party against whom enforcement is sought had at least seven days to review the agreement and seek a lawyer's advice; and (3) if the party against whom enforcement is sought did not have a lawyer, he or she was fully informed about the terms and effect of the agreement as well as any rights being sacrificed, and he or she signed an agreement to this effect)
- Agreement unconscionable when signed and prior to signing, party objecting to enforcement did not know other party's finances and was not given fair and reasonable disclosure
- Agreements about spousal support not enforceable if the party against whom enforcement is sought was not represented by a lawyer when the agreement was signed, or if the provision regarding spousal support is unconscionable at the time of enforcement

- Annulment of marriage, unless result would be inequitable
- Subject of agreement violates public policy or criminal law

Inheritance

Election Rights

- Surviving spouse is entitled to one-half of community property (Cal. Prob. Code §§ 100, 101)
- Deceased spouse may leave other half of the community property and all of his or her separate property as desired (Cal. Prob. Code § 6101)
- If one spouse attempts to leave more than half of the community property, surviving spouse may either accept the terms of the will or elect to take half of the community property (*Morrison v. Bowman*, 29 Cal. 337 (1865))
- Unless terms of the will show a contrary intent, surviving spouse can take community share as well any other property left under the will (*In re Prager's Estate*, 166 Cal. 450 (1913))
- If deceased spouse made an estate plan before marriage that didn't include surviving spouse, surviving spouse can claim all of the community property and up to one-half of the deceased spouse's separate property (Cal. Prob. Code § 21610)

Allowance Rights

- **Homestead.** Surviving spouse may choose and set apart a "probate homestead" to be used by the surviving spouse for a designated period of time, up to the surviving spouse's lifetime (Cal. Prob. Code §§ 6520 to 6526)
- **Family allowance.** Surviving spouse is entitled to maintenance during the estate administration process (Cal. Prob. Code § 654)

Waiver of Inheritance Rights

- Surviving spouse may waive inheritance or allowance rights by making a written contract (Cal. Prob. Code §§ 141, 142)
- The waiver is valid unless the surviving spouse proves either that (1) the surviving spouse did not receive fair and reasonable disclosure of the deceased spouse's finances (unless the surviving spouse waives disclosure after advice by separate legal counsel); or (2) the surviving spouse was not represented by independent legal counsel at the time of signing the waiver (Cal. Prob. Code § 143)

- If neither of the conditions above are met, a court may still enforce the waiver if it determines either that (1) at the time of signing, the waiver made a fair and equitable disposition of the rights of the surviving spouse; or (2) the surviving spouse had, or reasonably should have had, adequate knowledge of the deceased spouse's finances and the deceased spouse did not breach a fiduciary duty to the surviving spouse (Cal. Prob. Code § 144(a))
- The court may refuse to enforce all or part of the waiver if the court finds the waiver to be unconscionable (Cal. Prob. Code § 144(b))

Divorce

Division of Property at Divorce

Property division method: Community property

Marital fault considered: No

Factors affecting property division:

- Unless the spouses otherwise agree in writing or in open court, community property is divided equally (Cal. Fam. Code § 2550)
- If equal division results in inequitable conditions for either spouse, or if one spouse has deliberately misappropriated a portion of community property, additional share may be awarded (Cal. Fam. Code §§ 2601, 2602)
- If net value of community property is less than $5,000 and one party can't be located, other spouse may be awarded the whole share (Cal. Fam. Code § 2604)

Temporary Alimony

Cal. Fam. Code § 3600

- Either spouse may be ordered to pay support to the other during divorce proceedings

Permanent Alimony Award

Cal. Fam. Code § 4320

Marital fault considered: No

Factors affecting award:

- Whether the earning capacity of each spouse is sufficient to maintain standard of living established during marriage
- Marketable skills of the supported spouse, including time and expense required for supported spouse to obtain education or training to develop existing skills, or to acquire other skills or employment

- Extent to which supported spouse's earning capacity is impaired by long period of unemployment devoted to domestic duties
- Extent to which supported spouse contributed to supporting spouse's education, training, career position, or license
- Ability of the supporting spouse to pay alimony
- Needs of each spouse based on standard of living established during marriage
- Obligations and assets of each spouse
- Duration of the marriage
- Ability of supported spouse who is custodial parent to be gainfully employed without unduly interfering with the interests of the children
- Age and health of the spouses
- Domestic violence (as shown by documented evidence) including consideration of resulting emotional distress
- Tax consequences and balance of hardships to each spouse
- Goal that supported spouse be self-supporting within a reasonable period of time (generally limited to one-half the length of the marriage, with exceptions for marriages of more than ten years)
- Court may order party requesting support to be evaluated by a vocational training counselor (Cal. Fam. Code § 4331)

Circumstances That Terminate or Modify Alimony

Cal. Fam. Code §§ 4334 to 4337

- Death of either spouse
- Remarriage of spouse receiving alimony
- Spouses may agree in writing or orally in open court that spousal support is not subject to modification or termination

Debts

Cal. Fam. Code §§ 910 to 914

- Community property is liable for debts incurred by either spouse before or during marriage
- Earnings of one spouse during marriage are not liable for premarital debts of the other spouse, as long as earnings are kept in a separate account and not mixed with community property
- One spouse's separate property is not liable for debts the other spouse incurred before or during marriage

Colorado

Prenuptial Agreements

Legal term: marital Agreement

Has state adopted UPAA? No (Colorado's law is very similar to the UPAA, however)

State code sections: Colo. Rev. Stat. §§ 14-2-301 to 14-2-310, 15-11-204, 15-11-207

Required Formalities for Prenuptial Agreements

- In writing
- Signed by both parties

Permitted Subjects of Prenuptial Agreements

- Property rights
- Rights to sell, transfer, or control property
- What happens to property at divorce or separation
- What happens to property upon death
- Alimony (spousal support or spousal maintenance)
- Terms of wills, trusts, or other estate planning documents
- Life insurance ownership and arrangements
- Rights under retirement plan or other employee benefit plan
- Applicable state law
- Any other matter that does not violate public policy or criminal laws

What Makes a Prenuptial Agreement Unenforceable?

- Agreement not made voluntarily
- Agreement unconscionable as to spousal maintenance
- Annulment of marriage, unless result would be inequitable
- Subject of agreement violates public policy or criminal laws
- Party objecting to enforcement was not given fair and reasonable disclosure of other party's finances prior to signing

Inheritance

Election Rights

Colo. Rev. Stat. § 15-11-201

- Surviving spouse entitled to 5% of deceased spouse's augmented estate for each year of marriage (maximum of 50% reached at ten years)
- If elective share is less than $50,000, surviving spouse entitled to a supplemental share to bring total to $50,000

Allowance Rights

Surviving spouse entitled to:

- **Homestead.** Homestead exemption up to $45,000 (not considered an allowance) (Colo. Rev. Stat. §§ 38-41-204,15-11-402)
- **Exempt property.** $26,000 either in cash or in other property (Colo. Rev. Stat. § 15-11-403)
- **Family allowance.** Reasonable support for up to one year while estate is being settled (Colo. Rev. Stat. § 15-11-404)
- Property and family allowances are in addition to any elective share

Waiver of Inheritance Rights

(Colo. Rev. Stat. § 15-11-207

- May waive rights to elective share, exempt property, family allowance, and homestead exemption, wholly or in part, before or after marriage, by signing a written agreement after full disclosure of other spouse's assets and liabilities
- Waiver not enforceable if it would be unenforceable under premarital agreement laws (see above)
- Waiver of "all rights upon death" in the property or estate of a present or prospective spouse is waiver of: (1) election, exemption, and allowance rights; (2) priority to serve as personal representative, executor, or administrator of the estate; and (3) all benefits due by intestate succession or by provisions of any will executed before the waiver

Divorce

Division of Property at Divorce

Colo. Rev. Stat. § 14-10-113

Property division method: Equitable distribution

Marital fault considered: No

Factors affecting property division:

- Contribution of each spouse to the acquisition of marital property, including contribution of a homemaker
- Value of each spouse's separate property
- Economic circumstances of each spouse
- Desirability of awarding family home, or the right to live in it, to spouse with whom any children reside most of the time
- Any increase or decrease in value of the separate property of either spouse during marriage, or depletion of separate property for benefit of the marriage

Temporary Alimony

- During divorce proceedings, court may order either spouse to temporarily pay maintenance and debts, allow use of property, or pay attorneys fees (Colo. Rev. Stat. § 14-10-108)
- If combined annual gross income of both parties is $75,000 or less, spouse with higher income generally ordered to pay temporary support based on ability to pay and any prior spousal or child support obligations (Colo. Rev. Stat. § 14-10-114(2))
- If combined annual gross income of both parties is more than $75,000, same factors apply as those used to award permanent alimony (Colo. Rev. Stat. § 14-10-114(3),(4))

Permanent Alimony Award

Colo. Rev. Stat. § 14-10-114(3),(4)

Marital fault considered: No

Alimony awarded only if:

- Spouse seeking support lacks sufficient property, including share of marital property, to provide for own reasonable needs
- Spouse seeking support is unable to be self-supporting through appropriate employment or is custodian of a child who requires a stay-at-home parent

Other factors affecting award include:

- Financial resources of the spouse seeking maintenance and spouse's ability to meet needs independently
- Extent to which support for a child living with spouse seeking maintenance includes a sum for that spouse
- Time needed for spouse seeking maintenance to acquire sufficient education or training to find appropriate employment, and spouse's future earning capacity
- Duration of marriage and standard of living established during marriage
- Age and physical and emotional condition of spouse seeking maintenance
- Ability of spouse from whom maintenance is sought to meet own needs while meeting those of the other spouse

Circumstances That Terminate or Modify Alimony

Colo. Rev. Stat. § 14-10-122

- Circumstances have changed so much that the existing terms are unfair
- Death of either party or remarriage of party receiving alimony

Debts

- Wife's separate property is not liable for husband's debts (Colo. Rev. Stat. § 14-2-201)
- Separate property of both spouses is liable for family expenses and the education of children (Colo. Rev. Stat. § 14-6-110)

Connecticut

Prenuptial Agreements

Legal term: Premarital Agreement

Has state adopted UPAA? Yes

State code sections: Conn. Gen. Stat. Ann. §§ 46b-36a to 46b-36j; 45a-436(f)

Required Formalities for Prenuptial Agreements

- In writing
- Signed by both parties

Permitted Subjects of Prenuptial Agreements

- Property rights
- Rights to sell, transfer, or control property
- What happens to property at divorce or separation
- What happens to property upon death
- Alimony (spousal support or spousal maintenance)
- Terms of wills, trusts, or other estate planning documents
- Life insurance ownership and arrangements
- Applicable state law
- Any other matter that does not violate public policy or criminal laws
- Rights under retirement plan
- *Not permitted: child support restriction*

What Makes a Prenuptial Agreement Unenforceable?

- Agreement not made voluntarily
- Agreement unconscionable when agreement signed or at time of attempt to enforce
- Prior to signing, party objecting to enforcement did not know other party's finances, was not given fair and reasonable disclosure, and had no opportunity to consult with independent lawyer
- Alimony waiver, if it would cause waiving party to be eligible for public assistance
- Annulment of marriage, unless result would be inequitable
- Subject of agreement against public policy or criminal laws

Inheritance

Election Rights

Conn. Gen. Stat. Ann. § 45a-436

- Surviving spouse entitled to one-third of deceased spouse's real and personal property for life
- Surviving spouse may not take share until family allowance expires
- Surviving spouse may not take share if he or she abandoned deceased spouse or received property in lieu of elective share by written contract

Allowance Rights

Conn. Gen. Stat. Ann. § 45a-320

- **Family allowance.** Amount and terms set by probate court; may include use of family car

Waiver of Inheritance Rights

- No statute

Divorce

Division of Property at Divorce

Conn. Gen. Stat. Ann. § 46b-81

Property division method: Equitable distribution

Marital fault considered? Yes

Other factors affecting property division:

- Age, health, sources of income, employability, and skills of each spouse
- Prospects of each spouse for future acquisition of capital or income
- Contribution of each spouse to value of each spouse's separate property

Temporary Alimony

Conn. Gen. Stat. Ann. § 46b-83

- Awarded on same basis as permanent alimony, but marital fault is not considered

Permanent Alimony Award

Conn. Gen. Stat. Ann. § 46b-82

Marital fault considered? Yes

Other factors affecting award:

- Age, health, sources of income, employability, and skills of each spouse
- Need for spouse who is custodial parent to be at home
- Duration of marriage
- Marital property award

Circumstances That Terminate or Modify Alimony

Conn. Gen. Stat. Ann. § 46b-86

- Change in financial needs of spouse receiving alimony as a result of living with another person

Debts

Conn. Gen. Stat. Ann. § 46b-36

- Spouses are not responsible for each other's debts

Delaware

Prenuptial Agreements

Legal term: Premarital Agreement

Has state adopted UPAA? Yes

State code sections: Del. Code Ann. tit. 13, §§ 321 through 328

Required Formalities for Prenuptial Agreements

- In writing
- Signed by both parties

Permitted Subjects of Prenuptial Agreements

- Property rights
- Rights to sell, transfer, or control property
- What happens to property at divorce or separation
- What happens to property upon death
- Alimony (spousal support, spousal maintenance)
- Terms of wills, trusts, or other estate planning documents
- Life insurance ownership and arrangements
- Applicable state law
- Any other matter that does not violate public policy or criminal laws
- *Not permitted: child support restriction*

What Makes a Prenuptial Agreement Unenforceable?

- Agreement not made voluntarily
- Agreement unconscionable when signed and prior to signing, party objecting to enforcement did not know other party's finances and was not given fair and reasonable disclosure
- Annulment of marriage, unless result would be inequitable
- Subject of agreement against public policy or criminal laws

Inheritance

Election Rights

Del. Code Ann. tit. 12, § 901

- One-third of estate

Allowance Rights

Del. Code Ann. tit. 12, § 2308

- $2,000 cash

Waiver of Inheritance Rights

- May waive right to elective share and any other benefits or property that would be inherited either through intestate succession or a will executed before the waiver; waiver must be in writing and signed by the waiving spouse (Del. Code Ann. tit. 12, § 905)

Divorce

Division of Property at Divorce

Del. Code Ann. tit. 13, § 1513

Property division method: Equitable distribution

Marital fault considered? No

Factors affecting property division:

- Contribution of each spouse to value of property (includes homemaking) or responsibility of either spouse for depreciation of property value
- Current and projected economic circumstances of either spouse
- Duration of marriage or any previous marriage
- Custodial parent's and dependent children's need to remain in family home
- Either spouse's need for and ability to obtain life insurance

Temporary Alimony

- May be awarded to dependent party during divorce proceedings (Del. Code Ann. tit. 13, § 1512)

Permanent Alimony Award

Del. Code Ann. tit. 13, § 1513

Marital fault considered? No

Factors affecting award:

- Dependence on other spouse for support
- Whether spouse has sufficient separate or awarded property for support
- Whether spouse is unable to support self through employment or is custodial parent who needs to stay home with child
- Duration of marriage and standard of living established during marriage
- Either spouse's contribution to education, career, or earning capacity of other spouse, or postponement or sacrifice of economic, education, or career opportunities during marriage
- Time and money required to obtain education or training for appropriate employment.

Circumstances That Terminate or Modify Alimony

- Remarriage or cohabitation of spouse receiving alimony, without regard to any change in financial circumstances

Debts

- Neither spouse's separate property is liable for the separate debts of the other (Del. Code Ann. tit. 13, §§ 311, 314)

District of Columbia

Prenuptial Agreements

Legal term: Premarital Agreement

Has state adopted UPAA? Yes

State code sections: D.C. Code Ann. §§ 46-501 to 46-510; 19-113(f)

Required Formalities for Prenuptial Agreements

- In writing
- Signed by both parties

Permitted Subjects of Prenuptial Agreements

- Property rights
- Rights to sell, transfer, or control property
- What happens to property at divorce or separation
- What happens to property upon death
- Alimony (spousal support or spousal maintenance)
- Terms of wills, trusts, or other estate planning documents
- Life insurance ownership and arrangements
- Applicable state law
- Any other matter that does not violate public policy or criminal laws
- *Not permitted: child support restriction*

What Makes a Prenuptial Agreement Unenforceable?

- Agreement not made voluntarily
- Agreement unconscionable when signed and prior to signing, party objecting to enforcement did not know other party's finances and was not given fair and reasonable disclosure
- Alimony waiver, if it would cause waiving party to be eligible for public assistance
- Annulment of marriage, unless result would be inequitable and unless agreement provides that it is enforceable in the event of annulment
- Subject of agreement against public policy or criminal laws

Inheritance

Election Rights

D.C. Code Ann. § 19-113

- Surviving spouse entitled to up to one-half the net estate

Allowance Rights

D.C. Code Ann. §§19-101.02 to 19-101.04

- **Homestead.** Up to $15,000 (deceased must have been D.C. resident at the time of death)
- **Exempt property.** Up to $10,000 in furniture, personal effects, appliances, and automobiles (deceased must have been D.C. resident at the time of death)
- **Family allowance.** Reasonable support while estate is being administered

Waiver of Inheritance Rights

- May waive rights to deceased spouse's real and personal estate in a valid prenuptial agreement; waiver does not affect surviving spouse's right to benefits from any other bequest or provision (D.C. Code Ann. § 19-113(f))

Divorce

Division of Property at Divorce

D.C. Code Ann. § 16-910

Property division method: Equitable distribution

Marital fault considered? May be considered

Other factors affecting property division:

- All property accumulated during marriage is subject to division, whether title is held individually or jointly
- Duration of marriage and circumstances that contributed to estrangement
- Age, health, sources of income, employability, skills, assets, debts, and needs of each spouse, including opportunity for future acquisition of assets and income
- Custody of minor children
- Responsibility for children or spouse from prior marriage
- Contribution to other spouse's education and to family (includes homemaking)
- Each spouse's contribution to acquisition, appreciation, or depreciation of marital assets.

Temporary Alimony

D.C. Code Ann. § 16-911

- Court may award temporary alimony, child support for minor children, and costs and attorney fees to cover divorce proceedings
- Award considers same factors as permanent alimony (below)

Permanent Alimony Award

D.C. Code Ann. § 16-913

Marital fault considered? May be considered

Other factors affecting alimony award: The same as those considered for property division plus:

- Standard of living established during marriage
- Ability of either spouse to be self-supporting

- Time and money required for either spouse to obtain education or training needed for appropriate employment
- Financial needs and resources, including current and potential income, obligations, and eligibility for retirement benefits

Circumstances That Terminate or Modify Alimony

- Change in needs or financial resources of either party (*Alibrando v. Alibrando,* 375 A.2d 9, 1977)

Debts

D.C. Code Ann. § 46-601

- Neither spouse's separate property is liable for the other's debts
- Both spouses are liable for debts incurred during marriage for necessities or for support of dependent children

Florida

Prenuptial Agreements

Legal term: Antenuptial Agreement

Has state adopted UPAA? No

State code sections: Fla. Stat. Ann, §§ 61.14; 732.102

Important court cases: *Posner v. Posner,* 320 So.2d 455 (1975); *Casto v. Casto,* 508 So.2d 330 (1987)

Required Formalities for Prenuptial Agreements

- In writing
- Signed by both parties

Permitted Subjects of Prenuptial Agreements

- Property rights
- What happens to property at divorce or separation
- What happens to property upon death
- Alimony (spousal support or spousal maintenance), subject to modification if circumstances change unless modification rights waived
- Any other matter that does not violate public policy or criminal laws

What Makes a Prenuptial Agreement Unenforceable?

- Agreement was not made voluntarily or was made under fraud or duress
- Agreement was unreasonable when signed or when enforcement is sought
- Prior to signing, party objecting to enforcement was not given full disclosure of other party's finances
- Subject of agreement against public policy or criminal laws

Inheritance

Election Rights

Fla. Stat. Ann. § 732.2065

- 30% of estate

Allowance Rights

- **Homestead.** Right to homestead for life (Fla. Stat. Ann. § 732.401)
- **Exempt property.** Up to $10,000 in household furnishings and appliances from decedent's home; all family cars (Fla. Stat. Ann. § 732.402)
- **Family allowance.** Up to $18,000 (Fla. Stat. Ann. § 732.403)

Waiver of Inheritance Rights

- Antenuptial agreement that waives all inheritance rights includes waiver of statutory right to elective share *(De Garcia's Estate v. Garcia,* App. 3 Dist., 399 So.2d 486 (1981), rev. denied, 407 So.2d 1103)
- Waiver of all rights or partial rights is valid if written and signed in front of two witnesses (Fla. Stat. Ann. § 732.702)

Divorce

Division of Property at Divorce

Fla. Stat. Ann. § 61.075

Property division method: Equitable distribution

Marital fault considered: No

Other factors affecting property division:

- Duration of marriage
- Economic circumstances of the spouses
- Contribution to the marriage by each spouse, including child care and education, and homemaking services
- Interruption of personal career or educational opportunities, or contribution of one spouse to education or career of other
- Contribution of each spouse to the acquisition and improvement of, or the incurring of liabilities to, marital and nonmarital assets
- Intentional dissipation, depletion, or destruction of marital assets within two years before filing for divorce or after filing
- Desirability of keeping any asset intact and free from claim by the other spouse
- Need to maintain marital home as a residence for a dependent child or other person providing it is in their best interests and is equitable and financially feasible

Temporary Alimony

Fla. Stat. Ann. § 61.071

- Must make petition for alimony to pay for court costs ("suit money") when filing for divorce

Permanent Alimony Award

Fla. Stat. Ann. § 61.08

Marital fault considered? Adultery may be considered

Other factors affecting award:

- Duration of marriage and standard of living during marriage
- Age and physical and emotional condition of each spouse
- Financial resources of each spouse, including nonmarital and marital assets and liabilities
- Time required for either spouse to obtain education or training needed for appropriate employment

- Contribution of each spouse to the marriage, including services in homemaking, child care, education, and career development of the other spouse

Circumstances That Terminate or Modify Alimony

Fla. Stat. Ann. § 61.14

- Changed financial circumstances

Debts

- Husband not liable for premarital debts of wife (Fla. Stat. Ann. § 704.05)
- If wife gives separate property to secure husband's or marital debt, agreement must be in writing (Fla. Stat. Ann. §§ 704.08 to 704.10; *First Nat. Bank of Melbourne v. Berg,* 153 So.2d 331 Fla.App. 1963)

Georgia

Prenuptial Agreements

Legal term: Marriage Articles or Contract; Antenuptial Agreement

Has state adopted UPAA? No

State code sections: Ga. Code Ann. §§ 19-3-62 to 19-3-68

Important court cases: *Scherer v. Scherer,* 292 S.E.2d 662 (1982)

Required Formalities for Prenuptial Agreements

- Signed by both parties in front of two witnesses
- Notarized

Permitted Subjects of Prenuptial Agreements

- Property rights
- What happens to property at divorce or separation
- What happens to property upon death
- Alimony (spousal support or spousal maintenance)
- Terms of wills, trusts, or other estate planning documents
- Life insurance ownership and arrangements
- Any other matter that does not violate public policy or criminal laws

What Makes a Prenuptial Agreement Unenforceable?

- Agreement was not made voluntarily
- Agreement unconscionable
- One spouse failed to disclose material facts
- Subject of agreement against public policy or criminal laws
- Facts and circumstances changed so as to make enforcement unfair and unreasonable

Inheritance

Election Rights

Ga. Code Ann. § 53-2-1

- Entire estate if no children; or one-third to one-half estate depending on number of children

Allowance Rights

Ga. Code Ann. § 53-3-1

- **Family allowance.** Surviving spouse and minor children are entitled to one year's support

Waiver of Inheritance Rights

Ga. Code Ann. § 53-1-20

- Waiver must be in writing, describe property or benefit being renounced, and be signed by person making the waiver; waiver may also be filed with probate court and with county property records

Divorce

Division of Property at Divorce

Property division method: Equitable distribution

Marital fault considered? Yes

Other factors affecting property division:

- Court (jury) divides property in divorce verdict based on evidence heard in trial (Ga. Code Ann. § 19-5-13)

Temporary Alimony

Ga. Code Ann. § 19-6-3

- Based on cost of divorce and separate property of party seeking temporary alimony
- Court may consider causes of separation
- May include attorney's fees

Permanent Alimony Award

Ga. Code Ann. § 19-6-1

Marital fault considered? Adultery or desertion will prevent alimony award

Other factors affecting award:

- No alimony awarded if spouses live together during legal separation or while divorce is pending (temporary alimony will also be annulled) (Ga. Code Ann. § 19-6-12)
- Needs of spouse seeking alimony and ability of other spouse to pay
- Conduct of each spouse toward the other
- Duration of marriage and standard of living during marriage
- Age and physical and emotional condition of each spouse
- Financial resources of each spouse, including separate property, earning capacity, and fixed liabilities
- Time required for either spouse to obtain education or training needed for appropriate employment
- Contribution of each spouse to the marriage, including services in homemaking, child care, education, and career development of the other spouse.

Circumstances That Terminate or Modify Alimony

- Remarriage (Ga. Code Ann. § 19-6-5)
- Cohabitation with a third party (Ga. Code Ann. § 19-6-19)
- Change of financial circumstances (Ga. Code Ann. § 19-6-19)

Debts

- After permanent alimony awarded, spouse paying alimony is no longer liable for former spouse's debt (Ga. Code Ann. § 19-6-6)

- Separate property of each spouse remains separate and is not liable for other spouse's debts (Ga. Code Ann. § 19-3-9)

Hawaii

Prenuptial Agreements

Legal term: Premarital Agreement
Has state adopted UPAA? Yes
State code sections: Haw. Rev. Stat. §§ 572D-1 to 572D-11; 560:2 -213

Required Formalities for Prenuptial Agreements

- In writing
- Signed by both parties

Permitted Subjects of Prenuptial Agreements

- Property rights
- Rights to sell, transfer, or control property
- What happens to property at divorce or separation
- What happens to property upon death
- Alimony (spousal support, spousal maintenance)
- Terms of wills, trusts or other estate planning documents
- Life insurance ownership and arrangements
- Applicable state law
- Any other matter that does not violate public policy or criminal laws
- *Not permitted: child support restriction*

What Makes a Prenuptial Agreement Unenforceable?

- Agreement not made voluntarily
- Agreement unconscionable when signed and prior to signing, party objecting to enforcement did not know other party's finances and was not given fair and reasonable disclosure
- Alimony waiver, if it would cause waiving spouse to be eligible for public assistance
- Annulment of marriage, unless result would be inequitable
- Subject of agreement against public policy or criminal laws

Inheritance

Election Rights

- From 3% to 50% of the augmented estate depending on the length of the marriage (one year minimum up to 15 years for maximum percentage)
- If the amount of the elective share plus the value of any other property passing to the spouse by non-probate transfer, joint tenancy, or co-ownership is less than $50,000, the surviving spouse is entitled to a supplemental elective share that will bring the total to $50,000
- Taking elective share does not affect rights to exempt property, homestead, or family allowance (Haw. Rev. Stat. § 560:2-202)

Allowance Rights

- **Homestead allowance.** $15,000 (Haw. Rev. Stat. § 560:2-402)
- **Exempt property.** Up to $10,000 in household furniture, furnishings, appliances, automobiles, and personal effects (Haw. Rev. Stat. § 560:2-403)
- **Family allowance.** Reasonable maintenance for spouse and dependent children for up to one year while estate is being settled (Haw. Rev. Stat. § 560:2-404)

Waiver of Inheritance Rights

Haw. Rev. Stat. § 560:2-213

- All rights may be wholly or partially waived by written agreement or contract signed by person waiving right
- Waiver is not enforceable if: 1) it was not made voluntarily; 2) person executing waiver was not given fair disclosure of decedent's property or financial obligations, did not expressly waive right to such disclosure, and did not have or could not have had knowledge of property or obligations; or 3) waiver was unconscionable (court must decide this issue)
- Waiver of "all rights" presumes waiver of right to elective share, homestead, property, and family allowance

Divorce

Division of Property at Divorce

Haw. Rev. Stat. § 580-47(a)
Property division method: Equitable distribution
Marital fault considered? No
Factors affecting property division:

- Either spouse's contribution to the other spouse's acquisition of separate property or to the accumulation and preservation of marital property
- Relative abilities of each spouse
- Condition in which each spouse will be left by the divorce
- Responsibilities of each spouse in supporting and caring for the children

Temporary Alimony

Haw. Rev. Stat. § 580-9

- Reasonable advances to cover costs of divorce

Permanent Alimony Award

Haw. Rev. Stat. § 580-47(a)

Marital fault considered? No

Factors affecting permanent alimony award: Same factors as for property division, plus:

- Financial resources and needs of each spouse
- Age and physical and emotional condition of each spouse
- Ability of spouse seeking support to meet needs independently
- Vocational skills and employability of spouse seeking support
- Usual occupation of each spouse during marriage
- Duration of marriage and standard of living during marriage
- Custodial and child support responsibilities of each spouse
- Ability of spouse from whom support sought to meet own needs while paying alimony
- How long it will take the spouse seeking support to complete training or education necessary to qualify for appropriate employment as well as additional time needed to secure employment

Circumstances That Terminate or Modify Alimony

- Change in physical or financial circumstances (Haw. Rev. Stat. § 580-47(d))

Debts

Haw. Rev. Stat. §§ 572-21 to 572-25

- Neither spouse is liable for other spouse's debts
- Separate property of each spouse remains separate and can't be taken to pay spouse's debts

Idaho

Prenuptial Agreements

Legal term: Premarital Agreement

Has state adopted UPAA? Yes

State code sections: Idaho Code, §§ 32-921 to 32-929; 15-2-208

Required Formalities for Prenuptial Agreements

- In writing
- Signed by both parties
- Notarized

Permitted Subjects of Prenuptial Agreements

- Property rights
- Rights to sell, transfer, or control property
- What happens to property at divorce or separation
- What happens to property upon death
- Alimony (spousal support or spousal maintenance)
- Terms of wills, trusts, or other estate planning documents
- Life insurance ownership and arrangements
- Applicable state law
- Any other matter that does not violate public policy or criminal laws
- *Not permitted: child support restriction*

What Makes a Prenuptial Agreement Unenforceable?

- Agreement not made voluntarily
- Agreement unconscionable when signed and prior to signing, party objecting to enforcement did not know other party's finances and was not given fair and reasonable disclosure
- Alimony waiver, if it would cause waiving spouse to be eligible for public assistance
- Annulment of marriage, unless result would be inequitable
- Subject of agreement against public policy or criminal laws

Inheritance

Election Rights

- Surviving spouse is entitled to one-half of all community property; deceased spouse has right to dispose of separate property and his or her own half of the community property as desired (Idaho Code § 15-3-101)
- Surviving spouse has right to one-half of quasi-community property (the other half is subject to provisions of the deceased spouse's estate plan); if estate plan makes no provision, all quasi-community property goes to the surviving spouse (Idaho Code § 15-2-201)
- In some circumstances, if deceased spouse gave away quasi-community property, or sold it for less than its value, surviving spouse can demand that the property be returned to the deceased spouse's estate; surviving spouse can then claim half of that property (Idaho Code § 15-2-202 and following)

Allowance Rights

- **Homestead.** If the homestead is community property, it automatically passes to the surviving spouse; if it is not community property, surviving spouse is entitled to the value of the homestead or $50,000, whichever is less (Idaho Code §§ 15-2-402, 55-1010, 55-1003)
- **Exempt property.** Up to $10,000 in household furniture, automobiles, furnishings, appliances, and personal effects (Idaho Code § 15-2-403)
- **Family allowance.** Reasonable maintenance for spouse and dependent children for up to one year while estate is being settled (Idaho Code § 15-2-404)

Waiver of Inheritance Rights

Idaho Code § 15-2-208

- May waive all or partial rights to homestead allowance, exempt property, family allowance, and elective share
- Waiver must be a written contract, agreement, or waiver signed by the party waiving after fair disclosure

Divorce

Division of Property at Divorce

Idaho Code § 32-712

Property division method: Community property

Marital fault considered? No

- Community property divided equally unless there are compelling reasons not to do so
- Homestead may be awarded to one spouse as share of community property
- Age, health, occupation, amount and source of income, vocational skills, employability, present and potential earning capacity, retirement benefits, and liabilities of each spouse may be considered when dividing property
- Whether share of property is in addition to or instead of alimony

Temporary Alimony

Idaho Code § 32-704

- Court may order temporary support and maintenance
- Court may order a reasonable amount to pay costs of divorce

Permanent Alimony

Idaho Code § 32-705

Marital fault considered? May be considered

Other factors affecting award:

- Age and physical and emotional condition of spouse seeking support
- Financial resources of spouse seeking support, including share of marital property
- Ability of spouse seeking support to meet needs independently

Amount and duration of alimony may also be affected by:

- Time required for spouse seeking support to obtain education or training for appropriate employment
- Duration of marriage
- Ability of spouse from whom support is sought to meet own needs while paying alimony
- Tax consequences to each spouse

Circumstances That Terminate or Modify Alimony

Idaho Code § 32-709

- Substantial and material (physical and/or financial) change of circumstances

Debts

- Husband not responsible for wife's debts before marriage (Idaho Code § 32-910)
- Wife not responsible for husband's debts, both before and after marriage (Idaho Code § 32-911)

Illinois

Prenuptial Agreements

Legal term: Prenuptial Agreement

Has state adopted UPAA? Yes

State code sections: 750 Ill. Comp. Stat. §§ 10/1 to 10/11

Important court cases: *Estate of Ronald E. Anderson,* 552 N.E.2d 429 (1990)

Required Formalities for Prenuptial Agreements

- In writing
- Signed by both parties

Permitted Subjects of Prenuptial Agreements

- Property rights
- Rights to sell, transfer, or control property
- What happens to property at divorce or separation
- What happens to property upon death
- Alimony (spousal support or spousal maintenance)
- Terms of wills, trusts, or other estate planning documents
- Life insurance ownership and arrangements
- Applicable state law
- Any other matter that does not violate public policy or criminal laws
- *Not permitted: child support restriction*

What Makes a Prenuptial Agreement Unenforceable?

- Agreement not made voluntarily
- Agreement unconscionable when enforcement sought and prior to signing, party objecting to enforcement did not know other party's finances and was not given fair and reasonable disclosure
- Alimony waiver, if it would cause waiving spouse undue hardship
- Annulment, unless result would be inequitable
- Subject of agreement against public policy or criminal laws

Inheritance

Election Rights

755 Ill. Comp. Stat. § 5/2-8

- Surviving spouse entitled to one-half of deceased spouse's estate if deceased spouse has no descendants, or one-third if there are descendants

Allowance Rights

755 Ill. Comp. Stat. §§ 5/15-1 to 15-4

- **Family allowance.** Reasonable support for up to nine months while estate is being settled, but no less than

$10,000; spouse may choose allowance in cash or in goods not left by will

Waiver of Inheritance Rights

755 Ill. Comp. Stat. § 5/2-7

- Waiver must describe property being disclaimed and be signed by person waiving rights (or a representative)
- Signed copy of waiver may be filed with clerk of court in county where estate is likely to be settled
- If rights to real property waived, waiver may be filed with recorder in county where property located

Divorce

Division of Property at Divorce

750 Ill. Comp. Stat. § 5/503

Property division method: Equitable distribution

Marital fault considered? No

Factors affecting property division:

- Court will enforce any valid agreement made by spouses themselves, unless it is unconscionable
- Duration of marriage
- Contribution of each spouse to the acquisition, increase, or decrease in value of the marital or nonmarital property, including contribution as a homemaker,
- Dissipation by each spouse of marital or nonmarital property
- Value and tax consequences of the property assigned to each spouse
- Economic circumstances of each spouse, including the desirability of awarding the family home, or the right to live there, to the spouse having custody of the children
- Obligations and rights arising from a prior marriage
- Age, health, occupation, amount and sources of income, vocational skills, employability, opportunity for acquisition of assets and income, liabilities, and needs of each spouse
- Whether property award is instead of or in addition to alimony

Temporary Alimony

750 Ill. Comp. Stat. § 5/501

- Court may award temporary maintenance or child support
- Request must be accompanied by affidavit as providing facts that make temporary maintenance or support necessary

Permanent Alimony

750 Ill. Comp. Stat. § 5/504

Marital fault considered? No

Factors affecting award include:

- Age and physical and emotional condition of both spouses
- Income and property of each spouse, including marital property award
- Needs of each spouse
- Present and future earning capacity of each spouse
- Impairment to earning capacity of spouse seeking maintenance due to domestic duties or postponement or sacrifice of education, training, employment, or career opportunities because of the marriage
- Contributions by spouse seeking maintenance to education, training, career or career potential, or license of the other spouse
- Duration of marriage and standard of living during marriage
- Time needed for spouse seeking maintenance to acquire education, training, and employment
- Whether spouse seeking maintenance is able to be self-supporting through suitable employment, or has custody of a child and employment is not appropriate
- Any valid agreement of the spouses
- Any other factor that the court expressly finds to be just and equitable

Circumstances That Terminate or Modify Alimony

750 Ill. Comp. Stat. § 5/510

- Remarriage or cohabitation
- Substantial change in circumstances

Debts

750 Ill. Comp. Stat. § 65/5

- Neither spouse is liable for debts the other incurred before marriage
- Neither spouse is liable for the other's separate debts, nor can earnings, separate property, or income from property be subject to the other's debts

Indiana

Prenuptial Agreements

Legal term: Premarital Agreement

Has state adopted UPAA? Yes

State code sections: Ind. Code Ann. §§ 31-11-3-1 to 31-11-3-10; 29-1-2-13

Required Formalities for Prenuptial Agreements

- In writing
- Signed by both parties

Permitted Subjects of Prenuptial Agreements

- Property rights
- Rights to sell, transfer, or control property
- What happens to property at divorce or separation
- What happens to property upon death
- Alimony (spousal support or spousal maintenance)
- Terms of wills, trusts, or other estate planning documents
- Life insurance ownership and arrangements
- Applicable state law
- Any other matter that does not violate public policy or criminal laws
- *Not permitted: child support restriction*

What Makes a Prenuptial Agreement Unenforceable?

- Agreement not made voluntarily
- Agreement unconscionable when signed
- Alimony waiver, if it would cause waiving spouse extreme hardship
- Annulment, unless result would be inequitable
- Subject of agreement against public policy or criminal laws

Inheritance

Election Rights

Ind. Code Ann. § 29-1-3-1

- One-half of the net personal and real estate of the deceased spouse
- If surviving spouse is a second or subsequent spouse, there are no children of the marriage, and the deceased spouse has children by a previous marriage, then elective share is one-third of the net personal estate and a life interest in one-third of any real estate

Allowance Rights

Ind. Code Ann. § 29-1-4-1

- Surviving spouse entitled to an allowance of $25,000 (deceased spouse must have been living in Indiana at the time of death)

Waiver of Inheritance Rights

Ind. Code Ann. § 29-1-3-6

- Right to elective share may be waived by a written contract or agreement signed by the person waiving after a full disclosure of what is being waived
- Waiver may be recorded and filed with the clerk of the court where estate is likely to be settled

Divorce

Division of Property at Divorce

Ind. Code Ann. §§ 31-15-7-4 to 31-15-7-7

Property division method: Equitable distribution

Marital fault considered? No

Factors affecting property division: Court presumes that equal division of the marital property is just and reasonable, but will accept evidence that unequal division is fair based on these factors:

- Contribution of each spouse to the acquisition of the property
- Conduct of each spouse in the disposition or dissipation of the property
- Whether any property was acquired by each spouse before marriage or through inheritance or gift
- Economic circumstances, earnings, or earning ability of each spouse after division of property
- Tax consequences of the property division for each spouse's present and future economic circumstances
- Desirability of awarding family residence (or the right to live in it) to spouse who is custodial parent
- If there is little or no marital property, court may award either spouse a money judgment in recognition of that spouse's financial contribution toward tuition, books, and laboratory fees for the higher education of the other spouse (Ind. Code Ann. § 31-15-7-6)

Temporary Alimony

Ind. Code Ann. § 31-15-4-8

- Court may issue temporary alimony in amount that seems fair and just

Permanent Alimony

Ind. Code Ann. § 31-15-7-2

Marital fault considered? No

Factors affecting award include:

- Educational level of each spouse at time of marriage and time of filing for divorce
- Whether spouse lacks sufficient property, including awarded marital property, to provide for needs

- Whether one spouse is the custodial parent of a child whose physical or mental incapacity requires parent to forgo employment
- Interruption in the education, training, or employment of spouse seeking maintenance as a result of home-making and/or child care responsibilities
- Earning capacity of each spouse, including educational background, training, employment skills, work experience, and time in or away from the job market
- Time and expense required for spouse seeking maintenance to acquire education or training needed to find appropriate employment (spouse seeking support may be awarded rehabilitative maintenance, but for no longer than three years after the final decree)

- Whether one spouse is physically or mentally incapacitated and ability to support self is materially affected (alimony awarded during period of incapacity)

Circumstances That Terminate or Modify Alimony
Ind. Code Ann. § 31-15-7-3

- Substantial and continuing change in circumstances that makes current terms unreasonable

Debts
Ind. Code Ann. §§ 31-11-7-3, 31-11-7-4

- Married woman is responsible for own contracts and debts
- Husband not liable for wife's contracts and debts

Iowa

Prenuptial Agreements

Legal term: Premarital Agreement

Has state adopted UPAA? Yes

State code sections: Iowa Code §§ 596.1 to 596.12

Important court cases: *Estate of Spurgeon,* 572 N.W.2d 595 (1998)

Required Formalities for Prenuptial Agreements

- In writing
- Signed by both parties

Permitted Subjects of Prenuptial Agreements

- Property rights
- Rights to sell, transfer, or control property
- What happens to property at divorce or separation
- What happens to property upon death
- Terms of wills, trusts, or other estate planning documents
- Life insurance ownership and arrangements
- Applicable state law
- Any other matter that does not violate public policy or criminal laws
- *Not permitted: child support restriction; a spousal support restriction may be included in a prenuptial agreement but a court may decide not to enforce it*

What Makes a Prenuptial Agreement Unenforceable?

- Agreement not made voluntarily
- Agreement unconscionable when signed
- Prior to signing, party objecting to enforcement did not know other party's finances and was not given fair and reasonable disclosure
- Annulment of marriage, unless result would be inequitable
- Subject of agreement against public policy or criminal laws

Inheritance

Election Rights

Iowa Code § 633.238

- One-third of all real property; all personal property exempt from claims against estate; one-third of all other personal property if not needed to pay debts and expenses

Allowance Rights

- **Homestead.** Surviving spouse may choose to occupy homestead instead of retaining one-third interest in deceased spouse's real property; choosing homestead does not affect rights in personal property under elective share (Iowa Code § 633.240)
- **Family allowance.** Reasonable support for up to 12 months while estate being settled, even if surviving spouse remarries (Iowa Code § 633.374)

Waiver of Inheritance Rights

Matter of Estate of Spurgeon, 572 N.W.2d 595 (1998))

- Premarital agreement that waives inheritance rights is valid, but court has discretion to modify provisions regarding family allowance

Divorce

Division of Property at Divorce

Iowa Code § 598.21(1),(2)

Property division method: Equitable distribution

Marital fault considered? No

Factors affecting property division:

- Length of marriage
- Property each spouse brought to marriage
- Contribution of each spouse to marriage, giving appropriate economic value to homemaking and child care
- Contribution by one spouse to education, training, or increased earning power of the other
- Age and physical and emotional health of spouses
- Earning capacity of each spouse, including educational background, training, employment skills, work experience, and length of absence from job market
- Other economic circumstances of each spouse, including pension benefits, vested or unvested, and future interests
- Tax consequences to each spouse
- Custodial responsibilities for children
- Time and expense needed for custodial parent to acquire sufficient education or training to become self-supporting at a standard of living reasonably comparable to that enjoyed during marriage
- Desirability of awarding family home or right to live in it to custodial parent, or if parents have joint legal custody, to parent having physical custody
- Amount and duration of permanent alimony and whether property division is instead of or in addition to alimony
- Any written agreement made by the spouses concerning property distribution

- Court may set aside a portion of the property in a separate fund or conservatorship for the support, education, and general welfare of any minor children

Temporary Alimony

Iowa Code § 598.11

- Court may order either spouse to submit payment for other spouse's support and maintenance and divorce expenses
- Court may consider age of spouse seeking alimony, physical and economic condition of both spouses, and any other relevant facts

Permanent Alimony

Iowa Code § 598.21(3)

Marital fault considered? No

Factors affecting award include: Award, amount, and duration of permanent alimony based on same factors as those affecting property division, as well as:

- Distribution of marital property
- Educational level of each spouse at the time of marriage and at the time divorce proceedings begin
- Whether and when spouse seeking alimony can become self-supporting at a standard of living reasonably comparable to that enjoyed during marriage
- Any mutual agreement made by the spouses about contributions by one spouse with the expectation of future reciprocation or compensation by the other spouse

Circumstances That Terminate or Modify Alimony

Iowa Code § 598.21(8)

Changes in either spouse's:

- Employment, earning capacity, income, or resources
- Physical, mental, or emotional health
- Medical expenses
- Number or needs of dependents
- Residence

Other circumstances that may affect continuation of alimony award:

- Receipt of inheritance, pension, or other gift
- Remarriage
- Possible support by another person
- Changes in physical, emotional, or educational needs of a child whose support is governed by the order
- Violation of existing court orders

Debts

Iowa Code §§ 597.17 and following

- Neither spouse is liable for debts or liabilities the other spouse incurred before marriage or for separate debts contracted after marriage
- Neither spouse's wages, earnings, or property (or rent or income from the property) is liable for the other spouse's separate debts

Kansas

Prenuptial Agreements

Legal term: Premarital Agreement

Has state adopted UPAA? Yes

State code sections: Kan. Stat. Ann. §§ 23-801 to 23-811; 59-6a213

Required Formalities for Prenuptial Agreements

- In writing
- Signed by both parties

Permitted Subjects of Prenuptial Agreements

- Property rights
- Rights to sell, transfer, or control property
- What happens to property at divorce or separation
- What happens to property upon death
- Alimony (spousal support or spousal maintenance)
- Terms of wills, trusts, or other estate planning documents
- Life insurance ownership and arrangements
- Applicable state law
- Any other matter that does not violate public policy or criminal laws
- *Not permitted: child support restriction*

What Makes a Prenuptial Agreement Unenforceable?

- Agreement not made voluntarily
- Agreement unconscionable when signed and prior to signing, party objecting to enforcement did not know other party's finances and was not given fair and reasonable disclosure
- Alimony waiver, if it would cause waiving spouse to be eligible for public assistance
- Annulment of marriage, unless result would be inequitable
- Subject of agreement against public policy or criminal laws

Inheritance

Election Rights

Kan. Stat. Ann. § 59-6a202

- From 3% to 50% of the augmented estate depending on the length of the marriage (must be married at least one year for minimum; maximum reached at 15 years)
- If elective share plus value of any other property passing to the spouse by nonprobate transfer, joint tenancy, or co-ownership is less than $50,000, surviving spouse is entitled to a supplemental elective share to bring the total to $50,000

Allowance Rights

- **Homestead.** Surviving spouse entitled to homestead or may choose a homestead allowance of $35,000; homestead or homestead allowance is in addition to elective share (Kan. Stat. Ann. § 59-6a215)
- **Exempt property.** Clothing, family library, pictures, musical instruments, furniture and household goods, utensils and implements, one automobile, food, and fuel needed for support for one year (Kan. Stat. Ann. § 59-403)

Waiver of Inheritance Rights

Kan. Stat. Ann. § 59-6a213

- All rights, including elective share, may be wholly or partially waived by signed, written agreement
- To waive rights in homestead, homestead allowance, or family allowance, agreement must state clearly that any or all of these rights is waived with full knowledge
- Waiver is not enforceable if: 1) it was not made voluntarily; 2) person executing waiver was not given fair disclosure of decedent's property or financial obligations, did not expressly waive right to such disclosure, and did not have or could not have had knowledge of property or obligations; or 3) waiver was unconscionable

Divorce

Division of Property at Divorce

Kan. Stat. Ann. § 60-1610(b,1)

Property division method: Equitable distribution

Marital fault considered? No

Factors affecting property division:

- Age of spouses
- Duration of marriage
- Property owned by each spouse
- Present and future earning capacities
- Family ties and obligations
- Alimony award
- Dissipation of assets
- Tax consequences of the property division

Temporary Alimony

Kan. Stat. Ann. § 60-1607(a.3), (a.5)

- Either spouse may be awarded temporary support and expenses to cover cost of divorce and attorney's fees

Permanent Alimony

Kan. Stat. Ann. § 60-1610(b)(2)

Marital fault considered? No

Factors governing award:

- May be in a lump sum or installments, based on a percentage of earnings or on any other basis
- Either party may be awarded maintenance for up to 121 months; may petition for reinstatement of alimony, but no single term can be more than 121 months
- Either party may be awarded costs and attorney fees (Kan. Stat. Ann. § 60-1610(b)(4))

Circumstances That Terminate or Modify Alimony

Kan. Stat. Ann. § 60-1610(b)(2)

- No modification that increases original award will be made without consent of the party paying alimony

Debts

Kan. Stat. Ann. § 23-201

- Separate property of either spouse is not liable for debts of other

Kentucky

Prenuptial Agreements

Legal term: Antenuptial Agreement

Has state adopted UPAA? No

State code sections: Ky. Rev. Stat. Ann. §§ 371.010(5); 403.190(2)(d)

Important court cases: *Gentry v. Gentry,* 798 S.W.2d 928 (1990); *Edwardson v. Edwardson,* 798 S.W.2d 941 (1990); *Gaines v. Gaines' Administrator,* 173 S.W. 774 (1915)

Required Formalities for Prenuptial Agreements

- In writing

Permitted Subjects of Prenuptial Agreements

- Property rights
- What happens to property at divorce or separation
- What happens to property upon death
- Alimony (spousal support or spousal maintenance)
- Any other matter that does not violate public policy or criminal laws

What Makes a Prenuptial Agreement Unenforceable?

- Agreement not made voluntarily
- Agreement unconscionable when enforcement sought
- Prior to signing, party objecting to enforcement did not know other party's finances and was not given fair and reasonable disclosure
- Subject of agreement against public policy or criminal laws

Inheritance

Election Rights

Ky. Rev. Stat. Ann. §§ 392.020, 392.080

- One-half of deceased spouse's personal property; one-third of deceased spouse's real property; right to use one-third of any other real estate acquired during marriage for life
- In the event of divorce or adultery, surviving spouse may not claim any property from deceased spouse's estate (Ky. Rev. Stat. Ann. § 392.090)

Allowance Rights

Ky. Rev. Stat. Ann. § 391.030

- **Exempt property.** Up to $15,000 in cash or property; may withdraw $1,000 from any account belonging to deceased spouse (must get court order to release funds; any withdrawals will be deducted from the $15,000 worth of exempt property)

Waiver of Inheritance Rights

Ky. Rev. Stat. Ann. § 392.090

- No statute

Divorce

Division of Property at Divorce

Ky. Rev. Stat. Ann. § 403.190

Property division method: Equitable distribution

Marital fault considered? No

Factors affecting property division:

- Contribution of each spouse to acquisition of marital property, including contribution of a homemaker
- Value of property awarded to each spouse
- Duration of marriage
- Economic circumstances of each spouse after division of property
- Desirability of awarding family home or right to live in it to spouse who is custodial parent
- If retirement benefits of one spouse are excluded from marital property, then benefits of other spouse are also excluded

Temporary Alimony

Ky. Rev. Stat. Ann. § 403.160

- Either party may request temporary maintenance; requires affidavit providing facts that show need for support

Permanent Award

Ky. Rev. Stat. Ann. § 403.200(1)

Marital fault considered? No

Factors affecting award:

- Financial resources of spouse seeking maintenance and spouse's ability to meet needs independently
- Time necessary to acquire sufficient education or training so that spouse seeking maintenance can find appropriate employment
- Standard of living during marriage
- Duration of marriage
- Age and physical and emotional condition of the spouse seeking maintenance
- Ability of the spouse from whom maintenance is sought to meet own needs while paying alimony
- Spouse seeking award must lack sufficient property, including share of marital property, to provide for own reasonable needs
- Spouse seeking award must be unable to become self-supporting through appropriate employment or

be the custodial parent of a child whose condition or circumstances require parent to remain at home

Circumstances That Terminate or Modify Alimony

Ky. Rev. Stat. Ann. § 403.250

- Substantial and continuing change in circumstances that makes existing terms unconscionable
- Death or remarriage of one of the parties

Debts

Ky. Rev. Stat. Ann. § 404.010

- Married woman has complete right to property she acquired before or after marriage; wife's property is not liable for husband's debts
- Married woman is responsible for debts she incurred before or after marriage
- Husband is not liable for debts wife incurred before or after marriage, but is liable for her necessaries after marriage (Ky. Rev. Stat. Ann. § 404.040)

Louisiana

Prenuptial Agreements

Legal term: Premarital Contract; Antenuptial Agreement

Has state adopted UPAA? No

State code sections: La. Civ. Code Art. 2328 to 2336; 2369.8 to 2370

Important court cases: *Lamb v. Lamb,* 460 So.2d 634 (1984); *Holliday v. Holliday,* 358 So.2d 618 (1978)

Required Formalities for Prenuptial Agreements

- In writing
- Signed by both parties
- Notarized and witnessed

Permitted Subjects of Prenuptial Agreements

- Property rights
- What happens to property at divorce or separation
- What happens to property upon death
- Alimony (spousal support or spousal maintenance)
- Any other matter that does not violate public policy or criminal laws
- *Not permitted: Rights to sell, transfer, or control community property*

What Makes a Prenuptial Agreement Unenforceable?

- Agreement not made voluntarily
- Agreement waiving alimony is not enforceable if it encourages divorce

Inheritance

Election Rights

- **Community property.** Surviving spouse entitled to half of all community property. Deceased spouse may dispose of separate property and other half of community property. (La. Civ. Code Art. 2336, 2369.1)
- **Marital portion.** If value of deceased spouse's separate property is disproportionately greater than surviving spouse's separate property and share of community property, or if surviving spouse is left without adequate support, surviving spouse is entitled to: one-fourth of deceased spouse's separate property (if deceased spouse had no children); lifetime use of one-fourth of deceased spouse's separate property (if deceased spouse had three or fewer children); or lifetime use of the child's share of deceased spouse's separate property (if deceased spouse had more than three children). Any inheritance from will is deducted from marital portion, which may not exceed one million dollars (La. Civ. Code Art. 2432 to 2436)

Allowance Rights

- **Temporary allowance.** Surviving spouse who will be entitled to marital portion may receive allowance while estate is being settled; if allowance adds up to more than marital portion, surviving spouse is liable for deficiency (La. Civ. Code Art. 2437)

Waiver of Inheritance Rights

- Spouses may not renounce or alter the marital portion (La. Civ. Code Art. 2330)

Divorce

Division of Property at Divorce

La. Civ. Code Art. 2369.2, 2369.8, 2374

Property division method: Community Property

Marital fault considered? No

Factors affecting property division:

- Each spouse is entitled to 50% of all community property and its profits
- Any agreement that prevents division of community property is invalid

Temporary Alimony

- Court may award temporary support to spouse who is without fault (La. Civ. Code Art. 111)
- Award based on needs of spouse seeking support, ability of other spouse to pay, and standard of living during marriage (La. Civ. Code Art. 113)
- Temporary alimony ends when permanent alimony is awarded or denied or 180 days after divorce decree, whichever is sooner

Permanent Alimony

La. Civ. Code Art. 112

Marital fault considered? Yes

Other factors affecting award include:

- Duration of marriage
- Needs of each spouse
- Health and age of each spouse
- Income and assets of each spouse, including liquidity of assets
- Financial obligations of each spouse
- Earning capacity of each spouse and effect of child custody on earning capacity
- Time necessary for the spouse seeking support to acquire appropriate education, training, or employment
- Tax consequences
- Amount of award cannot exceed one-third of the paying spouse's net income

Circumstances That Terminate or Modify Alimony

La. Civ. Code Art. 114 to 115

- Material (physical or financial) change in circumstance of either spouse that makes support unnecessary
- Death of either spouse
- Remarriage or cohabitation (requires judicial determination) of party receiving support

Debts

La. Civ. Code Art. 2357 and following

- Debts incurred during marriage are presumed to be community debts payable from community property (La. Civ. Code Art. 2361)
- If one spouse incurs a debt before marriage, or during marriage but not for the benefit of both spouses or for the other spouse, it is a separate debt (La. Civ. Code Art. 2363)
- Costs of divorce and attorney's fees are debts payable from community property (La. Civ. Code Art. 2362.1)

Maine

Prenuptial Agreements

Legal term: Premarital Agreement

Has state adopted UPAA? Yes

State code sections: Me. Rev. Stat. Ann. tit. 19-A, §§ 601 to 611; tit. 18-A, § 2-204

Required Formalities for Prenuptial Agreements

- In writing
- Signed by both parties

Permitted Subjects of Prenuptial Agreements

- Property rights
- Rights to sell, transfer, or control property
- What happens to property at divorce or separation
- What happens to property upon death
- Alimony (spousal support or spousal maintenance)
- Terms of wills, trusts, or other estate planning documents
- Life insurance ownership and arrangements
- Applicable state law
- Any other matter that does not violate public policy or criminal laws
- *Not permitted: child support restriction*

What Makes a Prenuptial Agreement Unenforceable?

- Agreement not made voluntarily
- Agreement unconscionable when signed and prior to signing, party objecting to enforcement did not know other party's finances and was not given fair and reasonable disclosure
- Alimony waiver, if it would make waiving spouse eligible for public assistance
- Annulment of marriage, unless result would be inequitable
- Subject of agreement against public policy or criminal laws

Inheritance

Election Rights

- One-third of augmented estate, if deceased spouse was Maine resident at time of death (Me. Rev. Stat. Ann. tit. 18-A, § 2-201)
- Taking elective share does not affect surviving spouse's right to homestead and family allowance or exempt property (Me. Rev. Stat. Ann. tit. 18-A, § 2-206)

Allowance Rights

- **Homestead.** Surviving spouse entitled to homestead allowance of $10,000 (Me. Rev. Stat. Ann. tit. 18-A, § 2-401)
- **Exempt property.** Up to $7,000 in property (Me. Rev. Stat. Ann. tit. 18-A, § 2-402)
- **Family allowance.** Reasonable support for up to one year while estate is being settled (Me. Rev. Stat. Ann. tit. 18-A, § 2-403)

Waiver of Inheritance Rights

Me. Rev. Stat. Ann. tit. 18-A, § 2-204

- Rights may be wholly or partially waived by written agreement, contract, or waiver signed by the person waiving after full disclosure
- Waiver of "all rights" includes elective share, exempt property, homestead, and family allowance

Divorce

Division of Property at Divorce

Me. Rev. Stat. Ann. tit. 19-A, § 953

Property division method: Equitable distribution

Marital fault considered? No

Factors affecting property division:

- Contribution of each spouse to the acquisition of marital property, including the contribution of homemaker
- Value of property set apart to each spouse
- Economic circumstances of each spouse at the time of division of property
- Desirability of awarding family home or right to live in it to the spouse with custody of the children

Temporary Alimony

Me. Rev. Stat. Ann. tit. 19-A, § 951-A(2.E)

- May be awarded to support spouse during period of divorce proceeding or legal separation

Other Types of Alimony

Maine awards three different types of alimony:

General support (Me. Rev. Stat. Ann. tit. 19-A, § 951-A(2.A))

- Awarded to spouse with substantially less income potential than the other so that both can maintain a reasonable standard of living after the divorce
- Usually awarded only when spouses were married at least ten years, and for a period no longer than half the length of the marriage (longer award may

be made if spouses were married more than 20 years)

Transitional support

Me. Rev. Stat. Ann. tit. 19-A, § 951-A(2.B)

- To cover short-term needs resulting from financial hardships associated with divorce
- May cover expenses of reentry or advancement in the work force, including but not limited to physical or emotional rehabilitation services, vocational training, and education

Reimbursement support

Me. Rev. Stat. Ann. tit. 19-A, § 951-A(2.C)

- Awarded when spouses' financial circumstances are such that dividing marital property will not achieve equitable results
- May be awarded in response to "exceptional circumstances" such as economic misconduct by a spouse or substantial contributions by one spouse to the educational or occupational advancement of the other during the marriage

Factors Affecting Alimony Award

Me. Rev. Stat. Ann. tit. 19-A, § 951-A

Marital fault considered? No

Factors considered:

- Length of the marriage and standard of living during marriage
- Ability of each spouse to pay
- Age, health, and disabilities of each spouse
- Employment history and potential, income history and potential, education, and training of each spouse
- Retirement and health insurance benefits of each spouse
- Actual or potential income resulting from property division
- Tax consequences of support award and property division, including sale of marital home
- Contributions of either spouse as homemaker
- Contributions of either spouse to the education or earning potential of the other
- Economic misconduct by either spouse resulting in the diminution of marital property or income
- Ability of spouse seeking support to become self-supporting within a reasonable period
- Child support obligations

Circumstances That Terminate or Modify Alimony

Me. Rev. Stat. Ann. tit. 19-A, § 951-A(4)(5)

- "When it appears that justice requires," unless support order expressly limits future modification
- Support order must include any future limitations on increases or decreases in the amount and duration of alimony
- Support order must state whether alimony is subject to limitation upon remarriage or cohabitation of person receiving support

Debts

Me. Rev. Stat. Ann. tit. 19-A, § 804

- Neither spouse is liable for debts the other incurs before or after marriage

Maryland

Prenuptial Agreements

Legal term: Antenuptial Agreement

Has state adopted UPAA? No

State code sections: Md. Code Ann. [Est. & Trusts] § 3-205

Important court cases: *Martin v. Farber,* 68 Md.App. 137 (1986); *Frey v. Frey,* 298 Md. 552 (1984); *Hartz v. Hartz,* 248 Md. 47 (1967)

Required Formalities for Prenuptial Agreements

- In writing
- Signed by both parties

Permitted Subjects of Prenuptial Agreements

- Property rights
- What happens to property at divorce or separation
- What happens to property upon death
- Alimony (spousal support or spousal maintenance)
- Any other matter that does not violate public policy or criminal laws

What Makes a Prenuptial Agreement Unenforceable?

- Agreement not made voluntarily
- Agreement unconscionable when signed and prior to signing, party objecting to enforcement did not know other party's finances and was not given fair and reasonable disclosure
- Alimony waiver, if it would make waiving spouse eligible for public assistance
- Annulment, unless result would be inequitable
- Subject of agreement against public policy or criminal laws
- Agreement is not a "fair and reasonable" relinquishment of surviving spouse's rights and there was no "frank, full, and truthful" disclosure of rights being relinquished

Inheritance

Election Rights

Md. Code Ann. [Est. & Trusts] § 3-203

- Surviving spouse entitled to one-third net estate if the deceased spouse had children or one-half net estate if there are no children

Allowance Rights

Md. Code Ann. [Est. & Trusts] § 3-201

- Surviving spouse entitled to $5,000 for personal use

Waiver of Inheritance Rights

Md. Code Ann. [Est. & Trusts] § 3-205

- Right to elective share and allowance may be waived by written agreement, contract, or waiver signed by the person waiving
- A waiver of "all rights" presumes waiver of elective share and allowance
- Waiver is irrevocable

Divorce

Division of Property at Divorce

Md. Code Ann. [Fam. Law] § 8-205

Property division method: Equitable distribution

Marital fault considered? May be considered

Other factors affecting property division include:

- Duration of marriage
- Circumstances that contributed to estrangement of the spouses
- Age and physical and mental condition of each spouse
- Value of property interests and economic circumstances of each spouse
- Contributions, monetary and nonmonetary, of each spouse to the well-being of the family
- Pension, retirement, profit sharing, or deferred compensation plans of each or both spouses and contribution of each to value of plans
- Contribution by either spouse to the acquisition of real property held as tenants by the entirety
- Alimony award and any award concerning use of family home or family property

Special provisions concerning family home

Md. Code Ann. [Fam. Law] §§ 8-206 and following

- State policy is to allow children to remain in family home and to award temporary use of home and family property to custodial parent
- Interests of children take precedence over interests of spouses
- Spouse who does not live in home may still claim residence for tax purposes
- Award automatically terminates three years after decree or upon remarriage of spouse living in home, and home and family property become marital property

Temporary Alimony

Md. Code Ann. [Fam. Law] § 11-102

- May be awarded based on need for support while divorce pending

Permanent Alimony Award

Md. Code Ann. [Fam. Law] § 11-106

Marital fault considered? May be considered, but not automatic bar to award (Md. Code Ann. [Fam. Law] § 11-103)

Other factors affecting award include:

- Ability of spouse seeking alimony to be wholly or partly self-supporting
- Ability of spouse from whom alimony is sought to meet own needs while paying support
- Time necessary for spouse seeking alimony to obtain education or training required to find suitable employment
- Duration of marriage and standard of living during marriage
- Contributions, monetary and nonmonetary, of each spouse to the well-being of the family
- Circumstances that contributed to estrangement of the spouses
- Age and physical and mental condition of each spouse
- Financial needs, resources, and obligations of each spouse, including award of family home and property and right to receive retirement benefits

Circumstances That Terminate or Modify Alimony

Md. Code Ann. [Fam. Law] § 11-107

- Period of alimony may be extended if termination would lead to a "harsh and inequitable" result
- Award may be modified when "justice" requires

Debts

Md. Code Ann. [Fam. Law] § 4-301

- Neither spouse is liable for any debt the other incurs before marriage
- Husband not liable for any debts that wife incurs after marriage in her own name
- Wife's separate property, whether acquired before or after marriage, is not liable for husband's debts

Massachusetts

Prenuptial Agreements

Legal term: Antenuptial Settlement or Antenuptial Agreement

Has state adopted UPAA? No

State code sections: Mass. Gen. Laws. Ch. 209, §§ 25 and 26

Important court cases: *Osborne v. Osborne,* 384 Mass. 591 (1981); *Rosenberg v. Lipnick,* 389 N.E.2d 385 (1979)

Required Formalities for Prenuptial Agreements

- In writing
- Signed by both parties

Recorded in registry of deeds in county where husband lives

Permitted Subjects of Prenuptial Agreements

- Property rights
- What happens to property at divorce or separation
- What happens to property upon death
- Alimony (spousal support or spousal maintenance)
- Any other matter that does not violate public policy or criminal laws

What Makes a Prenuptial Agreement Unenforceable?

- Agreement not made voluntarily
- Terms of agreement not fair and reasonable at the time of signing
- Agreement signed without fair and full disclosure of finances
- Alimony waiver, if not fair and reasonable when enforcement sought
- Subject of agreement against public policy or criminal laws
- Failure to record agreement and to clearly note what property it covers

Inheritance

Election Rights

Mass. Gen. Laws ch. 191, § 15

- If deceased spouse has children, surviving spouse is entitled to one-third of personal and real property
- If deceased spouse has next of kin but no children, surviving spouse is entitled to $25,000 and one-half of remaining personal and real property up to $25,000 (entitled to interest only on personal and real property that exceeds $25,000)
- If deceased spouse has no children and no next of kin, surviving spouse is entitled to $25,000 and one-half of remaining personal and real property

Allowance Rights

- **Homestead.** Surviving spouse may remain in the home of deceased spouse rent-free for up to six months after death (Mass. Gen. Laws ch. 196, § 1)
- **Exempt property.** Whatever household and personal items are necessary for support of surviving spouse and for use of house (Mass. Gen. Laws ch. 196, § 2)

Waiver of Inheritance Rights

- No statute

Divorce

Division of Property at Divorce

Mass. Gen. Laws. Ch. 208, § 34

Property division method: Equitable distribution

Marital fault considered? Yes

Other factors affecting property division include:

- Duration of marriage
- Conduct of the spouses during the marriage
- Age, health, occupation, property, amount and sources of income, vocational skills, employability, liabilities, and needs of each spouse
- Opportunity of each spouse to acquire capital assets and income in the future
- Present and future needs of any dependent children
- Contribution of each spouse to the acquisition, preservation, or appreciation of each spouse's separate property
- Contribution of each spouse as a homemaker to the family unit
- In addition to or in place of alimony, court may award either spouse any portion of the other's property, including all retirement and pension, deferred compensation, and insurance benefits

Temporary Alimony

Mass. Gen. Laws. Ch. 208, § 17

- Either spouse may be awarded payment for costs of divorce and for support while divorce pending
- Includes provision to pay health insurance if spouse receiving alimony is not covered

Permanent Alimony Award

Mass. Gen. Laws. Ch. 208, § 34

Marital fault considered? Yes

Other factors affecting award include:

- Same factors as those used for Division of Property; see above

Circumstances That Terminate or Modify Alimony

Mass. Gen. Laws. Ch. 208, § 37

- Court decides; no circumstances specified

Debts

Mass. Gen. Laws. Ch. 209, §§ 1 and following

- Real and personal property of each spouse remain separate as if they were not married and cannot be held liable for the debts of the other

- Wife's earnings presumed to be her separate property
- Husband not liable for debts whether wife incurs before or after marriage

Michigan

Prenuptial Agreements

Legal term: Antenuptial Agreement or Contract
Has state adopted UPAA? No
State code sections: Mich. Comp. Laws §§ 557.28; 700.291
Important court cases: *Estate of Benker,* 416 Mich. 68 (1982)

Required Formalities for Prenuptial Agreements

- In writing
- Signed by both parties

Permitted Subjects of Prenuptial Agreements

- Property rights
- What happens to property at divorce or separation
- What happens to property upon death
- Alimony (spousal support or spousal maintenance)
- Any other matter that does not violate public policy or criminal laws

What Makes a Prenuptial Agreement Unenforceable?

- Agreement not made voluntarily, with each party understanding his or her rights
- Prior to signing, parties did not exchange fair and reasonable disclosure of finances
- Agreement not fair, equitable, and reasonable, in light of the surrounding circumstances
- Subject of agreement against public policy or criminal laws

Inheritance

Election Rights

Mich. Comp. Laws §§ 700.2202, 700.2102, 700.1210

- One-half of estate (if there are no children and no next of kin); or approximately $60,000 to $100,000 cash (depending on cost-of-living factors) plus one-fourth to one-half of remaining estate (depending on number of children and/or next of kin)
- Rights to allowances and exempt property are not affected by any provisions in the will or by taking an elective share (Mich. Comp. Laws § 700.2402)

Allowance Rights

- **Homestead.** Surviving spouse entitled to homestead allowance of $15,000 (Mich. Comp. Laws § 700.2402)
- **Family allowance.** Reasonable support for up to one year while estate is being settled (Mich. Comp. Laws § 700.2403)

- **Exempt property.** Up to $10,000 in household furniture, furnishings and appliances, automobiles, and personal effects (Mich. Comp. Laws § 700.2404)

Waiver of Inheritance Rights

Mich. Comp. Laws § 700.2205

- By written agreement signed by the waiving spouse after fair disclosure
- Rights to homestead allowance, elective share, exempt property, or family allowance may be wholly or partially waived
- A waiver of "all rights" presumes a waiver of all of the above

Divorce

Division of Property at Divorce

Mich. Comp. Laws §§ 552.18 and following; 552.101 and following
Property division method: Equitable distribution
Marital fault considered? No
Factors affecting property division:

- Pensions, retirement, and insurance benefits included in marital property
- Contributions by one spouse to the acquisition, improvement, or accumulation of the other spouse's separate property (Mich. Comp. Laws § 552.401)

Temporary Alimony

Mich. Comp. Laws § 552.13(1)

- May be awarded to allow one party to pay costs of divorce proceeding

Permanent Alimony Award

Mich. Comp. Laws §§ 552.18 and following; 552.23
Marital fault considered? May be considered
Other factors affecting award include:

- Sufficiency of property award to each spouse
- Ability of either spouse to pay
- Each spouse's situation and character (court decides based on circumstances of each case; no set list of considerations)

Circumstances That Terminate or Modify Alimony

Mich. Comp. Laws § 552.13(2)

- Remarriage of person receiving alimony unless divorce decree states otherwise

Debts

Mich. Comp. Laws § 557.21

- Wife's separate property and earnings are not liable for husband's debts

Minnesota

Prenuptial Agreements

Legal term: Antenuptial Agreement, Antenuptial Contract, or Antenuptial Settlement

Has state adopted UPAA? No

State code sections: Minn. Stat. Ann. §§ 518.54(5e); 519.11; 524.2-213

Important court cases: *Affiliated Banc Group, Ltd. v. Zehringer,* 527 N.W.2d 585 (App. 1995)

Required Formalities for Prenuptial Agreements

- In writing
- Signed by both parties
- Notarized

Permitted Subjects of Prenuptial Agreements

- Property rights
- What happens to property at divorce or separation
- What happens to property upon death
- Any other matter that does not violate public policy or criminal laws
- *Not permitted: child support restriction*

What Makes a Prenuptial Agreement Unenforceable?

- Agreement not made voluntarily
- Prior to signing, parties did not exchange full and fair disclosure of finances
- Subject of agreement against public policy or criminal laws
- Prior to signing, parties had no opportunity to consult with legal counsel of their own choice

Inheritance

Election Rights

Minn. Stat. Ann. § 524.2-202

- Up to 50% of augmented estate depending on the length of marriage (maximum reached at 15 years)
- If elective share plus value of any other property passing to spouse by nonprobate transfer, joint tenancy, or co-ownership is less than $50,000, surviving spouse is entitled to a supplemental elective share to bring the total to $50,000
- Right to homestead and other allowances are not affected by taking an elective share

Allowance Rights

- **Homestead.** Surviving spouse is entitled to homestead, including any manufactured home; if deceased spouse has no children, homestead passes to surviving spouse; if deceased spouse has children, surviving spouse has homestead for life, then it passes to children (Minn. Stat. Ann. § 524.2-402)
- **Exempt property.** Up to $10,000 in household furnishings, furniture, appliances, and personal effects; one automobile (no limit on value) (Minn. Stat. Ann. § 524.2-403)
- **Family allowance.** Reasonable support and maintenance for one year to 18 months, depending on whether estate can satisfy all claims against it; amount may not exceed $1,500 per month (Minn. Stat. Ann. § 524.2-404)

Waiver of Inheritance Rights

Minn. Stat. Ann. § 524.2-213

- By written agreement signed by the waiving spouse after fair disclosure
- The right of election and the rights to the homestead, exempt property, and family allowance may be wholly or partially waived
- Waiver must specify the rights being waived; a waiver of "all rights" is a waiver of only the right to the elective share

Divorce

Division of Property at Divorce

Minn. Stat. Ann. §§ 518.54, 518.58

Property division method: Equitable distribution

Marital fault considered? No

Factors affecting property division: (Minn. Stat. Ann. § 518.58)

- Duration of marriage and any prior marriage of a spouse
- Each spouse's age, health, occupation, amount and sources of income, vocational skills, employability, property, liabilities, needs, and opportunity to acquire capital assets and income in the future
- Contribution of each spouse to the acquisition, preservation, depreciation or appreciation in value of the marital property, including contribution of a spouse as a homemaker (court presumes that each spouse made a substantial contribution to the acquisition of income and property)
- If one spouse's property after division is so inadequate that it creates an "unfair hardship," court may grant that spouse a portion of the other spouse's separate property

Temporary Alimony

Minn. Stat. Ann. § 518.131 (Subd.1); 518.62

- Either spouse may be awarded temporary support, attorneys fees, and use of family home, car, and household goods
- Either spouse may be awarded household goods and furniture, whether or not acquired during the marriage
- Either spouse may be awarded right to occupy family home (Minn. Stat. Ann. § 518.63)

Permanent Alimony Award

Minn. Stat. Ann. §§ 518.55 and following

Marital fault considered? No

Factors affecting award include:

- Whether spouse seeking support lacks sufficient property, including portion of marital property, to provide for reasonable needs considering standard of living during marriage (especially during a period of training or education)
- Whether spouse seeking support is able to provide adequate self-support through appropriate employment, or is the custodial parent of a child whose condition or circumstances make it appropriate to remain home
- Financial resources of the spouse seeking maintenance, including marital property award and money awarded as custodial parent in child support order, and ability to meet needs independently
- Age and the physical and emotional condition of the spouse seeking maintenance
- Time necessary for spouse seeking maintenance to acquire sufficient education or training to find appropriate employment, and the probability, given age and skills, of completing education or training and becoming fully or partially self-supporting
- Duration of marriage and standard of living during marriage
- A homemaker's long absence from the workforce, with the result that education, skills, or experience are outmoded and earning capacity is permanently diminished
- Whether spouse seeking maintenance gave up earnings, seniority, retirement benefits, and other employment opportunities
- Ability of spouse from whom maintenance is sought to meet needs while paying alimony
- Contribution of each spouse to the acquisition, preservation, depreciation, or appreciation of the marital property, including contribution of homemaker to the other spouse's career or business

Circumstances That Terminate or Modify Alimony

Minn. Stat. Ann. § 518.64 (Subd. 2, Subd. 3)

- Substantially increased or decreased earnings or needs
- Receipt of assistance under AFDC (Aid to Families With Dependent Children)
- Change in the cost of living that makes existing terms unreasonable and unfair
- Addition of work- or education-related child care expenses or substantial increase or decrease in existing expenses
- Death of either party or remarriage of party receiving support (unless written agreement or divorce decree expressly provides otherwise)
- Court does not consider financial circumstances of either spouse's new spouse
- Court does not consider increase in income due to temporary or voluntary overtime

Debts

Minn. Stat. Ann. §§ 519.01 and following

- Wife's property is not liable for husband's debts, but is liable for her own
- Neither spouse is liable for the other's debts, but each is responsible for the other's necessary medical services and for household goods used by the family (Minn. Stat. Ann. § 519.05(a))

Mississippi

Prenuptial Agreements

Legal term: Antenuptial Agreement

Has state adopted UPAA? No

State code sections: None

Important court cases: *Smith v. Smith,* 656 So.2d 1143 (1995); *Estate of Hensley,* 524 So.2d 325 (1988); *Roberts v. Roberts,* 381 So.2d 1333 (1980)

Required Formalities for Prenuptial Agreements

- In writing
- Signed by both parties

Permitted Subjects of Prenuptial Agreements

- Property rights
- Rights to sell, transfer, or control property
- What happens to property at divorce or separation
- What happens to property upon death
- Alimony (spousal support or spousal maintenance)
- Any other matter that does not violate public policy or criminal laws

What Makes a Prenuptial Agreement Unenforceable?

- Agreement not made voluntarily
- Prior to signing, parties failed to make disclosure of finances
- Subject of agreement against public policy or criminal laws

Inheritance

Election Rights

- Up to one-half of deceased spouse's real or personal property (Miss. Code Ann. § 91-5-25)
- Surviving spouse who has separate property is entitled to elective share only if value of separate property is less than value of elective share. Percentage of elective share is determined by value of separate property, except that surviving spouse may take entire elective share if separate property is one-fifth or less of elective share (Miss. Code Ann. § 91-5-29)
- Homestead rights are not affected by taking elective share (*Matter of Estate of Hollaway,* 631 So.2d 127 (Miss. 1993))

Allowance Rights

- **Homestead.** If deceased spouse has no children or grandchildren, surviving spouse is entitled to entire homestead; otherwise, surviving spouse shares homestead as tenant-in-common with children and grandchildren. If surviving spouse owns a residence equal in value to the homestead, and deceased spouse has children or grandchildren from a former marriage, then homestead passes to them (Miss. Code Ann. § 91-1-19)
- **Family allowance.** "Comfortable support" for one year (amount is set by court); entitled to allowance for necessary clothing in addition to cash allowance (Miss. Code Ann. §§ 91-7-135, 91-7-141)

Waiver of Inheritance Rights

- No statute

Divorce

Division of Property at Divorce

Miss. Code Ann. § 95-5-23; see case notes below

Property division method: Equitable distribution

Marital fault considered? Yes, if it has a negative effect on "stability and harmony" of the marriage and family relationships

Other factors affecting property division: (*Ferguson v. Ferguson,* 639 So.2d 921 (Miss. 1994)):

- Substantial contribution to the accumulation of property through 1) direct or indirect economic contribution; 2) contribution to marriage and family stability and harmony as measured by time spent on family duties and duration of the marriage; and 3) contribution to the education, training, or other accomplishments that affected the earning power of the spouse accumulating the assets
- Degree to which each spouse spent, withdrew, or otherwise disposed of marital assets
- Market and emotional value of marital assets
- Value of each spouse's separate assets
- Tax and other economic consequences (including contractual or legal consequences to third parties) of the proposed property division
- Extent to which property division may eliminate alimony payments and other potential sources of future friction between the spouses
- Needs of the spouses for financial security, considering the combination of assets, income, and earning capacity
- Any other factor that would be equitable to consider

Temporary Alimony

Miss. Code Ann. § 95-5-17

- Court may award temporary alimony

- "Rehabilitative" alimony is fixed term of support to help one spouse in transition, usually prior to reentering workforce (*Hubbard v. Hubbard,* 656 So.2d 124 (Miss. 1995))

Permanent Alimony Award

Miss. Code Ann. § 95-5-23; see case notes

Marital fault considered? Yes

Other factors affecting award (*Armstrong v. Armstrong,* 618 So.2d 1278 (Miss. 1993)):

- Income and expenses of the spouses
- Health and earning capacities of the spouses
- Needs of each spouse
- Obligations and assets of each spouse
- Duration of marriage
- Presence or absence of minor children in the home

- Age of the spouses
- Standard of living of the spouses during marriage and at the time of the support determination
- Tax consequences of the spousal support order
- Fault or misconduct
- Wasteful dissipation of assets by either spouse
- Any other "just and equitable" factor

Circumstances That Terminate or Modify Alimony

Miss. Code Ann. § 95-5-23

- Substantial and material (financial or physical) change in circumstances

Debts

Miss. Code Ann. § 93 -3-1; see case notes

- Wife is responsible for her own debts

Missouri

Prenuptial Agreements

Legal term: Antenuptial Agreement

Has state adopted UPAA? No

State code sections: Mo. Rev. Stat. §§ 452.330; 474.120, 474.220

Important court cases: *Gould v. Rafaeli,* 822 S.W.2d 494 (1991)

Required Formalities for Prenuptial Agreements

- In writing
- Signed by both parties

Permitted Subjects of Prenuptial Agreements

- Property rights
- What happens to property at divorce or separation
- What happens to property upon death
- Alimony (spousal support or spousal maintenance)
- Any other matter that does not violate public policy or criminal laws

What Makes a Prenuptial Agreement Unenforceable?

- Agreement not made voluntarily
- Agreement unconscionable when signed
- Prior to signing, each party must have a full and complete understanding of the other's finances and must make full and complete disclosure of his/her own
- Subject of agreement against public policy or criminal laws

Inheritance

Election Rights

- Surviving spouse entitled to one-half of estate if there are no children, one-third of estate if there are children (Mo. Rev. Stat. § 474.160)
- Choosing elective share does not affect rights to family allowance or exempt property, but homestead allowance is offset against elective share (Mo. Rev. Stat. § 474.160, 474.230)

Allowance Rights

- **Homestead allowance.** Up to 50% of the estate value (excluding family allowance and exempt property) but no more than $15,000 (Mo. Rev. Stat. § 474.290)
- **Exempt property.** Family bible and other books; one motor vehicle; all clothing, household electrical appliances, musical and other amusement instruments, household and kitchen furniture, appliances, utensils, and implements (Mo. Rev. Stat. § 474.250)
- **Family allowance.** Up to one year's support while estate is being settled (Mo. Rev. Stat. § 474.260)

Waiver of Inheritance Rights

- May waive right to elective share by written agreement signed by the waiving spouse, after full disclosure of the rights being waived (Mo. Rev. Stat. § 474.220)

Divorce

Division of Property at Divorce

Mo. Rev. Stat. § 452.330

Property division method: Equitable distribution

Marital fault considered? Yes

Other factors affecting property division:

- Economic circumstances of each spouse
- Desirability of awarding family home or right to live in it to the spouse having custody of any children
- Contribution of each spouse to acquisition of marital property, including contribution of a homemaker
- Value of each spouse's share of nonmarital property
- Custodial arrangements for minor children

Temporary Alimony

Mo. Rev. Stat. § 452.355

- Court may order either party to pay the other's costs and attorney's fees during the divorce proceedings

Permanent Alimony Award

Mo. Rev. Stat. § 452.335

Marital fault considered? Yes

Alimony awarded only if:

- Spouse seeking maintenance lacks sufficient property, including share of marital property, to provide for own reasonable needs, and
- Spouse seeking maintenance is unable to be self-supporting through appropriate employment or is the custodial parent of a child whose condition or circumstances require parent to remain at home

Other factors affecting award:

- Financial resources of the spouse seeking maintenance and ability to meet needs independently
- Obligations and assets of each spouse, including marital property award and separate property
- Time necessary to acquire sufficient education or training so that spouse seeking maintenance can find appropriate employment
- Comparative earning capacity of each spouse

- Standard of living established during marriage
- Duration of the marriage
- Age and physical and emotional condition of the spouse seeking maintenance
- Ability of the spouse from whom maintenance is sought to meet own needs while paying alimony

Circumstances That Terminate or Modify Alimony

Mo. Rev. Stat. §§ 452.370, 452.335(3), 452.075

- Court order must state whether alimony can or cannot be modified; and may also set a termination date

- May be modified if substantial and continuing change of circumstances makes original terms unreasonable
- May be terminated upon remarriage of spouse receiving alimony or death of either spouse

Debts

Mo. Rev. Stat. §§ 451.250 and following

- Each spouse's personal property is exempt from debts the other spouse incurs before or during marriage
- Annual rent, income, or products from one spouse's personal real estate may be used to pay debts for necessities for the other spouse or for the family

Montana

Prenuptial Agreements

Legal term: Premarital Agreement

Has state adopted UPAA? Yes

State code sections: Mont. Code Ann. §§ 40-2-601 to 40-2-610; 72-2-224

Required Formalities for Prenuptial Agreements

- In writing
- Signed by both parties

Permitted Subjects of Prenuptial Agreements

- Property rights
- Rights to sell, transfer, or control property
- What happens to property at divorce or separation
- What happens to property upon death
- Alimony (spousal support or spousal maintenance)
- Terms of wills, trusts, or other estate planning documents
- Life insurance ownership and arrangements
- Applicable state law
- Any other matter that does not violate public policy or criminal laws
- *Not permitted: child support restriction*

What Makes a Prenuptial Agreement Unenforceable?

- Agreement not made voluntarily
- Agreement unconscionable when signed and prior to signing, party objecting to enforcement did not know other party's finances and was not given fair and reasonable disclosure
- Alimony waiver, if it would make waiving spouse eligible for public assistance
- Annulment, unless result would be inequitable
- Subject of agreement against public policy or criminal laws

Inheritance

Election Rights

Mont. Code Ann. § 72-2-221

- Up to 50% of the augmented estate depending on the length of the marriage (maximum reached at 15 years)
- If elective share plus value of any other property passing to the spouse by nonprobate transfer, joint tenancy, or co-ownership is less than $50,000, surviving spouse is entitled to a supplemental elective share to bring the total to $50,000

- Taking elective share does not affect rights to exempt property, homestead, or family allowance

Allowance Rights

- **Homestead.** Allowance of up to $20,000 (Mont. Code Ann. § 72-2-412)
- **Exempt property.** Up to $10,000 in household furniture, furnishings, appliances, automobiles, and personal effects (Mont. Code Ann. § 72-2-413)
- **Family allowance.** Reasonable maintenance for spouse and dependent children for up to one year while estate is being settled (Mont. Code Ann. § 72-2-414)

Waiver of Inheritance Rights

Mont. Code Ann. § 72-2-224

- All rights may be wholly or partially waived by signed, written agreement
- Waiver is not enforceable if: 1) it was not made voluntarily; 2) person executing waiver was not given fair disclosure of decedent's property or financial obligations, did not expressly waive right to such disclosure, and did not have or could not have had knowledge of property or obligations; or 3) waiver was unconscionable (court must decide this issue)

Divorce

Division of Property at Divorce

Mont. Code Ann. § 40-4-202

Property division method: Equitable distribution (court divides both marital and nonmarital property, whether title is held separately or by both parties)

Marital fault considered? No

Factors affecting property division:

- Duration of marriage and prior marriage of either spouse
- Age, health, occupation, amount and sources of income, vocational skills, employability, property, liabilities, and needs of each of the spouses
- Custody provisions and whether custodial parent receives payment
- Whether property division is instead of or in addition to alimony
- Opportunity of each spouse to acquire capital assets and income in the future
- Each spouse's contribution to (or dissipation of) the value of spouse's separate estate
- Contribution of a spouse as a homemaker or to the family unit and whether contribution increased the value of the other spouse's property

Temporary Alimony

Mont. Code Ann. § 40-4-121

- Either spouse may petition court for temporary support
- Must submit affidavit that includes the factual basis for the request, amounts requested, marital property liabilities, and a statement of each spouse's sources of income

Permanent Alimony Award

Mont. Code Ann. § 40-4-203

Marital fault considered? No

Awarded only if spouse seeking maintenance:

- Lacks sufficient property to provide for own reasonable needs, and
- Is unable to be self-supporting through appropriate employment or is the custodial parent of a child whose condition or circumstances require parent to remain at home

Factors affecting award include:

- Financial resources of the spouse seeking maintenance (including share of marital property) and ability to meet needs independently
- Whether spouse seeking maintenance is custodial parent, and whether child support includes a sum for custodian

- Time necessary for spouse seeking maintenance to acquire sufficient education or training to find appropriate employment
- Standard of living established during marriage
- Duration of the marriage
- Age and physical and emotional condition of the spouse seeking maintenance
- Ability of the spouse from whom maintenance is sought to meet own needs while paying alimony

Circumstances That Terminate or Modify Alimony

Mont. Code Ann. § 40-4-208

- Spouse receiving support remarries
- Either spouse dies
- Substantial and continuing change of circumstances that makes original terms unreasonable

Debts

Mont. Code Ann. §§ 40-2-102 to 40-2-210

- Except for necessities, each spouse's separate property or earnings is exempt from debts of the other spouse incurred before or during marriage

Nebraska

Prenuptial Agreements

Legal term: Premarital Agreement
Has state adopted UPAA? Yes
State code sections: Neb. Rev. Stat. §§ 42-1001 to 42-1011

Required Formalities for Prenuptial Agreements

- In writing
- Signed by both parties

Permitted Subjects of Prenuptial Agreements

- Property rights
- Rights to sell, transfer, or control property
- What happens to property at divorce or separation
- What happens to property upon death
- Alimony (spousal support or spousal maintenance)
- Terms of wills, trusts, or other estate planning documents
- Life insurance ownership and arrangements
- Applicable state law
- Any other matter that does not violate public policy or criminal laws
- *Not permitted: child support restriction*

What Makes a Prenuptial Agreement Unenforceable?

- Agreement not made voluntarily
- Agreement unconscionable when signed and prior to signing, party objecting to enforcement did not know other party's finances and was not given fair and reasonable disclosure
- Alimony waiver, if it would make waiving spouse eligible for public assistance
- Annulment of marriage, unless result would be inequitable
- Subject of agreement against public policy or criminal laws

Inheritance

Election Rights

Neb. Rev. Stat. § 30-2313

- Up to one-half of the augmented estate

Allowance Rights

- **Homestead.** Allowance to $7,500 (Neb. Rev. Stat. § 30-2322)
- **Exempt property.** Up to $5,000 in household furnishings, furniture, appliances, automobiles, and personal effects (Neb. Rev. Stat. § 30-2323)
- **Family allowance.** Up to one year's reasonable allowance for maintenance while estate is being settled (Neb. Rev. Stat. § 30-2324)

Waiver of Inheritance Rights

Neb. Rev. Stat. § 30-2316

- Any or all rights to elective share, homestead, exempt property, and family allowance may be waived by written agreement or contract signed by person waiving rights
- Waiver is not enforceable if: 1) it was not made voluntarily; 2) person executing waiver was not given fair disclosure of decedent's property or financial obligations, did not expressly waive right to such disclosure, and did not or could not have had knowledge of decedent's property or obligations; or 3) waiver was unconscionable (court must decide this issue)
- Waiver of "all rights" implies waiver of elective share, homestead, exempt property, and family allowance

Divorce

Division of Property at Divorce

Neb. Rev. Stat. § 42-365
Property division method: Equitable distribution
Marital fault considered: No
Factors affecting property division:

- Economic circumstances of spouses
- Duration of marriage
- Contributions to marriage by each spouse, including care and education of children, and interruption of personal careers or educational opportunities

Temporary Alimony

Neb. Rev. Stat. § 42-367

- While divorce is pending, court may require husband to pay wife whatever amount she needs to pursue legal action

Permanent Alimony Award

Neb. Rev. Stat. § 42-365
Marital fault considered? No
Factors affecting award:

- Economic circumstances of spouses
- Duration of marriage
- Contributions to marriage by each spouse, including care and education of children, and interruption of personal careers or educational opportunities
- Ability of spouse who is custodial parent to be gainfully employed without interfering with the interests of any minor children

Circumstances That Terminate or Modify Alimony

Neb. Rev. Stat. § 42-365

- "Good cause"
- Death of either spouse
- Remarriage of spouse receiving alimony
- If alimony not awarded in divorce decree, decree cannot be modified to include award

Debts

Neb. Rev. Stat. § 42-201 and following

- Wife's separate property and earnings are not liable for husband's debts
- Wife's separate property that is not exempt from judgment is liable for debts for family necessaries, if attempts to collect payment from husband are unsuccessful
- Husband's separate property is not liable for wife's debts prior to marriage (Neb. Rev. Stat. § 42-206)

Nevada

Prenuptial Agreements

Legal term: Premarital Agreement

Has state adopted UPAA? Yes

State code sections: Nev. Rev. Stat. Ann. 123A.010 to 123A.100

Important court cases: *Buettner v. Buettner,* 505 P.2d 600 (1973)

Required Formalities for Prenuptial Agreements

- In writing
- Signed by both parties

Permitted Subjects of Prenuptial Agreements

- Property rights
- Rights to sell, transfer, or control property
- What happens to property at divorce or separation
- What happens to property upon death
- Alimony (spousal support or spousal maintenance)
- Terms of wills, trusts, or other estate planning documents
- Life insurance ownership and arrangements
- Applicable state law
- Any other matter that does not violate public policy or criminal laws
- *Not permitted: child support restriction*

What Makes a Prenuptial Agreement Unenforceable?

- Agreement not made voluntarily
- Agreement unconscionable when signed and prior to signing, party objecting to enforcement did not know other party's finances and was not given fair and reasonable disclosure
- Alimony waiver, if it would make waiving spouse eligible for public assistance
- Annulment of marriage, unless result would be inequitable
- Subject of agreement against public policy or criminal laws

Inheritance

Election Rights

Nev. Rev. Stat. Ann. § 123.250

- Surviving spouse is entitled to one-half of community property
- Deceased spouse may leave other half of the community property and all his or her separate property as desired

Allowance Rights

- **Homestead.** Surviving spouse and children entitled to homestead (Nev. Rev. Stat. Ann. § 146.010)
- **Exempt property.** Surviving spouse and minor children entitled to all family clothing, food, and household furniture (Nev. Rev. Stat. Ann. § 146.010)
- **Family allowance.** If exempt property or surviving spouse's other income or property is insufficient for support and maintenance, surviving spouse is entitled to a reasonable allowance for up to one year while estate is being settled (Nev. Rev. Stat. Ann. § 146.030)

Waiver of Inheritance Rights

- May waive rights to share of deceased spouse's community and separate property (Nev. Rev. Stat. Ann. § 134.005)
- May waive rights to homestead, exempt property, and family allowance (Nev. Rev. Stat. Ann. § 146.005)

Divorce

Division of Property at Divorce

Nev. Rev. Stat. Ann. § 125.150

Property division method: Community property

Marital fault considered: No

Other factors affecting property division:

- Court will divide community property equally unless there is a "compelling reason" to do otherwise; court must give reasons in writing (Nev. Rev. Stat. Ann. § 125.150 (1)(b))
- Court may award a portion of either party's separate property for the support of the other (Nev. Rev. Stat. Ann. § 125.150(4))

Temporary Alimony

Nev. Rev. Stat. Ann. § 125.200

- Court may order either spouse to pay amount necessary for prosecuting the divorce action
- While divorce is pending, court may order either spouse to pay for support and maintenance of other spouse and children

Permanent Alimony Award

Nev. Rev. Stat. Ann. § 125.150

Marital fault considered? No

Factors affecting award: (Nev. Rev. Stat. Ann. § 125.150 (8), (9))

- One spouse needs alimony for the purpose of obtaining training or education relating to a job, career, or profession

- Spouse who would be paying obtained greater education or job skills during marriage
- Spouse who would be receiving provided financial support for the other's training or education
- Award may include payment for testing, evaluation, and career guidance as well as money for tuition or courses

Circumstances That Terminate or Modify Alimony

- Death of either spouse (Nev. Rev. Stat. Ann. § 125.150(5))
- Remarriage of the spouse receiving alimony (Nev. Rev. Stat. Ann. § 125.150(5))
- Changed circumstances, especially a reduction in income that leaves supporting spouse financially unable to make alimony payments (Nev. Rev. Stat. Ann. § 125.150(7))

Debts

- One spouse's separate property or share of community property is not liable for debts the other spouse incurred before marriage (Nev. Rev. Stat. Ann. § 123.050)
- Separate property of husband is liable for cost of necessaries to support wife, if community property is insufficient to cover debt (Nev. Rev. Stat. Ann. § 123.090)
- Wife must support husband out of her separate property if he does not have separate property, there is insufficient community property, and because of illness or disability, he cannot support himself (Nev. Rev. Stat. Ann. § 123.110)

New Hampshire

Prenuptial Agreements

Legal term: Antenuptial Agreement

Has state adopted UPAA? No

State code sections: N.H. Rev. Stat. Ann. §§ 458:52; 460:2-a; 560:15

Required Formalities for Prenuptial Agreements

- In writing
- Signed by both parties

Permitted Subjects of Prenuptial Agreements

- Property rights
- What happens to property at divorce or separation
- What happens to property upon death
- Alimony (spousal support or spousal maintenance)
- Any other matter that does not violate public policy or criminal laws

What Will Make a Prenuptial Agreement Unenforceable?

- Agreement not made voluntarily
- Agreement unconscionable
- Prior to signing, parties did not disclose material facts
- Subject of agreement against public policy or criminal laws
- Circumstances have changed since signing of agreement making it unenforceable because it "shocks the conscience"

Inheritance

Election Rights

N.H. Rev. Stat. Ann. § 560:10

- **Deceased spouse leaves children or grandchildren.** Surviving spouse is entitled to one-third of deceased spouse's personal and real property
- **Deceased spouse leaves parents or siblings, but no children or grandchildren.** Surviving spouse is entitled to $10,000 in personal property and $10,000 in real property, plus one-half of remainder over $10,000; if value of remaining personal or real property is less than $10,000, surviving spouse is entitled to all of it
- **Deceased spouse leaves no descendants or next of kin.** Surviving spouse is entitled to $10,000 in personal property, $10,000 in real property and $2,000 for each year of marriage, plus one-half of remainder over $10,000; if value of remaining personal or real property is less than $10,000, surviving spouse is entitled to all of it

Allowance Rights

- **Homestead.** Surviving spouse is entitled to stay in home for 40 days rent-free (N.H. Rev. Stat. Ann. § 560:2)
- **Family allowance.** Surviving spouse is entitled to a reasonable allowance set by the court; will be deducted from elective share (N.H. Rev. Stat. Ann. § 560:1)

Waiver of Inheritance Rights

N.H. Rev. Stat. Ann. § 560:14

- Waiver of elective share and homestead rights must be in writing
- Waiver should be filed in probate office and, if real estate is involved, recorded in county where property located

Divorce

Division of Property at Divorce

N.H. Rev. Stat. Ann. § 458:16-a

Property division method: Equitable distribution

Marital fault considered: Yes, if it caused breakdown of marriage and substantial pain and suffering or economic loss

Other factors affecting property division:

- Duration of marriage
- Age, health, social or economic status, occupation, skills, employability, separate property, amount and sources of income, needs, and liabilities of each spouse and opportunity for future acquisition of capital assets and income
- Ability of custodial parent to be gainfully employed without substantially interfering with interests of any minor children, and need of the custodial parent to occupy or own family home and to use or own its household effects
- Each spouse's contribution to growth or diminution in value of separate or marital property
- Significant disparity in contributions to marriage, including homemaking and childcare
- Direct or indirect contribution made by one spouse to help educate or develop the career or employability of the other spouse
- Interruption of either spouse's educational or personal career opportunities for benefit of other spouse's career, the marriage, or the children
- Expectation of pension or retirement rights acquired prior to or during marriage
- Tax consequences for each spouse

Temporary Alimony

N.H. Rev. Stat. Ann. § 458:16(I)(f)

- Court may order either spouse to pay allowance to the other while divorce is pending.

Permanent Alimony Award

N.H. Rev. Stat. Ann. § 458:19

Marital fault considered? Yes, if it caused breakdown of marriage and substantial pain and suffering or economic loss

Other factors affecting award:

- Spouse seeking alimony lacks sufficient income or property to meet reasonable needs, taking into account the style of living during the marriage
- Ability of spouse from whom alimony is sought to meet own needs while paying alimony, taking into account the style of living during the marriage
- Spouse seeking alimony is unable to be self-supporting through appropriate employment at a standard of living that meets reasonable needs or is custodian of a child whose condition or circumstances make it inappropriate to work outside the home
- In determining amount of award court considers length of marriage; age, health, social or economic status, occupation, amount and sources of income, property awarded, vocational skills, employability, estate, liabilities, and needs of each of the spouses; opportunity of each to acquire capital assets and income in the future; and federal tax consequences (N.H. Rev. Stat. Ann. § 458:19 (IV)(b))

Circumstances That Terminate or Modify Alimony

N.H. Rev. Stat. Ann. § 458:19(V)

- Unexpected changes to federal taxes or regulations

Debts

- Husband is not liable for debts wife incurred prior to marriage (N.H. Rev. Stat. Ann. § 460:3)

New Jersey

Prenuptial Agreements

Legal term: Premarital Agreement

Has state adopted UPAA? Yes

State code sections: N.J. Stat. Ann. §§ 37:2-31 to 37:2-41; 3B:8-10

Required Formalities for Prenuptial Agreements

- In writing
- Signed by both parties
- Statement of assets must be attached

Permitted Subjects of Prenuptial Agreements

- Property rights
- Rights to sell, transfer, or control property
- What happens to property at divorce or separation
- What happens to property upon death
- Alimony (spousal support or spousal maintenance)
- Terms of wills, trusts, or other estate planning documents
- Life insurance ownership and arrangements
- Applicable state law
- Any other matter that does not violate public policy or criminal laws
- *Not permitted: child support restriction*

What Makes a Prenuptial Agreement Unenforceable?

- Agreement not made voluntarily
- Agreement would leave spouse with less than adequate support when enforcement is sought
- Prior to signing, party objecting to enforcement of agreement did not know other party's finances, was not given fair and reasonable disclosure, and did not consult (or waive the right to consult) with independent counsel
- Alimony waiver, if it would make waiving spouse eligible for public assistance
- Annulment of marriage, unless result would be inequitable
- Subject of agreement against public policy or criminal laws

Inheritance

Election Rights

N.J. Stat. Ann. § 3B:8-1

- Surviving spouse entitled to one-third of augmented estate

Allowance Rights

N.J. Stat. Ann. § 3B:3-30

- **Family allowance.** If will is contested, court may award allowance for support and maintenance and to cover court expenses

Waiver of Inheritance Rights

N.J. Stat. Ann. § 3B:8-10

- Right to elective share may be waived by written agreement or contract, signed by the person waiving rights after fair disclosure
- Waiver of "all rights" presumes waiver of all benefits to which surviving spouse is entitled

Divorce

Division of Property at Divorce

N.J. Stat. Ann. § 2A:34-23.1

Property division method: Equitable distribution

Marital fault considered? No

Factors affecting property division:

- Duration of marriage and standard of living established
- Age and physical and emotional health of each spouse
- Income or property brought to the marriage by each spouse
- Debts and liabilities of each spouse
- Economic circumstances of each spouse when property division becomes effective
- Income and earning capacity of each spouse, including educational background, training, employment skills, work experience, length of absence from the job market, custodial responsibilities for children, and time and expense necessary to acquire sufficient education or training to enable either spouse to become self-supporting at a standard of living reasonably comparable to that established during marriage
- Contribution of each spouse to the education, training, or earning power of the other, and extent to which either spouse deferred achieving career goals
- Contribution of each spouse to the acquisition, dissipation, preservation, depreciation, or appreciation of marital property, including contribution of a homemaker
- Need of custodial parent to own or occupy family home and use or own household effects
- Need for creation of a trust to secure reasonably foreseeable medical or educational costs for a spouse

- Present value of property and tax consequences of proposed distribution

Temporary Alimony

N.J. Stat. Ann. § 2A:34-23

- Court may order one spouse to pay retainer fee for other spouse's legal services

Other Types of Alimony

Courts in New Jersey may consider three different types of alimony:

- **Limited duration.** Awarded for time it will reasonably take recipient to improve earning capacity so that alimony no longer needed (N.J. Stat. Ann. § 2A:34-23(c))
- **Rehabilitative.** Awarded based on a plan that details the scope, steps to be taken, and time frame of the rehabilitation (N.J. Stat. Ann. § 2A:34-23(d))
- **Reimbursement.** Awarded when one party supported the other through an advanced education degree with the expectation of sharing the benefits of increased earning capacity (N.J. Stat. Ann. § 2A:34-23(e))

Factors Affecting Alimony Award

Marital fault considered? May be considered, but is not the sole determining factor (N.J. Stat. Ann. § 2A:34-23(g))

Other factors considered: (N.J. Stat. Ann. § 2A:34-23(b))

- Actual need
- Ability of the spouses to pay
- Duration of marriage
- Age and physical and emotional health of the spouses
- Standard of living during the marriage and the likelihood that each spouse can maintain a reasonably comparable standard
- Earning capacities, educational levels, vocational skills, and employability of the spouses
- Length of absence from the job market of the spouse seeking maintenance
- Parental responsibilities for the children
- Time and expense necessary to acquire sufficient education or training to enable spouse seeking maintenance to find appropriate employment (including availability of training and employment)
- Financial or nonfinancial contributions to the marriage by each spouse, including care and education of children and interruption of career or educational opportunities
- Income available to either spouse from investment of personal assets
- Each spouse's opportunity to acquire capital assets and income in the future
- Tax treatment and consequences of any alimony award

Circumstances That Terminate or Modify Alimony

- Limited duration and rehabilitative alimony may be modified based on change of circumstances or nonoccurrence of circumstances upon which award was based (N.J. Stat. Ann. § 2A:34-23(c),(d))
- Permanent or limited duration alimony terminates upon remarriage of spouse receiving it; remarriage does not terminate rehabilitative or reimbursement alimony unless circumstances upon which award was based have not occurred or paying spouse shows good cause for termination (N.J. Stat. Ann. § 2A:34-25)
- Death of recipient spouse (N.J. Stat. Ann. § 2A:34-25)

Debts

- Married woman is responsible for debts she incurs before or during marriage (N.J. Stat. Ann. § 37:2-10)
- Wife's separate property and earnings are not liable for husband's debts (N.J. Stat. Ann. § 37:2-15)

New Mexico

Prenuptial Agreements

Legal term: Premarital Agreement

Has state adopted UPAA? Yes

State code sections: N.M. Stat. Ann. §§ 40-3A-1 to 40-3A-10, 40-2-4; 45-2-407

Required Formalities for Prenuptial Agreements:

- In writing
- Signed by both parties
- Notarized

Permitted Subjects of Prenuptial Agreements

- Property rights
- Rights to sell, transfer, or control property
- What happens to property at divorce or separation
- What happens to property upon death
- Alimony (spousal support or spousal maintenance)
- Terms of wills, trusts, or other estate planning documents
- Life insurance ownership and arrangements
- Applicable state law
- Any other matter that does not violate public policy
- *Not permitted: restrictions on child support, spousal support, child custody, visitation, choice of residence, or pursuit of a career*

What Makes a Prenuptial Agreement Unenforceable?

- Agreement not made voluntarily
- Agreement unconscionable when signed and prior to signing, party objecting to enforcement did not know other party's finances and was not given fair and reasonable disclosure
- Annulment of marriage, unless result would be inequitable
- Subject of agreement against public policy

Inheritance

Election Rights

N.M. Stat. Ann. §§ 45-2-805

- Surviving spouse is entitled to one-half of community property
- Deceased spouse may leave other half of community property and all his or her separate property as desired

Allowance Rights

- **Exempt property.** Surviving spouse entitled to $15,000 in household furniture, furnishings, appliances, automobiles, and personal effects; if value of exempt property is less than $15,000, other assets may be used to make up difference (N.M. Stat. Ann. § 45-2-403)
- **Family allowance.** Surviving spouse entitled to $30,000 (N.M. Stat. Ann. § 45-2-402)
- Allowance rights are in addition to any intestate share or benefit from the will (N.M. Stat. Ann. §§ 45-2-402 to 45-2-403)

Waiver of Inheritance Rights

N.M. Stat. Ann. § 45-2-407

- All rights may be wholly or partially waived by written agreement or contract signed by waiving spouse
- Waiver is not enforceable if: 1) it was not made voluntarily; 2) person executing waiver was not given fair disclosure of decedent's property or financial obligations, did not expressly waive right to such disclosure, and did not have or could not have had knowledge of property or obligations; or 3) waiver was unconscionable (court must decide this issue)
- Waiver of "all rights" presumes waiver of right to exempt property, family allowance, and any other benefit that would pass by intestate succession or by will

Divorce

Division of Property at Divorce

N.M. Stat. Ann. § 40-4-7

Property division method: Community property

Marital fault considered? No

Factors affecting property division:

- Quasi-community property treated as community property if both spouses are living in New Mexico when they file for divorce or legal separation (N.M. Stat. Ann. § 40-3-8(D))
- Court may award a portion of either spouse's separate property as spousal support (N.M. Stat. Ann. § 40-4-12)

Temporary Alimony

N.M. Stat. Ann. § 40-4-7(A)

- Court may award to either spouse for support during divorce proceeding and for expenses to ensure efficient preparation and presentation of case

Other Types of Alimony

N.M. Stat. Ann. § 40-4-7(B)

Courts in New Mexico may consider three types of spousal support:

- **Rehabilitative.** Provides education, training, work experience, or other forms of rehabilitation that increase receiving spouse's ability to earn income and become self-supporting; court may include a specific rehabilitation plan with award and make continuation of support contingent upon compliance

- **Transitional.** Supplements receiving spouse's income for a limited period of time (time period must be clearly stated in the order)
- **Indefinite duration.** No time limit

Factors Affecting Alimony Award

Marital fault considered? No

Factors considered: (N.M. Stat. Ann. § 40-4-7(E))

- Age and health of both spouses
- Means of support, current and future earnings, and earning capacity of both spouses
- Amount of property awarded or confirmed to both spouses and income from property (potential proceeds from sale of separate property are not considered unless required by exceptional circumstances and need to be fair to both spouses)
- Assets and liabilities of both spouses
- Good-faith efforts of both spouses to maintain employment or become self-supporting

- Reasonable needs of both spouses, including standard of living during the marriage and maintenance of medical insurance
- Duration of marriage (court has jurisdiction over continuing support payment proceedings in marriages of 20 years or more) (N.M. Stat. Ann. § 40-4-7(F))

Circumstances That Terminate or Modify Alimony

- Death of either spouse (N.M. Stat. Ann. § 40-4-7(D))
- Circumstances court finds appropriate for modification, unless decree states that award cannot be modified (N.M. Stat. Ann. § 40-4-7(B,2))

Debts

- Community property is not liable for any debts unless contract signed by both spouses (N.M. Stat. Ann. § 40-3-4)
- Debt incurred by either spouse before marriage, in one spouse's name only, or as a result of legal gambling, is a separate debt (N.M. Stat. Ann. §§ 40-3-9, 40-3-9.1)
- Neither spouse's separate property or share of community property is liable for the separate debt of the other spouse (N.M. Stat. Ann. § 40-3-10)

New York

Prenuptial Agreements

Legal term: Antenuptial Agreement or Antenuptial Contract

Has state adopted UPAA? No

State code sections: N.Y. Dom. Rel. Law § 236; Part B3; N.Y. Gen. Oblig. Law § 3-303; N.Y. Est. Powers & Trusts Law § 5-1.1

Important court cases: *Hoffman v. Hoffman,* 474 N.Y.S.2d 621 (1984)

Required Formalities for Prenuptial Agreements

- In writing
- Signed by both parties
- Notarized (agreement may be acknowledged by anyone authorized to conduct a marriage ceremony)
- Separate lawyer for each party

Permitted Subjects of Prenuptial Agreements

- Property rights
- What happens to property at divorce or separation
- What happens to property upon death
- Any other matter that does not violate public policy or criminal laws

What Makes a Prenuptial Agreement Unenforceable?

- Subject of agreement against public policy or criminal laws
- Terms were unfair and unreasonable when agreement was made or are unconscionable at time of divorce decree (N.Y. Dom. Rel. Law § 236; Part B3)

Inheritance

Election Rights

N.Y. Est. Powers & Trusts Law § 5-1.1-A

- Surviving spouse is entitled to $50,000 or one-third of the net estate, whichever is greater; spouse is entitled to entire estate if it is worth less than $50,000

Allowance Rights

N.Y. Est. Powers & Trusts Law § 5-3.1

- Housekeeping utensils, household furniture and appliances, musical instruments, computers and electronic devices, fuel, food, and clothing worth up to $10,000 total
- A family bible, books, pictures, videotapes, computer tapes, discs, and software worth up to $1,000 total
- Domestic animals, feed for 60 days, farm machinery, one tractor, and one lawn tractor worth up to $15,000 total
- One motor vehicle worth up to $15,000 total. Surviving spouse may pay excess value to estate and acquire decedent's motor vehicle worth more than $15,000, or may take $15,000 in cash instead of motor vehicle
- Money or personal effects worth up to $15,000 (less any funeral expenses if there is not enough money in the estate to cover them)

Waiver of Inheritance Rights

N.Y. Est. Powers & Trusts Law § 5-1.1-A(e)

- May waive right to elective share in a written agreement or release signed by waiving spouse
- A waiver of "all rights" presumes waiver of elective share
- Waiver must be notarized

Divorce

Division of Property at Divorce

N.Y. Dom. Rel. Law §§ 234, 236(5)

Property division method: Equitable distribution

Marital fault considered? No

Factors affecting property division: (N.Y. Dom. Rel. Law § 236(5)(d))

- Income and property of each spouse
- Duration of marriage
- Age and health of each spouse
- Custodial parent's need to occupy or own the family home and to use or own its household effects (court may award home without regard to the form of ownership (N.Y. Dom. Rel. Law § 236(5)(f))
- Loss of inheritance and pension rights upon divorce
- Alimony award
- Any equitable claim to, interest in, or contribution to acquisition of marital property by the spouse not having title, including services as a spouse, parent, wage earner, and homemaker, and contributions to the career or career potential of the other spouse
- Liquid or nonliquid status of marital assets
- Wasteful dissipation of assets by either spouse
- Transfer or encumbrance of separate property made on account of the marriage without fair compensation
- Probable future financial circumstances of each spouse
- Tax consequences to each spouse
- Possibility of property division being a barrier to remarriage of either spouse (N.Y. Dom. Rel. Law § 236(5)(h))

- Difficulty of evaluating any partial asset or an interest in a business, corporation, or profession, and economic desirability of keeping it intact and free from claim or interference by the other spouse
- If equitable distribution is impractical or burdensome or distribution of a business interest would be contrary to law, court must make a distributive award to achieve equity between spouses; court may also make an award to supplement or facilitate distribution of marital property (N.Y. Dom. Rel. Law § 236(5)(e))

Temporary Alimony

- Either spouse may be ordered to pay court costs and attorney fees if necessary to allow other spouse to continue with the divorce proceeding (N.Y. Dom. Rel. Law § 237)

Permanent Alimony Award

N.Y. Dom. Rel. Law § 236(6)(a)

Marital fault considered? May be considered

Other factors affecting award include:

- Same factors as those affecting property division, when applicable
- Standard of living of the spouses during marriage
- Spouse who will receive alimony lacks sufficient property and income to provide for own reasonable needs
- Spouse who will pay alimony has sufficient property or income to provide for the other's reasonable needs

- Income and property of both spouses, including any marital property award
- Ability of the spouse seeking alimony to become self-supporting, and the length and cost of training needed
- Reduced or lost lifetime earning capacity of the spouse seeking alimony because of giving up or postponing education, training, employment, or career opportunities during the marriage
- Presence of children of the marriage in the home of either spouse

Circumstances That Terminate or Modify Alimony

- Death of either spouse (N.Y. Dom. Rel. Law § 236(6)(c))
- Remarriage of spouse receiving alimony (N.Y. Dom. Rel. Law § 236(6)(c))
- Cohabitation of spouse receiving alimony (statute refers to wife only) (N.Y. Dom. Rel. Law § 248)

Debts

- Wife's personal and real property, whether acquired before or during marriage, is not liable for husband's debts (N.Y. Dom. Rel. Law § 50)
- Debt contracted by wife does not obligate husband or his separate property (N.Y. Gen. Oblig. Law § 305)
- Husband who acquires property from wife through antenuptial agreement or upon marriage is liable for her antenuptial debts up to the value of the acquired property (N.Y. Gen. Oblig. Law § 307)

North Carolina

Prenuptial Agreements

Legal term: Premarital Agreement

Has state adopted UPAA? Yes

State code sections: N.C. Gen. Stat. §§ 52B-1 to 52B-11; 30-3

Required Formalities for Prenuptial Agreements

- In writing
- Signed by both parties

Permitted Subjects of Prenuptial Agreements

- Property rights
- Rights to sell, transfer, or control property
- What happens to property at divorce or separation
- What happens to property upon death
- Alimony (spousal support or spousal maintenance)
- Terms of wills, trusts, or other estate planning documents
- Life insurance ownership and arrangements
- Applicable state law
- Any other matter that does not violate public policy or criminal laws
- *Not permitted: child support restriction*

What Makes a Prenuptial Agreement Unenforceable?

- Agreement not made voluntarily
- Agreement unconscionable when signed and prior to signing, party objecting to enforcement did not know other party's finances and was not given fair and reasonable disclosure
- Alimony waiver, if it would make waiving spouse eligible for public assistance
- Annulment of marriage, unless result would be inequitable
- Subject of agreement against public policy or criminal laws

Inheritance

Election Rights

N.C. Gen. Stat. § 30-3.1

- If deceased spouse has no surviving children, one child, or grandchildren from one child: surviving spouse is entitled to one-half of total net assets, minus the value of property passing to the surviving spouse
- If deceased spouse has two or more children, grandchildren from two or more children, or one child and grandchildren from one or more children: surviving spouse entitled to one-third of total net assets, minus the value of property passing to the surviving spouse
- If surviving spouse has been married before, and deceased spouse has children from a prior marriage but none with surviving spouse, the surviving spouse's share is reduced by 50%
- Instead of elective share, surviving spouse may choose life interest in one-third of value of real property acquired by deceased spouse during marriage (N.C. Gen. Stat. § 29-30)
- Divorce, abandonment, or adultery bar right to elective share (N.C. Gen. Stat. § 31A-1)

Allowance Rights

- **Homestead.** Surviving spouse is entitled to rents and profits from the homestead, if there are no minor children and surviving spouse does not own a separate homestead; homestead is exempt from claims against the estate; homestead rights cease upon remarriage (N.C. Const. Art. X, § 2)
- **Family allowance.** Surviving spouse is entitled to $10,000 allowance for one year; value of elective share is reduced by amount of allowance (N.C. Gen. Stat. § 30-15)
- Divorce, abandonment, or adultery bar right to homestead or family allowance (N.C. Gen. Stat. § 31A-1)

Waiver of Inheritance Rights

N.C. Gen. Stat. § 30-3.6

- May waive all or partial rights to elective share in a signed written waiver
- Not enforceable if waiver was not made voluntarily, or if person waiving rights was not given a fair and reasonable disclosure of deceased's property and financial obligations, unless there is also a written waiver of right to such disclosure

Divorce

Division of Property at Divorce

N.C. Gen. Stat. § 50-20

Property division method: Equitable distribution

Marital fault considered? No

Factors affecting property division:

- Income, property, and liabilities of each spouse
- Any obligation for support from prior marriage
- Duration of marriage
- Age and physical and mental health of both spouses
- Need of a custodial parent to occupy or own family home and use or own its household effects

- Expectation of pension, retirement, or other deferred compensation rights not included in marital property
- Any equitable claim to, interest in, or contribution to the acquisition of marital property by the spouse not having title, including contributions and services as a spouse, parent, wage earner, or homemaker
- Contribution made by one spouse to help educate or develop the career potential of the other spouse
- Direct contribution to increase in value of other spouse's separate property during the course of the marriage
- Liquid or nonliquid character of all marital and divisible property
- Difficulty of evaluating any partial asset or an interest in a business, corporation, or profession, and economic desirability of keeping it intact and free from claim or interference by the other spouse
- Tax consequences to each spouse
- Acts of either party to maintain, preserve, develop, expand, waste, neglect, devalue, or convert the marital property or divisible property during the period after separation and before the time of distribution
- If certain assets or types of property cannot be equitably divided, court must make a distributive award to achieve equity between spouses; court may also make a distributive award to supplement or facilitate distribution of marital property (N.C. Gen. Stat. § 50-20(e))
- Equitable distribution of property is made without regard to alimony award (N.C. Gen. Stat. § 50-20(f))

Temporary Alimony

N.C. Gen. Stat. § 50-16.2A

Marital fault considered? Yes

Other factors considered when awarding temporary alimony:

- Financial needs of each spouse, based on accustomed standard of living, and expenses reasonably necessary for support
- Employment income, other recurring earnings, and income-earning abilities of each spouse
- Separate and marital debt obligations, and each spouse's legal obligation to support others
- Barring marital fault, dependent spouse is entitled to post-separation support award if his or her resources are not adequate to meet reasonable needs and the supporting spouse has the ability to pay

Permanent Alimony Award

N.C. Gen. Stat. § 50-16.3A

Marital fault considered? Yes ("Illicit sexual behavior" on part of dependent spouse precludes alimony award; supporting spouse who is at fault will be obligated to pay alimony)

Other factors affecting award include:

- Similar factors to those affecting property division
- Age and the physical, mental, and emotional conditions of the spouses
- Amount and sources of earned and unearned income, including dividends and medical, retirement, insurance, Social Security, or other benefits
- Duration of the marriage and standard of living during marriage
- Whether child custody affects the earning power, expenses, or financial obligations of a spouse
- Education of the spouses and the time necessary for spouse seeking alimony to acquire sufficient education or training to find employment that meets reasonable economic needs
- Assets and liabilities of the spouses and debt service requirements, including legal obligations of support
- Property brought to the marriage by either spouse
- Contribution of a spouse as homemaker
- Relative needs of the spouses
- Federal, state, and local tax ramifications of the alimony award
- Alimony may be awarded for a specified or indefinite term and amount of marital property distribution may be considered

Circumstances That Terminate or Modify Alimony

N.C. Gen. Stat. § 50-16.9

- Change of financial circumstances
- Dependent spouse's remarriage or cohabitation

Debts

- Neither spouse is liable for the other spouse's premarital debts (N.C. Gen. Stat. § 52-11)

North Dakota

Prenuptial Agreements

Legal term: Premarital Agreement

Has state adopted UPAA? Yes

State code sections: N.D. Cent. Code §§ 14-03.1-01 to 14-03.1-09; 30.1-05-07

Required Formalities for Prenuptial Agreements

- In writing
- Signed by both parties

Permitted Subjects of Prenuptial Agreements

- Property rights
- Rights to sell, transfer, or control property
- What happens to property at divorce or separation
- What happens to property upon death
- Alimony (spousal support or spousal maintenance)
- Terms of wills, trusts, or other estate planning documents
- Life insurance ownership and arrangements
- Applicable state law
- Any other matter that does not violate public policy or criminal laws
- *Not permitted: child support restriction*

What Makes a Prenuptial Agreement Unenforceable?

- Agreement not made voluntarily
- Agreement unconscionable when signed or when enforcement sought, if party objecting to enforcement did not know other party's finances and was not given fair and reasonable disclosure prior to signing
- Alimony waiver, if it makes waiving spouse eligible for public assistance
- Annulment of marriage, unless result would be inequitable
- Subject of agreement against public policy or criminal laws

Inheritance

Election Rights (N.D. Cent. Code § 30.1-05-01)

- Surviving spouse is entitled to one-half of augmented estate
- If the amount of the elective share plus the value of any other property passing to the spouse by non-probate transfer, joint tenancy, or co-ownership is less than $50,000, the surviving spouse is entitled to a supplemental elective share that will bring the total to $50,000

- Taking elective share does not affect rights to exempt property, homestead, or family allowance

Allowance Rights

- **Homestead.** Up to $80,000 in house, land, and improvements used as residence (N.D. Cent. Code § 47-18-01)
- **Exempt property.** Up to $10,000 in household furniture, furnishings, appliances, automobiles, and personal effects (N.D. Cent. Code § 30.1-07-01)
- **Family allowance.** Reasonable maintenance for spouse and dependent children for up to one year while estate is being settled (N.D. Cent. Code § 30.1-07-02)

Waiver of Inheritance Rights

N.D. Cent. Code § 30.1-05-07

- All rights may be wholly or partially waived by written agreement or contract signed by the waiving spouse
- Waiver not enforceable if: 1) it was not made voluntarily; 2) person executing waiver was not given fair disclosure of decedent's property or financial obligations, did not expressly waive right to such disclosure, and did not have or could not have had knowledge of property or obligations; or 3) waiver was unconscionable (court must decide this issue)
- Waiver not enforceable if it would reduce surviving spouse's income to level eligible for public assistance

Divorce

Division of Property at Divorce

N.D. Cent. Code § 14-05-24

Property division method: Equitable distribution

Marital fault considered? No

Factors affecting property division:

- None specified; distribution is based on property rights

Temporary Alimony

N.D. Cent. Code § 14-05-23

- May be awarded to either party for support and attorney's fees while divorce is pending

Permanent Alimony Award

N.D. Cent. Code §§ 14-05-24.1 to 14-05-25

Marital fault considered? May be considered, especially in deciding which party may occupy or possess family residence

Other factors affecting award:

- "Circumstances of the parties"

- If either spouse has sufficient separate property to be self-supporting, the court may decide not to award alimony out of the other spouse's separate property

Circumstances That Terminate or Modify Alimony

N.D. Cent. Code § 14-05-25

- None specified; all support orders are subject to modification

Debts

N.D. Cent. Code § 14-07-08

- Neither spouse is liable for the other's debts
- Each spouse's separate property and earnings belong to that spouse alone and cannot be taken to pay the other's debts

Ohio

Prenuptial Agreements

Legal term: Antenuptial Agreement

Has state adopted UPAA? No

Important court cases: *In re Mize,* 611 N.E.2d 460 (1992); *Gross v. Gross,* 492 N.E.2d 476 (1984); *Troha v. Sneller,* 159 N.E.2d 899 (1959)

Required Formalities for Prenuptial Agreements

- In writing
- Signed by both parties

Permitted Subjects of Prenuptial Agreements

- Property rights
- What happens to property at divorce or separation (premarital property only)
- What happens to property upon death
- Alimony (spousal support or spousal maintenance)
- Any other matter that does not violate public policy or criminal laws

What Makes a Prenuptial Agreement Unenforceable?

- Agreement not made voluntarily
- Agreement not fair and reasonable under all attendant circumstances
- Prior to signing, party objecting to enforcement did not know other party's finances and was not given full disclosure
- Alimony waiver, if it is not fair and reasonable under all attendant circumstances
- Subject of agreement against public policy or criminal laws

Inheritance

Election Rights

Ohio Rev. Code Ann. §§ 2106.01

- Surviving spouse's share may not exceed one-half of the net estate; if deceased spouse has two or more children, share may not exceed one-third
- If surviving spouse's share would be equal to or less than deceased spouse's share of homestead ("mansion house"), surviving spouse may also choose that share of the homestead

Allowance Rights

- **Homestead.** Surviving spouse is entitled to deceased spouse's share of homestead, including adjacent farm-lands and household furnishings, either as part of elective share or as part of allowance rights (Ohio Rev. Code Ann. §§ 2106.10, 2106.01)
- **Right to live in homestead.** Surviving spouse is entitled to live in homestead rent-free for one year; if homestead must be sold to satisfy claims against estate, surviving spouse is entitled to compensation equal to value of rent for remaining term (Ohio Rev. Code Ann. § 2106.15)
- **Family allowance.** $40,000 in cash or property; if deceased spouse had minor children who are not also children of the surviving spouse, court will distribute $40,000 equitably (Ohio Rev. Code Ann. § 2106.13)
- **Motor vehicles.** Surviving spouse may choose up to two automobiles that have a combined value of no more than $40,000; the lower of the two vehicle values is deducted from the family allowance (Ohio Rev. Code Ann. §§ 2106.18, 2106.13)
- **Boats.** Surviving spouse has right to one boat ("watercraft"), one outboard motor, or one of each (Ohio Rev. Code Ann. § 2106.19)

Waiver of Inheritance Rights

- May waive rights to elective share or any other rights, if agreement or contract clearly states that intention. (*Hook v. Hook*, 431 N.E.2d 667 (1982))
- "Strong and unmistakable language" is necessary to deprive a surviving spouse of the elective share conferred by statute (*Troha v. Sneller*, 159 N.E.2d 899 (1959))

Divorce

Division of Property at Divorce

Ohio Rev. Code Ann. § 3105.171

Property division method: Equitable distribution

Marital fault considered? Economic misconduct considered

Other factors affecting property division: (Ohio Rev. Code Ann. § 3105.171(F))

- Duration of marriage
- Assets and liabilities of spouses
- Desirability of awarding family home, or the right to reside in it, to the spouse with custody of the children
- Liquidity of the property to be distributed
- Economic desirability of keeping an asset intact
- Tax consequences of property division
- Costs of sale, if an asset must be sold to achieve an equitable distribution of property

Temporary Alimony

Ohio Rev. Code Ann. § 3105.18(B), (H)

- Either spouse may be awarded reasonable support while divorce or legal separation is pending
- Either spouse may be awarded reasonable attorney's fees at any stage of divorce proceedings if court determines that the spouse ordered to pay fees has the ability to do so, and the receiving spouse will not be able to protect his or her rights and interests unless awarded attorney's fees

Permanent Alimony Award

Ohio Rev. Code Ann. § 3105.18(C)

Marital fault considered? No

Factors affecting award:

- Income of the spouses from all sources, including retirement benefits and marital property award
- Relative assets and liabilities of the spouses, including any court-ordered payments
- Relative earning ability and education of the spouses
- Age and physical, mental, and emotional condition of the spouses
- Duration of marriage and standard of living during marriage
- Whether it is appropriate for custodial parent of minor child to work outside the home
- Contribution of either spouse to the education, acquisition of a professional degree, training, or earning ability of the other spouse
- Lost income-producing capacity of either spouse as a result of marital responsibilities
- Time and expense necessary for spouse seeking support to acquire education, training, or job experience to be qualified to obtain appropriate employment (spouse must actually acquire necessary skills and seek employment)
- Tax consequences for each spouse
- When determining whether alimony is reasonable and determining the amount and terms of payment, court assumes each spouse has contributed equally to the production of marital income

Circumstances That Terminate or Modify Alimony

- Death of either spouse (Ohio Rev. Code Ann. § 3105.18(B))
- Change of economic circumstances, including increase or involuntary decrease in wages, salary, bonuses, living expenses, or medical expenses (Ohio Rev. Code Ann. § 3105.18(F))
- Divorce decree must specifically authorize court to modify alimony terms or payments (Ohio Rev. Code Ann. § 3105.18(E))

Debts

- Each spouse is liable for necessaries for support of the other (Ohio Rev. Code Ann. § 3103.03(C))
- Neither spouse is responsible for the other's debts (Ohio Rev. Code Ann. § 3103.08)

Oklahoma

Prenuptial Agreements

Legal term: Antenuptial Contract or Antenuptial Agreement

Has state adopted UPAA? No

State code sections: Okla. Stat. Ann. tit. 43, § 121; tit. 84, § 44

Important court cases: *Estate of Burgess,* 646 P.2d 623 (1982); *Freeman v. Freeman,* 565 P.2d 365 (1977)

Required Formalities for Prenuptial Agreements

- In writing
- Signed by both parties

Permitted Subjects of Prenuptial Agreements

- Property rights
- What happens to property at divorce or separation
- What happens to property upon death
- Any other matter that does not violate public policy or criminal laws

What Makes a Prenuptial Agreement Unenforceable?

- Agreement not made voluntarily
- Agreement not just and reasonable at time of signing
- Prior to signing, party objecting to enforcement did not know other party's finances and was not given full disclosure
- Subject of agreement against public policy or criminal laws

Inheritance

Election Rights

Okla. Stat. Ann. tit. 84, § 44

- Surviving spouse is entitled to one-half of all property acquired by the joint work of both spouses during the marriage

Allowance Rights

- **Homestead.** Surviving spouse is entitled to live in and own homestead (Okla. Stat. Ann. tit. 58, § 311)
- **Exempt property.** Family pictures; family bible, school books, and all other books in family library to value of $100; church pew; burial plot; clothing; one year's food and fuel; all household furniture and appliances; all other property that is legally exempt from creditor's claims (Okla. Stat. Ann. tit. 58, §§ 311, 312)
- If there are minor children, surviving spouse is entitled to one-half of exempt property; if surviving spouse has income equal to value of property, then all property will go to children except for the homestead (Okla. Stat. Ann. tit. 58, §§ 316, 318)
- **Family allowance.** If there is insufficient exempt property to support surviving spouse and family, court may set aside a reasonable allowance for up to one year while estate is being settled (Okla. Stat. Ann. tit. 58, § 314)

Waiver of Inheritance Rights

- Waiver permitted as part of an antenuptial contract; no special requirements specified

Divorce

Division of Property at Divorce

Okla. Stat. Ann. tit. 43, § 121

Property division method: Equitable distribution

Marital fault considered? No

Factors affecting property division:

- Property division is at the discretion of the court; the only consideration is that the distribution is fair, just, and reasonable
- If divorce decree awards money payment, it must clearly distinguish between payment as part of property division (which cannot be revoked or modified and must continue until completed) and payment for alimony (Okla. Stat. Ann. tit. 43, § 134(A))

Temporary Alimony

Okla. Stat. Ann. tit. 43, § 110

- During divorce proceeding, either spouse may request temporary maintenance
- Court may require either spouse to maintain health, property, and life insurance policies

Permanent Alimony Award

Okla. Stat. Ann. tit. 43, § 121

Marital fault considered? No

Other factors affecting award:

- Either spouse may be awarded alimony that is reasonable in relation to the value of the supporting spouse's property
- Determining factors are needs of spouse receiving alimony and ability of other spouse to pay (*Smith v. Smith,* 847 P.2d 827 (Okla. App.1993))

Circumstances That Terminate or Modify Alimony

Okla. Stat. Ann. tit. 43, § 134(B) to (D)

- Death of either spouse
- Remarriage or cohabitation of spouse receiving support

- Substantial and continuing changed circumstances relating to the need for support or ability to support, which make the terms of the decree unreasonable to either spouse

Debts
Okla. Stat. Ann. tit. 43, § 208

- Neither spouse is responsible for the other's debts
- Each spouse's separate property is liable for that spouse's own debts
- Separate property of one spouse is not liable for the prenuptial debts of the other spouse

Oregon

Prenuptial Agreements

Legal term: Premarital Agreement

Has state adopted UPAA? Yes

State code sections: Or. Rev. Stat. §§ 108.700 to 108.740; 114.115

Required Formalities for Premarital Agreement

- In writing
- Signed by both parties

Permitted Subjects of Prenuptial Agreements

- Property rights
- Rights to sell, transfer, or control property
- What happens to property at divorce or separation
- What happens to property upon death
- Alimony (spousal support or spousal maintenance)
- Terms of wills, trusts, or other estate planning documents
- Life insurance ownership and arrangements
- Applicable state law
- Any other matter that does not violate public policy or criminal laws
- *Not permitted: child support restriction*

What Makes a Prenuptial Agreement Unenforceable?

- Agreement not made voluntarily
- Agreement unconscionable when signed
- Prior to signing, party objecting to enforcement did not know other party's finances and was not given fair and reasonable disclosure
- Alimony waiver, if it would make waiving spouse eligible for public assistance
- Annulment of marriage, unless result would be inequitable
- Subject of agreement against public policy or criminal laws

Inheritance

Election Rights

Or. Rev. Stat. §§ 114.105, 114.125

- One-fourth of net estate, minus the value of various types of income and property currently owned by, or transferred to, surviving spouse

Allowance Rights

- **Homestead.** Surviving spouse is entitled to occupy homestead for one year after death of spouse (Or. Rev. Stat. § 114.005)
- **Family allowance.** Court must order necessary and reasonable support; court may allow temporary support pending final order (Or. Rev. Stat. § 114.015, 114.035)

Waiver of Inheritance Rights

- Right to elective share may be waived by agreement signed by both spouses (Or. Rev. Stat. § 114.115)
- Right to allowance or support may be waived by premarital agreement (*Simmons v. Simmons,* 728 P.2d 921 (1986))

Divorce

Division of Property at Divorce

Or. Rev. Stat. § 107.105(e)

Property division method: Equitable distribution

Marital fault considered? No

Factors affecting property division:

- Contribution of spouse as homemaker
- Reasonable costs of selling assets
- Tax consequences of division
- Whether alimony or support will be awarded instead of a share of property

Temporary Alimony

Or. Rev. Stat. § 107.095(1)(a)

- One spouse may be ordered to pay necessary support, maintenance, and court costs to other spouse to allow other spouse to prosecute or defend divorce action

Permanent Alimony Award

Or. Rev. Stat. § 107.105(d)

Marital fault considered? No

Oregon awards three types of alimony: transitional, compensatory, and maintenance. Slightly different factors affect each type of award. Factors affecting all three types are:

- Duration of marriage
- Tax consequences to each spouse

Transitional spousal support. Awarded so that one spouse can attain education and training necessary to reenter or advance in the job market.

Factors affecting award:

- Training, employment skills, and work experience of spouse seeking support
- Custodial and child support responsibilities of spouse seeking support
- Financial needs and resources of each spouse

Compensatory spousal support. Awarded when one spouse has made a significant financial or other contribution to the education, training, skills, career, or earning capacity of the other.

Factors affecting award:

- Amount, duration, and nature of the contribution
- Extent to which marital estate already benefited from the contribution
- Relative earning capacity of the spouses

Spousal maintenance. A contribution by one spouse to the support of the other for a specified or an indefinite period.

Factors affecting award:

- Age and health of the spouses, including their physical, mental, and emotional condition
- Standard of living established during marriage
- Relative income and earning capacity of the spouses (wage earner's income is evaluated differently from income supported spouse may receive from share of marital property)
- Training, employment skills, and work experience of spouse seeking support
- Financial needs and resources of each spouse

Circumstances That Terminate or Modify Alimony
Or. Rev. Stat. § 107.135

- Substantial change in economic circumstances including: substantial change in the cost of reasonable and necessary expenses to either spouse; good faith career change that reduces paying spouse's income; inability of spouse receiving alimony to get anticipated retirement or other pension benefits
- When reviewing change in circumstances, court will compare each spouse's income opportunities and benefits, including likelihood of acquiring future income and assets, retirement, travel, recreational, and medical benefits
- Compensatory spousal support may be modified only if there is an involuntary, extraordinary, and unanticipated change in circumstances that reduces the earning capacity of the paying spouse

Debts
Or. Rev. Stat. § 108.020

- Neither spouse is liable for debts the other spouse incurred before marriage or for the other spouse's separate debts incurred during marriage
- Separate property (and income or rents derived from it) of one spouse is not liable for debts of the other spouse
- Both husband and wife are jointly and separately responsible for family expenses and education of the children (Or. Rev. Stat. § 108.040)

Pennsylvania

Prenuptial Agreements

Legal term: Antenuptial Agreement

Has state adopted UPAA? No

State code sections: 23 Pa. Cons. Stat. Ann. § 3104

Important court cases: *Karkaria v. Karkaria,* 592 A.2d 64 (1991); *Estate of Geyer,* 516 Pa. 492, 533 A.2d 423 (1987)

Required Formalities for Prenuptial Agreements

- In writing

Permitted Subjects of Prenuptial Agreements

- Property rights
- What happens to property at divorce or separation
- What happens to property upon death
- Alimony (spousal support or spousal maintenance)
- Any other matter that does not violate public policy or criminal laws

What Makes a Prenuptial Agreement Unenforceable?

- Agreement not made voluntarily
- Agreement not signed until enforcement is sought
- Prior to signing, party objecting to enforcement did not know other party's finances and was not given fair and reasonable disclosure
- Subject of agreement against public policy or criminal laws

Inheritance

Election Rights

20 Pa. Cons. Stat. Ann. § 2203

- Surviving spouse is entitled to one-third of deceased spouse's estate; also entitled to one-third of any property already conveyed by deceased spouse if: 1) deceased spouse still had power at time of death to withdraw conveyance; and 2) surviving spouse had not jointly conveyed property or given consent to conveyance
- Elective share does not include proceeds of life insurance or employee benefit plan

Allowance Rights

20 Pa. Cons. Stat. Ann. § 3121

- **Exempt property.** $3,500 worth of real or personal property or both.

Waiver of Inheritance Rights

20 Pa. Cons. Stat. Ann. § 2207

- Right to elective share may be waived entirely or partially; no special requirements specified

Divorce

Division of Property at Divorce

23 Pa. Cons. Stat. Ann. § 3502

Property division method: Equitable distribution

Marital fault considered? No

Other factors affecting property division:

- Duration of marriage and standard of living during marriage
- Any prior marriage of either spouse
- Age, health, amount and sources of income, vocational skills, employability, estate, liabilities, and needs of each spouse
- Contribution by one spouse to the education, training, or increased earning power of the other
- Sources of income of both spouses, including medical, retirement, insurance, or other benefits and opportunities for future acquisitions of capital assets and income
- Contribution of each spouse to the acquisition, preservation, depreciation, or appreciation, or dissipation of marital property, including contribution of a homemaker
- Value of marital property distributed to each spouse
- Economic circumstances of each spouse, including federal, state, and local tax ramifications, at the time division of property is to become effective
- Either spouse's responsibilities as custodial parent of dependent minor children

Temporary Alimony

23 Pa. Cons. Stat. Ann. § 3702

- Either spouse may be awarded reasonable attorney's fees and expenses during divorce proceeding
- Supporting spouse may be ordered to pay reasonable support and to maintain hospital and medical insurance for dependent spouse

Permanent Alimony Award

23 Pa. Cons. Stat. Ann. § 3701

Marital fault considered? Yes

Other factors affecting award:

- Relative earnings and earning capacities of the spouses
- Relative assets, liabilities, and needs of the spouses
- Ages and the physical, mental, and emotional conditions of the spouses
- Sources of income of both spouses, including medical, retirement, insurance, or other benefits, expectancies, and inheritances
- Duration of marriage and standard of living during marriage

- Contribution by one spouse to the other's education, training, or increased earning power
- Extent to which being a custodial parent will affect the earning power, expenses, or financial obligations of either spouse
- Relative education of the spouses and the time needed for spouse seeking alimony to acquire sufficient education or training to find appropriate employment
- Spouse seeking alimony lacks sufficient property, including share of marital property, to provide for reasonable needs and is incapable of self-support through appropriate employment
- Property brought to the marriage by either spouse
- Contribution of a spouse as homemaker
- Federal, state, and local tax ramifications of award

Circumstances That Terminate or Modify Alimony
23 Pa. Cons. Stat. Ann. § 3701(e)

- Remarriage of spouse receiving alimony
- Substantial and continuing changed economic circumstances of either spouse
- Cohabitation of spouse receiving alimony (23 Pa. Cons. Stat. Ann. § 3706)
- Death of either spouse (23 Pa. Cons. Stat. Ann. § 3707)

Debts
23 Pa. Cons. Stat. Ann. §§ 4101 and following

- Spouse is not liable for debts the other spouse incurred before marriage

Rhode Island

Prenuptial Agreements

Legal term: Premarital Agreement
Has state adopted UPAA? Yes
State code sections: R.I. Gen. Laws §§ 15-17-1 to 15-17-11
Important court cases: *Penhallow v. Penhallow,* 649 A.2d 1016 (1994); *Peck v. Peck,* 12 R.I. 485 (1880)

Required Formalities for Prenuptial Agreements

- In writing
- Signed by both parties

Permitted Subjects of Prenuptial Agreements

- Property rights
- Rights to sell, transfer, or control property
- What happens to property at divorce or separation
- What happens to property upon death
- Alimony (spousal support or spousal maintenance)
- Terms of wills, trusts, or other estate planning documents
- Life insurance ownership and arrangements
- Applicable state law
- Any other matter that does not violate public policy or criminal laws
- *Not permitted: child support restriction*

What Makes a Prenuptial Agreement Unenforceable?

- Agreement not made voluntarily
- Agreement unconscionable when signed and prior to signing, party objecting to enforcement did not know other party's finances and was not given fair and reasonable disclosure
- Alimony waiver, if it would make waiving spouse eligible for public assistance
- Annulment of marriage, unless result would be inequitable
- Subject of agreement against public policy or criminal laws

Inheritance

Election Rights

R.I. Gen. Laws §§ 33-35-2 to -5

- Surviving spouse is entitled to lifetime use of all real estate owned by deceased spouse; must renounce any other gift of real property in order to claim election

Allowance Rights

- **Exempt property.** Clothing, household furnishings, and any other property exempt by law from creditors' claims (R.I. Gen. Laws § 33-10-1)
- **Family allowance.** Court may order "reasonable allowance" for support for six months while estate being settled; may be extended for another six months if estate is still in probate (R.I. Gen. Laws § 33-10-3)
- **Additional support.** If deceased spouse left no children, probate court may set aside a portion of real estate for support of surviving spouse (R.I. Gen. Laws § 33-10-4)

Waiver of Inheritance Rights

R.I. Gen. Laws § 15-17-6

- Waiver must be voluntary
- Spouse waiving rights must 1) have knowledge of other spouse's property and financial obligations; 2) be given fair disclosure of property and obligations; or 3) expressly waive right to such disclosure
- Waiver may not be unconscionable (court decides this issue)

Divorce

Division of Property at Divorce

R.I. Gen. Laws § 15-5-16.1
Property division method: Equitable distribution
Marital fault considered? Yes
Income or appreciation in value of separate property may be subject to division. Other factors affecting property division include:

- Duration of marriage
- Contribution by each spouse to the acquisition, preservation, or appreciation of their separate property
- Contribution and services of either spouse as a homemaker
- Health, age, occupation, employability, and amount and sources of income of each spouse
- Opportunity of each spouse to acquire capital assets and income in the future
- Contribution by one spouse to the education, training, licensure, business, or increased earning power of the other
- Custodial parent's need to occupy or own family home and household effects, taking into account the best interests of the children
- Either spouse's wasteful dissipation of assets or transfer or encumbrance of assets made in contemplation of divorce

Temporary Alimony

R.I. Gen. Laws § 15-5-16(f)

- Court may order support for either spouse while divorce pending

Permanent Alimony Award

R.I. Gen. Laws § 15-5-16(b)

Marital fault considered? Yes

Other factors affecting award include:

- Duration of marriage and standard of living established
- Health, age, occupation, amount and sources of income, vocational skills, and employability of each spouse
- Liabilities and needs of each spouse
- Opportunity of either spouse to acquire capital assets and income in the future
- Either spouse's inability to earn a living based on custody of a child whose condition or circumstances require parent to stay at home, or be employed only part- or flex-time
- Either spouse was away from job market while fulfilling homemaking responsibilities, and education, skills, or experience are outmoded and earning capacity diminished

- Time and expense required for supported spouse to acquire education or training to develop marketable skills and find appropriate employment
- Probability, given supported party's age and skills, of completing education or training and becoming self-supporting
- Duration of award based on how long it takes supported spouse to become financially independent
- Supporting spouse's ability to pay, based on earning capacity, earned and unearned income, assets, debts, and standard of living

Circumstances That Terminate or Modify Alimony

R.I. Gen. Laws § 15-5-16(c)

- Substantial change in circumstances
- Remarriage of spouse receiving alimony

Debts

R.I. Gen. Laws § 15-4-12

- Neither spouse is liable for debts the other incurred before or during marriage

South Carolina

Prenuptial Agreements

Legal term: Antenuptial Agreement

Has state adopted UPAA? No

State code sections: S.C. Code §§ 20-7-473; 20-5-50; 62-2-204

Required Formalities for Prenuptial Agreements

- In writing
- Signed by both parties
- Notarized
- Schedule of property attached

Permitted Subjects of Prenuptial Agreements

- Property rights
- What happens to property at divorce or separation
- What happens to property upon death
- Any other matter that does not violate public policy or criminal laws

What Makes a Prenuptial Agreement Unenforceable?

- Agreement not made voluntarily
- Prior to signing, party objecting to enforcement was not given fair and reasonable disclosure and was not represented by separate counsel
- Subject of agreement against public policy or criminal laws

Inheritance

Election Rights

- Surviving spouse is entitled to one-third of deceased spouse's estate (S.C. Code Ann. § 62-2-201)
- Homestead allowance and exempt property rights are still available, but value will be deducted from elective share (S.C. Code Ann. § 62-2-206)

Allowance Rights

- **Homestead.** Up to $5,000 in real property used as a residence (S.C. Code Ann. § 15-41-30)
- **Exempt property.** $5,000 in household furnishings, furniture, appliances, automobiles, and personal effects. If property value is less than $5,000, other estate assets may be used to make up the difference (S.C. Code Ann. § 62-2-401)

Waiver of Inheritance Rights

S.C. Code Ann. § 62-2-204

- Rights may be wholly or partially waived in a written agreement signed by the person waiving after fair disclosure

- Agreement that waives "all rights" to property or estate assumes waiver of elective share, homestead allowance, and exempt property rights

Divorce

Division of Property at Divorce

S.C. Code Ann. § 20-7-472

Property division method: Equitable distribution

Marital fault considered? Yes

Other factors affecting property division include:

- Duration of marriage
- Ages and physical and emotional health of the spouses
- Contribution by each spouse to the acquisition, preservation, depreciation, or appreciation in value of marital property, including contribution of a homemaker
- Each spouse's income, earning potential, and opportunity for future acquisition of capital assets
- Need of either spouse for additional training or education in order to achieve income potential
- NonMarital property and vested retirement benefits of each spouse
- Desirability of awarding family home or right to live in it to spouse having custody of any children
- Tax consequences to each spouse
- Existence and extent of either spouse's prior support obligations
- Liens and other encumbrances upon marital or separate property, and any other joint or separate debts incurred during the marriage

Temporary Alimony

- Court may grant maintenance and support to either spouse during divorce proceedings (S.C. Code Ann. § 20-3-130(A))
- Fault is a factor in awarding temporary alimony (S.C. Code Ann. § 20-3-130(A))
- Court may award attorney, expert witness, and investigation fees based on spouses' financial resources and marital fault (S.C. Code Ann. § 20-3-130(H))

Permanent Alimony Award

S.C. Code Ann. § 20-3-130

Marital fault considered? Yes (no alimony awarded to spouse who commits adultery)

South Carolina defines four types of permanent alimony:

- **Periodic alimony.** Support that is ongoing, but may be modified or terminated
- **Lump-sum alimony.** Finite amount that may not be modified
- **Rehabilitative alimony.** Finite sum based on how long it will take supported spouse to become self-sufficient after completion of required job training or education
- **Reimbursement alimony.** Finite sum awarded from future earnings of one spouse based on contributions of the other during the marriage

Factors affecting these awards:

- Duration of marriage and standard of living during marriage
- Ages of the spouses at the time of the marriage and at the time of the divorce
- Physical and emotional condition of each spouse
- Educational background of each spouse, including need for additional training or education to achieve his or her income potential
- Employment history and earning potential of each spouse
- Current and reasonably anticipated earnings, expenses, and needs, and support obligations of both spouses

- Marital and separate property of each spouse (including property division as result of divorce)
- Custody of any children, especially where conditions or circumstances make it appropriate for parent to seek only limited or no employment outside the home
- Misconduct of either spouse that affects parties' economic circumstances
- Tax consequences to each spouse of the particular form of support awarded

Circumstances That Terminate or Modify Alimony
S.C. Code Ann. §§ 20-3-130(B), 20-3-150

- Except for lump-sum alimony, support terminates on death of either spouse or on remarriage or continued cohabitation of supported spouse
- "Continued cohabitation" is defined as living with someone in a romantic relationship for at least 90 days
- Change in financial circumstances of either spouse (S.C. Code Ann. § 20-3-170)

Debts

- Wife's separate property is not subject to husband's debts (S.C. Code Ann. § 20-5-30)
- Husband is not responsible for debts wife incurred before or during marriage (S.C. Code Ann. § 20-5-60)

South Dakota

Prenuptial Agreements

Legal term: Premarital Agreement

Has state adopted UPAA? Yes

State code sections: S.D. Codified Laws, §§ 25-2-16 to 25-2-25; 29A-2-213

Important court cases: *Connolly v. Connolly*, 270 N.W.2d 44 (1978)

Required Formalities for Prenuptial Agreements

- In writing
- Signed by both parties

Permitted Subjects of Prenuptial Agreements

- Property rights
- Rights to sell, transfer, or control property
- What happens to property at divorce or separation
- What happens to property upon death
- Terms of wills, trusts, or other estate planning documents
- Life insurance ownership and arrangements
- Applicable state law
- Any other matter that does not violate public policy or criminal laws
- *Not permitted: child support restriction; spousal support restriction*

What Makes a Prenuptial Agreement Unenforceable?

- Agreement not made voluntarily
- Agreement unconscionable at time of signing
- Prior to signing, party objecting to enforcement did not know other party's finances and was not given fair and reasonable disclosure
- Annulment of marriage, unless result would be inequitable
- Subject of agreement against public policy or criminal laws

Inheritance

Election Rights

S.D. Codified Laws Ann. § 29A-2-202

- Up to 50% of the augmented estate depending on the length of the marriage (maximum reached at 15 years)
- If the elective share plus the value of any other property passing to spouse by nonprobate transfer, joint tenancy, or co-ownership is less than $50,000, surviving spouse is entitled to a supplemental elective share to bring the total to $50,000
- Taking elective share does not affect rights to exempt property, homestead, or family allowance

Allowance Rights

- **Homestead.** Surviving spouse is entitled to home used as residence, including mobile home, or up to $30,000 from sale of homestead (no limit for those who are at least 70 years old) (S.D. Codified Laws Ann. §§ 29A-2-402, 43-31-13, 43-45-3)
- **Exempt property.** Family pictures; church seat or pew; burial plot; family Bible, schoolbooks and $200 worth of other books in family library; clothing; food and fuel for one year (S.D. Codified Laws Ann. § 43-45-2)
- Up to $6,000 if surviving spouse is head of a family ($4,000 if not) (S.D. Codified Laws Ann. § 43-45-4)
- **Family allowance.** Reasonable maintenance while estate is being settled (up to $1,800 total or $1,500 per month for one year may be paid without court approval) (S.D. Codified Laws Ann. § 29A-2-403)

Waiver of Inheritance Rights

S.D. Codified Laws Ann. § 29A-2-213

- All rights may be wholly or partially waived by written agreement or contract signed by the person waiving rights
- A waiver of "all rights" in property or estate presumes waiver of right to elective share, homestead, exempt property, and family allowance
- Waiver is not enforceable if: 1) it was not made voluntarily; or 2) person executing waiver was not given fair disclosure of decedent's property or financial obligations, did not expressly waive right to such disclosure, or did not have or could not have had knowledge of property or obligations; or 3) waiver was unconscionable (court must decide this issue)

Divorce

Division of Property at Divorce

S.D. Codified Laws Ann. §§ 25-4-44, 25-4-45.1

- Duration of marriage
- Age and health of the spouses
- Ability of each spouse to earn a living
- Contribution of each spouse to the accumulation of property
- Value of property owned by the spouses
- Income-producing capacity of the spouses' assets

Temporary Alimony

S.D. Codified Laws Ann. § 25-4-38

- While divorce is pending, court may require either party to pay support and costs of defending or prosecuting divorce action

Permanent Alimony Award

S.D. Codified Laws Ann. § 25-4-41

- Duration of marriage
- Respective earning capacity of spouses and respective financial condition after the property division
- Spouses' age, health, and physical condition
- Spouses' station in life or social standing

- Relative fault in the termination of the marriage

Circumstances That Terminate or Modify Alimony

S.D. Codified Laws Ann. § 25-4-41

- Change in economic circumstances (see *Olson v. Olson,* 1996 S.D. 90, 552 N.W.2d 396 (1996))

Debts

- Separate property of one spouse is not liable for debts other spouse incurred before or after marriage (S.D. Codified Laws Ann. § 25-2-6)
- Earnings of one spouse are not liable for debts of other spouse (S.D. Codified Laws Ann. § 25-2-12)

Tennessee

Prenuptial Agreements

Legal term: Antenuptial or Prenuptial Agreement

Has state adopted UPAA? No

State code sections: Tenn. Code Ann. §§ 36-3-501; 31-1-102

Important court cases: *Randolf v. Randolf*, 937 S.W. 2d 815 (1996) *Uhrig v. Pulliam*, 713 S.W. 2d 649 (1986)

Required Formalities for Prenuptial Agreements

- In writing
- Signed by both parties
- Notarized
- Separate lawyer for each party

Permitted Subjects of Prenuptial Agreements

- Property rights
- What happens to property at divorce or separation
- What happens to property upon death
- Any other matter that does not violate public policy or criminal laws

What Makes a Prenuptial Agreement Unenforceable?

- Agreement not made voluntarily
- Prior to signing, party objecting to enforcement did not know other party's finances and was not given full and fair disclosure
- Subject of agreement against public policy or criminal laws

Inheritance

Election Rights

Tenn. Code Ann. § 31-4-101

- Up to 40% of net estate depending on length of marriage (maximum reached at nine years)

Allowance Rights

- **Homestead.** Life use of homestead (Tenn. Code Ann. § 31-1-104)
- **Exempt property.** Up to $50,000 worth of any personal property or motor vehicles not used in business or for investment purposes (Tenn. Code Ann. § 30-2-101)
- **Family allowance.** Reasonable maintenance for up to one year while estate is being settled (Tenn. Code Ann. § 30-2-102)

Waiver of Inheritance Rights

- Antenuptial agreement that waives all rights in estate is valid waiver of elective share and other statutory rights (*Uhrig v. Pulliam*, 713 S.W.2d 649 (1986))

- Without fair disclosure of property and resources, antenuptial agreement cannot waive right to elective share (*Williams v. Williams*, 868 S.W.2d 616 (1992))

Divorce

Division of Property at Divorce

Tenn. Code Ann. § 36-4-121

- Duration of marriage
- Age, physical and mental health, vocational skills, employability, earning capacity, assets, financial liabilities, and financial needs of each spouse
- Economic circumstances of each spouse
- Social Security benefits available to each spouse
- Each spouse's opportunity to acquire capital assets and income in the future
- Contribution by one spouse to education, training, or increased earning power of other spouse
- Contribution by each spouse to acquisition, appreciation, depreciation, or dissipation of marital or separate property, including contribution of homemaker, parent, or wage earner
- Value of each spouse's separate property at time of marriage and at time of property division
- Tax consequences to each spouse, reasonably foreseeable costs, and expenses associated with sales or maintenance of assets
- Spouse with physical custody of any children is likely to be awarded family home and household effects

Temporary Alimony

Tenn. Code Ann. § 36-5-101(i)

- May order either spouse to pay for other's support and maintenance and for expenses of conducting divorce
- Support may include expenses of job training and education
- Factors affecting award are financial needs of each spouse, and each spouse's ability to meet those needs and pay for divorce proceedings

Permanent Alimony Award

Tenn. Code Ann. § 36-5-101(d)

- **Rehabilitative support.** Temporary award until economically disadvantaged spouse can become self-supporting at a standard of living comparable to that of the marriage or that of the other spouse
- **Long-term periodic alimony.** Awarded when rehabilitation is not feasible, or when an economically disadvantaged spouse can be only partially rehabilitated

- **Transitional alimony.** Awarded for a finite period when rehabilitation is not necessary, but economically disadvantaged spouse needs assistance adjusting to economic consequences of divorce
- Relative earning capacity, obligations, needs, and financial resources of each spouse
- Relative education and training of each spouse, or ability and opportunity to obtain education and training
- Need of one spouse for further education and training to improve his or her earning capacity
- Duration of marriage and standard of living during marriage
- Age and mental and physical condition of each spouse
- Whether it would be undesirable for custodial parent of a minor child to seek employment outside the home
- Each party's separate assets and share of marital property

- Each spouse's tangible and intangible, monetary and homemaking, contributions to the marriage and to the education, training, or increased earning power of other spouse
- Any other factors, including tax consequences, relevant to achieving equity between the spouses

Circumstances That Terminate or Modify Alimony
Tenn. Code Ann. § 36-5-101(a)
- Substantial change in circumstances that affects finances
- Death or remarriage of person receiving alimony
- Alimony recipient is living with a "third person" (unless he or she can prove that alimony is still needed)

Debts
- Husband is not liable for debts wife incurred before marriage (Tenn. Code Ann. § 36-3-503)
- Neither spouse is liable for the other's credit card debts or charge accounts, unless both spouses signed credit application (Tenn. Code Ann. § 47-18-805)

Texas

Prenuptial Agreements

Legal term: Premarital Agreement
Has state adopted UPAA? Yes
State code sections: Tex. Fam. Code Ann. §§ 4.001 to 4.010
Important court cases: *Williams v. Williams,* 569 S.W. 2d 867 (1978)

Required Formalities for Prenuptial Agreements

- In writing
- Signed by both parties

Permitted Subjects of Prenuptial Agreements

- Property rights
- Rights to sell, transfer, or control property
- What happens to property at divorce or separation
- What happens to property upon death
- Alimony (spousal support or spousal maintenance)
- Terms of wills, trusts, or other estate planning documents
- Life insurance ownership and arrangements
- Applicable state law
- Any other matter that does not violate public policy or criminal laws
- *Not permitted: child support restriction*

What Makes a Prenuptial Agreement Unenforceable?

- Agreement not made voluntarily
- Agreement unconscionable when signed and prior to signing, party objecting to enforcement did not know other party's finances and was not given fair and reasonable disclosure
- Annulment, unless result would be inequitable
- Subject of agreement against public policy or criminal laws

Inheritance

Election Rights

Tex. Fam. Code Ann. §§ 3.101, 3.102

- Surviving spouse is entitled to one-half of community property regardless of how title held; each spouse has right to dispose of his or her own separate property

Allowance Rights

- **Homestead.** Surviving spouse has homestead rights regardless of whether homestead is community or separate property (Tex. Prob. Code Ann. § 283) Homestead cannot be used to pay estate debts except for mortgage payments, property taxes, and liens; if there is no homestead, court will make reasonable cash allowance up to $15,000 (Tex. Prob. Code Ann. §§ 270, 273)
- **Exempt property.** Surviving spouse is entitled to all property that is exempt from sale to satisfy creditors or judgments; if there is no exempt property, court will make reasonable cash allowance up to $5,000 (Tex. Prob. Code Ann. §§ 271, 273)
- **Family allowance.** Sufficient maintenance for up to one year; if surviving spouse has adequate separate property, court will not grant allowance. Surviving spouse may choose to take property instead of allowance (Tex. Prob. Code Ann. §§ 286 to 292)

Waiver of Inheritance Rights

- No statute

Divorce

Division of Property at Divorce

Tex. Fam. Code Ann. § 7.001

- Relative earnings, financial condition, and obligations of each spouse
- Relative income and earning capacity of each spouse
- Size and nature of separate property of each spouse
- Relative ages and physical conditions of each spouse
- Benefits that spouse not at fault would have received if marriage had continued

Temporary Alimony

Tex. Fam. Code Ann. § 6.502

- Court may order either spouse to pay support and reasonable attorney's fees and expenses
- Court may award either spouse exclusive use of family home and control of joint business while divorce is pending

Permanent Alimony Award

- Duration of marriage was ten years or longer
- Spouse seeking support lacks sufficient property or earning ability to provide for minimum reasonable needs
- Spouse seeking support is unable to become self-supporting through appropriate employment because of an incapacitating physical or mental disability
- Spouse seeking support is custodian of child who requires substantial care and supervision, which precludes spouse from employment outside the home, or
- Spouse seeking support makes a diligent effort to find suitable employment or to develop skills needed to

become self-supporting during period of separation and while divorce is pending (Tex. Fam. Code Ann. § 8.053)

- Financial resources of each spouse, including share of community and separate property (and debts) and medical, retirement, insurance, or other benefits
- Ability of spouse seeking support to meet needs independently
- Education and employment skills of the spouses
- Time needed for spouse seeking support to acquire sufficient education or training to find appropriate employment
- Duration of marriage
- Age, employment history, earning ability, and physical and emotional condition of spouse seeking support
- Ability of spouse from whom alimony is sought to meet own personal needs and any child support obligations while providing support to other spouse
- Either spouse's excessive or abnormal expenditures or destruction, concealment, or fraudulent disposition of community property or other property held in common
- Contribution by one spouse to education, training, or increased earning power of the other
- Property brought to marriage by either spouse
- Contribution of a spouse as homemaker
- Efforts of spouse seeking alimony to pursue employment counseling

Circumstances That Terminate or Modify Alimony
Tex. Fam. Code Ann. §§ 8.056, 8.057

- Death of either party
- Remarriage or cohabitation of party receiving support
- Substantial change in financial circumstances (disability that develops after marriage does not qualify a party to start receiving alimony)

Debts
Tex. Fam. Code Ann. § 3.202

- Neither spouse's separate property is liable for the debts of the other spouse
- Neither spouse's interest in community property is liable for debts the other spouse incurred before or during marriage
- Each spouse's interest in community property is liable for debts that spouse incurred before or during marriage

Utah

Prenuptial Agreements

Legal term: Premarital Agreement

Has state adopted UPAA? Yes

State code sections: Utah Code Ann. §§ 30-8-1 to 30-8-9; 75-2-213

Required Formalities for Prenuptial Agreements

- In writing
- Signed by both parties

Permitted Subjects of Prenuptial Agreements

- Property rights
- Rights to sell, transfer, or control property
- What happens to property at divorce or separation
- What happens to property upon death
- Alimony (spousal support or spousal maintenance)
- Life insurance ownership and arrangements
- Applicable state law
- Any other matter that does not violate public policy or criminal laws
- *Not permitted: child support restriction*

What Makes a Prenuptial Agreement Unenforceable?

- Agreement not made voluntarily
- Agreement fraudulent when signed
- Prior to signing, party objecting to enforcement did not know other party's finances and was not given reasonable disclosure
- Alimony waiver, if it would make waiving spouse eligible for public assistance
- Annulment of marriage, unless result would be inequitable
- Subject of agreement against public policy or criminal laws

Inheritance

Election Rights

Utah Code Ann. § 75-2-202

- One-third of augmented estate
- If elective share plus value of any other property passing to spouse is less than $25,000, surviving spouse is entitled to a supplemental share to bring total to $25,000
- Homestead allowance, exempt property, and family allowance are deducted from elective share

Allowance Rights

- **Homestead.** Surviving spouse is entitled to allowance of $15,000 (Utah Code Ann. § 75-2-402)
- **Exempt property.** $10,000 in household furniture, furnishings, appliances, automobiles, and personal effects; if value of exempt property is less than $10,000, spouse may use other estate assets to make up the difference (Utah Code Ann. § 75-2-403)
- **Family allowance.** Reasonable maintenance for up to one year while estate is being settled (Utah Code Ann. § 75-2-404)

Waiver of Inheritance Rights

Utah Code Ann. § 75-2-213

- All rights may be wholly or partially waived by signed written agreement or by contract signed by person waiving rights
- Waiver not enforceable if: 1) it was not made voluntarily; 2) person executing waiver was not given fair disclosure of decedent's property or financial obligations, did not expressly waive right to such disclosure, or did not have or could not have had knowledge of property or obligations; or 3) waiver was unconscionable (court decides this issue)
- Waiver of "all rights" in property or estate presumes waiver of elective share, homestead, exempt property, and family allowance.

Divorce

Division of Property at Divorce

Utah Code Ann. § 30-3-5(8)(d),(e)

- Whether achieving equality between spouses' standard of living is appropriate
- Whether one spouse's earning capacity was greatly enhanced due to efforts of both spouses
- Dissolution of long-standing marriage where one spouse is about to experience a major increase in income due to efforts of both spouses

Temporary Alimony

Utah Code Ann. § 30-3-3

- Either spouse may be ordered to pay the other's costs of pursuing divorce action
- Either spouse may be awarded support and maintenance while divorce is pending

Permanent Alimony Award

Utah Code Ann. § 30-3-5(8)

- Financial condition and needs of recipient spouse

- Ability of paying spouse to provide support
- Recipient's earning capacity or ability to produce income
- Duration of marriage
- Standard of living at time of separation or time of divorce
- Whether spouse seeking alimony has custody of minor children requiring support
- Whether spouse worked for little or no pay in business owned or operated by other spouse
- Whether spouse directly contributed to increase in other's skills by paying for education or allowing spouse to attend school during the marriage
- Whether one spouse's earning capacity was greatly enhanced due to efforts of both spouses

- Marriage of long duration, and divorce sought when income of one spouse is about to undergo a major increase due to efforts of both spouses
- Alimony may not last longer than duration of marriage, unless circumstances justify extending support

Circumstances That Terminate or Modify Alimony
Utah Code Ann. § 30-3-5(8)(g),(9),(10)
- Substantial change in economic circumstances
- Death of either party
- Cohabitation or remarriage of spouse receiving alimony

Debts
Utah Code Ann. § 30-2-5
- Property, wages, earnings, or other income of one spouse is liable for debts the other incurred before or after marriage

Vermont

Prenuptial Agreements

Legal term: Antenuptial Agreement

Has state adopted UPAA? No

State code sections: Vt. Stat. Ann. tit. 14, § 465; tit. 15, § 1205

Important court cases: *Bassler v. Bassler,* 593 A. 2d 82 (1991)

Note: Parties to a civil union under Vermont law may enter into an antenuptial agreement.

Required Formalities for Prenuptial Agreements

- In writing
- Signed by both parties

Permitted Subjects of Prenuptial Agreements

- Property rights
- What happens to property at divorce or separation
- What happens to property upon death
- Applicable state law
- Any other matter that does not violate public policy or criminal laws
- *Not permitted: child support restriction*

What Makes a Prenuptial Agreement Unenforceable?

- Agreement not made voluntarily and freely
- Agreement unconscionable when signed and prior to signing, party objecting to enforcement did not know other party's finances and was not given fair and reasonable disclosure
- Alimony waiver, if it would make waiving spouse eligible for public assistance or leave spouse far below the standard of living both enjoyed during marriage
- Subject of agreement against public policy or criminal laws

Inheritance

Election Rights

Vt. Stat. Ann. tit. 14, § 402

- If there are no children, surviving spouse is entitled to entire estate if it is valued at $25,000 or less; otherwise entitled to $25,000 and one-half of remaining estate.
- If surviving spouse chooses elective share, it is instead of interest in real estate (see below)

Allowance Rights

- **Real estate.** Surviving spouse is entitled to one-third interest in real estate owned and mortgaged by deceased spouse; if there are no children or only one child (who is also the child of surviving spouse), spouse is entitled to one-half interest (Vt. Stat. Ann. tit. 14, §§ 461, 462); surviving spouse may live in family residence and collect one-third of rents owed deceased spouse, until interest in real property distributed (Vt. Stat. Ann. tit. 14, § 470)
- **Personal property.** If there is no provision in the will, surviving spouse is entitled to all of deceased spouse's clothing and accessories (Vt. Stat. Ann. tit. 14, § 401); if property needed to pay for estate expenses or debts, surviving spouse is entitled to at least one-third (Vt. Stat. Ann. tit. 14, § 401)
- **Household property.** If there is no provision in the will and no children, surviving spouse is entitled to all household goods and furniture; property is in addition to share of real estate (Vt. Stat. Ann. tit. 14, § 403)
- **Boat, snowmobile, or ATV.** If there is no provision in the will, title passes to surviving spouse (Vt. Stat. Ann. tit. 14, § 403a)
- **Family allowance.** Reasonable allowance for maintenance for up to eight months while estate being settled (Vt. Stat. Ann. tit. 14, § 404)

Waiver of Inheritance Rights

- Antenuptial agreement may waive rights to elective share and share in real property (Vt. Stat. Ann. tit. 14, §§ 402, 465)

Divorce

Division of Property at Divorce

Vt. Stat. Ann. tit. 15, § 751

- Duration of marriage
- Age and health of spouses
- Occupation, source and amount of income, vocational skills, and employability of each spouse
- Contribution by one spouse to the other's education, training, or increased earning power
- Value of each spouse's property interests, liabilities, and needs
- Whether property settlement is instead of or in addition to alimony
- Opportunity for each spouse to acquire capital assets and income in the future
- Desirability of awarding family home or right to live in it to spouse having custody of any children
- Contribution by each spouse to acquisition, preservation, depreciation, or appreciation in value of joint or separate property, including contribution of homemaker

Temporary Alimony

Vt. Stat. Ann. tit. 15, § 594a

- Either spouse may apply for support while divorce is pending
- Court may assign family home to either spouse based largely on best interests of any children

Permanent Alimony Award

Vt. Stat. Ann. tit. 15, § 752

- Spouse seeking maintenance lacks income or property, including share of distributed property, to provide for reasonable needs
- Spouse seeking maintenance can't meet standard of living established during marriage or is custodial parent of a minor child
- Financial resources and property distributed to spouse seeking maintenance
- Ability of spouse seeking maintenance to meet needs independently
- Extent to which child support includes payment to custodial parent

- Time and expense required for spouse seeking maintenance to obtain education or training needed to find appropriate employment
- Duration of marriage and standard of living during marriage
- Age and physical and emotional condition of each spouse
- Ability of spouse from whom maintenance is sought to meet own reasonable needs while meeting those of spouse seeking maintenance
- Inflation with relation to the cost of living

Circumstances That Terminate or Modify Alimony

Vt. Stat. Ann. tit. 15, § 758

- Substantial and unanticipated change in financial circumstances

Debts

Vt. Stat. Ann. tit. 15, §§ 66 and following

- Wife's separate property and income are not liable for husband's debts
- Husband is not liable for wife's premarital debts

Virginia

Prenuptial Agreements

Legal term: Premarital Agreement

Has state adopted UPAA? Yes

State code sections: Va. Code Ann. §§ 20-147 to 20-155

Important court cases: *Batleman v. Rubin,* 98 S.E. 2d 519 (1957)

Required Formalities for Prenuptial Agreements

- In writing
- Signed by both parties

Permitted Subjects of Prenuptial Agreements

- Property rights
- Rights to sell, transfer, or control property
- What happens to property at divorce or separation
- What happens to property upon death
- Alimony (spousal support or spousal maintenance)
- Terms of wills, trusts, or other estate planning documents
- Life insurance ownership and arrangements
- Applicable state law
- Any other matter that does not violate public policy or criminal laws

What Makes a Prenuptial Agreement Unenforceable?

- Agreement not made voluntarily
- Agreement unconscionable when signed
- Prior to signing, party objecting to enforcement was not given fair and reasonable disclosure of other party's finances
- Annulment of marriage, unless result would be inequitable
- Subject of agreement against public policy or criminal laws

Inheritance

Election Rights

- Surviving spouse is entitled to one-half of estate if the deceased spouse has no children; one-third if there are children (Va. Code Ann. § 64.1-16)

Allowance Rights

- **Homestead.** Surviving spouse is entitled to homestead allowance of $15,000; if homestead is worth less than $15,000, surviving spouse is entitled to allowance that will add up to $15,000 (Va. Code Ann. § 64.1-151.3); surviving spouse is entitled to live in family residence while homestead rights being settled (Va. Code Ann. § 64.1-16.4); no allowance if surviving spouse takes elective share (Va. Code Ann. § 64.1-151.3)
- **Exempt property.** $15,000 in household furniture, furnishings, appliances, automobiles, and personal effects; if value of exempt property is less than $15,000, other estate assets may be used to make up the difference (Va. Code Ann. § 64.1-151.2)
- **Family allowance.** Reasonable maintenance for up to one year while estate is settled (Va. Code Ann. § 64.1-151.1)

Waiver of Inheritance Rights

- No statute

Divorce

Division of Property at Divorce

Va. Code Ann. § 20-107.3

- Each spouse's contribution to the well-being of the family
- Each spouse's contribution to the acquisition, care, and maintenance of marital property
- Duration of marriage
- Age and physical and mental condition of each spouse
- How and when specific items of marital property were acquired
- Debts and liabilities of each spouse, basis for debts and liabilities, and property that may serve as security
- Liquid or nonliquid character of marital property
- Tax consequences to each spouse
- Marital property is distributed without taking any alimony award into account, but alimony award may be revised or modified after property division

Temporary Alimony

Va. Code Ann. § 20-103

- Court may order one spouse to pay support and maintenance (including health insurance) to spouse filing for divorce
- Spouse filing for divorce may be awarded money needed to carry on the suit
- Either spouse may be awarded exclusive use of family home while divorce is pending

Permanent Alimony Award

Va. Code Ann. § 20-107.1

- Obligations, needs, and financial resources of each spouse, including income from all pension, profit sharing, or retirement plans

- Duration of marriage and standard of living during marriage
- Age and physical and mental condition of each spouse
- Any special circumstances of the family
- Extent to which age or physical or mental condition of any child make it inappropriate for one spouse to seek employment outside of the home
- Contributions, monetary and nonmonetary, of each spouse to family's well-being
- Property interests of each spouse, including share of marital property
- Earning capacity, skills, education, training, and current employment opportunities of each spouse
- Time and costs required for either spouse to acquire education, training, and skills needed to enhance earning ability or to obtain employment
- What effect decisions regarding employment, career, economics, education, and parenting arrangements had on each spouse's present and future earning potential, including length of absence from the job market
- Extent to which one spouse contributed to other spouse's attainment of education, training, career position, or profession
- Any other factors, including tax consequences, relevant to establishing equity between the spouses

Circumstances That Terminate or Modify Alimony
Va. Code Ann. § 20-109

- Spouse receiving alimony has been cohabiting with another person in a marriage-like relationship for at least one year
- Considerable, unanticipated change in circumstances
- Death of either spouse or remarriage of spouse receiving alimony

Debts
Va. Code Ann. § 55-37

- Neither spouse is liable for debts for the other incurred before or after marriage

Washington

Prenuptial Agreements

Legal term: Prenuptial Agreement

Has state adopted UPAA? No

Important court cases: *Marriage of Fox,* 795 P. 2d 1170 (1990); *Estate of Crawford,* 730 P. 2d 675 (1986) *Friedlander v. Friedlander,* 494 P. 2d 208 (1972)

Required Formalities for Prenuptial Agreements

- In writing
- Signed by both parties

Permitted Subjects of Prenuptial Agreements

- Property rights
- What happens to property at divorce or separation
- What happens to property upon death
- Any matter that does not violate public policy or criminal law

What Makes a Prenuptial Agreement Unenforceable?

- Agreement not made freely and voluntarily
- Agreement not fair and reasonable when enforcement sought and prior to signing, party objecting to enforcement was not given full and fair disclosure of other party's finances, with competent and independent advice from a separate lawyer
- Subject of agreement against public policy or criminal laws
- Agreement was not followed during the marriage and circumstances indicate that the spouses intended to revoke it

Inheritance

Election Rights

- One-half of all community property belongs to surviving spouse; deceased spouse may dispose of other half (Wash. Rev. Code Ann. § 11.02.070)
- One-half of quasi-community property belongs to surviving spouse (Wash. Rev. Code Ann. §§ 26.16.220, 26.16.230)
- Deceased spouse may dispose of separate property as desired (Wash. Rev. Code Ann. §§ 26.16.010, 26.16.020)

Allowance Rights

- **Homestead.** Total net value of personal residence and land it is on, improvements, mobile homes, or other personal property used as a residence, or $40,000 in residence, land, improvements, and mobile home, whichever is less (Wash. Rev. Code Ann. §§ 6.13.010, 6.13.030)
- **Family allowance.** In place of homestead rights, surviving spouse may request award equal to dollar value of homestead allowance (Wash. Rev. Code Ann. §§ 11.54.020 and foll.); allowance may be paid from either community property or deceased spouse's separate property (Wash. Rev. Code Ann. § 11.54.020)

Waiver of Inheritance Rights

- Right to receive share of quasi-community property may be waived by written agreement signed by both spouses (Wash. Rev. Code Ann. § 26.16.250)

Divorce

Division of Property at Divorce

Wash. Rev. Code Ann. § 26.09.080

- Nature and extent of the community and separate property
- Duration of marriage
- Economic circumstances of each spouse
- Desirability of awarding the family home, or the right to stay in it, to spouse with whom children live most of the time

Temporary Alimony

Wash. Rev. Code Ann. § 26.09.060(1)(b)

- Either party may request temporary maintenance during divorce proceedings; may submit affidavit stating facts that make support necessary

Permanent Alimony Award

Wash. Rev. Code Ann. § 26.09.090

- Financial resources of spouse seeking support, including separate or community property and any payment received as a custodial parent
- Ability of spouse seeking support to meet needs independently
- Time required for spouse seeking support to acquire education or training to find employment appropriate to his or her skills, interests, and style of life
- Duration of marriage and standard of living during marriage
- Age, physical and emotional condition, and financial obligations of spouse seeking support
- Ability of spouse from whom alimony is sought to meet own needs and financial obligations while meeting those of the other spouse

Circumstances That Terminate or Modify Alimony

Wash. Rev. Code Ann. § 26.09.170

- Substantial change of circumstances
- Death of either spouse or remarriage of spouse receiving alimony
- Couple may create a separation agreement that says alimony may not be modified or terminated (Wash. Rev. Code Ann. § 26.09.070)

Debts

- Neither spouse's separate property, the income from it, nor personal earnings is liable for the other's debts (Wash. Rev. Code Ann. §§ 26.16.010, 26.16.020, 26.16.200)
- Neither spouse is liable for the separate debts the other incurred before or during marriage (Wash. Rev. Code Ann. § 26.16. 200)

West Virginia

Prenuptial Agreements

Legal term: Antenuptial or Prenuptial Agreement

Has state adopted UPAA? No

State code sections: W.Va. Code §§ 48-1-203; 48-6-101(b); 42-3-3a

Important court cases: *Gant v. Gant,* 329 S.E. 2d 106 (1985)

Required Formalities for Prenuptial Agreements

- In writing
- Signed by both parties
- Notarized
- Separate lawyer for each party

Permitted Subjects of Prenuptial Agreements

- Property rights
- Rights to sell, transfer, or control property
- What happens to property at divorce or separation
- What happens to property upon death
- Alimony (spousal support or spousal maintenance)
- Any other matter that does not violate public policy or criminal laws

What Makes a Prenuptial Agreement Unenforceable?

- Agreement not made voluntarily
- Agreement unconscionable when signed
- Prior to signing, party objecting to enforcement did not know other party's finances and was not given fair and reasonable disclosure with opportunity to consult with independent counsel
- Subject of agreement against public policy or criminal laws

Inheritance

Election Rights

W.Va. Code § 42-3-1

- Up to 50% of augmented estate depending on the length of the marriage (maximum reached at 15 years)
- If elective share plus value of any other property passing to surviving spouse is less than $25,000, surviving spouse entitled to a supplemental share to bring total to $25,000

Allowance Rights

- **Homestead.** $5,000 homestead exemption (not included in augmented estate calculation) (W.Va. Const. Art. 6, § 48)
- **Exempt property.** $1,000 in personal property (not included in augmented estate calculation) (W.Va. Const. Art. 6, § 48); food and fuel on hand; livestock used for food (W.Va. Code § 44-1-17)

Waiver of Inheritance Rights

W.Va. Code § 42-3-3a

- All rights may be wholly or partially waived by signed, written agreement or contract signed by the person waiving rights
- Waiver is not enforceable if 1) it was not made voluntarily, 2) person executing waiver was not given fair disclosure of decedent's property or financial obligations, did not expressly waive right to disclosure, or did not have or could not have had knowledge of property or obligations, or 3) waiver was unconscionable (court decides this issue)

Divorce

Division of Property at Divorce

W.Va. Code §§ 48-7-101, 48-7-103

- Each spouse's monetary contribution to the acquisition, preservation, maintenance, or increase in value of marital property
- Each spouse's nonmonetary contribution, including homemaking and child care; working for no or little pay in family business or other business in which either spouse has an interest; maintaining or improving tangible marital property; or managing or investing marital property assets
- Extent to which either spouse limited or decreased own income-earning ability by giving up employment or other income-earning opportunity
- Extent to which either spouse increased the other's income-earning ability by direct or indirect contributions to the other's education or training

Temporary Alimony

W.Va. Code §§ 48-5-502 to 48-5-507

- Either spouse may be ordered to pay maintenance (in lump sum or installments)
- Either spouse may be ordered to maintain health and hospitalization insurance for other party
- Either spouse may be awarded expenses of pursuing divorce action
- Either spouse may be awarded use of family home and motor vehicles

Permanent Alimony Award

W. Va. Code § 48-8-101

- **Permanent.** Periodic payments where total amount and duration are not predetermined; subject to modification or termination (see below)
- **Temporary.** While divorce is pending (see above)
- **Rehabilitative.** Awarded for a limited period of time to allow recipient spouse to become self-supporting through training or study; may terminate before rehabilitation completed under certain circumstances (see below) (W.Va. Code § 48-8-105)
- **Spousal support "in gross."** Definite amount paid in one sum or for a specific time period; not subject to termination or modification (W.Va. Code § 48-1-243)
- Duration of marriage and length of time spouses lived together as husband and wife
- Standard of living during marriage
- Financial needs of each spouse and legal obligations to support self or any other person
- Current employment income and other regular earnings of each spouse
- Distribution of marital property as it affects each spouse's ability to pay or need for support
- Income-earning abilities of each spouse, based upon education, training, employment skills, work experience, length of absence from job market, and custodial responsibilities for children
- Age and physical, mental, and emotional condition of each spouse
- Likelihood that spouse seeking support can substantially increase income-earning abilities within a reasonable time by acquiring additional education or training (and cost of obtaining it)
- Extent to which it would be inappropriate for spouse who has custody of a minor child to seek employment outside the home
- Contribution made by either spouse to education, training, vocational skills, career, or earning capacity of other party
- Whether one spouse gave up or postponed economic, education, or employment opportunities during marriage
- Costs of providing health care for each of the spouses (court may order either party to provide) (W.Va. Code § 48-5-606))
- Tax consequences to each spouse

Circumstances That Terminate or Modify Periodic or Rehabilitative Alimony

- Change in needs or circumstances of either spouse (W.Va. Code § 48-8-103)
- Spouse receiving support cohabiting in a stable, marriage-like relationship (does not terminate rehabilitative alimony) (W.Va. Code § 48-5-707)
- Remarriage of spouse receiving support (rehabilitative alimony cannot be terminated during first four years of rehabilitation) (W.Va. Code § 48-6-203)
- Death of either party (rehabilitative alimony terminates only on death of recipient) (W.Va. Code § 48-6-202)

Debts

W. Va. Code § 48-29-105

- Neither spouse is liable for the other's debts

Wisconsin

Prenuptial Agreements

Legal term: Marital Property Agreement, Premartial Agreement

Has state adopted UPAA? No

State code sections: Wis. Stat. Ann. §§ 766.58 to 766.588 (includes forms); 767.255(L); 861.10

Required Formalities for Prenuptial Agreements

- In writing
- Signed by both parties

Permitted Subjects of Prenuptial Agreements

- Property rights
- Rights to sell, transfer, or control property
- What happens to property at divorce or separation
- What happens to property upon death
- Alimony (spousal support or spousal maintenance)
- Terms of wills, trusts, or other estate planning documents
- Life insurance ownership and arrangements
- Applicable state law
- Any other matter that does not violate public policy or criminal laws
- Nonprobate transfers of property
- *Not permitted: child support restriction*

What Makes a Prenuptial Agreement Unenforceable?

- Agreement not made voluntarily
- Agreement unconscionable when signed
- Prior to signing, party objecting to enforcement did not know other party's finances and was not given fair and reasonable disclosure
- Terms of property division are inequitable to either party
- Alimony waiver, if it would leave spouse waiving rights with less than necessary and adequate support or eligible for public assistance
- Subject of agreement against public policy or criminal laws

Inheritance

Election Rights

- **Marital (community) property.** Surviving spouse is entitled to one-half of marital property (Wis. Stat. Ann. § 861.01)
- **Deferred marital property.** Surviving spouse may elect to take one-half of augmented deferred marital property estate (the total value of the deferred marital property of both spouses, including gifts of deferred marital property made by the deceased spouse during the two years before death) (Wis. Stat. Ann. § 861.02)

Allowance Rights

- **Homestead.** Surviving spouse has right to deceased spouse's share in any residence or dwelling that surviving spouse occupies or intends to occupy; must petition the court to receive share and must pay for any part of the share that doesn't automatically go to surviving spouse by law (Wis. Stat. Ann. § 861.21)
- **Exempt property.** Clothing and jewelry; automobile; household furniture, furnishings, and appliances; up to $3,000 worth of other personal property not used in agriculture or business (Wis. Stat. Ann. § 861.33)
- **Family allowance.** Payment needed for support for up to one year while estate is being settled; may be extended for longer period; family allowance may be deducted from elective share (Wis. Stat. Ann. § 861.31)

Waiver of Inheritance Rights

Wis. Stat. Ann. §§ 861.10, 766.58

- Right to elect share of deferred marital property may be waived in a written agreement signed by both spouses.
- Waiver is not enforceable if 1) it was not made voluntarily, 2) person executing waiver did not receive fair disclosure or did not have knowledge of decedent's property or financial obligations, or 3) waiver was unconscionable (court decides this issue)
- A waiver of "all rights" in property or estate presumes waiver of right to elective share

Divorce

Division of Property at Divorce

Wis. Stat. Ann. § 767.255

- Duration of marriage
- Property each spouse brought to marriage
- Whether one spouse has substantial assets not subject to division by the court
- Age and physical and emotional health of each spouse
- Contribution by each spouse to marriage, giving appropriate economic value to homemaking and child care
- Contribution by one spouse to education, training, or increased earning power of the other
- Earning capacity of each spouse, including educational background, training, employment skills and experi-

ence, length of absence from job market, and custodial responsibilities for children

- Time and cost of acquiring education or training to become self-supporting at a standard of living comparable to that during marriage
- Desirability of awarding family home or right to live in it to spouse that has physical custody of children for the greater period of time
- Amount and duration of spousal or family support payments, and whether property division is instead of or in addition to alimony
- Economic circumstances of each spouse, including pension benefits and future interests
- Tax consequences to each spouse

Temporary Alimony

Wis. Stat. Ann. § 767.23(d)

- Either spouse may be required to pay maintenance for the other spouse
- Maintenance may include attorney fees and costs of conducting divorce action

Permanent Alimony Award

Wis. Stat. Ann. § 767.26

- Duration of marriage
- Share of property division
- Age and physical and emotional health of each spouse
- Educational level of each spouse at time of marriage and at time of filing for divorce
- Earning capacity of spouse seeking support, including education, training, skills, experience, absence from job market, custodial responsibilities for children, and

time and expense of obtaining education or training needed to find appropriate employment

- Feasibility of spouse seeking maintenance becoming self-supporting at a standard of living comparable to that during marriage, and time required to achieve this goal
- Tax consequences to each spouse
- Contribution by one spouse to education, training, or increased earning power of the other
- Financial or service contributions made by one spouse to the other, where future repayment or other compensation was mutually agreed upon, but has not been made

Circumstances That Terminate or Modify Alimony

Wis. Stat. Ann. § 767.32

- Substantial change in either spouse's cost of living
- Remarriage of spouse receiving alimony

Debts

Wis. Stat. Ann. §§ 766.55 to .555

- Community property is liable for debts incurred by one spouse in interest of family or marriage; if community property is insufficient, then separate property of spouse incurring debt is liable
- Debts incurred before marriage by one spouse are the liability of that spouse's separate property or share of community property that would be still be separate property if not married
- Individual debts incurred by one spouse during marriage are the liability of that spouse's separate property and share of community property

Wyoming

Prenuptial Agreements

Legal term: Antenuptial agreement or Contract
Has state adopted UPAA? No
State code sections: Wyo. Stat. §§ 1-23-105; 2-5-102
Important court cases: *Laird v. Laird,* 597 P. 2d 463 (1979)

Required Formalities for Prenuptial Agreements

- In writing
- Signed by both parties

Permitted Subjects of Prenuptial Agreements

- Property rights
- What happens to property at divorce or separation
- What happens to property upon death
- Any matter that does not violate public policy or criminal laws

What Makes a Prenuptial Agreement Unenforceable?

- Agreement not understandingly and freely made
- Agreement "overreaching" when signed and prior to signing, party objecting to enforcement did not know other party's finances and was not given fair disclosure
- Alimony waiver, if it would make waiving spouse eligible for public assistance
- Annulment of marriage, unless result would be in-equitable
- Subject of agreement against public policy or criminal laws

Inheritance

Election Rights

Wyo. Stat. § 2-5-101

- If the deceased spouse has no children, elective share is one-half of net estate
- If surviving spouse is not the parent of any of the deceased spouse's children, elective share is one-fourth of net estate.

Allowance Rights

- **Homestead.** Surviving spouse may live in home and have use of all household furniture and clothing until estate is settled (Wyo. Stat. § 2-5-501); surviving spouse is entitled to homestead allowance of $30,000 (Wyo. Stat. §§ 2-5-501, 2-5-508)
- **Exempt property.** Surviving spouse is entitled to all property that is exempt from creditors; if deceased spouse had minor children who are not children of surviving spouse, then surviving spouse is entitled to one-half of that property (Wyo. Stat. § 2-5-504)
- **Family allowance.** Surviving spouse is entitled to reasonable support while estate is being settled (Wyo. Stat. § 2-5-502)

Waiver of Inheritance Rights

Wyo. Stat. § 2-5-102

- The rights to elective share, homestead allowance, exempt property, and family allowance may be waived totally or partially by a written contract or agreement signed by the party waiving rights
- Party waiving must receive fair disclosure of decedent's assets and liabilities
- A waiver of "all rights" assumes waiver of rights to elective share, homestead allowance, exempt property, and family allowance

Divorce

Division of Property at Divorce

Wyo. Stat. § 20-2-114

- Effect of divorce on each spouse's economic condition
- Which spouse acquired property
- Family debts or other obligations paid for by property

Temporary Alimony

Wyo. Stat. § 20-2-111

- Court may order either spouse to pay for support of other spouse and for expenses of pursuing or defending divorce

Permanent Alimony Award

Wyo. Stat. § 20-2-114

- Property award
- Ability of one spouse to pay
- Need of other spouse for support

Circumstances That Terminate or Modify Alimony

Wyo. Stat. § 20-2-116

- Substantial change in circumstances affecting ability to pay or need to receive alimony

Debts

Wyo. Stat. §§ 20-1-201 to –202

- Neither spouse's separate property is liable for the other's debts
- Each spouse is liable for own premarital debts

Index

Q

R

S

more from
N O L O
Law for All

Quicken WillMaker Plus 2004

Windows CD-ROM

Software

WQP4/$79.95

Handle many routine legal matters with *Quicken WillMaker Plus*! Whether you need to create a fully developed estate plan, or just want to leave the kids with the neighbors for an evening, this powerful software package helps you get the paperwork done, quickly and easily. It also helps you to:

Write a Will
- *Provide for family, friends and charities*
- *Name a personal guardian to care for minor children*
- *Specify the executors of your estate*
- *Make a new will whenever you like*

Create a Living Trust
- *Make a basic trust*
- *Use an AB (bypass) trust and spare heirs from potentially heavy estate taxes*
- *Create subtrusts for minor children and young adults*
- *Change or revoke a trust at any time*

Make a Financial Power of Attorney
- *Name someone to make financial decisions*
- *Appoint a replacement if that person cannot serve*

Make a Living Will (Healthcare Directive)
- *Specify whether to extend life through artificial means*
- *Outline medical procedures desired*

Record Final Arrangements
- *Plan a funeral or other ceremony*
- *Choose between a cremation or burial*

Leave Documents for Executors
- *Provide the forms and other documents that personal representatives will need to handle an estate, including a Request for Death Certificate and Notice to Insurance Companies*

Use Everyday Legal Forms
- *Generate authorizations, agreements and other documents, including an Authorization to Drive a Motor Vehicle, Child Care Agreement and Elder Care Agreement*

Create Promissory Notes
- *Create legally binding loan documents when you lend or borrow money.*

Quicken WillMaker Plus lets anyone create valid estate planning documents for all states except Louisiana.

Want a big discount on *Quicken WillMaker Plus?*

ORDER IT ONLINE AT WWW.NOLO.COM

800-728-3555 or www.nolo.com

more from
N O L O
Law for All

Plan Your Estate
by Attorneys Denis Clifford & Cora Jordan

Plan Your Estate covers everything from the basics of wills and living trusts to sophisticated tax-saving strategies. It provides straightforward, plain-English explanations of every significant estate-planning option available, so you can make the best decisions for you and those you love. The book covers:

- federal estate and gift taxes
- trusts used to control property
- funerals and burials

- durable powers of attorney
- charitable remainder trusts left to beneficiaries
- living wills

Good in all states except Louisiana.

$44.99/NEST

Make Your Own Living Trust
by Attorney Denis Clifford
Book with CD-ROM

Create your own living trust. You will find out how a living trust works, how to establish one, and how to determine what kind of trust is right for you. Contains all the forms and instructions you need to:

- transfer property quickly & easily
- eliminate attorney fees

- cut estate taxes with an A-B trust

Good in all states except Louisiana.

$39.99/LITR

Estate Planning Basics
by Attorney Denis Clifford

This book provides straightforward explanations of the major components of estate planning, so that you don't have to spend hours wading through endless options. Learn about:

- choosing beneficiaries
- other probate-avoidance methods
- wills

- estate planning by parents with minor children
- estate taxes, and tax reduction methods
- living trusts

Good in all states except Louisiana.

$21.99/ESPN

8 Ways to Avoid Probate
by Attorney Mary Randolph

Probate court proceedings can take years, and cost your family a bundle. With *8 Ways to Avoid Probate*, learn how to take advantage of eight important probate-avoidance strategies, including:

- setting up payable-on-death bank accounts
- registering stocks & bonds, and vehicles, in transfer-on-death forms
- creating a living trust
- giving away property now

- naming a beneficiary for retirement accounts
- taking advantage of special procedures for small estates
- holding property in joint ownership

$19.99/PRO8

800-728-3555 or www.nolo.com

CATALOG

...more from Nolo

	PRICE	CODE

BUSINESS

	PRICE	CODE
Buy-Sell Agreement Handbook:		
Plan Ahead for Changes in the Ownership of Your Business (Book w/CD-ROM)	$49.99	BSAG
The CA Nonprofit Corporation Kit (Binder w/CD-ROM)	$59.95	CNP
Consultant & Independent Contractor Agreements (Book w/CD-ROM)	$29.99	CICA
The Corporate Minutes Book (Book w/CD-ROM)	$69.99	CORMI
Create Your Own Employee Handbook	$49.99	EMHA
Dealing With Problem Employees	$44.99	PROBM
Drive a Modest Car & 16 Other Keys to Small Business Sucess	$24.99	DRIV
The Employer's Legal Handbook	$39.99	EMPL
Everyday Employment Law	$29.99	ELBA
Federal Employment Laws	$49.99	FELW
Form Your Own Limited Liability Company (Book w/CD-ROM)	$44.99	LIAB
Hiring Independent Contractors: The Employer's Legal Guide (Book w/CD-ROM)	$34.99	HICI
How to Create a Noncompete Agreement	$44.95	NOCMP
How to Form a California Professional Corporation (Book w/CD-ROM)	$59.95	PROF
How to Form a Nonprofit Corporation (Book w/CD-ROM)—National Edition	$44.99	NNP
How to Form a Nonprofit Corporation in California (Book w/CD-ROM)	$44.99	NON
How to Form Your Own California Corporation (Binder w/CD-ROM)	$59.99	CACI
How to Form Your Own California Corporation (Book w/CD-ROM)	$34.99	CCOR
How to Get Your Business on the Web	$29.99	WEBS
How to Write a Business Plan	$34.99	SBS
Incorporate Your Business	$49.95	NIBS
The Independent Paralegal's Handbook	$29.95	PARA
Leasing Space for Your Small Business	$34.95	LESP
Legal Guide for Starting & Running a Small Business	$34.99	RUNS
Legal Forms for Starting & Running a Small Business (Book w/CD-ROM)	$29.99	RUNS2
Marketing Without Advertising	$24.00	MWAD
Music Law (Book w/CD-ROM)	$34.99	ML
Nolo's Guide to Social Security Disability	$29.99	QSS
Nolo's Quick LLC	$24.99	LLCQ
Nondisclosure Agreements	$39.95	NAG
The Small Business Start-up Kit (Book w/CD-ROM)	$29.99	SMBU

Prices subject to change.

ORDER 24 HOURS A DAY @ www.nolo.com
Call 800-728-3555 • Mail or fax the order form in this book

ORDER 24 HOURS A DAY @ www.nolo.com
Call 800-728-3555 • Mail or fax the order form in this book

	PRICE	CODE

GOING TO COURT

Beat Your Ticket: Go To Court and Win! (National Edition)	$19.99	BEYT
The Criminal Law Handbook: Know Your Rights, Survive the System	$34.99	KYR
Everybody's Guide to Small Claims Court (National Edition)	$26.99	NSCC
Everybody's Guide to Small Claims Court in California	$26.99	CSCC
Fight Your Ticket ... and Win! (California Edition)	$29.99	FYT
How to Change Your Name in California	$34.95	NAME
How to Collect When You Win a Lawsuit (California Edition)	$29.99	JUDG
How to Seal Your Juvenile & Criminal Records (California Edition)	$34.95	CRIM
The Lawsuit Survival Guide	$29.99	UNCL
Nolo's Deposition Handbook	$29.99	DEP
Represent Yourself in Court: How to Prepare & Try a Winning Case	$34.99	RYC
Sue in California Without a Lawyer	$34.99	SLWY

HOMEOWNERS, LANDLORDS & TENANTS

California Tenants' Rights	$27.99	CTEN
Deeds for California Real Estate	$24.99	DEED
Dog Law	$21.95	DOG
Every Landlord's Legal Guide (National Edition, Book w/CD-ROM)	$44.99	ELLI
Every Tenant's Legal Guide	$29.99	EVTEN
For Sale by Owner in California	$29.99	FSBO
How to Buy a House in California	$34.99	BHCA
The California Landlord's Law Book: Rights & Responsibilities (Book w/CD-ROM)	$44.99	LBRT
The California Landlord's Law Book: Evictions (Book w/CD-ROM)	$44.99	LBEV
Leases & Rental Agreements	$29.99	LEAR
Neighbor Law: Fences, Trees, Boundaries & Noise	$26.99	NEI
The New York Landlord's Law Book (Book w/CD-ROM)	$39.99	NYLL
New York Tenants' Rights	$27.99	NYTEN
Renters' Rights (National Edition)	$24.99	RENT
Stop Foreclosure Now in California	$29.95	CLOS

HUMOR

Poetic Justice	$9.95	PJ

IMMIGRATION

Becoming A U.S. Citizen: A Guide to the Law, Exam and Interview	$24.99	USCIT
Fiancé & Marriage Visas	$44.95	IMAR
How to Get a Green Card	$29.99	GRN
Student & Tourist Visas	$29.99	ISTU
U.S. Immigration Made Easy	$44.99	IMEZ

ORDER 24 HOURS A DAY @ www.nolo.com
Call 800-728-3555 • Mail or fax the order form in this book

	PRICE	CODE

MONEY MATTERS

	PRICE	CODE
101 Law Forms for Personal Use (Book w/CD-ROM)	$29.99	SPOT
Bankruptcy: Is It the Right Solution to Your Debt Problems?	$19.99	BRS
Chapter 13 Bankruptcy: Repay Your Debts	$34.99	CH13
Creating Your Own Retirement Plan	$29.99	YROP
Credit Repair (Quick & Legal Series, Book w/CD-ROM)	$24.99	CREP
Getting Paid: How to Collect form Bankrupt Debtors	$29.99	CRBNK
How to File for Chapter 7 Bankruptcy	$34.99	HFB
IRAs, 401(k)s & Other Retirement Plans: Taking Your Money Out	$34.99	RET
Money Troubles: Legal Strategies to Cope With Your Debts	$29.99	MT
Stand Up to the IRS	$24.99	SIRS
Surviving an IRS Tax Audit	$24.95	SAUD
Take Control of Your Student Loan Debt	$26.95	SLOAN

PATENTS AND COPYRIGHTS

	PRICE	CODE
The Copyright Handbook: How to Protect and Use Written Works (Book w/CD-ROM)	$39.99	COHA
Copyright Your Software	$34.95	CYS
Domain Names	$26.95	DOM
Getting Permission: How to License and Clear Copyrighted Materials Online and Off (Book w/CD-ROM)	$34.99	RIPER
How to Make Patent Drawings Yourself	$29.99	DRAW
Inventor's Guide to Law, Business and Taxes	$34.99	ILAX
The Inventor's Notebook	$24.99	INOT
Nolo's Patents for Beginners	$29.99	QPAT
License Your Invention (Book w/CD-ROM)	$39.99	LICE
Patent, Copyright & Trademark	$39.99	PCTM
Patent It Yourself	$49.99	PAT
Patent Pending in 24 Hours	$29.99	PEND
Patent Searching Made Easy	$29.95	PATSE
The Public Domain	$34.95	PUBL
Trademark: Legal Care for Your Business and Product Name	$39.95	TRD
Web and Software Development: A Legal Guide (Book w/ CD-ROM)	$44.95	SFT

RESEARCH & REFERENCE

	PRICE	CODE
Legal Research: How to Find & Understand the Law	$39.99	LRES

	PRICE	CODE

SENIORS

Choose the Right Long-Term Care: Home Care, Assisted Living & Nursing Homes	$21.99	ELD
The Conservatorship Book for California	$44.99	CNSV
Social Security, Medicare & Goverment Pensions	$29.99	SOA

SOFTWARE

**Call or check our website at www.nolo.com
for special discounts on Software!**

LeaseWriter CD—Windows	$129.95	LWD1
LLC Maker—Windows	$89.95	LLP1
PatentPro Plus—Windows	$399.99	PAPL
Personal RecordKeeper 5.0 CD—Windows	$59.95	RKD5
Quicken Legal Business Pro 2004—Windows	$79.95	SBQB4
Quicken WillMaker Plus 2004—Windows	$79.95	WQP4

Special Upgrade Offer

Save 35% on the latest edition of your Nolo book

Because laws and legal procedures change often, we update our books regularly. To help keep you up-to-date, we are extending this special upgrade offer. Cut out and mail the title portion of the cover of your old Nolo book and we'll give you **35% off** the retail price of the NEW EDITION of that book when you purchase directly from Nolo. This offer is to individuals only.

Call us today at 1-800-728-3555

Prices and offer subject to change without notice.

Order Form

Name _____

Address _____

City _____

State, Zip _____

Daytime Phone _____

E-mail _____

Our "No-Hassle" Guarantee

Return anything you buy directly from Nolo for any reason and we'll cheerfully refund your purchase price. No ifs, ands or buts.

☐ Check here if you do not wish to receive mailings from other companies

Item Code	Quantity	Item	Unit Price	Total Price

Subtotal	
Add your local sales tax (California only)	
Shipping: RUSH $9, Basic $5 (See below)	
"I bought 3, ship it to me FREE!"(Ground shipping only)	
TOTAL	

Method of payment

☐ Check   ☐ VISA   ☐ MasterCard
☐ Discover Card   ☐ American Express

Account Number _____

Expiration Date _____

Signature _____

Shipping and Handling

Rush Delivery—Only $9

We'll ship any order to any street address in the U.S. by UPS 2nd Day Air* for only $9!

* Order by noon Pacific Time and get your order in 2 business days. Orders placed after noon Pacific Time will arrive in 3 business days. P.O. boxes and S.F. Bay Area use basic shipping. Alaska and Hawaii use 2nd Day Air or Priority Mail.

Basic Shipping—$5

Use for P.O. Boxes, Northern California and Ground Service.

Allow 1-2 weeks for delivery. U.S. addresses only.

For faster service, use your credit card and our toll-free numbers

**Call our customer service group
Monday thru Friday 7am to 7pm PST**

Phone   1-800-728-3555
Fax   1-800-645-0895
Mail   Nolo
         950 Parker St.
         Berkeley, CA 94710

Order 24 hours a day @
www.nolo.com

Little publishers have big ears.
We really listen to you.

Take 2 Minutes & Give Us Your 2 cents

Your comments make a big difference in the development and revision of Nolo books and software. Please take a few minutes and register your Nolo product—and your comments—with us. Not only will your input make a difference, you'll receive special offers available only to registered owners of Nolo products on our newest books and software. Register now by:

PHONE
1-800-728-3555

FAX
1-800-645-0895

EMAIL
cs@nolo.com

or **MAIL** us
this registration card

fold here

Registration Card

NAME _____ DATE _____

ADDRESS _____

_____

CITY _____ STATE _____ ZIP _____

PHONE _____ E-MAIL _____

WHERE DID YOU HEAR ABOUT THIS PRODUCT? _____

WHERE DID YOU PURCHASE THIS PRODUCT? _____

DID YOU CONSULT A LAWYER? (PLEASE CIRCLE ONE)   YES   NO   NOT APPLICABLE

DID YOU FIND THIS BOOK HELPFUL?   (VERY)   5   4   3   2   1   (NOT AT ALL)

COMMENTS _____

_____

_____

WAS IT EASY TO USE?   (VERY EASY)   5   4   3   2   1   (VERY DIFFICULT)

We occasionally make our mailing list available to carefully selected companies whose products may be of interest to you.

❑   If you do not wish to receive mailings from these companies, please check this box.

❑   You can quote me in future Nolo promotional materials.
Daytime phone number _____.

PNUP 1.0

Nolo in the NEWS

"Nolo helps lay people perform legal tasks without the aid—or fees—of lawyers."

—USA TODAY

Nolo books are ..."written in plain language, free of legal mumbo jumbo, and spiced with witty personal observations."

—ASSOCIATED PRESS

"...Nolo publications...guide people simply through the how, when, where and why of law."

—WASHINGTON POST

"Increasingly, people who are not lawyers are performing tasks usually regarded as legal work... And consumers, using books like Nolo's, do routine legal work themselves."

—NEW YORK TIMES

"...All of [Nolo's] books are easy-to-understand, are updated regularly, provide pull-out forms...and are often quite moving in their sense of compassion for the struggles of the lay reader."

—SAN FRANCISCO CHRONICLE

------------------------------- fold here -------------------------------

Place
stamp here

Nolo
950 Parker Street
Berkeley, CA 94710-9867

Attn: PNUP 1.0